People of Faith

A book in the series
Latin America In Translation / En Traducción / Em Tradução
Sponsored by the Duke–University of North Carolina
Program in Latin American Studies

PEOPLE OF FAITH

Slavery and African Catholics in
Eighteenth-Century Rio de Janeiro

MARIZA DE CARVALHO SOARES

TRANSLATED BY JERRY D. METZ

DUKE UNIVERSITY PRESS
Durham & London 2011

© 2011 Duke University Press
All rights reserved

Printed in the United States of America on
acid-free paper ∞ Designed by Jennifer Hill.
Typeset in Quadraat by Keystone Typesetting, Inc.

Library of Congress Cataloging-in-Publication
Data appear on the last printed page of this book.

For Bruno and Juliana,
Sources of inspiration for my work and my life

CONTENTS

TABLES

ACKNOWLEDGMENTS

The initial version of what would become this book was my
doctoral dissertation for the Department of History at the Federal Fluminense University, Rio de Janeiro. I thank the History
Department, where I already worked, for allowing me two years of unen-
cumbered time to organize and write the dissertation. In particular, I thank
my colleagues at the Laboratório de História Oral e Imagem, where my
relationships with Ana Maria Mauad, Ângela de Castro Gomes, Hebe Mattos, Ismênia de Lima Martins, and Paulo Knauss always provided attentive
and fruitful collaborations. In compiling and organizing data from a range
of sources, I was ably assisted by Fluminense history students Luciana
Gandelman, Mônica Monteiro, and Juliana Barreto Farias.

I gained access to critical documents through the friendly generosity of
the members of the Brotherhood of Santo Elesbão and Santa Efigênia,
especially Américo Bispo da Silveira and Roberto Machado Passos. I also
wish to express thanks to the staffs of the other archives and libraries
where I carried out research, of which the personnel at the Arquivo da Cúria
Metropolitana do Rio de Janeiro deserve particular recognition. Of course I
am also indebted to all the authors whose works I have cited in the following pages, but I feel a fundamental obligation to those writers whose works
shaped my questions, research, and analysis in a more indirect or un-
noticed way; undoubtedly, my bibliography would be more complete if my
memory were a bit better.

Manolo Florentino and Luciana Villas-Boas were responsible for bringing attention to this work and fostering its publication in Brazil in 2000. Since then, many people and institutions have engaged with it, and in the process brought wider attention to it. I will highlight only some: Bernard Vincent wrote a flattering review in *Cahiers du Brésil Contemporain*; Ambassador Alberto da Costa e Silva read the text with exquisite care; with Hebe Mattos and Silvia Lara I shared my work and permanent friendship. I owe my utmost gratitude to my students, and to the great majority of my readers, who are personally unknown to me. They have consistently provided the most meaningful recognition and incentive to do better.

The barriers of distance and language can appear formidable, but *Devotos*, as my book came to be called in Brazil, was able to cross them in the present edition thanks to the efforts of several scholars and institutions. Stuart Schwartz, A. J. R. Russell-Wood, and Mary Karasch were among the first non-Brazilian historians to lend the book some prominent encouragement. In 2001 I achieved my first "foreign" visit, at the History Department at the University of Maryland, College Park, thanks in particular to Barbara Weinstein. This position provided me a valuable opportunity to begin establishing contacts with American universities, and since then I have often traveled to the United States and Canada; I am very grateful to the various institutions that have supported these academic exchanges. In 2003, thanks to a postdoctorate grant from Coordenação de Aperfeiçoamento de Pessoal de Nível Superior—CAPES/Brazil, I spent a year at the History Department of Vanderbilt University; Marshall Eakin, the chair at that time, was tireless in his support. During that year I enjoyed frequent visits to York University at the Harriet Tubman Resource Centre on the African Diaspora (presently Harriet Tubman Institute), where I served as an associate. During those years Jane Landers, Paul Lovejoy, and Elisée Soumonni became colleagues and friends. My first papers were published in the United States thanks to Toyin Falola and Matt Childs (*The Yoruba Diaspora in the Atlantic World*, 2004), and to Gwyn Campbell, Suzanne Miers, and Joseph C. Miller (*Women and Slavery*, 2008).

Finally, if the arrival of this English edition of *Devotos da Cor* (whose original title could not be translated directly into English without losing some force) is an expression of the book's success in Brazil, its fortunes in this new form will depend on a much wider circle of readers, critics, and interrogators. I am grateful to all those participants at workshops and conferences who heard my ideas and, even when debating them, encouraged me to continue. The final revisions for this edition were completed at the Gilder Lehman Center of Yale University, thanks to a fellowship in March of 2007. I thank the staff of the center, especially Dana Schaffer. During this period, the friendship of Íris Kantor, Maria Jordan Arroyo, and Stuart Schwartz was indispensable.

At last I want to thanks Jerry Metz for his translation and constant conversation; Leia Pereira and Monica Carneiro for helping to prepare the folder with the images; and the team of editors at Duke University Press.

I paid my first visit to the Church of Santo Elesbão and Santa Efigênia one Wednesday morning, back in 1989, and it was an appointment with a friend that happened to take me there. The church fronts onto a bustling street in central Rio de Janeiro, lined with stores offering inexpensive clothing, shoes, and housewares. The din of commerce is constant; enthusiastic inducements to buy blare from tinny speakers mounted on shopfronts, and from sidewalk amplifiers. But inside, the church maintains an air of quiet, inconspicuous reserve, its serenity protected by a stately wooden panel standing in its open entrance that discreetly buffers the noise while preventing passersby from glancing toward the pews. Architecturally, it is small and unremarkable, especially when one compares it to the other more sumptuous examples of eighteenth-century churches nearby; and perhaps because of this, it is not well known. I had gone to meet Alberto Lobo, who suggested the location. "Seu Lobo," as he was also known, was born around 1900 and had come to Rio de Janeiro from Bahia (in northeastern Brazil) around 1930. He was a practitioner of *candomblé* (a Brazilian religion with an African background),[1] and had also joined the Church of Santo Elesbão and Santa Efigênia soon after arriving in Rio. I was working on my master's thesis, and I hoped to share with him some of my discoveries and uncertainties about the history of religious practices in Brazil—and to learn, in turn, from his stories and perspective.

As it happened, we would have several delightful and (for me) helpful conversations, speaking in hushed voices as we sat in the benches of the old church. But Seu Lobo passed away the following year. I thought of him regularly, especially when I began doctoral work in 1994. I often replayed our discussions in my mind, looking for hints of insight or ideas that I had not grasped at the time, but I never returned to the Church of Santo Elesbão and Santa Efigênia.

However, a chance discovery, also in 1994, raised a series of questions that would ultimately lead me back to an exploration of the humble little church. I happened to pick up a copy of the *Guia Brasileiro de Fontes para a História da África, da Escravidão Negra e do Negro na Sociedade Atual* (Brazilian Guide to Sources on the History of Africa, Slavery, and the Negro in Contemporary Society), published by the National Archive. I was intrigued to notice an unusual reference to the "Statutes of the Congregation of the Minas Makii Blacks in Rio de Janeiro (1786), copy of document in the National Library (1907)."[2] The 1907 document I read at the National Archive was a handmade copy of part of a 1786 manuscript whose whereabouts were uncertain. When I inquired at the National Library, the staff could determine only that the information pertaining to the document's accession (such as date and method of acquisition) had been lost. The catalog had the description of the document,[3] with two call numbers for it, an older—BN(MA)5,3,12—and a newer—BN(MA)9,3,11. There was also another form of numeric descriptor, 11447, which turned out to be a registration number from the important Exhibition of Brazilian History in 1882. The document had been displayed in a section related to Brazilian ethnography (specifically, "Classe X Natural History/2nd Ethnography and Linguistics/A. Brazilian Ethnography"), rather than to slavery or religious organizations. Indeed, it was classified as belonging to the study of so-called heathen peoples, utterly disconnected from the histories of slavery or the Catholic Church. Based on the exhibition catalog,[4] it seemed certain that the document had been maintained at the library at least since the exhibition. Through fruitless searches, my curiosity grew.

Upon the first reading, I was unaware that this document, substantial as it was—nearly seventy pages—would transform the premises of my research. It had been written by a member of a congregation of enslaved and freed Africans referred to in the text as the "Kingdom of Maki" (or "Mahi," according to modern spelling), which, I was astonished to learn on the thirteenth page, was based in the very Church of Santo Elesbão and Santa Efigênia where I had met with Seu Lobo two centuries later. Structurally, the Mahi Manuscript contains two separate narratives (actually two dialogues).[5] The first recounts the election and administration of Francisco Alves de Souza as the leader of the Mahi Congregation, and includes a statute, dated 1786, that lays out the congregation's devotional activities. The second dialogue (undated but probably from the same period) describes the Mina Coast, with attention not only to its ports and castles but to the various groups of people that lived there. This type of account was common to the era and popularly known as a *derrota*.[6]

For the better part of a year I pored over the Mahi Manuscript, intrigued by the challenge to reconcile its components and situate the whole document geographically and historically. At one point, the writer claimed that the congregation numbered some 200 people in 1786, all of them originally from the "kingdom" of Mahi on the Mina Coast. Drawing on what literature on the history of Africa I could compile, I determined that the Mahi came from the hinterland of the Bight of Benin, north of the ancient Kingdom of Dahomey. These Mahi arriving in Rio de Janeiro from the Mina Coast were considered members of the Mina "nation," whatever their actual provenience. Since at least 1740, the Mina that composed the Mina Congregation had elected a king to govern them, and that king had been without exception a Mina himself. But one of the great surprises the Manuscript offers is its portrayal of a group of Africans in Brazil, many of them freed and all converted to Catholicism and deeply concerned for the salvation of their kinfolk in Africa who had remained dedicated to their pagan beliefs. I came to doubt much that I had studied previously about African slavery in Rio de Janeiro, and gradually realized that—whatever my previous, tentative ideas for dissertation topics had been—the project emerging from the provocations of the Mahi Manuscript clearly focused on the meanings and importance of Mahi identity within the African community of eighteenth-century Rio.[7]

The first problem was to find additional sources that could help illuminate the nature of the city in that era, and the composition of its slave and freed populations. Most of the research on Rio's urban slavery focused on a later period, while works on the slave trade to colonial Brazil rarely acknowledge the presence of West Africans in the captaincy of Rio de Janeiro in the eighteenth century. Almost without exception, Brazilian studies of slavery concentrated narrowly on the work relations and daily life of slaves without considering the larger context of diaspora, and the transfer and negotiation of identity among transplanted Africans. Anthropologists have highlighted the fundamental contributions of peoples from the Bight of Benin to Afro-Brazilian religious practice, but as historical societies these peoples remain strangely anonymous. Thus it was by both interest and necessity that I turned to the history of Africa, although this was still fairly uncharted terrain for me and for most Brazilian historians at the time.

The Mahi are part of the Gbe language groups, and shared their territory with different Yoruba speakers.[8] Gbe speakers were and still are in what are today Togo and Benin, and came to be called Jêje in Brazil, while Yoruba peoples extend today across Nigeria into Benin and Togo, and were usually termed Nagô in Brazil.[9] But these terms could be combined, as in the expressions Jêje-Nagô and Jêje-Mahi found in the candomblé practiced in Bahia.[10] Still, while one must never ignore the dangers inherent in imputing ethnic veracity to classificatory terms from colonial sources, occasional specific references to the Mahi in anthropological literature support the notion that there were Mahi elements in the foundation of Bahian candomblé. In a collection of African myths related to the orixás (deities) of candomblé, Pierre Verger relates the story of Obaluaê-Xapanã (the orixá associated with smallpox) who with his warriors left Empé, the region of Nupe (called Tapa in Brazil), to lay waste to the Mahi. Before the attack, the Mahi consulted an oracle, who suggested certain offerings be made to Obaluaê-Xapanã. The offerings carried out, the deity was not only placated but charmed into dwelling with the Mahi; and since that time, the Mahi kingdom prospered.[11] Perhaps the Manuscript refers to such tales, as well as to the somewhat more easily verifiable episodes of fierce resistance to invasion by neighboring forces, when it asserts that the Mahi Kingdom was one of the "most powerful of the Mina Coast."

Although there is also evidence of the Mahi in Bahia by the middle of the eighteenth century, we have been unable to trace their arrival or existence earlier than the 1740s, when the Manuscript clearly indicates that they were not merely present but actively organizing. A preliminary survey of the growing literature on African history shows that Mahi people probably constituted less a kingdom than a series of dispersed small villages, with no centralized authority or government. It also seems that during this period, the Mahi were caught up in the expansion of both the kingdom of Dahomey and the slave trade; the historian Akinjogbin notes that traders were coming to consider the general region that included the Mahi lands as one continuous "hunting ground" for human captives.[12] According to Verger, there was a marked presence of Dahomeans in Bahia from the late seventeenth century until 1735.[13] From around 1730 onward, the frequent incursions on Mahi land by Dahomean aggressors led to a gradual but consistent increase in the numbers of Mahi shipped to Bahia throughout the remainder of the century; this demographic wave included one Francisco Alves de Souza, who arrived at the port of Salvador, Bahia. When he went to Rio in 1748, he fell in with a group of so-called Mina blacks, all of whom originally came from the Bight of Benin and spoke the "general tongue of Mina."[14] Souza would later become head of the Mahi Congregation, and would author the Mahi Manuscript.

Nina Rodrigues, a Bahian medical doctor and scholar of African cultures in Brazil, referred to the dwindling population of Mahi in the city of Salvador at the end of the nineteenth century:

The number of Jêjes [Ewe or Eves] has markedly diminished in Bahia.[15] Those that remain lack a proper district or headquarters of their own in the city, and wander dispersed here and there, some in Campo Grande, some in the Rua dos Sapateiros. The population seems to be evenly split among males and females. I have encountered a few from Dahomey, but almost all are from the coast, having left behind the cities of Ajudá, Ouidah, Popo, Agbomi, and Kotonu. Many of them say they are Efan, and display their distinctiveness from the Dahomeans with a characteristic tattoo that includes a small burn mark. Others are Maí, a small group residing to the north of Dahomey that has suffered cruel persecution from its southern neighbor. Two Maí families that lived near the fountain on São Pedro hill furnished me with much valuable information on the history of Bahia's jêje colony; but today, those two families are reduced to one aged survivor.[16]

My own research also benefited from the kindness of informants. At the Church of Santo Elesbão and Santa Efigênia I conducted several helpful interviews. I also came across a bound folio containing (in painstaking transcription) the brotherhood's compromisso, or foundational statutes[17]—

in Portuguese—as well as the complete ecclesiastical correspondence between the worshippers of Santo Elesbão, the bishop of Rio de Janeiro, and the Tribunal of Conscience and Orders in Lisbon, from 1740 to 1767, pertaining to their approval. Unfortunately, the volume lacks information about its own origins—date of compilation, name of author, or any mention of how or where the transcription of the statutes took place; despite repeated efforts, I could not locate the original documents. The compromisso states that the brotherhood had been organized by a diverse group of Africans from the Mina Coast, Cape Verde, the island of São Tomé, and Mozambique. It also specifies that "blacks from Angola" would never be permitted membership in the brotherhood. This is notable because at least since the sixteenth century, so-called blacks from Angola had held leadership positions in the Irmandade de Nossa Senhora do Rosário dos Homens Pretos (Brotherhood of Our Lady of the Rosário of the Black Men), established since the 1720s in Rio's "Church of Rosário."

While researching Portuguese archive catalogs, I came across entries referring to a proposal to form a congregation dedicated to Our Lady of Remédios, also in the Church of Santo Elesbão and Santa Efigênia, dating from 1788. The first reference appeared in the records of M. A. Hedwig Fitzler and Ernesto Enes, published in 1928; the other was included in the inventories of the Arquivo Histórico Ultramarino in Lisbon.[18] In both archives, the document is catalogued the same way,[19] which helped me locate it on microfilm at the National Library in Lisbon. Examining it, I began to perceive a connection between the three Mahi Catholic organizations—the Mahi Congregation, the Devotion to the Souls of Purgatory, and the Fraternity of Nossa Senhora dos Remédios—all within the Church of Santo Elesbão and Santa Efigênia. Rarely have scholars been able to identify such organizations, and pursue their histories through diverse primary sources, at such an early period in the Americas. Of course, the ultimate goal is to go beyond identifying and listing these organizations, and to use the range of documentary evidence surrounding them to begin to reconstruct how they were conceived, negotiated, and lived by their members. Indeed, this far-flung set of documents not only contains information about the Mahi associations but was for the most part actually written by them as well. These documents, particularly the Mahi Manuscript, can be read as something of an "ethnic text" whose analytic possibilities extend far beyond the parameters of this study.[20]

But I had a more immediate question to address. What could I make of this substantial presence of slaves from the Mina Coast in eighteenth-century Rio de Janeiro, a city where Bantu peoples had long been assumed to be the principal, perhaps near-exclusive African group? Where could I get a more complete portrait of the Africans brought to Rio in the early and middle parts of the century? I first turned to the baptismal records of slaves at the Archive of the Cúria Metropolitana in Rio de Janeiro—ACMRJ.[21] It can be difficult to explain to nonhistorians why baptismal records are something to be excited about; but particularly in Brazil, before the 1890s, they not merely documented the performance of baptisms but served the key function of identifying people—free, freed, or slave—in detailed ways. They also provided a medium in which other important events or commemorations touching colonial families could be inscribed,[22] as in the case of one newborn slave whose master freed him in the baptismal basin because he was "the first progeny of the household."

The *Constituições Primeiras do Arcebispado da Bahia* (1719), the first official book of guidelines for ecclesiastical practice in Brazil, includes regulations for baptismal records but does not substantively address how to record the conversions or baptisms of African slaves; in this, it echoes an omission in the earlier *Ordenações Filipinas* (1604).[23] Still, the general instructions for record keeping are clear: there should be a bound book, with numbered pages, each page signed at the top by the vicar or attendants; the front and back cover of the book should indicate the number of pages. In the form of a statement by the priest performing the baptism, a record should contain the date of the ceremony, the parish in which it occurred, and the name of the child as well as the names of his or her parents and godparents.[24] This model was standard for recording baptisms in Brazil throughout the eighteenth century, but in practice the existing notations often included information about the juridical status of the enslaved or freed individuals undergoing the ceremony. Close reading of entries can also help us hear the individual authorial voice of the functionaries who wrote the books, making the basic exercise of comparing and contrasting their content quite rewarding. It is at once the standardization of the information required by the book, combined with baptismal records' subtle peculiarities of detail, which suggested to me that they are one of the conceptual and legal spaces where colonial society constructed slave identity. For this reason I turned to them in hopes of better understanding the composition of slave demographics in Rio de Janeiro, and, proceeding from there, in evaluating the nature of Mahi identity within the city's cultural tapestry.

But again, whatever the potential of such a research method, its success depends on solid and abundant sources; and despite the heroic efforts of many librarians, there were predictable frustrations in this regard. I had access to only three books containing slave baptism records from the two parishes of Rio in the first half of the eighteenth century: *Livro de Batismo de Escravos, Freguesia da Sé* (the seventh Baptism Book of Captive Slaves of the Parish of Sé, 1718–26); and two others, lacking covers or titles—*Livro de Batismo de Escravos, Freguesia da Sé, 1744–61*, and *Livro de Batismo de Escravos, Freguesia da Candelária, 1745–44* (from the Parish of Candelária). Other books dated from 1751 or later, when the city added two more parishes: for example, *Livro de Batismo de Escravos, Freguesia de São José, 1751–90* (records from the Parishes of São José), and *Livro de Batismo de Escravos, Freguesia de Santa Rita, 1751–99* (Santa Rita, 1751–99). In the last-mentioned book, the effects of humidity had rendered illegible all the pages for 1751, and some of those for 1752.

From this incomplete series, I framed my collection of data within two periods—before 1751, and the decade from 1751 to 1760. The earlier period must be characterized more tentatively, since its analysis is based on data first only from the Parish of Sé (1718–26) and then on both Sé (1744–50) and Candelária (1744–50). The second period is a shorter time frame but includes the whole city, which is vital for comprehension of the spatial distribution of Mina slaves across Rio's urban landscape. In the end, there are a total of 9,578 registered baptisms of supposed slaves whose masters lived within the four parishes of the city. I say "supposed" because there are occasionally children of freed slaves among the lists, or a few children of indigenous mothers who should not be recorded as slaves. Where there were significant doubts, those cases were excluded, reducing the total to 9,269. It should also be noted that the number of individual registers will be larger than the number of records of baptism ceremonies, which often included more than one individual participant.[25] Those 9,269 registers can be broken down in the following manner as seen in table 1.

All the calculations used throughout the study are based on the 9,269 registers considered valid for analysis. Still, although a large and verifiable number seems to offer a certain reassurance to the researcher, far more

Table 1. Total Slave Baptisms Valid for Analysis, 1718–1760

PARISH AND YEARS	BAPTISMS		TOTAL
	Baptism with Mother	*Baptism of Adults*	
Sé (1), 1718–26	983	855	1,838
Sé (2), 1744–50	1,381	283	1,664
Sé (3) 1751–60	893	324	1,217
Candelária, 1751–60	1,648	586	2,234
São José, 1751–60	1,117	321	1,438
Santa Rita, 1751–60	587	291	878
Total	6,609	2,660	9,269

Source: ACMRJ, *Livro de Batismo de Escravos*, Rio de Janeiro: Sé, 1718–26, 1744–61; Candelária, 1745–74; São José, 1751–90; Santa Rita, 1751–99. The parishes of São José and Santa Rita were created in 1751.

profound questions hover over this data. For instance, how are we to interpret such descriptive labels as "gentio ("heathen" [literally "gentile"]) from Mina" or "Mina nation," which are common not only in the parochial books but in all the ecclesiastical documentation? How did the Mahi arrive in Rio de Janeiro? How did they begin to organize? What was the significance of religious organizations in the life of urban slaves in the eighteenth century? And what does the historiography say, or not say, about such questions? These were the overarching concerns of my research project. Following the trail of Africans from the Bight of Benin to Rio de Janeiro involved making lists of countless names and miniscule details which might, or might not, provide key connections later. This book is the product of two years' worth of coaxing tiny pieces around in an Atlantic-sized jigsaw puzzle; the emerging image was finally clear enough, at least, to draw some conclusions from this phase of the research.

One of the greatest challenges I faced was in grappling with the composite names given to Africans, which combined Christian first names (with or without a last name) with kingdoms, locales, or some other geographic allusion: "Maria Antunes of the heathens of Guinea," "Pedro, black of the Mina nation," "Elório Cabinda." There is always some sort of group designation to these names, indicating that beyond the utility of individual identification the names were partly a strategy to classify Africans brought as slaves to Brazil into recognized categories of physical aspect, behavior, ancestry, language, or beliefs. Of course, it was not only a Brazilian phenomenon. The French artist Jean-Baptiste Debret, who lived in Rio from 1816 to 1831, drew a street vendor of cornmeal who, he wrote, "looks to be Congo, judging by the shaved head and the attitude of the turban." When the famed naturalist Louis Agassiz and his wife, Elizabeth Agassiz, visited Rio in 1865, she commented that "Mina women are very pretty . . . with an almost noble bearing."[26] Such descriptions were part of the general practice for constructing ethnic-functional "types" by which Africans were comprehended and inserted into colonial society—as domestic workers, field hands, miners, or, for the women (lest one forget), as desirable sexual partners. A plethora of such terms composed a crude system for conceiving, evaluating, and representing themes of such complexity that we still lack the basic theoretical and methodological approaches to grasp them.

This quandary is not alleviated by recourse to the Brazilian historiography, which has been far more concerned with tracing the expansion of Europeans in Brazil than in looking closely at the Africans and their particular situations. Neither have historians been immune to more recent and broad-based generalizations about racial and cultural diversity, at least when applied to African-born peoples. The three concepts of race, ethnicity, and origins have come to refer almost inextricably to each other, although each subject has different theoretical requirements and, while their empirical terrains may overlap, they are not interchangeable. Acceptance of the study of ethnic identity has come to historians slowly, through the gradual interdisciplinary transformation of social science as a whole. Since the 1980s interest has grown in understanding the social and cultural diversity of the African populations brought to Brazil. While new sources are necessary, it is also critical to interrogate known sources in light of these new queries and sensitivities. Three scholars in particular were pioneers in the field: Stuart Schwartz, A. J. R. Russell-Wood, and Mary Karasch. Perhaps it is not a coincidence that they work in institutions in the United States, where the study of African history is far better established than in Brazil. However, two other influential scholars, Pierre Verger and João José Reis, have explored the history of slavery and Africans in Bahia, where the presence of slaves from the Bight of Benin was quite marked.[27]

Rather than purely following these authors' leads and creating a social history of Mina slaves in Rio de Janeiro, I elected to base my study in religious behavior—more specifically, in the participation of Africans (slaves or freed) in Catholic organizations such as the black lay brotherhoods. Lay brotherhoods have been a newly emergent theme in the Brazilian historiography, with works by Julita Scarano and Caio C. Boschi focusing on Minas Gerais.[28] Religiosity is an example of what Fernand Braudel calls "mental frames" of long duration,[29] but here the conversion of Africans under slavery in the Americas is treated as a source of infinite possibilities that can only be perceived in the short term. To that point, Braudel's notion of the danger hidden in everyday occurrences has influenced the tone of my work.[30] But the brief moment of disputes, tensions, and conflicts—so viscerally present in the proceedings of the Mahi Congregation—emerged from the long run of history. My work is placed squarely at that temporal intersection, with the objective of viewing in their integrity both the particular circumstances of the religious activity of the Mina in Rio, and the long unfolding of slavery, the slave trade, and the African Diaspora that surrounds it.

Anthropological theory, notably from such Latin American anthropologists as Roberto Cardoso de Oliveira, João Pacheco de Oliveira, and Miguel Bartolomé, has informed my interdisciplinary approach to history. By emphasizing the fundamental relations between ethnic identity and culture, these and other anthropologists help demonstrate that a historiography excluding the long, diverse, and often violent episodes involving African-born slaves in Brazil, or in any other place in the Americas, will be only an impressionistic outline.[31] Norbert Elias's classic sociological work on France,[32] delicately transposed to colonial Rio de Janeiro, has helped me imagine the textures of a society pervaded by the rules of sociability of the ancien régime. In Rio, as throughout the Portuguese empire, black lay brotherhoods engaged in expressions of imperial pomp through elaborate festivals, processions and funerals, the election of kings and queens, and the organization of royal courts, all within their ethnic and provenience groups. This book, by focusing on the establishment of lay brotherhoods among freed and enslaved Mina linked to the Church of Santo Elesbão and Santa Efigênia from the early 1740s to the late 1780s, attempts to comprehend the importance of Catholicism in the new social configurations these people adopted living under slavery.

The diversity of sources I encountered enabled me to follow a relatively small group—around 200 people in the Mahi Congregation, and several thousand Mina dispersed around the city—for a fifty-year period. Notwithstanding my interdisciplinary approach, this work is grounded in the empirical standards and methods of history. My overarching concern is to understand how Mina people in general, and the Mahi in particular, assembled and organized themselves through meaningful religious activity under slavery.[33] Thus I read widely in the history of slavery and of the Catholic Church in Brazil. The historiography of Brazil and Brazilian slavery provided the contours of the "historical situation" where my questions of ethnic and religious identity would be directed.[34] Slavery, ethnicity, and religiosity are essential factors in how a group of Africans in colonial Rio de Janeiro constructed their identity and social organization, dialoguing with the past and the new rules and determinants of a Brazilian slave society.[35]

Another central challenge I faced was to compose a sufficiently rich and meaningful portrait of the era, which would be the stage on which these various actors lived their lives and engaged each other. I was reminded many times of Boschi's advice:

> If one endeavors to study religion in the colonial setting, one cannot keep as a parameter or yardstick the historical norms of doctrinal Catholicism, uttered by theologians and canonical law. If indeed this parameter ever existed, the Portuguese colony in the Americas would have been an unlikely setting for their realization. Rather, what one sees here is a popular Catholicism characterized by both the precarious conditions of evangelism and expanded devotional and protective spheres. Thus, analysis of colonial religion has to somehow get inside this pretended exteriority. Only in that way can one begin to comprehend, for example, the real meanings of sacred festivals in that context; and to identify, under the diaphanous mantle of superficiality, the original expression that is a hallmark of Brazilian colonial religiosity.[36]

Studies of slavery in Brazil were another framework to be considered. I traversed the different moments of the historiography, including classics by João Lúcio de Azevedo, Maurício Goulart, Pierre Verger, and newer work by Manolo Florentino (who is the first author to explore in depth the commerce of slaves in the city of Rio de Janeiro). Still, none of these scholars dwelled overlong on the commercial relations between Rio and the Mina Coast in the first half of the eighteenth century.[37] Florentino does look at the Atlantic slave trade, especially the dealings between Angola and Rio in the years after 1790, when the documentation is more substantial. Works treating the years before 1790, such as Luiz Felipe de Alencastro's on the seventeenth century and Herbert S. Klein's on the mid- to late eighteenth, have also tended to focus on Angola.[38]

Inspired by Hebe Mattos's analysis of the *Das Cores do Silêncio* (silence of color) in the nineteenth century,[39] I could observe something different in the eighteenth century—a period in which social status was determined overwhelmingly by color. Elites were supposedly "white" and of "clean blood," and the "blacks" were slaves or slaves who had been liberated. Occasionally there were *pardos*, somewhere in between the two extremes but difficult to grasp in a comprehensive way from the sources. In this era, color bespoke social condition and one's place in the social hierarchy. Take the woman known as Páscoa (Easter), said to be "preta mina forra" (freed Mina black): Before being identified as from Mina, she was called "black," and even though she was a freed woman her freedom comes last in her name, after the insistent "preta mina."

I relied on the period chroniclers of city life who showed an interest in the religious practices of Rio's African population. Among them, Augusto Maurício recorded much insightful information about churches, and quoted from eighteenth-century documents. Other authors—such as Monsenhor Pizarro, Moreira de Azevedo, Padre Perereca, Vieira Fazenda, and Vivaldo Coaracy—helped fill in the gaps in the documentation about the brotherhoods or the city itself.[40] When taken as a whole and read in sequence, these sources are also extraordinarily challenging because they not only regrettably refrain from citing the additional material they draw from, but they often address comments, allusions, and arguments to each other in a style of partially closed or coded conversation. All these writers shared the goal of creating a consensus about the past, whose doubts or mysteries would be gradually resolved as knowledge was accumulated in a methodical (if dangerous) procedure. This may explain why one author often seemed to address or refer to another with whom he agreed, while ignoring or grumbling about an author who held a divergent position. Such intertextuality has to be kept in mind to analyze or contextualize any given single document from the group of chronicles.[41]

Images and engravings are rare for this period, and the few that do exist still await concentrated analysis. Lygia da Fonseca Fernandes Cunha should be recognized for, among other things, publishing the plates of Carlos Julião that are likely from the 1780s. Maps are rather more numerous and have been studied by Gilberto Ferrez and Eduardo Canabrava Barreiros. Occasionally I refer to images from the first decades of the nineteenth century, but only when the images convey what were understood to be places or practices that dated from the eighteenth century. Still, even these images are rarely unaccompanied by text that "explains" them, whether the image is meant to illustrate something in the text or (as in the case of Debret's work) the text is meant to provide context to the image.[42]

One of the risks for historians in the recent trend to "read" images for what written text does not or cannot articulate is that the content of the image can be unmoored, forced to do interpretive work far from its own historical circumstances. For instance, we have no record of how the Mina people in eighteenth-century Rio dressed, or arranged their hair, or applied physical markings; for the period, there are only Julião's images of unidentified Africans involved in special festive events. The Mina woman pointed out for praise by Elizabeth Agassiz was seen on the streets of Rio in the middle of the nineteenth century. Demographics suggest that that woman was a Nagô, that is, Yoruba speaker, who had likely come to Rio from Bahia after the Malê uprising.[43] In the era I address, Gbe speakers were predominant in the city compared to Yoruba-speaking people. These are distinct languages, traditions, and cultures, which likely had an influence on local social identities and strategies adopted to cope with slavery. But still, since I lack images to create more complete portraits, the people in this book must remain to an extent faceless. All historical research projects contain omissions, but this is one I particularly regret.

I make one final comment about the appearance of period texts. Although transliteration is a common practice today, I opted to transcribe directly, because it seems that to change the words of authors from a distant century adds an additional interpretive burden to the historian already struggling to understand them in their fullest historical context.[44] Nonetheless, punctuation has been made current, and obvious errors in grammar or orthography have been corrected. In this edition all the English translations are written in correct modern English.

The narrative exposition of a research project must differ from the nonlinear, sometimes chaotic, and often highly obscure process of researching itself. Therefore, although I began the investigation long ago with the transcription of the Mahi Manuscript, that document is specifically addressed only in chapter 6. The chapters can be imagined as a series of six photographs taken of the same subject, each with a tighter zoom and sharper central focus: starting with European exploratory formulations of Africa and the Mina Coast, and ending with the Mahi community in Rio de Janeiro that formed a lay brotherhood in 1786.[45]

The book is further organized into two parts. The first presents the Mina Coast, the commerce of slaves to Brazil, and the formation of what I call *grupos de procedência* (provenience groups). Chapter 1 analyzes the conquest of Guinea in the fifteenth and sixteenth centuries; it also attempts to trace how designations such as Guinea and Mina were selectively applied in practice, and how they came to be lodged in Western thought. Chapter 2 looks at the slave trade from the Mina Coast to Rio de Janeiro in the eighteenth century to begin to understand who were the so-called Mina heathen in the city, and where they came from. Chapter 3 considers the Mina from the perspective of the classifications used by the church, such as baptism records, to try to tease out some averages for population size, their diverse relationships, and the texture of their presence in Rio. Key to this discussion is the period term *gentio*, (heathen), which appears throughout the book because of frequent use in the documentation; it refers to people ignorant of the ways and teachings of Christianity (unlike pagans, who learn about but reject baptism).

Part two situates the Mina within the panorama of enslaved and freed Africans in the city, with particular attention to religious practice and internal organization. Chapter 4 focuses on the development of black lay brotherhoods in Rio during the seventeenth and eighteenth centuries. Chapter 5 articulates an analysis of the twenty-year process of constructing the compromisso of the Brotherhood of Santo Elesbão and Santa Efigênia and the multiple negotiations involving members of the brotherhood themselves and the representatives of the Portuguese Crown. Chapter 6 details the organization of the Mahi Congregation, as well as issues that arose from their ethnic identity, exploring the Mahi Manuscript for hints of how the process of identity construction intersected with strategies for power.

My research goal was to find a consistent path through diverse documents that pointed to a new understanding of African slavery in the Portuguese Empire. Twelve years after the dissertation was written, I have been able to augment the African dimensions of the research. As I carried out research in the 1990s, there was still an almost total lack of interest in African history in the Brazilian academy, which also meant that essential books on the subject written in other languages remained inaccessible to readers of Portuguese. All of that is certainly changing, although not as quickly or substantially as some of us would like. Still, to have included references here to all the related, expanding themes and bibliographies— from the history of slavery and of Africa, to diaspora studies and the Atlantic world—would have doubled the size of this book, or demanded a second one. For that reason, I decided to leave the text almost as it was already published in Brazil—with the addition of a postscript that contains details about the Mahi that I have subsequently learned. My last fifteen years of effort have been dedicated to understanding the specific experiences of Africans taken as slaves to the Americas, and how they collectively reconstructed their lives within, and at times apart from, captivity. This book emphasizes the importance of groups, and not isolated individuals, in this historical context. I hope it stimulates scholarly debate but, also and especially, more research into ethnic identity and provenience groups among the Africans in the New World.

Finally, I'd like to note that in the Brazilian edition of this book, I used the term "*procedência*" (provenance) to refer to the trajectories of captive Africans, from the starting points of their journeys until landing in Brazil. The term was borrowed from Nina Rodrigues, one of the founders of this type of study in Brazil; I extended its application from individuals to groups, called *grupos de procedência* (that analysis appears here in chapter 3). For the American publication, however, I opted for the term "provenience" utilized by Melville Herskovits. Thus I use "provenience group" to designate the form of organization created by Africans in the New World that is rooted in the reference to a shared provenience.

PART ONE

As Renaissance Europe probed its southern frontier through trade networks branching across the Mediterranean, its merchants, scholars, royalty, and commoners alike gazed in delighted wonder at the bags, chests, and bundles arriving from distant lands by ship and caravan. Precious metals, ivory, ostrich feathers, strange furs, and hides—these and other exotic stuffs were joined (and often physically conveyed) by dark-skinned slaves, who were themselves both a highly valued import commodity and a provocative object of study for Renaissance elites eager to situate themselves at the apex of a world market-geography as yet incompletely formulated.

In this period, knowledge of faraway realms was mostly obtained through the voyagers' accounts that had been accumulating in the literature since antiquity. According to Herodotus (fifth century BCE), beyond the Saharan Desert sands one could reach a region of great forests and bogs, with a vast river full of crocodiles that swam upstream, in a river flowing from the sunset to the Levant (supposedly the Niger River). The Greek historian had also alluded to entire cities of black people there; and he gave an account of the formidable Garamantes, who spent their days hunting the Troglodytes—a strange people who subsisted on snake meat and communicated with batlike squeals. Four centuries later, another Greek, the geographer Strabo (I BCE–ACE I), provided a harrowing description of the "numerous deserts" that formed a barrier to the exploration of "the country of the Occidental Ethiopes." By the beginning of the

Christian era, Roman explorers and philosophers added their own accounts to the Greek repertoire. With those writings in hand, Pliny the Elder (first century ACE) devised his own list of the peoples inhabiting the remote area south of the Sahara.[1]

Until the early fifteenth century, Europeans based their understanding of far-off lands and peoples on materials such as these. They had traveled only as far as the Mediterranean coast, parts of Egypt, the edge of the Sahara, and the northern stretch of the western coast of Africa (up to the Atlantic archipelagos). The Portuguese, however, were soon to open a new era in Atlantic exploration in general, and African exploration in particular. Their conquest in 1415 of Ceuta (today an enclave in Morocco), a strategic port city in North Africa, eventually came to be a vital Portuguese commercial base with established links to the Muslim world. Portugal thus had new access to the caravan routes that fanned across the north, west, and east of Africa, while it took advantage of Ceuta's seaside location to launch its own navigational forays up and down the African coast. It would be through a combination of their own actual exploration and the assimilation of Muslim familiarity with the region's physical and astronomical features that the Portuguese could, in the mid-fifteenth century, start to devise a new African geography.[2]

To the south, the Sahara separated Portugal and North Africa from the city of Timbuktu (in modern Mali), already an important center of learning in the early fifteenth century as well as a key trading post where caravans would exchange cargo, haggle for supplies, and water their camels. The city's location—near the banks of the Niger River, and at the intersection of trade arteries bearing salt, gold, and other goods—was favorable for both culture and commerce. Salt, extracted from the mines at Taghaza (in today's Mali), was conveyed from Timbuktu on to West Africa, south of the Sahara. In exchange for the salt, as well as for other merchandise imported into West Africa, the black kingdoms sent back to Timbuktu gold, slaves,[3] and ivory, along with particular commodities prized by the Mediterranean market (such as black pepper, cola nuts, and amber). The west coast was accessed by three land routes: one leading to Arguin (off Mauritania); one to the city of Safi; in Morocco, and one to Cantor, in the Lower Gambia. Renaissance maps suggest that due east of the Guinea Coast, if one could cross or circumnavigate the entire African landmass, lay Oriental Ethiopia, a place of Christian kingdoms where Santo Elesbão (Ethiopia) and Santa Efigênia (Nubia) originated. According to these cartographies, Guinea denominated a narrow slice of the western coast, situated at around the fifteenth parallel.[4] Little was known of the surrounding territories or the people that inhabited them, particularly south of the Saharan sands. That would begin to change with the Portuguese arrival on the Mina Coast in 1470.

If one compares the depictions of Africa produced by European cartographers during the first half of the fifteenth century to those produced a century before, the similarity implies that European conceptions of African geography had scarcely changed in a hundred years' time. Even by the 1450s and 1460s, exploratory expeditions did not penetrate far enough to revise the boundaries established during antiquity. But if the early cartographic limits were not as yet being challenged in a fundamental way, increasing contact between explorers and the so-called native forest peoples, who had been known only from their fabulous descriptions in ancient texts, would soon transform European thought and society.

To understand this process, it is appropriate to begin with the writings of an influential contemporary, the crown's royal chronicler Gomes Eanes de Zurara (1410–74). Whatever his personal opinions or intentions, Zurara's work constitutes a detailed toponymy that gave narrative form and lexical texture to the West Coast of Africa. In a sense, Zurara initiated the entire scheme of categories and classifications that would underpin the way slavery was understood in the Portuguese Empire.[5] The expression *terra de negros* (land of the negroes) already appears in his writing in the middle part of the century, designating the region to the south of what is today called the Senegal River.

THE LAND OF THE BLACK MOORS

Gomes Eanes de Zurara was the author of many books, including the *Crônicas de Guiné* (*Chronicles of Guinea*), which remained as a manuscript until 1841. The chronicle had been written at the request of King Afonso V. João de Barros cited the *Chronicles* in 1552, but by 1556, Damião de Góis claimed that it had been lost; the Manuscript was ultimately discovered by Ferdinand Denis in the Paris Library in 1837, and published in 1841.[6] The book contains ninety-seven chapters, of which the first seven are devoted to lauding the notable deeds of Infante Dom Henrique (1394–1460, also known as Henry the Navigator), organizer of Portugal's seaborne expeditions of Africa. While listing Henry's lofty motivations to "search for the lands of Guinea" (gain true knowledge of the region, assess the power of the moors, search for Christian princes, save the souls of heathen), Zurara found a delicate way to suggest that Henry's underlying personal inspiration came from a different dimension altogether:

> It is because his ascendant sign was Aires, which is the house of Mars, and is the exaltation of the Sun, and his Master is in the eleventh house, accompanied by the Sun. And the aforementioned Mars was in Aquarius, which is the house of Saturn, and in a place of hope, which meant that he should struggle to accomplish great feats, especially seeking things hidden to other men, and secrets according to the quality of Saturn, in whose house he is. And because he was accompanied by the Sun, and the Sun was in the house of Jupiter, he knew all of his achievements would be faithfully and gracefully done, to the pleasure of his king.[7]

From the eighth chapter on, Zurara recounted various expeditions along the African coast. It should be emphasized that since around 1440 in Portugal, the conquest of new lands and the commerce in both gold and slaves had been tightly associated. This association had developed out of earlier strategies and victories, such as the taking of Ceuta, an important trading city, from the Spanish in 1415; and the successful crossing in 1434 of the "sea of darkness" that had swallowed many European ships around Cape Bojador, the Bulging Coast of North Africa. The first African gold in Portugal arrived in 1442 in the form of a ransom for two Moorish hostages;[8] the gold arrived with "ten black slaves, and some trinkets produced on the coast."[9] In 1443, when Portuguese navigators made it to the island of Arguin, a base was established to trade with the caravans for a variety of goods such as wheat, horses, pitchers, bowls, combs, bracelets, shawls, linens, eyeglasses, and needles.[10] A year later the expeditions reached Cantor, near the borders of (as the chronicles told it) the "land of the negroes," or Guinea; it is here that the Portuguese began assembling large shipments of slaves. An African enterprise in the region lived handsomely for years through the commerce of slaves to Algarve, in the south of Portugal.

The expedition reports that Zurara compiled allowed him to interpret and demarcate the transition from Islamic Africa (including the Sahara) to the "land of the negroes" (equatorial Africa). Zurara commented on the passage of the navigator Dinis Dias across the border:

> He arrived in the land of the negroes, who are called Guineans. And as we have had occasion to say several times in this narration, Guinea was the other place where the pioneers explored. We by necessity write of the land as continuous from the north to the south, but there are in essence two distinct places, marked by great differences, and lying far apart from each other.[11]

Drawing from Dias, Zurara specified a physical marker of the border between the two regions—a pair of palm trees—which aided the explorers who soon followed, such as Gonçalo de Sintra, who took this path to pass from the "land of the moors" (Sahara) to the "land of the negroes" (Guinea). Zurara related de Sintra's journey: "The caravels having left behind the lands of the Sahara, they soon espied the two palm trees which Dias identified as the beginning of the land of the negroes."[12] And he emphasized that "the peoples of this green land are all black [negros], and that is why it is called the land of the negroes, or Guinea, and the people are called Guineans, which means the same thing as negro."[13] In these writings, Guinea was emerging as the uncharted land between the better-known regions of coastal Northwest Africa, and Christian Ethiopia far to the east.

Zurara terminated his account in 1448, when he replaced Fernão Lopes as the principal royal chronicler of the House of Bragança. That move was probably not unrelated to Lisbon's creation of the House of Guinea (Casa de Guiné) in the southern Portuguese city of Lagos in 1445 to better administrate its oversea activities, in particular on the African coast. Zurara soon complained that there had been a regrettable change in Portuguese strategy with respect to maritime expansion and African exploration, a deterioration that the mostly commercial functions of the House of Guinea represented.[14] It is clear that Zurara had the ambitious sense of being the chronicler of Portugal, not merely the biographer of Dom Henrique.[15] Nevertheless, he reiterated the broader spiritual goals attributed to Henry the Navigator in looking for Guinea in the first place, such as the possibilities of finding Christian kingdoms and of saving souls, and misconstrued the new era and its commercial goals.

This helps us understand why he would come to insist in the *Chronicles* on describing the inhabitants of the "land of the negroes" as Moors, a curious fact which has already caught scholars' attention.[16] However, I argue that Zurara was neither careless nor ingenuous. The roots of his argument lie in the papal bulls of the period. The *Dum Diversas* of 1452 conceded the right to Portugal to conquer the Moors; and the deeply "imperialist" 1454 *Romanus Pontifex* gave to the Portuguese royalty all the lands discovered beyond the Capes Bojador and Num, while extending the permission to conquer "Indians" as well as Moors. Finally, the *Inter Coetera* of 1456 gave to the Order of Christ (with Henry the Navigator as their Grand Master) the legal and spiritual authority over lands discovered to be non-Christian.[17] Thus, Zurara gave the Guineans the unlikely designation of Moors so that the 1452 papal bull could be used to justify and legitimize their conquest by the Portuguese Crown.

Zurara's preoccupation with nomenclature in turn helps us date the completion of the original edition of his *Chronicles of Guinea*, a point of contention in the Portuguese historiography. A. J. Costa has argued that the texts were written in their entirety after the death of Dom Henrique, between 1464 and 1468, while Duarte Leite suggested that Zurara began writing in 1451 and finished between 1460 and 1466.[18] My research suggests that Leite is more accurate. But Zurara would have written his chronicles for the king after the 1452 *Dum Diversas*, and before the 1454 *Romanus Pontifex*, which is why his discourse assumed the programmatic conversion of Moors but not of Indians or heathens.[19]

If Zurara knew how to distinguish Moors from heathens, he also called for a project to convert "Indians" (permission for which would be granted in the 1454 bull). He suggested that Indians are more easily converted than Moors because they "do not come from the lineage of Moors, but of heathen [*gentios*]"; thus they are more readily brought to the path of salvation.[20] But to demonstrate how those black Africans who might not be Moors still could and should be converted, Zurara reminded his readers of how effortlessly several young boys and girls born of black African "gentio" families in the city of Lagos (in Portugal) had become "good and true Christians."[21]

To the extent that the Portuguese efforts of the first half of the fifteenth century were, as Zurara claimed in the *Chronicles*, to gain true knowledge of the region of Guinea, the second half of the century would be marked by an intensification of commercial relations and the insertion of the "discovered" peoples into networks of imperial and religious power. These three imperatives were perhaps less distinguishable than Zurara tried to maintain, and he holds a complex, ambivalent legacy at the center of them.

THE MINA OF GUINEA

Zurara was later replaced as royal chronicler of the House of Bragança and High Guard of the Tower of the Tombo by Rui de Pina (1440–1523), who wrote accounts of the contemporary conquest of Kongo as well as continuing to compile information about Guinea. Two other coeval writers added to the corpus of knowledge about Guinea: Duarte Pacheco Pereira (dates of birth and death unknown), and João de Barros (1496–1570).[22] Pereira—soldier, navigator, knight of the house of Dom João II, and inventor of the cosmograph—finished his *Esmeraldo de Situ Orbis* between 1506 and 1508. Named captain of the Fort of São Jorge in Mina (also known as Mina Castle) in 1519, he resided there from 1520 until 1522, when he was accused of various malfeasances and taken back to Lisbon in chains. João de Barros, manager of the Portuguese administrations for the House of India and for Mina, wrote extensively on history, although some of his work has been lost. In *Asia* 1ª. *Década*, he also recounted the conquest of the West African coast and furnished detailed descriptions of Mina in particular.

By the mid-1450s, after the caravels had first reached the island of Arguin, they were continuing their southward explorations past the estuary of the Gambia River.[23] At the time, Portugal was receiving around 800 slaves a year. In 1460, as the expeditions reached what is today Sierra Leone, Henry the Navigator died. Because he had no descendants, the crown incorporated his patrimony, which took nine years to complete; that same year, 1469, a substantial contract to develop both slave commerce and Portuguese territory in Guinea was awarded to Fernão Gomes. The five-year contract stipulated that annually, Gomes had to secure 100 more leagues of land beyond the region of modern Sierra Leone.[24] Acting to fulfill this contract, João de Santarém and Pero Escobar reached modern Ghana by 1470, bartering for gold there, and by 1472 had arrived at the islands of São Tomé and Príncipe.

Of course, Portugal was not the only European power exploring the region. A Flemish ship landed on the Mina Coast in 1475, but the Portuguese accounts declare that "the negroes ate all thirty-five Flemings on board."[25] In 1479, the Treaty de Alcáçovas, which brought to an end the War of the Castilian Succession, gave to Portugal the dominion over Guinea, Madeira, the Azores, and Cape Verde, reserving the Canary Islands for Castela. Anxious to centralize its control over the growing commerce in gold and slaves, the Portuguese Crown in 1481 created the House of Slaves in Lisbon to regulate and tax the trade. A year later, in 1482, they ordered the construction of a fort on the Mina Coast, in today's Ghana, to protect the trade from other nations (especially Spain).

The task of building the fort was assigned to Diogo de Azambuja, a royal knight and commentator of the Order of São Bento (Benedictine Order). He chose to name the fort for São Jorge (Saint George), of whom King João II was a votarist. According to Duarte Pacheco Pereira, all the material used to build the Mina Castle, every stone of it, was brought from Portugal. Final touches to the construction of the first major European building in tropical Africa were performed in 1486. Anchored by the fort, the Portuguese conception of the Mina Coast began to coalesce around this extension of Iberian identity and bureaucracy into what had been Guinea's vast and diffuse complex of ports, ethnic groups, business deals, and maritime routes. By late 1486 the growing population of Portuguese and converted Africans in the environs of the fort led to the designation of a city there, also named Mina.

From the first, the Portuguese allied themselves with particular groups of amenable natives who might be seen less as local agents than as partners in a globalizing commercial system based on gold and slaves. Individual dealers carried the gold to the fort, and little was communicated or recorded about its origins, although most of it seems to have come from west of the Portuguese outpost. We do know that as early as the beginning of the sixteenth century, slaves were being taken from various kingdoms along the coast, principally Benin but also those farther southeast, into coastal Central Africa and beyond. But the central importance of the kingdom of Benin as a reliable, nearby source of slaves quickened the interest of Portuguese traders and explorers. Even before the Mina fort had been completed in 1486, João Afonso de Aveiro had been awarded a contract to establish Portuguese-controlled trade in a region favored by slave hunters, neighboring the kingdom of Benin, east of the fort. No less than the king of Benin himself agreed to supervise the capturing of slaves for sale to João Afonso, who agreed to build a warehouse (*feitoria*) in a nearby place called Guato. From there, the slaves would be marched to the fort and either traded to other merchants for gold, or dispatched on a waiting ship for Portugal.

Africans were the middlemen in a system that seemed to benefit everyone, except of course the slaves. An African could capture slaves for political reasons, but the presence of Europeans eager to barter offered additional motivations or conveniences. Even those African traders who dealt in other forms of merchandise could use slaves to carry their goods in caravans, only to trade those slaves at the end of the route for the gold also prized by Europeans. In global partnership, these complicated local networks produced a voluminous commerce of human beings that by the 1600s led the whole region, from the falls of the Volta River to the Niger estuary, to be designated the "slave coast."

But in the midst of all this, the Africans who negotiated with the Portuguese were also, from the beginning, targets of missionary efforts aimed at their conversion to Christianity.[26] Somewhat more rarely, locals could also request conversion, as occurred during the period João Afonso was negotiating with the king of Benin. A representative of the king approached the missionaries, asking for a group indoctrination into the Catholic faith. This was apparently unsuccessful because the king had to be converted first in order to then convert his subjects, but according to João de Barros, "The King was too attached to his idolatries." When João Afonso died in 1486, the contract was suspended and the missionaries abandoned the area, but the slave trade continued.[27]

The coast of Kongo was first reached early in the 1470s. Regular contact with the Kongo Kingdom and Angola was established later, by Diogo Cão, in 1482. Historians have noted that the Portuguese presence in this part of Africa was characterized by violence and an expansion of slave trading, despite all efforts to introduce the Catholic Church there.[28] Arriving in Kongo, the Portuguese realized that what they called Guinea (the realm between the Islamic Sahara and the Catholic Ethiopia) was in fact much longer than Zurara's writings had led them to anticipate. Whatever the case, the discovery of these territories unknown to previous explorers and cartographers stretched the geographical concept of Guinea to encompass both the Mina Coast (including the islands of the archipelago of Cape Verde), and the south-central area of Kongo and Angola. Changing conceptions of the scale and composition of the area are reflected in the words of the royal chronicler Rui de Pina, who located the kingdom of Kongo "in Guinea, far beyond Mina."[29] This toponymy also justified the addition of another title to the King of Portugal: Lord of Guinea (attributed in the 1479 Treaty of Alcáçovas, but adopted by Dom João II in 1485): "King John, by God's Grace King of Portugal and the Algarves, whose dominion covers both sides of the Sea, Lord of Guinea in Africa." Rui de Pina argued that the title was valid because of the growing importance of the region in the Portuguese Empire: "Kings can legitimately lay claim to a dominion through its contributions and Apostolic concessions; but in the past, until very recently, Guinea was a very small thing, and not worthy of being claimed by a King."[30] Once Guinea was no longer a "very small thing," a new royal title was in order.

The first shipments of slaves leaving the Kongo were routed through the fort at Mina to be resold. Soon another commercial route was established, with stops in São Tomé, to accommodate the growing numbers of slaves from the area. The increasing importance of the Mina Castle was not only financial but symbolic, coming to represent the robust Portuguese colonial initiative. Other forts were soon constructed at strategic locations in the empire, such as Luanda, Mozambique, Goa, Macau, and Itamaracá.

The Portuguese missionary project gained a nominal victory with the conversion of the king of Kongo, baptized as Dom João I, around 1491. The king soon abandoned Christianity, but his son, baptized Dom Afonso I, stayed truer to the faith and worked to continue conversions in the kingdom early in the 1500s.[31] Still, the apparent fickleness of Africans with respect to Christianity was not the only limitation faced by the Catholic Church. It was simply not easy to find missionaries willing to risk the area's inhospitable conditions and many diseases to work there. Afonso's son D. Henrique was educated in Portugal and made a bishop in 1520, but he never returned to Kongo. Portugal's suggestion to instruct converted Africans to teach the catechism was deemed too dangerous to ever put into practice.

In 1488, with the rounding of a notorious rocky headland off modern South Africa, the so-called Cape of Torments or Cape of Storms was renamed the Cape of Good Hope. With this achievement, the entire West Coast of Africa had been effectively delineated by Portuguese navigators, and Guinea could be accessed by a series of Portuguese ports. The new sea routes to the Orient that this made possible were crowded and disputed by Portuguese, Dutch, French, and English ships; meanwhile, forts, towns, and factories of various European nations dotted the coastal territories. The new maritime routes transformed not only coastal linkages but also helped expand trade into the West African hinterland. Between 1450 and 1500, Portugal's inventory of slaves traded across the Atlantic totaled approximately 150,000 people.[32] In a classic study of Atlantic history, the French scholar Pierre Chaunu observed that "black Africa was definitively sundered from the Maghrib and set adrift in the sea."[33] Of course, there were no concrete new divisions between coastal and Saharan Africa, but the connections between them had been remade.

Renaissance maps of the African landmass would have to be redrawn, and period maps depicted an Africa growing in detailed complexity with every generation of cartographers. The Insularium Illustratum, a planisphere drawn by Henricus Martellus in 1489, shows the southern coast as traced by Bartolomeu Dias. From the Cape of Good Hope onward, lack of information left the drawing vague, and the eastern coast lacks the island of Madagascar (that would first be called São Lourenço). For their part, the contours of Asia still largely resemble what Ptolemy had imagined. Soon, however, the increasing expeditions toward both Asia and the Americas resulted in an innovative 1502 planisphere called Cantino's Map, after its creator, Alberto Cantino. This work shows the Southern Hemisphere, including the American continent and the Caribbean, in remarkable detail, and includes a recognizable depiction of North America.[34]

Across the Portuguese empire by the sixteenth century, the word Guinea becomes a generic label for the source of slaves. Requests for slaves in Brazil, for instance, never indicated a specific region from which slaves should be drawn. The letter to the king from Duarte Coelho Pereira (1485–1554), donatary captain of the captaincy of Pernambuco, was typical in asking for "some slaves from Guinea." Padre Manoel da Nóbrega similarly appealed for "Guinea negroes" to work at the Colégio dos Jesuítas in

Bahia. But within the royal administration that regulated the slave trade through such controls as licensing and taxation, the record keeping was more precise. This body responded to the accumulating requests from Brazilian colonists for "Guinea slaves" by authorizing the captain at São Tomé, in 1559, to send up to 120 "slaves from Kongo" to each plantation owner who received certification from the governor of Brazil.[35]

The city of São Paulo de Luanda, founded in 1575, reflects how the commerce in slaves had come to give both form and direction to the Portuguese presence in Africa. Between 1575 and 1591, Angola exported some 50,000 slaves to Portugal, Spain, and their respective colonies.[36] By contrast, the trade in both slaves and gold from the Mina Coast that had produced such notable riches for Portugal the previous century was in evident decline. In 1585, the crown attempted to lease this part of its commercial holdings to suitable investors for 24 *contos* per year; once the first contract had expired, given the lack of interested parties, Mina reverted to the king's control.[37]

During the period of the Union of the Iberian Crowns (1580–1640), the Portuguese explorer and merchant Duarte Lopes proposed the construction of two new principal facilities to rationalize the warehousing and marketing of slaves in each country: one in Lisbon, focusing on slaves from Kongo, São Tomé, and Angola; and the other in Seville, handling slaves from Cape Verde and the so-called Guinea Rivers.[38] His proposal was not acted upon, but it indicates the growing demarcation between two general geographical sources of slaves on the West Coast of Africa—and it also reflects Portugal's sharpening interest in the central part of the coast. This is further revealed in Duarte's exertions to create a bishopric in the Kongo city of São Salvador, where he lived for several years; the bishopric was approved in 1596. By the beginning of the seventeenth century, both commercial and religious activity had divided the formerly shapeless Guinea into two distinct realms: the Mina Coast, and Kongo/Angola, both of them advanced posts in the Portuguese Empire.

A wide survey of maps, official sources of various kinds, and even period literature about the Portuguese vision of Africa in the fifteenth and sixteenth centuries has left me with two overall conclusions. First, it is unwise for a historian to adopt phrases such as "Guinea Coast" or "Guinea slaves," which are common in Brazilian documents until the eighteenth century, without first carrying out a vigorous study of the meanings of the label "Guinea" in the particular contexts involved. Second, and whatever Guinea can be understood to signify, by the early fifteenth century the Mina Coast had already taken on a distinct identity in Portugal's toponymy of the western African coast. It is possible to conceptualize it as a territory corresponding to a stage of conquest (the contract of Fernão Gomes); a determined constellation of African "nations" that together constitute the "heathens of Mina"; and the fort, often called the Mina Castle, which both symbolized and inspired the Portuguese colonial project.

THE MAP OF AFRICA IN THE HISTORIOGRAPHY OF THE SLAVE TRADE

The changing Portuguese presence in Africa can be viewed in a series of four phases: first, the expeditions advancing along the coast, as Zurara recounted—1415–48; second, arrival in the "land of the negroes" and the recognition of Guinea—1448–69; third, growing commercial bases in the Mina Coast, São Tomé and Kongo, described by Rui de Pina, and administered by a burgeoning royal authority—1469–82; and fourth, the exploration of Angola, after 1482. As the geographical concept of Guinea grew during this period, the western boundaries of a Christian Ethiopia, anticipated by Zurara, were never reached. At the same time, older topographical characterizations of the western coast were enriched by a new multiplicity of villages, ports, ethnic groups, and commercial relations.

Based on this perspective of the history of Portugal in Africa, I decided to examine some of the classic texts on Brazilian slavery and slave commerce to both isolate their underlying visions of Portuguese expansion, and raise points of contrast with the present work. I start, in chronological order, with the positivist historian Francisco Adolfo de Varnhagen (1816–78). He cited Guinea, the Mina Coast, and Kongo (here probably including Angola), but highlighted the events and importance of the Mina Coast. Incorrectly, he attributed to this region the "nations" of Nagô speakers,[39] who were heavily represented in the shipments of slaves to Brazil in the first half of the nineteenth century, during the years when Varnhagen was completing his education. Given his interests in politics and power, he gave greater emphasis to the nation as the fundamental identifying unit of local (political) organization than to the categories of "heathens" or "pagans," which open into sociocultural and religious dimensions.[40]

Nina Rodrigues (1862–1906) was a medical doctor and observer of the so-called human races, a popular theme in the waning years of the nineteenth century. A pioneer in calling for the serious study of the provenience of African slaves in Brazil, he cites Varnhagen as an example of the deficiencies of extant historiography. At the same time, like the previous author he linked provenience with nationality. Thus the "kingdom of Guinea," which continued to mushroom through "Portuguese colonial grandiosity . . . from the Senegal to the Orange Rivers"[41]—that is, from modern Senegal to South Africa—contained within its purportedly discrete boundaries numerous places from which slaves were taken. But there was never a kingdom of Guinea, either of African extraction or by Portuguese extension (the only real Portuguese occupation was in Angola).

In a 1906 essay, Sílvio Romero (1851–1914)—philosopher, literary critic, and scholar of African influences in Brazilian culture—indicted what he viewed as bias in the historiography, as well as in Brazilian society:

> No one has deigned to concentrate on the negroes, which is a most abominable expression of ingratitude. What was the ethnographic map of Africa when Brazil began to import slaves from beyond the seas? And in the eighteenth century, when this enterprise continued? And in the nineteenth, until 1850, when this terrible trade overpassed the previous centuries? What about the classification of races, and the political situation of African states? What about the social organization of those people? From which tribes did we take slaves, and in what number? What do we owe them, in economic, social, and political terms?[42]

Interestingly, despite the assertion of African cultural diversity in this passage, Romero's writings as a whole betray the assumption of the existence of a sort of blanket Bantu unity that contradicts his own occasional claims (as well as those of Rodrigues).

The historian João Lúcio de Azevedo (1855–1933) drew heavily from the chronicles of Zurara to describe a changing geography of color and belief across Africa, emphasizing the rainbowlike diversity of the first generation of captives: "bright whites to more or less tarnished; mixed-bloods to negroes, the dark hue a measure of whence along the southward expeditions they were taken. Islamic at the start, and by the end a gleaming black, all barbarous idolaters."[43] This recalls Zurara's reference to the progressive darkening of the native peoples of Guinea.

The most important historian of the Atlantic commerce of slaves in Brazil was Maurício Goulart (1908–83), a pioneer in attempting to estimate the total numbers involved in the trade.[44] But he was less interested in comprehending the diverse cultural and geographic proveniences of the slaves in Brazil than he was in defending the notion of four historically dominant trading routes across the ocean: from High Guinea, Mina Coast, Angola, and Mozambique (or east coast). Of the sixteenth century he stated, "In popular conception there was no Africa, there was Guinea. The entire region from which negroes were ransomed, the West Coast of Africa, from top to bottom was Guinea."[45] Still, because his ultimate goal was an estimate of the numbers of slaves sent to Brazil, his distinctions were few. He delineated the two main commercial origins, Mina Coast and Angola, and suggested where the majority of slaves from each source was sent—Mina slaves to Bahia and Angola slaves to Rio de Janeiro. Even more recent authors have been satisfied to stay within this dualistic version of the proveniences of Brazilian slaves, a perspective that was not born with Goulart but that emerged in the sixteenth century with the way Portugal established and conceptualized its African possessions and trade routes. Period maps, such as that of Sebastião Lopes (1558), accentuate the principal features of Portuguese Africa: the Mina Castle and the Catholic Church erected in Kongo.[46]

Charles R. Boxer (1904–2000), an English historian with many substantial contributions to the history of colonial Brazil, analyzed Portuguese slave trading in Angola but largely ignored the Mina Coast.[47] To the degree that he was interested in the Portuguese empire, his preference for Angola is comprehensible, given the larger Portuguese presence there. But the effect was to exclude the Mina Coast from his analysis of Portuguese history. (His brief consideration of the Mina Coast focuses on the Dutch presence.)

There are several reasons why the historiography has been built with recurring gaps and shadows over the circumstances that created commercial and cultural ties between Brazil and the Mina Coast in the sixteenth and seventeenth centuries. When Frédéric Mauro wrote his highly influential book about the Portuguese Atlantic of the seventeenth century, little information was accessible about either the Mina Coast or São Tomé. The resulting imbalance, or difference in emphasis, perhaps contributed in its own way to the historians of the period that followed in Mauro's wake.[48] The historiography on the slave trade to Bahia is mostly dedicated to the eighteenth century and later, an era for which documentation is comparatively abundant.[49] For Rio de Janeiro, the connection to Mina has been practically ignored. The ties between Rio and Angola in the seventeenth century —embodied in the figure of Salvador de Sá, a theme expertly studied by Boxer—have left the illusion of exclusivity and continuity that do not hold for the eighteenth century, when (as shown in the tables of chapter 2), a significant number of Africans were brought to the city from the Bight of Benin.[50]

It should be noted that the complex question of the cultural diversity of African slaves has been of more interest to the social sciences generally than to history proper. Following Rodrigues's lead, Arthur Ramos was the first to attempt an elaborate map of cultural origins as well as an evaluation of academic production on the topic. The French sociologist Roger Bastide, working within the cultural approach of Herskovits, produced important work with a consistent focus on religion. Rodrigues, Ramos, and Bastide are, each in his own manner and time, the principal names of what we might call the Bahian school of Afro-Brazilian studies.

Arthur Ramos (1903–49) presented, in 1936, the first general classification of the African peoples brought to Brazil. His work criticized the partiality of Rodrigues (for the Sudanese Africans) and Romero (for the Bantu); he chided Romero for not answering his own forceful questions on the study of origins, and proposed responding to them himself. Deploying a range of racial and cultural criteria, he reformulated the two basic groups of Africans familiar to scholars—Sudanese and Bantu—into four new cultural categories: Sudanese (Yoruba, Dahomean, Fanti-Ashanti, and others); Guinean-Islamic Sudanese (Fula, Mandinga, Haussa, and others); Angola-Kongo Bantu; and East African Bantu. In his map of the Brazilian distribution of these groups, he situated the Bantu in Maranhão, Pernambuco, Alagoas, Minas Gerais, and Rio de Janeiro. Sudanese groups joined the Bantu in Maranhão, but they were the dominant African population in Bahia.[51]

The anthropologist Melville Herskovits (1895–1963) led a group of American researchers to Brazil, by way of Africa, to study the acculturation of Africans and their descendants. Herskovits had studied at Columbia University under Franz Boas, as had Gilberto Freyre; both these men were deeply influenced by the teachings of the elder anthropologist. In Brazil, Herskovits and his team observed among Afro-Brazilians what they called survivals, or the surviving traits of early African cultures. Their conclusion was that because the Fon and especially the Yoruba (from modern Benin and Nigeria) had been among the last African peoples to be taken to Brazil as slaves, between the late eighteenth century and mid-nineteenth, their cultural memories were more intact and perceptible.

Herskovits's project on the transfer of African peoples and cultures was the largest and most widely discussed such study to date. It produced an impressive documentation in the 1930s of the historical conditions surrounding the transfer of African populations to Brazil, along with maps to suggest the origins and destinations of these populations. Herskovits published two books about Dahomey—Outline of Dahomean Religious Belief (1933) and Dahomey (1938)[52]—whose influence Karl Polanyi explicitly acknowledged in his own important historical study, Dahomey and the Slave Trade.[53] However, the fact remains that despite the interest Herskovits expressed in Fon speakers in Africa, and their descendants in Brazil, his curiosity did not inspire substantive studies (by him or his contemporaries) either of slaves from that region, or of the "Jêje candomblés" of Bahia. Indeed, anthropologists as well as historians in the first half of the twentieth century concentrated on Yoruba speakers, neighbors of the Fon, and their descendants in Brazil. If historians tended to focus on the history of slavery, not of Africa, anthropologists often homed in on the religious and cultural heritage of Yoruba derivation.

Such was the case with Roger Bastide (1898–1974), a French sociologist who arrived in Bahia in 1940. He published extensively, but is perhaps best known for the 1958 O Candomblé da Bahia (Rito Nagô) and the 1960 As Religiões Africanas no Brasil, books in which he applied first an ethnographic and then a historical-sociological perspective to the religiosity of slaves and their descendants in Brazil. Bastide envisioned a continuum of religious culture extending from Africa to Bahia. From there it went to Rio de Janeiro, where it was broken down and assimilated into such syncretized Brazilian forms as "macumba." Both books privilege the purity and authenticity of the Nagô legacy—a predilection that is implicit in the first work, and explicit (even insistent) in the second.[54]

In *Religiões Africanas*, Bastide included a critical survey of the literature on the Atlantic commerce of African slaves, and suggested that Arthur Ramos had glimpsed the "definitive solution" to the problem of classifying African cultures. He proposed one qualification to Ramos's four cultural categories—subdividing the Angola-Kongo Bantu group into eastern and western—and then proceeded to a succinct century-by-century chronology of how the Portuguese slave trade mapped Africa: sixteenth century, the exploration of Guinea (then including what would be known as Angola); seventeenth century, the establishment of primary commercial relations with Angola; eighteenth century, the reversion of the commercial base to the Mina Coast, and the replacement of shipments of mostly Bantu by "Mina or Sudanese"; nineteenth century, Angola's distinction once again as the center of the trade. Bastide made the following observation about the designation of slave origins:

> In the beginning all the African slaves sent to Brazil were called "Guinea negroes," but one should not read too much into this because in the sixteenth century Guinea extended from Senegal to Orange. The so-called "Guineas" arriving in Brazil were most likely Bantus. After all, do not the records of the Inquisition in Bahia often include references to the "Guinea negro, son of the Angola race"? However, it's probable that during the first years of colonization most slaves came from regions above the Equator.[55]

Bastide did not sufficiently explain why the slave trade of the sixteenth century should be understood as mostly Bantu, and his recycling of stereotypes and undefended assertions contribute little to the historical problems at hand. If anything, the popularity and influence of his work have acted to discourage research programs that might challenge such inherited views.

In sum, we can derive from the above authors three basic chronological criteria that they applied in different ways to the task of locating the sources of Brazil's slave trade across time. First, there is the perspective of stages of Portuguese expansionism, starting with the approach to Guinea (as described by Zurara) and the occupation of the Mina Coast, followed by the drying up of Mina's gold trade and Portugal's growing relations with

Kongo and Angola. Although these authors all seemed to recognize that the construction of the Mina Castle was contemporaneous with the conquest of the central-western coast, they wrote as though these were successive events and represent distinct historical epochs.

Second, there is the perspective of differentiating ethnic or provenience groups by "nation." Period documents use the terms *gentios* (heathens) and *nações* (nations), although they are not interchangeable. Heathen from Angola might also have been considered a nation, from the point of view of Portuguese or Brazilian observers, but the reverse is not true, since a nation was a broader social construct that could have contained both heathens and converted individuals. And while there were "Guinea heathen" in general, there never existed a Guinea nation. Guinea, a term of toponymy from the fifteenth century, corresponded only to a heathen person of generic ethnicity from West Africa. Over a relatively short span of time the term fell into disuse and was progressively substituted by *nação* (nation) in the colonial documentation.

Finally, there is the periodization of the Portuguese historiography that emerged with the Avis dynasty. This corresponds to the reigns of Dom Afonso V (1438–81),[56] and of Dom João II (1477/81–1495), who were principally responsible for impelling the explorations to the Mina Coast and Kongo/Angola.[57] These two kingdoms were associated with different strategies and geographies of maritime expansion. If the mysteries of Guinea were first penetrated under Dom Afonso V, the more targeted efforts of João II led to the construction of Mina Castle (1482–86), the first forays up the Congo River (1482–85), and the occupation of Angola's coast (1486).

Whereas some of the authors discussed above used these criteria to discuss the commerce of slaves, others applied them to the study of African cultures and contact between cultures in the colonial setting. But it is notable that none of them attempted to question what is a sort of received consensus about the spatial distribution of African peoples. Certainly all were concerned with the proveniences of the African slaves who were sent to Brazil, but they all also tended to forget or ignore the histories of these peoples and the contours of both short-term and long-term change— before but especially during the eras of European contact. Slave trafficking, whether for external sale or for the myriad internal political disputes between African groups, was one force affecting the movements and distribution of people; other primary factors included droughts and the spread of Islam. But even beyond spatial distribution, these forces could have impacted the social organization and cultural expression of these peoples. We confront the possibility that while much of the west African coastal region has been mapped by the historiography, the populations who lived there may themselves remain quite unknown to us, as they changed and regrouped and adapted throughout the nearly five centuries of the Atlantic slave trade. Nina Rodrigues was keenly aware of the need to better comprehend Africa, and the lives of people there, throughout the period.

> In the records of the trade in human flesh, customs receipts should have indicated the provenience (procedência) of each tragic shipment, at least with reference to the port in Africa where they were loaded aboard ship. But this was rarely done, and when done, rarely with accuracy. The best one could hope to see was an indication of the port, and this says nothing of the hunting grounds from which the slaves were snatched, by war or by fraud; nor of the central markets where the slaves were taken to be sold before being herded to port. It is only with such information that one could discern, in the cold statistics of black immigration, the provenience of the people brought to Brazil in the slavers' holds.[58]

In the dialogue, or absence of a dialogue, between these authors we can see the distance imposed by their different theoretical starting points, but also by the methods of analysis adopted by each one. For a long time, historians of Brazil paid little attention to culture. The Brazilian historians Francisco Adolfo Varnhagen and João Pandiá Calógeras reflected the preoccupations of their era in their focus on politics and diplomacy. Rodrigues was in a certain sense the most modern and ambitious in his work, but he was hindered by polarized period debates over the meaning and verifiability of true knowledge. Avoiding the tendency of some historians to embrace oral histories of elderly Africans as a means of studying the past, he went the opposite way, deferring to official documents (and he loudly protested the destruction of the archives of the slave trade after abolition). In distinct ways both he and Romero suggested provocative alternative methods and sources to present-day historians—Rodrigues in his focus on migrations, using oral reports of older Africans in Brazil, and Romero in his deep immersion in the African influences in folklore and national culture.

I cannot enter here into the various historiographical impasses over race, ethnicity, and color in the general field of slavery in Brazil. My intention in this chapter has been to demonstrate that all of these important authors grappled with one particular problematic—the relations between Africa and Brazil—and the possibility of identifying continuities from one place to another. Texts and maps of the fifteenth and sixteenth centuries construct an idea of Guinea that was based on Portuguese conceptions of African geography and African culture. They served as the basis for the struggles of modern social scientists to comprehend the African presence in Brazil. The use of African and Portuguese toponymies could be alternated or combined, as with the formulaic social description reproduced by Bastide, "Guinea negro, son of the Angola race."[59]

Several points should be emphasized before we begin to look more closely at the slave trade in the Mina Coast. First, as should be clear by now, the phrases in documents of the fifteenth through seventeenth centuries that mention Guinea—such as "Guinea Coast" or *gentio de Guiné* (heathen of Guinea)—must be understood within their particular historical contexts. Effective studies of the changing meanings and borders of "Guinea" have yet to be undertaken. Second, the Mina Coast emerges by the end of the fifteenth century as a distinct place within Guinea, characterized by the construction of the Mina Castle, the development of a settlement there, and the initiation of a cyclical and complex relation of global commerce and power. Finally, I am not asserting that social scientists of the period who have highlighted the importance for Brazil of Angola, while downplaying that of the Mina Coast, are somehow simply wrong or benighted. Few historians could argue with the general claims that Mina was less important than Angola within Portuguese America; and that in the case of Rio de Janeiro, Angola was the source of most slaves both to the captaincy and the city. But by focusing on the connections between Mina and the city of Rio de Janeiro, I hope to reformulate the Portuguese colonial world in a more complex way than such general claims allow, while at the same time linking that research to a previously untold story of how some individual Africans remade their lives in the diaspora.

The physical act of slavery—capture, dislocation to the markets, commercialization, forced labor—directly impacted millions of Americans, Africans, and Asians throughout the Portuguese Empire from the fifteenth century through the nineteenth. In the higher echelons of Portuguese society, the nature of those enslaved was a topic of contentious debate not only among merchants, plantation owners, and tax collectors, but also the Catholic Church. What were the slaves' moral and intellectual capacities, and what were owners' responsibilities toward their slaves? When and how should spiritual values be allowed to override financial concerns?

SLAVE TRADING IN THE SEVENTEENTH CENTURY

On 30 July 1609, during the union of the Portuguese and Spanish Crowns (1580–1640), Felipe III of Spain (Portugal's Felipe II) stunned most Brazilians—not least the slaveholding class—when he declared that all the indigenous slaves (called Indians or *gentio da terra*, "native heathen") there were to be freed. According to the decree, they should be placed under the jurisdiction of the Jesuits, who would instruct them in the catechism and "civilize" them (to prepare them to live as vassals of the Portuguese Crown).[1] Thus began a juridical dispute that would last centuries.

The law was greeted with loud protest in the captaincy of Rio de Janeiro, where agricultural labor provided by converted indigenous people was indispensable. Slave and free Indians toiled not only in mills and plantations; they carried out a range of critical functions in the city of Rio de Janeiro, from the household delivery of water to construction and public works. Local clamor against the law was such that in 1611 another law was written to permit enslavement of Indians, by "fair war" (sometimes called "just war") for a period of ten years—a term that was rarely observed in practice.[2] The second law incited a rush across south-central Brazil: expeditions set out from Rio de Janeiro to capture Indians in the Paraíba Valley, while explorers and Indian hunters departing from São Paulo made it as far as the Paraguay basin.

At this time, Rio de Janeiro had around 3,850 inhabitants, who were then referred to as "souls": roughly 750 Portuguese, 100 Africans, and 3,000 Indians and mestiços (mixed-bloods).[3] The African demographic was increasing, but historians have neither a clear sense of its patterns early in the seventeenth century, nor of its relations to the progressive decline of the indigenous population from the captaincy of Rio de Janeiro as a whole. The smallpox epidemic of 1613 that decimated most of the indigenous in the region might have been a factor encouraging the importation of Africans. Three clues about the presence of Africans in the captaincy in the following years suggest that the profile of the local slave population was undergoing a transformation soon after 1613. First, in his massive account of the history of the captaincy, Monsenhor Pizarro mentioned an early contract for the importation of slaves from the Mina Coast. He did not provide a date for the contract, but did state that the initial request had been approved by official permit in 1615.[4] Second, in 1618, Governor Rui Vaz Pinto gave his brother Duarte Vaz the privilege of using African slaves to load and unload ships at port.[5] Third, a local 1625 law, eloquent in its implications for both the size and the restiveness of the African population, established a reward for the capture of fugitive black slaves.[6]

The present challenge is to interrogate available sources to assess the proportions of slaves from different African proveniences imported into the city of Rio de Janeiro. We know that in this period there were three principal maritime routes: from Kongo/Angola, often stopping in São Tomé; from Mina; and from so-called High Guinea (where the trade was centered along the Cacheu River in modern Guinea-Bissau), with a regular stop in Cape Verde.[7] Unfortunately, data indicating the numbers of slaves traded along these routes in the period are not reliable. And specific data for how many slaves went through which routes to the captaincy of Rio de Janeiro seem to be nonexistent. There were few local surveys or demographic studies, and no population censuses, all of which makes comprehending the general population of the city of Rio—much less its assemblage of African slaves—an unlikely feat. The only claim that can be made with relative certainty is that by the second decade of the seventeenth century, a population of African slaves—most of whom were probably taken from Kongo/Angola[8]—were working alongside indigenous slaves around the Guanabara Bay, both within Rio de Janeiro proper and throughout the city's outlying fields and hollows.

In 1632, one Father Dr. Lourenço de Mendonça arrived in Rio de Janeiro to serve as the prelate of Sé. He quickly aligned himself with the Jesuits of the local mission in their stance against the enslavement of Indians. In swift response came the predictable protests and hectoring of the prelate, but the force of local antipathy to Mendonça's position was expressed when his house, liberally dusted with gunpowder from a barrel carried boldly up to his door, was set ablaze. Mendonça survived, making him more fortunate than his predecessor Mateus da Costa Aborim, who was killed by poisoning in 1629 for, it was said, defending the cause of indigenous emancipation.[9] Such events suggest the determination of Rio's residents, particularly its landholding classes, to protect their access to Indian labor. These conflicts were occurring at the same time that the Portuguese were struggling to maintain control of their factories at different slave ports in Africa, defending them from attacks (especially by the Dutch). The future of Brazil's labor force seemed increasingly insecure. Religious commitments were constricting the possibility of relying on Indian slaves, while clashes between European powers threatened to disrupt Brazil's acquisition of Africans.

The Dutch provoked the Portuguese with a series of affronts. They had created the West India Company in 1621, and within a few years were dealing in slaves for the lucrative Caribbean market. In 1625 they attacked Bahia. In 1637, they took possession of the Mina Castle on the Mina Coast. In 1639 they occupied Pernambuco, and in 1641 Angola too went under Dutch control. Simultaneously, piracy corroded Portuguese authority and profits in the various Atlantic routes between Lisbon, the West African coast, Rio de Janeiro, and Bahia. The French, for their part, created the Compagnie des Îles d'Amérique in 1635 and began the occupation of Guadalupe. In 1638, they founded the city of Saint Louis in modern Senegal, where they engaged in the profitable export of gum arabic (a water-soluble binder derived from certain species of the acacia tree). Stretches of land in the French-held island of Martinique were converted to sugar cane fields in 1654, after seedlings were spirited there by Dutch Jews angered at their expulsion from Brazil; ten years later, using profits from its sugar exports, France formed the Compagnie des Indes Occidentales. The entire Portuguese imperial project seemed at risk.

In the midst of these tensions, Portugal confronted Spain to restore the Portuguese Crown (1640) and attempted to reassert its relevance in the Atlantic trade between Africa and the Americas. The Dutch occupation of Luanda a year later was both a symbolic and strategic blow to the Portuguese Empire, since Luanda was the principal supplier of slaves to Brazil.[10] The captaincy of Rio de Janeiro was affected by the lack not only of slaves, but of other merchandise that was carried along the human-trading routes. The increasing disarray that gripped Portugal's Atlantic commerce is reflected in the definitive insertion of the Dutch into the slave trade to the Americas—and also in the establishment of a competing sugar market in the Dutch Antilles, which served England and France as well as Holland, with plants taken from Portuguese holdings. Brazilian planters were hurt twice over, as Dutch sugar forced them to lower prices on their own exports while the demand for slave labor to cultivate and process the sugar in the Antilles raised the costs of importing slaves.[11] To centralize its efforts to regain control of its Atlantic possessions, Portugal created the Conselho Ultramarino (Oversea Council) between 1642 and 1643. One of the council's first recommendations was that trade between Portugal and Brazil must no longer be carried out in a piecemeal fashion, with small groups of ships that were easily attacked. The mercantile ships should be organized into fleets, protected by accompanying armed galleons.

One person closely following these developments was Salvador Correia de Sá, a landowner with possessions in Brazil (farther south, near the Prata River) and in Angola. A scion of Estácio de Sá, founder of the city of Rio de Janeiro, Salvador de Sá and his family controlled great swathes of land in the captaincy of Rio de Janeiro, and they dominated local politics in Rio. He served as governor of the captaincy several times, starting in 1637. In 1643, he wrote to the king in response to a royal inquiry about the best means to open trade relations with the Prata region, especially Buenos Aires. He observed that in the face of the Dutch occupation of Portuguese Angola, it would be difficult to trade with the Spanish in Buenos Aires, since the merchandise most sought after there was African slaves. It would therefore be better to retake Luanda first. He urged action, reminding the king both of the need for the meat and leather that the Spanish offered, and of the fact that a Portuguese presence along the Prata River would open access for Brazil to the silver mines at Potosí.[12]

Although there was a clear intention by the crown to make all trade more organized, efficient, and safe, in practice the powerful merchants linked to trading monopolies had more sway than individual businessmen, who either had to appeal their much smaller contracts and licenses to royal authorities, or who sought other ways to get what they needed more cheaply. An example of Salvador de Sá's influence in this regard can be seen in his response to local protest over the new law prohibiting trading ships to operate outside of the official fleets. These naval convoys sailed only twice a year between Lisbon and Brazil. To attempt an Atlantic crossing without the protection they offered would leave ships isolated and vulnerable to pirates, but Rio's businessmen evidently preferred this risk to what they saw as too egregious a constraint on their abilities to operate. In 1645 Salvador de Sá, then the captain-major of the captaincy of Rio de Janeiro,[13] even though he was residing in Lisbon, went to Rio to confront the protest. Soon after gathering in assembly to debate the law with him, local merchants declared their unified opposition and revolted against the law.[14] Salvador de Sá negotiated a few small concessions but sided with the crown in maintaining the overall structure of the law; by a curious coincidence, he was quickly named the fleets' commander, which included being given all the rights and privileges of a military general.[15] Dumbstruck, residents of Rio de Janeiro carried accusations of corruption against him to the Finance Council in Lisbon, which was persuaded to call for the opening of a formal inquiry.[16] Resisting the accusations, Salvador de Sá was ultimately nominated governor of the captaincy of Rio de Janeiro. All of this suggests that the crown and the powerful shipping monopolies were at least as concerned about clamping down on what may have been a thriving informal system of Atlantic commerce as they were about protecting Portuguese trade in general from pirates and international competitors.

Rather than staying in Rio de Janeiro, Salvador de Sá raised funds and organized a squadron to battle the Dutch in Angola. He helped retake the colony in 1648, and stayed on there as governor. In 1649, he, the renowned Jesuit priest Antônio Vieira, and other notables raised capital from private investors (especially from the Portuguese New Christian network) and created the General Company of the State of Brazil. Their first fleet was sent to Brazil in 1650, a vivid demonstration of the victory of large-business interests, including their representatives in Rio de Janeiro, over less power-ful commercial segments in the city. A private company, with few tangible connections to the crown or royal commerce, the General Company's fleets traversed the Atlantic on their own schedules, circulating merchandise (including slaves) throughout the Portuguese colonies.[17]

Mina Coast in the seventeenth century experienced a growing demand for slaves for the expanding American market, and the solidification of commercial networks increasingly linked it to the Atlantic world. Early in the century the kingdom of Hueda, in modern Benin, encouraged European traders to focus slave-hunting efforts in the Bight of Benin. Soon all of the different European nations that were present on the Mina Coast had estab-lished alliances with groups of local people to facilitate both access to slaves and the occupation of coastal territory. In this era many "castles" resembling Portugal's São Jorge da Mina were built on the littoral of mod-ern Ghana to serve a similar dual function: defense (as a fort) and com-merce (as a factory). In 1665 the English claimed Cape Corso, where a century earlier the Portuguese had constructed a modest fort. They reno-vated that old building into what came to be called Cape Coast Castle, and it served as the base of operations for expanding English interests in the area. Christiansborg Castle, constructed by the Danes in 1679, was purchased by the Portuguese and renamed São Francisco Xavier. A contingent from Bran-denburg-Prussia also built a fort, Friedrichsburg, in 1683. Some less im-posing structures were also erected along the coast to facilitate and defend slave trading, such as the French warehouse placed in Ouidah in 1671.

Three stretches of the Mina Coast became especially important in the trade: the Gold Coast, where Mina Castle sits and where the scale of trade began to mount after 1660; the kingdom of Allada, east of Mina Castle, incorporated into trading patterns after 1670; and the kingdom of Hueda, whose people were significant participants in augmenting the trade by the end of the seventeenth century. By the early eighteenth century, they had lured away many of the European trading partners of the kingdom of Allada.[18]

The historian Karl Polanyi has described the Gold Coast as a long, rain-drenched strip of sand separating the mountains from the sea. The region is intercut with lagoons, where in the sixteenth century the Portuguese encountered communities of fishing villages with little apparent political centralization. The origins of Portugal's Gold Coast slave trade were here, with most of the early negotiations involving only a few slaves (even one or two) offered by the natives directly to the Portuguese; the gold trade began under similar circumstances.[19] But it was precisely this loose form of social organization, poorly observed among fishermen in the wetlands, that the Europeans would assume were kingdoms, with discrete boundaries and authoritative central governments. The political system that the Portuguese projected onto local communities was one highly conducive to the expansion of slave commerce. Thus began a complex relationship between the emergence in the region of territorial states with centralized power, the voracious demand for slaves in the Americas, and the infrastructure and networks that developed around the business of slave commerce through ports throughout West Africa.

This was the context surrounding the first shipments of slaves to Brazil from the Bight of Benin around 1670. In the same period, in 1675, a group of merchants created the Cacheu Company to coordinate Portuguese commercial relations in High Guinea. But the Dutch intervention had been decisive, and Holland, occupying Mina Castle, soon became the dominant player in West Africa's European slave trade.[20] An insightful portrait of the era comes from William Bosman, who relocated to the area late in the seventeenth century as subcommander of the Dutch West India Company. In 1705, Bosman published a book called *Voyage to Guinea*, which includes numerous stories and asides about the West India Company as well as the Royal African Company (founded 1660 in England) and the Company of Senegal (founded 1673 in France). He believed that these three European companies, each of which from the beginning had scrambled to outflank the others, finally succeeded in destroying each other. Still, the abundant riches produced by trading in African gold and slaves meant that Holland,

England, and France all came out well ahead in the end. Bosman also observed that the most desirable slaves from the Mina Coast region were under the age of thirty-five; that the price of women was 20 percent less than that of men; and that Dutch ships usually carried between 600 and 700 captives per trip.[21]

In the eighteenth century, the most formidable kingdom of the Gold Coast was that of the Ashanti. Located in the interior, they skirmished incessantly with their southern coastal neighbors, the Akim, who sat on the source of the gold considered by European merchants to be the finest in the region.[22] As the Ashanti battled to enlarge their territory, and the Akim to defend theirs, English merchants were fortuitously situated to benefit from the additional flows of gold and slaves resulting from the strife. This was contemporaneous with the bloody but profitable struggles raging west of the Gold Coast, where the kingdom of Dahomey was fighting its way to the littoral, killing or displacing people of the Allada and Hueda kingdoms to control the maritime commerce of the Slave Coast. Directly or indirectly, both the Ashanti and Dahomey kingdoms were fighting over not only ports but the myriad land routes used to march slaves through the interior to waiting European pens and ships.

The Portuguese presence on the Mina Coast, limited after the mid-1600s, was even further diminished by these developments. A booming Atlantic demand for African slaves, combined with the power consolidation of several dominant African groups on the coast, led to a redefinition of relations between Europeans and West Africans to which the Portuguese were mostly a distant witness. They were losing their grip not only within the European commercial circuit, but also on the trade to Brazil. There, local merchants and investors, principally from Bahia, were underwriting their own slave-buying trips to the Bight of Benin to help meet a demand that the ports of Kongo and Angola seemed increasingly unable to satisfy. Portugal, unable to regulate or even effectively participate in the commerce of slaves across the Atlantic, while it was still sharply restricting access to indigenous labor in Brazil, helped usher in a transformation of labor relations in Portuguese America. Now, African slavery, obtained by local means if necessary, was looking like the definitive solution to the labor shortage afflicting some regions of Brazil—among them the captaincy of Rio de Janeiro.

In the city of Rio, disputes between Jesuits and residents over whether

Brazil's indigenous should be subject to forced labor had continued throughout the seventeenth century. In 1680 the Prince Regent and future Dom Pedro II of Portugal decreed once again the liberty of Indians, provoking yet more violent local protests. That law was modified in 1684 to allow for Indians to be maintained in relationships of private "administration," as long as they were instructed in the Catholic faith and incorporated into the church. Meanwhile, the increasingly urgent calls for importing more African slaves to the captaincy were silenced by a virulent epidemic in Angola that temporarily choked the trade, to Bahia as well as Rio de Janeiro. It was in this context that, in 1685, approval was granted by the governor of Bahia to a proposal, submitted by local merchants, to send a ship to the Mina Coast on a slave-buying trip. The initial petition made reference to the "news that comes from Angola that smallpox has so direly afflicted it, one may fear that in many years the loss of negroes dead of the disease will not be recouped." Smallpox wrought devastation in Angola during the 1680s, and it is not surprising that the epidemic should be adduced in the arguments for turning to the Mina Coast, especially the Bight of Benin. It is notable that the Bahian slave traders sought authorized access to the ports of Mina. At any rate, their preferred mode of conveyance, the *patacho*—a nimble but small vessel with only two masts—could carry but a miniscule proportion of the human cargo handled by the large European shipping companies of the day.[23]

RIO DE JANEIRO'S SLAVE TRADE
IN THE EIGHTEENTH CENTURY

In his analysis of the evolution of Rio de Janeiro's commercial activity from the eighteenth century to the nineteenth, the historian Manolo Florentino shows how the centrality of local traders to the city's development, in its myriad aspects, often led to conflicts of interest with the Portuguese Crown.[24] This was also the case in the seventeenth century. Even if the documents for the earlier period are less abundant, they are quite expressive of such tensions and indicate how they could persist and multiply with the passage of time.

Late in the seventeenth century, a call went out to send slaves to the new mining region north of Rio de Janeiro proper, a place increasingly referred to as "Minas" (referring to the gold mine lands) and later "Minas Gerais" (General Mines), where gold had been discovered. In 1699, the crown legalized slave trading from the Mina Coast to Brazil, creating what quickly became a busy and prosperous circuit of gold and slaves flowing between Minas (the mines in Brazil's central interior) and Mina (the Bight of Benin in West Africa). Pernambuco, Bahia, and Rio also partook in the trade, anxious for access to slave labor. In the immediate rush, however, proper taxes—principally the quinto ("fifth")—were not always paid to Portugal. This allegation was the premise of a letter written by D. Rodrigo Costa, governor of Bahia (1702–5), to the crown on 20 June 1703. In a rambling diatribe, Costa accused the traders in Rio of having maximized their personal gain in recent years by not only avoiding or underpaying the taxes, but by using the gold carted to its ports from Minas Gerais to buy slaves from other European brokers instead of from Portugal's appointed agents in Benin.[25] Whether Costa's motivations stemmed from personal loyalty to the crown or indignation at what he saw as unfair competition remains unclear.

However, the response was prompt. That same year, 1703, King Pedro II prohibited the departure of slavers from Rio de Janeiro for the Mina Coast, and instituted quotas for the allocation of Mina slaves between Rio, Bahia, Pernambuco, and the gold mines of Minas, with the additional stipulation that all slaves should be imported through Bahia. This measure was intended not so much to limit the importation of slaves as to more closely regulate the movement of Brazilian gold, with the objective of keeping it out of the hands of foreign establishments plying the Mina Coast trade. Bahia's primacy in the region did not last too long. The 1703 law was never fully complied with, and it was abolished in 1715 in the face of a rapid expansion of mining in the area and a concomitant need for more slaves.[26] It is unclear how many slaves the traders in Rio de Janeiro helped bring to Minas Gerais between 1703 and 1715, and targeted research is urgently needed to illuminate this poorly known chapter of Brazil's commerce with the Mina Coast.

Meanwhile, Rio's merchants were locking horns with the colonial administration over what they argued was prejudicial treatment. In 1704, officials from the city council sent a representative to the Oversea Council in Portugal to denounce alleged abuses of power by then governor, D.

Álvaro da Silveira e Albuquerque (1702–4). According to the letter drawn up by the council, which included some of Rio's most important local businessmen,

> The officials of the City Council of Rio de Janeiro inform His Majesty that when several vessels arrived into that port carrying shipments of slaves from Mina Coast and São Tomé, Governor D. Álvaro da Silveira obliged the ships to remove themselves to a deserted island to be examined for contagious diseases. He did not permit the ships to disembark in the city until each one had provided him with the best negro specimen on board, all of which slaves being then informed they were property of the Governor, and commanded to hoist him on his *palanquim* [sedan] and carry him to and fro.[27] Beyond this offense he demanded the right for himself and his family to buy the best of the remaining slaves for a trifle, and they then sold these slaves to the people of the city at a profit, each person making at least 40,000 or 50,000 réis. When they do this again, with the ships coming from Angola, we will deliver another letter of complaint to His Majesty.[28]

This curious manner of advertising a future complaint about the same offenses should not be taken to indicate that traders maintained exclusive relationships with the different sources of slaves—that is, that some merchants in Rio de Janeiro dealt only with Mina slaves, and others only with Angola slaves, so that a distinct set of merchants would be hurt by the governor's actions in each case. Rather, the letter indicates the formation of complex political alliances and interest groups in the city, for whom a campaign of letter-writing to the Oversea Council represented a strategic move. Unfortunately, I could not discover what the council made of this communication. But, coincidence or no, Álvaro da Silveira was replaced as governor of the captaincy that very same year, with D. Fernando Martins Mascarenhas taking his place.

In 1706, D. Rodrigo da Costa, the ex-governor of Bahia, was still preoccupied with Rio de Janeiro and the slave trade even as he headed back to Lisbon. In a letter he wrote to the king ostensibly about Brazil's gold mines, he quickly returned to the themes of commerce with the Mina Coast and Rio's evasion of the royal fifth. In this context he also alerted the king to the apparent fact that slaves in the mining region were worth two to three times more than they were in the plantations. He went so far as to propose the outright prohibition of any shipment of slaves to Rio de Janeiro, be they "from Angola or the Mina Coast, Bahia, Pernambuco, Paraíba, the Islands, Lisbon, Mozambique, India, or any other place in or out of the royal dominions of His Majesty."[29] The ex-governor suggested mandating the trading of slaves through the Cacheu Company, a Portuguese concern boasting a substantial naval fleet that was already active in the trade. (Slaves arriving at Bahia usually had departed from the Bight of Benin, but at least some of those in Pernambuco and Paraíba came from the region called High Guinea, and appeared in the documentation in Rio de Janeiro as *cacheos* or *cacheus*.) Again, the idea was less to limit the absolute numbers of imported slaves than to channel the trade into the hands of the so-called *Junta de Cacheu* (Cacheu Council), an assortment of rich merchants, politicians, and insiders who owned the company. In fact, as an investor in the company, D. Rodrigo had a personal interest in seeing the Cacheu Council gain exclusive slave-trading rights. He was exasperated at all the business lost to local traders and smugglers in Brazil,[30] especially in Rio, although in his missives to the king he tended to dwell on the argument of the unpaid taxes. It remains unclear the extent to which local traders may have participated in larger commercial and financial networks, including Portugal and even other European countries.[31] Apparently swayed by D. Rodrigo's insistence, the Oversea Council threatened, in a 1706 document, to denounce "in public or in private" all plantation owners in Brazil who sold their slaves to the mines for an untaxed profit.[32] A reading of various related documentation indicates that the ministers of the Oversea Council were increasingly amenable to the idea of reinstating the "exclusive system," in which large Portuguese companies would dominate the trafficking of slaves to Brazil and local autonomy to trade externally or within the colony would be diminished.

By the first years of the eighteenth century, there existed two routes linking Minas Gerais with Atlantic trade. One went south-southwest from Salvador, crossing the interior scrublands, following when possible the course of several rivers until arriving at the villages of Minas, especially Vila Rica (later named Ouro Preto) and Vila do Carmo (later Mariana), the location of the principal gold mines of the time—often called the *Caminho do Sertão*, a hinterland route described by Antonio Andreoni. He was a Jesuit who published under the name André João Antonil while living in Bahia in the late seventeenth century and early eighteenth. The second route extended north from Rio de Janeiro by sea until Parati, then across the Mantiqueira mountain range to the same villages in Minas. It has received comparatively less study, although it is makes an appearance in the narrative of the travels of the Count of Assumar, who arrived as the governor of Minas in 1717.[33]

The trading of slaves within Brazil was not as pervasive as its critics intimated, although there were internal commercial routes based on the rough trails linking Rio de Janeiro, Minas Gerais, and Bahia. These terrestrial routes were also the final stage of an Atlantic journey bringing slaves from Africa to the mines at Minas. In the first half of the eighteenth century, according to Maurício Goulart, some 2,000 captives a year were marched from Salvador to Minas down the Interior Trail. Between 1728 and 1748, 40 percent of the slaves arriving in Salvador were destined for the mines. The same author has demonstrated that starting in 1715, somewhat more than 2,200 slaves a year passed through the port at Rio de Janeiro from the Mina Coast on their way to Minas. Between 1725 and 1727, around 5,700 captives a year arrived in Rio from the Mina Coast and Cape Verde; of these, 2,300 were dispatched to Minas. The rest were divided in various ways between the captaincy of Rio de Janeiro and the cities of Rio and São Paulo.[34]

There are no systematic studies of the Parati route that linked Rio de Janeiro and Minas Gerais. Historians seem to have dismissed its importance in the larger networks of trade connecting Brazil to the Atlantic world. This neglect echoes the longstanding lack of interest in the presence of Mina slaves in Rio de Janeiro. That the two phenomena are related in complex ways encouraged me to explore the available primary sources more widely, and apply the insight or evidence gained about one of the historical problems back to the other, thereby keeping them in dialogue. This is where baptism records helped fill in some of the gaps left in the data on Rio's slave imports and the city's retention of a small percentage of those sent on to Minas. Where it exists, baptism data tend to be relatively reliable because of the nature of the ritual and the singular importance it held for contemporaries. Of course, when adult African slaves were baptized, broader data appealing to subsequent researchers (such as the proportion of baptized versus nonbaptized slaves in the parish or city, or the identity of the company or merchant that brought a given slave to the city) were hardly ever included in the record books. Nonetheless, these records constituted a critical source of information for my inquiries.

In the first half of the eighteenth century, the city of Rio de Janeiro contained two urban parishes: Sé and Candelária. The oldest record book of slave baptisms available to me at the time of research was the 7° *Livro de Batismo de Pretos Cativos da Freguesia da Sé* (Seventh Book of Baptisms of Black Captives in Sé Parish), covering the years from 1718 to 1726. Data from the earlier period (1702–17), when slaves began arriving in Rio in substantial numbers, would have been extremely helpful. Even still, suggestive trends emerged from these records that could be correlated elsewhere. Over the period covered by the records, significantly more baptisms were performed for adult slaves brought from the Mina Coast than from any other provenience (even though it is well established that more slaves were arriving from Angola than from anywhere else),[35] and these numbers were especially concentrated in the years 1722 and 1724.

Those were years of intense conflict along the Slave Coast. The kingdom of Dahomey invaded the kingdom of Allada in 1724, and the kingdom of Hueda in 1727, and took control of the commerce of slaves along a vast expanse of prized coastline. According to Polanyi, at this time French and English traders operated individually or in small associations up and down the coast, while the Portuguese and the Dutch—accustomed to the "exclusive system" of large organized companies—tended to negotiate their cargoes in the Bight of Biafra (in modern Nigeria) or in Kongo.[36] This approach might explain why the importation of slaves from the Bight of Benin to Rio de Janeiro went into sharp decline after 1725, although it had been falling gradually for several years. The instability of full-out war in the region, combined with Portugal's current preference for other sources of slaves, led to a slowdown in the local trade to Brazil. By late 1730 or early 1731, the kingdom of Dahomey had secured the coast and had reversed its battle maneuvers to push northward, into the hinterlands of the Bight of Benin and deeper in the interior, where it lay siege against the kingdom of Oyo. This was also where the Mahi territory lay, and the region soon became, as the historian Akinjogbin observed, a "hunting ground" for the Dahomean incursions to gather prisoners, slaves, or both.[37]

Pierre Verger analyzed the inventories kept by Bahian slave owners be-

Table 2. Baptisms of Adult Africans in Sé Parish, 1718–1726

YEAR	PROVENIENCE													TOTAL	
	Mina		Guinea		Central West		Cabo Verde		Cacheo		East Coast				
	#	%	#	%	#	%	#	%	#	%	#	%	#	%
1718	57	7.2	1	0.1	2	0.3	1	0.1	0	0.0	0	0.0	61	7.7
1719	64	8.1	5	0.6	7	0.9	1	0.1	0	0.0	0	0.0	77	9.7
1720	50	6.3	5	0.6	5	0.6	1	0.1	0	0.0	6	0.8	67	8.5
1721	95	12.0	13	1.6	2	0.3	0	0.0	1	0.1	11	1.4	122	15.4
1722	107	13.5	5	0.6	0	0.0	0	0.0	1	0.1	2	0.3	115	14.6
1723	73	9.2	11	1.4	0	0.0	0	0.0	0	0.0	0	0.0	84	10.6
1724	125	15.8	19	2.4	0	0.0	0	0.0	0	0.0	0	0.0	144	18.2
1725	79	10.0	9	1.1	0	0.0	0	0.0	0	0.0	0	0.0	88	11.1
1726	31	3.9	1	0.1	0	0.0	0	0.0	0	0.0	0	0.0	32	4.1
Total[a]	681	86.2	69	8.7	16	2.0	3	0.3	2	0.2	19	2.4	790	100.0

Source: ACMRJ, Livro de Batismo de Escravos, Freguesia da Sé, 1718–26. Calculations were made based on the proveniences declared in the record; these designations are analyzed in chapter 3. The column "Central West Coast" corresponds to slaves imported from that region, including such designations as Kongo, Luanda, Angola, Benguela, and Quissamã. The column "East Coast" includes slaves imported from Mozambique and the island of São Lourenço (modern Madagascar). As noted in the text, the higher percentage of Mina baptisms is explained by the Portuguese practice of baptizing slaves in Angola before taking them from Africa to Brazil.
[a]Rounding of decimals accounts for discrepancies in some of the totals.

tween 1737 and 1841. Out of a total of 187 Africans clearly originating from Dahomey, Verger identified 180 "Jêjes," three "mondobi," one "ladá," two "maquim (maí)," and one "savanu." He isolated thirty-one other slaves identified only as "minas," and one as "guiné," denominations which he considered vague enough to refer to either "Dahomeans" or "Yorubas."[38] Somewhat earlier, in Rio de Janeiro, the growing number of adult slave baptisms in the 1720s might be a function of the demand for slaves in Minas Gerais, or also of the local demand in Rio. The city was growing as its trading functions expanded, which occurred in large part due to the discoveries at Minas. Table 2 presents the Africans baptized in Sé Parish between 1718 and 1726, which gives an idea of the distribution of proveniences of slave imports to Rio de Janeiro in the period. The great variation from one year to another prevents us from drawing associations between import levels and distributions and the wars in the Bight of Benin.

While Portuguese companies were already struggling to maintain their share of the slave trade in the 1720s—in an Atlantic Ocean crowded with Dutch, English, and French ships—internal disputes between merchants in Portugal and in Brazil were beginning to heat up. In the twenty years between 1720 and 1740, traders based in Lisbon and in Bahia engaged in raucous conflict over control of the traffic to Brazil. In 1721, the Portuguese constructed a fort, São João Batista de Ajudá, in Ouidah (it was more of a warehouse, although it was often referred to as a fort). The fort went under the dominion of Dahomey in 1727, when the Dahomeans conquered the kingdom of Hueda containing the fort, and its occupation marked a new phase in the commercial relationships between African kingdoms and Portuguese and Brazilian traders. The Portuguese had long allied themselves with the kingdom of Allada, now defunct, and suffered stormy relations with a newly powerful kingdom of Dahomey. Nonetheless, the fort (called Ajudá, Judá, Uidá, Ouidah, or Whidah, depending on the document) remained the principal Portuguese commercial structure on the Mina Coast until around 1770.[39]

Most current analyses indicate that the wars waged by the Dahomeans to control sources of gold and slaves, as well as territorial routes and coastal access, resulted in mass imprisonments of men and women who were ultimately sold as slaves on the international market. However, table 2 shows a reduction in the appearance of slaves from the Mina Coast in Rio de Janeiro after 1724. Turning once again to Polanyi, we get a bit more perspective on this drop-off. He suggested that the wars' turbulence directly impacted the capacity of local traders to successfully negotiate with nervous European traders, even if the absolute number of slaves available for sale might have been increasing. And one should not take the latter point as a given. Many of the prisoners would have been disposed of by other means, either through ritual sacrifice or through local slavery on the fields of the Dahomey Kingdom. Before the attacks bore down on the realm of Allada, that kingdom was probably responsible for the sale of around 20,000 slaves a year through Ouidah. Polanyi doubted that the subsequent commerce run by the Dahomeans reached similar levels.[40] Those are all reasonable assumptions. But we are left with the puzzling coincidence of the baptism of no fewer than

144 Mina slaves in Sé Parish in Rio de Janeiro in 1724, one year after Dahomey laid siege to Allada. Since the numbers decreased to 79 in 1725, and to 31 in 1726, were these slaves the bitter fruit of that war, or were they the last harvest before the wars began?

I could find no contracts, receipts, or other specific primary sources relative to the buying, selling, or internal redistribution of slaves before 1725, but the documents from that year provide an outline of how the transactions were undertaken. In 1725, Jerônimo Lobo Guimarães was granted a new contract, which he managed to extend for three years, to administer the apportionment of slaves entering Rio de Janeiro from Mina Coast and Cape Verde.[41] In another three-year contract, dated a month later, the Oversea Council instructed Guimarães to send most of these slaves on to Minas Gerais.[42] Guimarães cropped up in an earlier document, from 1723, petitioning for multiple contracts to distribute slaves from ports at Bahia, Pernambuco, Paraíba, and Rio de Janeiro to the gold mines at Minas.[43]

The various correspondence pertaining to Guimarães reveals that his achievement of those two contracts in 1725 was met with skepticism and dissension among other merchants, and even among members of the Oversea Council itself. That very year, doubts were raised about the contractor in the council of the Treasury in Lisbon,[44] and provoked the governor of Rio de Janeiro to convene discussions with the local representatives of the Portuguese Treasury.[45] For his part, Guimarães sent five petitions defending his honor and demanding the observance of his contract.[46] He was allowed to appear before the commission in Rio, although the denunciations continued, many coming from disgruntled contenders for the choice contract Guimarães had won.[47] In October of 1725, an irate Guimarães succeeded in lodging a formal complaint against the Treasury for the damages he claimed the public mudslinging had caused him; soon after, his contract was guaranteed until 1727.[48] We can only imagine the reaction of the Oversea Council in 1726, when one André da Costa Faria petitioned the council to be recognized as Guimarães's personally nominated representative in Rio de Janeiro, and thus as the effective administrator of the contract which the embattled Guimarães had clung to so tenaciously.[49]

This episode is eloquent in its implications for how the social webs of contracts, influences, negotiations, and reputations encircled and complicated the official slave trade from the Mina Coast to the city of Rio de Janeiro and beyond. The scope and nature of all the transactions (legal or otherwise) directly and indirectly associated with the commerce of slaves remain much harder to tease out of the documents. After 1730, voyages from Brazil to the Bight of Benin required the prior permission of the viceroy. Whether Portugal's intention was to limit local autonomy or more pointedly to clamp down on smuggling, the clandestine trades (which had reached levels shocking to officials in Lisbon) clearly continued. By 1734–35, the illicit trading of gold to West Africa to buy slaves had grown almost too obvious to deny. It was discovered that not only individual smugglers but a highly organized secret company operated in the trade. One had agents based in Bahia, Pernambuco, Rio de Janeiro, Sacramento, São Paulo, and the island of São Tomé, where no less than the local judge was arrested as one of the outfit's masterminds.

The African slave trade to Brazil was carried out through the singular deals of freewheeling merchants and adventurers; official contracts, obscurely awarded but loudly disputed; and clandestine enterprises spread across the Atlantic. There was constant tension between free commerce and the exclusive system of the Portuguese monopolies, but both forms of the trade were implicated in the shadowy transfer of Brazilian gold to other European traders.[50] However the myriad actors went about the business of trading in human captives, all involved sought privileges, personal advancement, and riches. In that sense, the slaves themselves were viewed less as living beings than as merchandise, a means to an end.

The numbers in table 3 present baptism records from the Parish of Sé in the city of Rio de Janeiro from 1744 through 1750. They can be cautiously compared with the data in table 2 for a sense of the flux of imports of Mina slaves in particular. Some hints about the general decrease in total numbers might be derived from an earlier document, from 1738, that mentions a reduction of slaving voyages from Rio to the Mina Coast.[51]

The numbers in tables 2 and 3 need further contextualization, of which I can provide only a preliminary sketch. Maurício Goulart found that between 1735 and 1740, the slave population of Minas Gerais remains stable, although it had been clearly growing in previous decades. There is even a slight decline perceptible after 1740.[52] Over the same period in the city of Rio de Janeiro, there was a continued increase in the levels of Mina slaves

Table 3. Baptisms of Adult Africans in Sé Parish, 1744–1750

YEAR	PROVENIENCE													TOTAL	
	Mina		Guinea		Central West		Cabo Verde		Cacheo		East Coast				
	#	%	#	%	#	%	#	%	#	%	#	%		#	%
1744	12	4.5	1	0.4	3	1.1	3	1.1	0	0.0	0	0		19	7.2
1745	12	4.5	0	0.0	0	0.0	3	1.1	0	0.0	0	0		15	5.7
1746	33	12.5	0	0.0	1	0.4	6	2.3	0	0.0	0	0		40	15.1
1747	24	9.1	0	0.0	1	0.4	0	0.0	1	0.4	0	0		26	9.8
1748	37	14.0	0	0.0	0	0.0	4	1.5	0	0.0	0	0		41	15.5
1749	49	18.5	2	0.8	0	0.0	0	0.0	0	0.0	0	0		51	19.2
1750	68	25.7	2	0.8	0	0.0	3	1.1	0	0.0	0	0		73	27.5
Total[a]	235	88.7	5	1.9	5	1.9	19	7.2	1	0.4	0	0		265	100.0

Source: ACMRJ, Livro de Batismo de Escravos, Freguesia da Sé, 1744–61. See the additional explanations in source note for table 2.

[a] Rounding of decimals accounts for discrepancies in some of the totals.

that roughly tracks with the growth of the city proper. The number of Mina adult slaves baptized in Sé went from 12 in 1744 to 68 in 1750, while the total baptisms for all African adults grew from 19 to 73 in those years. The increase between 1744 and 1750 in the absolute number of slaves in the city might be attributed to the slight lowering in the price of slaves, which might itself be a reflection of a tapering off of demand in Minas Gerais. But more likely the main factor was the rapid transformation of Rio de Janeiro, in terms of new urban development, population growth, and businesses; as well as the creation in 1751 of the second High Court in Brazil (the first was in Salvador, the colonial capital until Rio earned that distinction in 1763).[53] Just as slaves imported from the Mina Coast had been introduced to meet an urgent demand in the mines, which the trade with Angola appeared insufficient to satisfy, so would Mina slaves in later years be brought to serve the needs of the new capital of the colony.

After 1730, the decline of direct commerce between Rio and the Mina Coast is probably based on the requirement for prior authorization from the viceroy, associated with the machinations of the powerful Bahian traders whose interests the restriction served. According to a survey carried out by Pierre Verger in the Hague, between 1724 and 1740 there were 212 pass-ports awarded by the Dutch West India Company to "Portuguese vessels" docking at the Mina Castle: 129 of them were from Bahia, 73 from Pernam-buco, 9 from Paraíba, and 1 from Rio de Janeiro.[54] Even granting the steep decline in baptisms of Mina slaves from 1725–26 (110) to 1744–45 (down to 24), the appearance of these new arrivals needs to be comprehended. The likeliest explanations are that they were brought from unlicensed ships between Rio and the Mina Coast, or that they had first arrived at port in Brazil in a different city, such as Salvador or Recife.

THE TRADE IN GOLD AND TOBACCO

We enter very briefly here into the ways that historical documents describe slaves who derive from different regions (and I must refrain from pursuing how such ideas ultimately fed into the wider colonial-era processes of identifying Africans in both Brazil and Africa). Boxer linked the trading of slaves from the Mina Coast at the end of the seventeenth century with the impelling demand at the gold mines, but also with the physical force of Mina slaves perceived by contemporary observers.[55] Referring to roughly the same period, from 1700 to 1730, Russell-Wood suggested that the bad reputation of Mina slaves in Bahia created downward pressure on their prices, which made them appealing when Angola slaves could not be produced in sufficient number to satisfy local demand.[56] But a letter from the governor of Rio de Janeiro to the crown in 1726 plays up their ostensibly unique and valuable knowledge: "No miner can live without a Mina Black; it is said that only with them is there good luck."[57] Along those very lines, an eighteenth-century manuscript, cited by Scarano, highlighted the sup-posed familiarity these slaves had with the methods of prospecting: "The Mina Blacks from the Tombuo Bambui Kingdoms are generally the best miners of gold in Brazil, and perhaps it was they who instructed the Portuguese on how to remove the gold from the alluvium, since it is so like a method they already know."[58] This line is highly valuable, since it indi-cates that the Portuguese searched out specialists in gold mining from the region of Timbuktu. Although it might be utterly anecdotal, it (and other references to a magical ability of "Mina blacks" to sniff out gold) reinforces the idea that West Africans were known for gold mining, which suggests that this might have been the motive for choosing slaves from the Mina Coast region to work in the mines of Brazil. It was an idea with little substance behind it, since most of these slaves had never mined in Africa. But in a form of popular alchemy, their very presence came to connote good luck, good fortune, and happy endings to those eagerly running the mining and wildcatting operations in Brazil.

The question of the particular qualities accorded to slaves by provenience must be treated with care because, as Russell-Wood pointed out, the qualities attributed to such groups by those in power vary with place and epoch. For instance, we know that most slaves sent from Bahia to Minas Gerais early in the eighteenth century walked off ships that had come from the Mina Coast; and we have a sense why, based on the previous paragraphs. But I am also interested in the practical dimensions of the trade in these people—the financial, mercantile, and shipping logistics involved in their commerce, the different merchants and agents they connected, who distributes them where and why—because it is only when considered in this totality can we begin to comprehend the meanings and values that different African peoples held for plantation owners and mine operators. This level of research and analysis remains largely an ideal.

If the Portuguese perspective of the slave trade to Brazil in the eighteenth century involved a tightening of the reins on colonial upstart traders, from the point of view of Rio de Janeiro the goal seems to have been to continually try to thwart metropolitan controls. From the early decades of the century, gold was packed into vessels waiting in Rio's port to embark for the slave markets of the Mina Coast without the slightest concern for the royal fifth, or other taxes—much less for the need, articulated later, for official permission to make the route. Brazil's main ports all participated, as Boxer argued: "Gold was smuggled out by unfrequented rivers and paths through the sertão to Rio de Janeiro, Bahia, and Recife (whence some of it was again diverted illegally to the slave trade in West Africa)."[59] Unlike Bahia, which could use its tobacco as a homegrown resource in the trade with African kingdoms, the city of Rio de Janeiro relied on Minas gold— and, increasingly, Bahian tobacco, in its commerce with the Mina Coast.[60] Even though it depended on carrying goods from other Brazilian regions across the Atlantic, this trade, in concert with Rio's other mercantile endeavors, created many rich men in the city. The Pereira de Abreu family had long roots in the slave trade, but when Cristóvão Pereira de Abreu began combining commerce in tobacco and slaves in the first half of the eighteenth century, he increased the family's wealth. His heir Joaquim José Pereira de Abreu continued in Cristóvão's gilded footsteps and traded in slaves until well into the nineteenth century.[61]

Tobacco from Brazil, principally Bahia, was prized all over the world, from Europe and China to Dahomey.[62] In his book published in 1711, Andreoni stated that Rio de Janeiro was receiving 3,000 *arrobas* of Bahian tobacco a year at the time.[63] I encountered a permit dated 1 April 1712 authorizing the use for trade on the Mina Coast of tobacco "of the third category," which was prohibited in Europe, as long as the rolls did not exceed two and a half arrobas in weight.

Rio de Janeiro's trade in tobacco was plainly inferior to Bahia's,[64] but it is not without interest to the present study, because the African kingdoms on the Bight of Benin were well-known customers of the commodity. The city's first contract for brokering tobacco was created in 1695, by way of a royal decree that had been solicited by Rio's legislative assembly (the *Câmara*) in order to help pay for city staff. On 28 April 1728, Manoel Corrêa Bandeira won the tobacco contract for Rio de Janeiro from the Oversea Council, which authorized him to take possession of 4,000 arrobas of Bahian tobacco; the contract was valid for three years, based on the payment of 35,000 *cruzados* and 50,000 réis.[65] A law of 10 January 1757 mandated the opening of the city's tobacco contract to competition, and also authorized the local planting and selling of the crop.[66] The Duarte Nunes Almanac of 1799 indicates that in 1794, there were twenty-four merchants focused on reselling tobacco, a number that jumped to thirty-five by 1798.[67] But if we go all the way back to the first waves of voyages from Rio de Janeiro to the Mina Coast to exchange gold for slaves, it is possible that tobacco was also on board those ships as a trade good. Its visibility to official record keepers would have been lower in the seventeenth century than later, and it had the additional virtue of being directly appealing to African slave traders themselves, whereas European brokers in charge of much of the slave trade would have demanded gold.

What remains to be done in this chapter is to suggest how the church hierarchy, lay religious brotherhoods, tobacco merchants, and Mina slaves all intersected in the city of Rio de Janeiro throughout the eighteenth century. One perspective on this network comes from a letter written in 1709 from the bishop of Rio de Janeiro, D. Francisco de São Jerônimo, to D. João V, the king of Portugal. D. Jerônimo served as temporary governor of Rio de Janeiro three times—during the years 1704, 1708, and 1709. He wrote to ask the king for financial support to construct a new church in Sé Parish, and he offered a proposal that shows a canny awareness of both Rio's trading activity and the metropolitan bureaucracy. Rather than transferring funds from the treasury in Portugal, which D. Jerônimo noted faced "so many expenses," the bishop-cum-governor suggested that permission be granted for Rio's merchants to take 700 arrobas of Bahian tobacco beyond what the contracts allowed for. This way the crown would pay nothing directly, and D. Jerônimo could discreetly mention that the contract for tobacco as it stood was insufficient for local needs: "For many months the warehouse sits empty, causing great harm to the whites but even worse damage to the blacks, who sustain themselves with the precious smoke of the dried leaves."[68]

The letter describes the decadence of the aging Church of São Sebastião (Saint Sebastian), constructed in the sixteenth century when the city of Rio de Janeiro was founded atop a hill overlooking the bay. During the seventeenth century the city expanded to the lowlands, and many of the important families of the area began to visit the newer churches, built by lay brotherhoods along the plain. There was more autonomy in those churches than in the older Church of São Sebastião, where the bishop kept the faithful under a tight rein—especially since it was there he had established the Cabido da Sé, or administration of the bishopric. Soon this church, also referred to as Sé, came to be frequented almost exclusively by the poor population that lived in the surrounding area, and especially by the blacks and pardos who had installed their brotherhoods there. The first years of the eighteenth century had been marked by intense conflict between the diocese and the black brotherhoods. During the period from 1700 to 1704, the bishop had expulsed one association outright—the Brotherhood of São Domingos, directed by men said to have come from "Guinea heathen"—and had struggled to get rid of the Brotherhoods of Our Lady of the Rosário and of São Benedito (Saint Benedict from Palermo, also known as "the Moor") led by "Angola blacks." There is no information about brotherhoods of Mina slaves at this time; the first notice is from 1716. But the bishop's reference to blacks' benefiting from commerce in tobacco suggests the possibility that those individuals might have been so-called Mina blacks, brought to Rio on the same boats that had carried tobacco to the Bight of Benin.

The letter thus hints provocatively at the relations between traders of tobacco and slaves, slaves and free blacks, and the bishop who was trying to gain something himself from the network.[69] The proposed increase of 700 arrobas of Bahian tobacco over the contracted 3,000 suggests that the potential margin, as contributed by the traders, would have been substantial. Indeed, the bishop intimated that this contribution from the increased local trade would be worth more than the 30,000 cruzados the royal treasury had committed to pay. The bishop further emphasized that the current amount of tobacco stipulated in the contract was not sufficient "for the expenses that the merchants have in the city," and alerted the crown of the fiscal dangers facing not only white but black traders. This implies that already in 1709 there was an assortment of whites and blacks, free and slave, connected with each other through the tobacco trade and through proximity or fealty to the Church of Sé. Who those people were, what they did, how and for how long, were fascinating questions that I could only begin to answer within the limits of this book.

Nowhere in the documents that address the identity or activity of Rio's merchants in the first half of the eighteenth century could I find allusions to the existence of blacks from the Mina Coast, who were freed, working, and residing in the city.[70] However, the existence of such a group is suggested by the participation of freed Africans in the lay religious brotherhoods. By 1740, we can determine that there was a group of freed Mina blacks living in the Parish of Candelária who organized their devotion to Santo Elesbão and Santa Efigênia in a brotherhood.[71]

The ties that are just perceptible in Rio between the bishopric and the tobacco merchants are even clearer in Bahia. In 1745, Teodósio Rodrigues de Faria, a captain in the Portuguese navy who had arrived in Salvador five years earlier, founded there the Brotherhood of Senhor do Bonfim. A successful and notable man, president of the Tobacco Commission, Faria quickly found the support necessary to construct a church.[72] Between 1751 and 1759, the director of the Portuguese fort at Ouidah was a Portuguese soldier named Teodósio Rodrigues—perhaps a kin of the same name, but perhaps it was the benefactor of Senhor do Bonfim himself.[73] The spheres of commerce and religion overlap again in the case of Felix Simões de Azevedo, administrator of the contract for Mina Coast slaves. In 1763, Felix Simões donated to the Brotherhood of Senhor Bom Jesus dos Martírios in Salvador—an association composed of "Jêje" Africans, recent arrivals from the Bight of Benin—a chapel in the neighborhood of Barroquinha, which came to be one of the more popular sanctuaries in the city.[74]

It is important to remember that it was not only traders linked to the Mina Coast who had the habit of financing or participating in brotherhoods; nor was it a recent practice. The relation between economic activity and religious devotion is old and diverse. In Rio, one could mention the Brotherhood of Santo Pedro Gonçalves, created in the seventeenth century by a consortium of wealthy navigators. In the eighteenth century, a humbler group of merchants constructed a public oratory containing the image of Our Lady of Lapa (Our Lady of the Cave). Years later they united with another coalition of merchants to form the grander Brotherhood under the name Our Lady of Lapa dos Mercadores (Our Lady of the Cave of the Merchants).

In Rio, by 1740 or before, there existed at least four established Catholic devotions among the Mina blacks: two in the Church of Our Lady of the Rosário (Santo Antônio da Mouraria, Saint Anthony of the Moors; and Our Lady of Lampadosa, Our Lady of the Candle) and two in the Church of São Domingos (Santo Elesbão and Santa Efigênia, and Menino Jesus). The Brotherhoods of Our Lady of Lampadosa and Santo Elesbão and Santa Efigênia were the wealthiest and most popular; by the late 1740s, both had raised sufficient funds to begin constructing their own chapels.[75] The Mina who associated in Santo Elesbão and Santa Efigênia seem to have been especially well endowed, since they inaugurated their new church a mere eight years after receiving authorization to begin breaking ground.[76] It hardly seems conceivable that a chapel could be built in such a short time with only the contributions of slaves and poor freed blacks. There must have been other sources of capital, whether from allied devout patrons or from more heterogeneous methods of acquisition. This is where the bishop's letter to the crown about the renovation of the church at Sé appears especially relevant. The construction of a chapel meant something more than any other building could have in this historical context. It demonstrated a solid economic base, openly recognized connections with the

Catholic Church, and the strategic capacity to attract allies in both devotion and other dimensions of public life. These would have been acknowledged by anyone in Rio at the time, black or white, slave or free, as real advantages.

The slave trade involved more than the displacement of Africans to Brazil; it constructed an extensive, complex network of commercial intermediaries and interested parties, from the moment of capture until the slave arrived to make his or her way on Brazilian soil. The gaps and partialities of record keeping on the trade prevent us from being certain about where, not just individual slaves, but entire groups of slaves came from. We cannot know for sure where the slaves called "Mina" in eighteenth-century Rio came from, or to what ethnic groups they belonged. Europeans were little preoccupied with these details, and perhaps the only agent within the trade who knew anything about particular slaves were their African captors, probably from neighboring groups, who had first caught and imprisoned them. At the same time, it is the African groups who engaged with the Europeans as trading partners and local agents (such as the Dahomeans) that were the best known, because Europeans dealt with them directly and had shared business concerns to protect. That is, the most helpful information in period documents is about African peoples who practiced the trade, and not about those who suffered it. Polanyi's fine book, for example, focuses with admirable sensitivity and insight on the Dahomeans as a slave-trading people. But about the peoples whom they traded, Polanyi had less to say. He noted that the strip of land corresponding to Dahomey was made up of disorganized, mutable territories (except Ouidah and Porto Novo) and diverse, rebellious tribes, many of them habitually battling each other.[77]

Given the lack of African sources, New World documentation obviously holds more promise for the historian interested in slave provenience as well as in the ways that captive peoples confronted slavery in a new society. That this is a complicated trajectory to reconstruct with imperfect sources is a truism that the researcher learns and relearns every day. Sometimes, a people could change from being slave traders to the slaves being traded by others, or vice versa. This was the case of the Dahomeans, who were the principal source of human merchandise when the kingdom of Allada dominated the Portuguese commerce. Later, the Dahomeans conquered Allada and became the largest exporter of slaves on the Bight of Benin.

It appears that the Brotherhood of Santo Elesbão and Santa Efigênia in

In colonial Brazil, as throughout the Portuguese Empire, there was not a clear distinction between civil and religious administration. This apparent ambiguity was part of the structure of the *Padroado*, a pact between the Catholic Church and the Portuguese Crown, which gave a religious dimension to the political bureaucracies of the king and also allowed the church to be active in civil affairs.[1] Baptism records are an example of how the Catholic Church acted to order the social lives and identities of people (in large part because the church assumed that everyone in the population was or would be a Catholic). A baptism record is a written register of the occurrence of the religious ritual on such-and-such a date, at so-and-so a place. But more than that, in the absence of any secular civil registers, the baptism document often provided the only official written information attesting to a person's identity. It listed such basic information as the names of parents and godparents or, in the case of slaves, the name of the owner.[2] These records can begin to reveal how informal, individual choice—in areas of personal names, selection of godparents, family relations—bumped up against or interfered with the official sphere of an obligation to abstract norms.[3]

Slave names are a rich source for comprehending the personal values or social calculations of their masters, who gave them those names. There were innumerable slaves, many facing especially tragic destinies, who were baptized under the beatific designations of Felicidade (Happiness), Ventura (Venture), and Esperança (Hope). Another trend, emerging from the documents of the Parish of Sé, was the significant number of slaves baptized under the unusual name Hyeronimo. This was probably in homage to D. Hyeronimo Barbosa, an adjunct to the bishop, who was responsible for most of the baptisms at the time. Records for slaves who had come from Africa typically mention the provenince of the slave, what they usually refer as his or her *nação* (nation). In the case of slaves born in the city and baptized as infants, records regularly mention the provenience of the mother, that means, her nation. Thus, the parochial books are helpful not only for indicating how the size of the local slave population changed with the arrivals and births of new slaves, but for showing the categories by which each new individual is absorbed into the conceptual structure of Brazil's slave society. Those categories, in particular *gentio* (heathen) and *nação* (nation) will be scrutinized in the following section "African Heathens and Nations." As I have shown earlier, the criteria for identifying slaves started to be formed during the first years of the Portuguese presence in Guinea, with the preliminary organization of the Atlantic slave commerce. Those identities were officialized in the parishes of Brazil, when baptisms were performed and recorded.

The most fundamental point that distinguished slaves from each other in the colonial context is whether they were born within Brazilian territory or outside it, in Africa. The first group is categorized by color in the parish records, with three predominant terms: *preto, pardo, branco* (black, pardo, white). Two words that modern readers might expect, *mulato* (mixed-race) and *negro*, did not appear in the documents; but the distinctions of preto, pardo, and branco were widely recognized and socially accepted in the era under study. If their conceptualization and ascription may sometimes seem vague or inconsistent from our perspective, they were nonetheless carefully assessed by contemporaries and had meanings and ramifications throughout colonial society. For instance, the Brotherhood of Santo José (Saint Joseph) only admitted brancos; pretos and pardos had their own associations, such as the Brotherhood of Our Lady of the Rosário and São Benedito of Black Men, or the Brotherhood of Our Lady of the Conception and Boa Morte (Good Death) of Pardo Men. It was common to refer to Africans in Brazil as pretos, although the term was not only applied to them. An intensive study of the internal social relations, forms of identification, and broader social hierarchies that cohered around these divisions is beyond the scope of this work. I focus on the other subgroup of slaves that colonial society created: those born beyond the reach of Portuguese colonial society, who arrived in Brazil by ship, and who were categorized there on the basis of a presumed nation or provenience group.

Typically historians have worked with a slightly different set of parameters, in which creole slaves were those born in the New World, versus natural-born Africans, who in this case might also be referred to as pretos, and were imported. But the documents reveal that some slaves born in Africa were called creoles, and not *gentios* (heathens). At the same time, indigenous slaves in Brazil—often called *negros da terra* (native negroes) or "native heathen"—were obviously born in Brazil, but not within the world framed by colonial references and mores; and they were sometimes called gentios, the same as Africans were. The existence of these variations in the documents suggests to me that the underlying criteria for choosing designations that include or exclude have to do with the perceived limits or boundaries of colonial society and the Portuguese Empire. The simultaneous possibility of, as documents reveal, creole slaves born in Pernambuco, Braga (Portugal) and Angola indicates the fragmented identity of Portuguese society in the eighteenth century—but it also shows that the society was seen as genuine in certain realms beyond Portugal and Brazil. We can only guess at how much critical mass it took to be implicitly recognized as a branch of society rather than as a mere outpost in the wilds. That I never found reference to a Mina creole might be a reflection of the precarious Portuguese presence in that part of Africa, unlike in Angola.[4]

The *Constituições Primeiras*[5]—rules that carefully regulated the formats for recording baptisms, weddings, and deaths—did not require doing anything dramatically different for slaves; but they did incorporate the current means of identifying African peoples: Guinea, Mina, Angola, and so on. The frequent use of phrases such as "of the *gentio* of X" or "of the nation X" in parochial documents shows the preoccupation with including this information. At times the curate, vicar, or whoever was writing the record would have to ask around to determine the proper label of derivation for the slave being baptized. When an adult slave was being baptized, his or her own participation in the ritual depended on his or her comprehension of the Portuguese language and level of Christian indoctrination. On such occasions the position of authority held by the priest (of which the power to write was a critical part) permitted the religious functionary to impose, even if involuntarily, the conditions by which the record was created.[6] Thus, through the lens of the baptism records, it is possible to envision how the church participated in reinforcing, combining, highlighting, or obscuring differences and variations in the composition of Rio de Janeiro's slave population.

The *Livro de Batismo de Escravos, Freguesia da Sé* (Book of Slave Baptisms from Sé Parish) of 1744–61, contains records taken down by a number of different people, starting with the curate Manoel Rodrigues Cruz (1744–46), who seems to have adopted the expression "*Gentios* from Guinea" from its use in earlier books. By 1753, after several other functionaries had contributed records, the priest Manoel Fazenda de Castro began a relatively lengthy tenure behind the pen. In 1753 and 1754, he distinguished himself from the other scribes by noting all of the newborn slaves as creoles but without an indication of the mother's provenience. From 1755 onward, he methodically included the mother's provenience in all the records of infant baptisms. This change reflects the importance of the maternal derivation in identifying the child, and also reinforces the definition of creole as the first generation born of an African mother within the limits of colonial society.[7] It was curious that, starting in 1750, the standard expression "João of the Angola nation" or "João of the Mina nation" was substituted by "João Angola" or "João Mina," with the provenience incorporated into the personal name. All of this implies that there was a fairly wide margin within which the ecclesiastics could take records, a fact which should be kept in mind when it comes to comparing data across time or performing statistical analyses. It also seems that there was a learning process that each record taker went through, determining what was appropriate to include and how precisely to do it—a process in which the regulations in the *Constituições Primeiras* would have played a significant but not all-encompassing role. When the nation or provenience group of a slave was not declared, for instance, the ecclesiastic was usually required to recognize the external marks and physical attributes of each common group, or at the least speak with other slaves about where the individual might have come from, in order to include that reference in the register. It should be emphasized that listing the nation of a baptized slave was not a required part of the norms for baptism records. It more likely therefore derived from some sort of local

Table 4. Total Baptisms of Slaves in Rio de Janeiro, 1718–1860

| PARISH | BAPTISM | | | | TOTAL | |
| | Children (with Mother) | | Adults | | | |
	#	%	#	%	#	%
Sé, 1718–26	983	10.6	855	9.2	1,838	19.8
Sé, 1744–50	1,381	14.9	283	3.1	1,664	18.0
Sé, 1751–60	893	9.6	324	3.5	1,217	13.1
Candelária, 1751–60	1,648	17.8	586	6.3	2,234	24.1
São José, 1751–60	1,117	12.1	321	3.5	1,438	15.5
Santa Rita, 1751–60	587	6.3	291	3.1	878	9.5
Total	6,609	71.3	2,660	28.7	9,269	100

Source: ACMRJ, *Livros de Batismo de Escravos, Rio de Janeiro*: Sé, 1718–26, 1744–61; Candelária, 1745–74; São José, 1751–90; Santa Rita, 1751–99.

social imperative, especially given that the importance of these records as the central mode of noting and implementing official identity.

Although there was a substantial proportion of freed slaves in the brotherhoods, the books of slave baptisms provide the best source of information relative to the provenience of Africans in the city. They also maintain the basic distinction mentioned earlier about slave groupings: gentios versus creoles, or those born within the ambit of colonial society. They show that the first group was typically composed of adults, and the second of children or infants. Table 4 presents a total of 9,269 individual registers of slave baptisms from 1718 to 1860, including 6,609 children born in Rio de Janeiro and 2,660 adult African gentios.[8]

The analysis presented here takes as its base these two basic groupings. In the case of children born in the city, the focus of attention turns to the mothers. One qualification needs to be made about the category of mothers: women could be counted multiple times if, for example, a woman with three children returned for three separate ceremonies. The category is thus artificial, but accurate insofar as it suggests the distribution of proveniences encountered in the city—assuming that women from particular provenience groups did not have more or less children than women from other groups.[9] The category of "adults," on the other hand, effectively corresponds to the numbers of adults baptized. Another point to be raised is that among mothers, there would have been both Africans (*gentios*, or "heathens") and creoles, while the adults contained only Africans. This chapter is dedicated to the analysis of African gentios by way of the slave baptism records, with special attention to those called Mina blacks (or simply Mina). Before that can be done, however, we need to more fully consider the female slaves born within the ambit of colonial society.

FEMALE SLAVES BORN IN THE PORTUGUESE EMPIRE

These women were usually described as *crioulas* (female creoles), *pardas*, *cabras* (variations of race mixture), *pretas*,[10] or simply as "a female slave belonging to ——." For the years between 1718 and 1726 I found a total of 267 registers divided as follows: 126 pardas, 47 crioulas, 5 cabras, 2 pretas, 85 labeled only "slave" and 2 freed women.[11] The term *creole* typically referred to a male of female slave, born to a *gentia* (female heathen) mother within colonial society; a creole was often assumed to be the first generation born in the city, who nonetheless maintained connections with the mother's native language and culture. In the designation of creole identity there was a connotation both of the past, and of current or racial and social ascendance —details of which would be adduced in the register. We read, for instance, of Magdalena Costa, a "freed creole black," the natural daughter of Josepha da Costa, "Mina black." Magdalena had her own small boy, Custódio, who was baptized in 1745; he was first entered in the "Book of Captives," but that entry was annulled and placed in the "Book of Emancipated."[12] Whatever the story of Custódio, other sources also suggest that there might have been only one generation of creoles per lineage, with the next offspring reverting to the category of slave (but not African or gentio). Perhaps that is one reason why there were only 47 explicitly creole mothers in the data, compared to 267 born within the limits of colonial society. The phrase "creole nation" occurred, but very infrequently. The creoles constitute a coherent group from the point of view of statistics, but in terms of social relations and shared interests they are much more difficult to recognize and comprehend.[13] For the purposes of analysis, I counted mothers as slaves only when they seemed not to fit any other available category.

The group of children born within the ambit of colonial society presents a double gradation: from black to white, passing through pardo, and from slave to free, passing through emancipated status. The baptism records show how complicated these paths were. Most fundamentally, the book in which each child's baptism was registered—that of the captives or the emancipated—was already a critical and durable indication of the place in the social hierarchy in which each "innocent" had been born. The majority of slave emancipations involved colonial Portuguese or Brazilian women liberating the children of female slaves they owned, which might indicate a certain proximity between mistress and slave. That remains a tentative supposition.

Until 1871, parishes in the Bishopric of Rio de Janeiro maintained two different books in which to record baptisms.[14] One was called the Livro de Batismo de Pretos Cativos (Book of Baptisms of Black Captives). The other was called the Livro de Batismo de Brancos (Book of Baptisms of Whites), which refers to people of Portuguese or European descent, born free. But this book had a dual role that exemplifies the complexity of racial and social designations in colonial Brazil. When a slave child was emancipated in the baptismal basin, his or her baptism should have been registered in the Book of Baptisms of Whites, but that very same book in these situations was called by a different name. It was referred to—in annotations within those two books, or in other documents—as the Livro dos Forros (Book of the Freed). However, some of these freed individuals were listed in the Book of Black Captives instead, for no apparent reason. The complications involved in freeing a slave, in social and normative terms, can in a sense be measured by the frequent, occasionally testy annotations scribbled along the margins of a page when such an act was performed during the baptismal ritual and had to be recorded. In one situation, a woman declared to the vicar Ignacio Manoel "with a letter, written in her hand and recognized, that she had given liberty to a slave and wanted him baptized in his freedom." To the extent that the required baptism represented an act of freedom or not, it was clear that the slave had been freed, but the register of the event went straight into the Book of Captives. A subsequent annotation by the vicar even included the amount of money paid to free the slave, young Agostinho, as if to substantiate the circumspect and official liberation of the boy. But the register stayed where it was, in the Book of Captives, and in this case did not even include the facile gesture of a note that the record of Agostinho's baptism and the proof of his emancipation should be transferred to the Book of the Freed.[15]

Sometimes, with no added commentary, a register was annulled from the Book of Captives and placed in the Book of Whites.[16] One inevitable conclusion that these incidents suggest is that there was reluctance on the part of ecclesiastical authorities to bear witness to the bureaucratic and symbolic transformation of a black to a white. Even when the documents offer abundant proof that church officials knew of the changed legal status of the child, the register could persist in the Book of Captives, which shows that emancipation represented a substantial step in the social hierarchy. In actually passing from slave to freed, a slave had to effect the similarly unlikely passage from one church book to another; emancipation in the baptismal basin was only considered complete when it was recorded in the Book of Whites. But even when a register of such an event was placed there, reference is made to the book as the Book of the Freed to maintain the critical differentiation between freed blacks and free whites. The new juridical status of a freed slave was certainly valuable, but in and of itself it had little capacity to challenge colonial social hierarchies.

The question of pardos also deserves attention here, not least because it can be especially difficult to separate them from the black population.[17] We know that in Bahia at around the same time, pardos never reached more than 10 percent of the slave numbers.[18] There are no equivalent data from Rio de Janeiro, but the figures for mothers with children registered in the city between 1718 and 1726 can give a rough idea of the distribution of pardos. The 983 registers from Sé in those years (table 4) correspond to 716 mothers with an African nation attributed (72.8 percent), 126 pardas (12.8 percent), 47 creoles (4.8 percent), and 94 with other designations, most of them slaves (9.6 percent). However rightly or wrongly, these limited numbers are in accord with the findings for Bahia. Studies are clearly needed to shine light on the identities and social circumstances of the pardos, but the present work is based on the clear predominance of blacks whose designation included reference to African nations or gentios.

AFRICAN HEATHENS AND NATIONS

One thing the historiography on African slavery in Brazil lacks, and which I cannot provide, is a detailed historical and etymological study of the words *gentio* and *nação*. I have had to develop my own interpretations, based on extant discussions in the historiography, as well as the nuances discovered in my own research. In documents from the seventeenth century, these words apply both to Africans and to indigenous Brazilians. A 1680 law mentions "defensive or offensive war, against a nation of Indians." In 1680, the crown resolved to "find a convenient way to reduzir [attract, assemble and convert] the Gentio of the State of Maranhão," which involved bringing "these gentios to the embrace of the Church."[19]

As discussed in chapter 1, use of the term gentio (heathen) derives from the earliest epochs of Portuguese expansion in Africa, and persists through the baptismal records of slaves in Rio de Janeiro in the eighteenth century. The word nação (nation) also appears in those records, and a casual glance at the documents would suggest that the terms were used interchangeably. But they represent two distinct classificatory systems for colonized peoples: gentios is consistently used to describe those who were to be catechized, whereas nations refers to different groupings of people that the Portuguese interact with in the process of colonial expansion. The overlap is clear, but awareness of the distinction is vital to any close analysis of period documents.

The word gentio (heathen) was usually used to describe peoples located outside the scope of the Catholic Church—people who had never been exposed to a Christian religion and who were considered easier to convert (as noted in chapter 1). Nação (nation), on the other hand, dealt with any people who occupied a given territory, and a shared language, laws, customs, and systems of governance. The term was often used in the period context of race and caste.[20] In this sense nation refers to a people united in common interests and understandings, which may broadly include Christians, Jews, Muslims, pagans, or gentios.[21] A nation could be any unit of people—gentio, pagan, or Christian, politically centralized or not—with whom the Portuguese related, at the time usually for diplomacy or commerce, in times of war or peace. Nation was also used to identify those who were enslaved, whether or not they were black or African. I was able to observe that the word nação appears in ecclesiastical records from the fifteenth century to the nineteenth, while gentio, also present in the fifteenth, disappears from most documents along the course of the eighteenth century.

I found no mention of a "Guinea nation." The reference to Guinea was always intended to describe or situate a gentio, although ambivalence as to its particular geographical setting is apparent throughout the documents. Consider two of the slaving contracts awarded to the merchant Bartolomeu Marchione in the late fifteenth century. One permitted Marchione to operate in the Slave River (1486–93), which was a well-known waterway that gave access to the kingdom of Benin. Another contract (1490–95) was for slaving in the Guinea Rivers, with little additional information about where they were.[22] Making matters more complex for the historian is the fact that, as shown in the first chapter, the region called Guinea in the fifteenth century did not match up with the Guinea of the eighteenth century. A map published in 1781 bore the title *Carte de Guinée contenant les isles du Cap Verd, le Senegal, la Côte de Guinée poprement dite, les royaumes de Loango, Congo, Angola, et Benguela avec les pays voisins autant qu'ils sont connus*. That is, this map of Guinea depicted an area from Cabo Verde to Angola, although somewhere in the middle was a region actually referred to as Guinea.[23]

The terms *gentio* and *nação* did not necessarily refer to an ethnic group, since they were applied to assemblages of people of possibly numerous ethnic groups arriving together at the same port (in the case of Africans) or gathered within the same village (in the case of indigenous). For Africans, these are often place names that should not be taken as ethnic or tribal indicators, but as the place where the ship picked up the slaves in Africa (hence such names as Angola, Loango, Benguela, Mina). Similarly, natives were referred to by place names such as Carijó, Guarani, Botocudo, and Caeté. It bears emphasizing again that *gentio* and *nação* were equally applied to the indigenous and to Africans, whether or not they were slaves. And the word *negro* could describe an African or a Brazilian native, while the concept of *índio* (Indian, American native) included natives from anywhere, as long as they were in their proper cultural and geographical environment. By the time they reached Brazil, the Portuguese had developed a sort of commercial anthropology for understanding and classifying peoples in the Orient and in Africa, a perspective that they essentially transferred whole onto Brazil's indigenous peoples.[24] In that sense, any analysis of the disappearance of the term *gentio* to describe African slaves in the eighteenth century would also have to consider the term's trajectory in relation to indigenous peoples (who were called, among other things, *gentio "da terra"* that means "local" or "native" heathen," in this case, American natives).[25]

Table 5. Principal Proveniences of Slaves in Rio de Janeiro, 1718–1760
(with percentages for each period)

PARISH	PROVENIENCE						TOTAL	
	Guinea		Mina		Angola			
	#	%	#	%	#	%	#	%
Sé, 1718–26	516	75.2	107	15.6	63	9.2	686	100
Sé, 1744–50	442	54.8	189	23.4	175	21.7	806	100
Sé, 1751–60	45	22.6	62	31.2	92	46.2	199	100
Candelária, 1751–60	5	7.7	34	52.3	26	40.0	65	100
Santa Rita, 1751–60	4	1.3	88	28.2	220	70.5	312	100
São José, 1751–60	60	9.8	150	24.5	402	65.7	612	100
Total	1,072	40.0	630	23.5	978	36.5	2,680	100

Source: ACMRJ, *Livros de Batismo de Escravos, Rio de Janeiro*: Sé, 1718–26, 1744–61;
Candelária, 1745–74; São José, 1751–90; Santa Rita, 1751–99.

In the baptism books from Rio de Janeiro in the early eighteenth century, some personal information about slaves was often left out (such as birthdates), but the slave's provenience was always included. A slave was identified by a composite appellation listing the baptism name, provenience (in terms of nation or gentio), followed by the full name of his or her owner: for example, "Josepha of the Mina Heathen, slave of . . ." The name of the owner could change in the documents or even disappear over time, but the slave's provenience, once entered in the baptism records, became a permanent attribute of the slave's name and public identity even if the slave managed to attain freedom.

Of the African mothers from principal gentio groups who had their children baptized in Rio de Janeiro's Sé Parish between 1718 and 1726, 75.2 percent were called Gentio of Guinea; 15.6 percent Gentio of Mina; and 9.2 percent Gentio of Angola (see table 5 for these and the following figures). Between 1744 and 1750, also among African mothers in Sé, those proportions had changed to 54.8 percent Guinea, 23.4 percent Mina, and 21.7 percent Angola.[26]

In Rio de Janeiro the term *gentio* was common in baptismal records early in the eighteenth century; by the end of the century, it had all but vanished. In Sé from 1718 to 1723, nearly all the entries were written by priest Hyeron-

Table 6. Principal Proveniences of Slaves in Rio de Janeiro, 1718–1760
(with percentages of the total sample)

PARISH	PROVENIENCE						TOTAL	
	Guinea		Mina		Angola			
	#	%	#	%	#	%	#	%
Sé, 1718–26	516	19.3	107	4.0	63	2.4	686	25.6
Sé, 1744–50	442	16.5	189	7.1	175	6.5	806	30.1
Sé, 1751–60	45	1.7	62	2.3	92	3.4	199	7.4
Candelária, 1751–60	5	0.2	34	1.3	26	1.0	65	2.4
Santa Rita, 1751–60	4	0.1	88	3.3	220	8.2	312	11.6
São José, 1751–60	60	2.2	150	5.6	402	15.0	612	22.8
Total	1,072	40.0	630	23.5	978	36.5	2,680	100.0

Source: ACMRJ, *Livros de Batismo de Escravos, Rio de Janeiro*: Sé, 1718–26, 1744–61; Candelária, 1745–74; São José, 1751–90; Santa Rita, 1751–99.

imo Barbosa, who regularly used the expressions Guinea Gentio, Mina Gentio, and Angola Gentio. The first use of *nação* appears to be from the pen of the curate Manoel Rodrigues Cruz in mid-1725,[27] and as it grew in prominence over the years, the specific expression "Guinea Gentio" notably receded. If we look at who was called a Guinea Gentio, most were mothers present to register their children, while the slaves called Mina (who had passed from gentio to nation) were almost all adults being baptized. The category of Guinea slaves had been present in the city over a longer period of time and was as a group more socialized to the ways of colonial society. That might also explain why, for most of the legitimate children of married slaves recorded in the period, both parents were Guinea Gentios (forty-three out of sixty-two).[28]

Although the period of 1744 to 1761 was relatively short, it saw the greatest number of births (806, or 30.1 percent; see table 6), a fact that correlates with the patterns of Rio de Janeiro's growth overall. Baptisms of the children of mothers who were Mina slaves represented 23.5 percent of all baptisms. Looking more closely at the Parish of Candelária in the decade of the 1750s, the presence of Mina slave mothers reached 52.5 percent of the total for that period. This parish, which included the city's port, had a conspicuously large population of Mina slaves compared to the other parishes. The number of male Mina slaves, not only female, was proportionally higher here too, as the records of adult baptisms indicate.

Comparing data from the first half of the century with that of the 1750s involves as much art as science on the part of the researcher. Two related phenomena affected records for the later period: the expansion of the city, and the creation of two new parishes to serve it. In simple terms, part of Sé was separated and called Santo José, and Candelária was similarly divided to create a new parish called Santa Rita. One can derive a rough estimate for Sé's demographics across the 1740s and the 1750s by comparing the original Sé in the years 1744–50 with the combined figures for the new, smaller Sé and its offshoot, Santo José, for the 1750s. There remain the problems of city growth that are complicated to factor in, not to mention that there exist data for only seven years of the 1740s, compared to ten years in the 1750s. Given all those qualifications, the numbers of baptisms of children whose mothers were slaves of the three main African categories for the two time periods in Sé are as follows: 105 Guinea (45 vs. 60); 212 Mina (62 vs. 150); and 494 Angola (92 vs. 402), for a total of 811 (199 vs. 612).

Taken all together, the numbers in tables 5 and 6 show a general tendency for the Guinea Gentio slave identity to disappear from the baptismal records over the period 1718–60, while the Angola identity enjoyed a dramatic increase, and the Minas a slight one. Part of the effect here was overall demographic change from urban growth, but part also must have been the normative reallocation of slaves who would earlier have been considered Guinea Gentios into the Angola nation. All the evidence suggests that most of the Africans called Guinea Gentios had come from the central-western coast, and probably more specifically from Luanda in Angola; commerce with the ports of Benguela and Cabinda would reach a significant scale only decades later.[29] Some of the Mina had been called gentios, but not many, and they were more easily absorbed into the category of Mina nation.

These trends lend support to the argument advanced in the previous chapter about the progressive delineation of western Africa in Portugal's worldview: the contours of Guinea were increasingly difficult to delimit (conceptually and on the map), while the Mina Coast had relatively clear boundaries and features. Slaves who would have been called Guinea Gentios would need to be redistributed into the African "nations" that were emerging in the universe of Portuguese colonial and commercial relations. The term *gentio*—applied initially to heathen peoples or communities who should be converted, enslaved, or both—was replaced by *nação*—still a generic term, but one whose meanings better fit the demands of the rapidly expanding slave trade. The discourse was secularized. The individual heathen or slave was no longer identified by his or her position within a project of Catholic evangelism. The new parameters by which such individuals would be officially recognized took on a geographical refinement that, if flawed in its accuracy (with the consolidation of purported "nations" around African ports of call serving the trade), was also strategic in its awareness of a vast, diverse tapestry of colonial relations in the Atlantic world. The gradual substitution of terms in Rio's baptismal records thus expresses much larger transformations in the social and commercial exchanges throughout the Portuguese Empire.

THE "NATIONS," OR
AFRICAN PROVENIENCES

The words used in official documents to describe a slave's provenience point to a heterogeneous assortment of places and social entities—from islands and ports, to kingdoms and small villages, to cultural or kinship groupings. Not infrequently I encountered in the declared provenience of a given slave a reference to a specific locale or group that was impossible to find in other sources. The provenience terms should not necessarily be interpreted as implying the status of an ethnic group, although wider studies indicate that a few African groups semantically preserved by colonial society—the Cobu, Coura, and Mahi—might qualify. For instance, the literature on African history mentions Cabu, Caabu, Kabu, Ngaabu, Caaabu, and similar variations of Cobu (although not precisely Cobu itself) as a subgroup of the Mande, in the region of Senegambia.[30] There was little naval traffic between this part of West Africa and Rio de Janeiro, but it is known that slaves from throughout the region were shipped out to Brazil through the island hub of Cape Verde (although they were often described as Mina, not Guinea). The Coura or Couranos, shown in the work of Luiz Mott to have been present among the slave population of Minas Gerais,[31] were a subgroup of the Mina "nation," as were the Mahi. The Mahi inhabited a mountainous region north of the kingdom of Dahomey, as I stated earlier, and the final chapter of this book will address them in more depth.

The slave baptism records from Rio de Janeiro present a lexicological rainbow of proveniences and derivations. There was of course the Mina from the Bight of Benin, including its subgroups,[32] and the Cacheu, coming from the port of Cacheu on the São Domingos River in the captaincy of Cacheu, in modern Guinea-Bissau. The central-western coast of Africa was typically imagined as divided into two regions, each a distinct source of slaves. From Kongo, principal subgroups included Muxicongo, Loango, Cabinda, and Monjolo. Angola's subgroups included Loanda (later Luanda), the port city, as well as Kasanje (or Cassange), Massangano, Rebolo, Cabundá, Quissamã, and Ambaca. Benguela expanded the colonial topography of African social diversity when it became a third distinct region later in the eighteenth century.[33] The island of São Tomé, whose Portuguese presence dates to 1485, was a vital node of Atlantic slave trading; for centuries it served as a warehouse and factory for the commerce of Africans from the Bights of Benin and Biafra, Kongo, and Angola. But perhaps because of São Tomé's isolated island geography and well-known clearinghouse functions, its name seems to have been adopted only as a nation, not a gentio group, in the documents.

Between 1745 and 1761 in the Church of Candelária, nearly all the entries for slave baptisms were written by the vicar Ignacio Manoel. In his detailed inscriptions we see a pattern of recording the rituals for Mina slaves and Kongo or Angola slaves in different ways. For Mina slaves, who were probably reasonably assumed to be undergoing the ritual for the first time, the entry was typically concise: "I baptized and placed the Holy waters on So-and-So, Mina adult." But for slaves from the central-western coast, where the Portuguese missionary project had long and deep roots, the ritual was more elaborate. It had to be done *sub conditione*, or under the condition of a verbal guarantee from the slave that he or she had not been baptized before.[34] To the extent that this more complex interaction might reflect a different attitude toward the Central African slave, whose proveniences were in a region where the church was present and active, is a question awaiting careful analysis.

In the baptisms of adult slaves throughout the various parishes of Rio de Janeiro, slaves from the Mina Coast were predominant (2,063 out of a total of 2,660); as a rule it was their masters who instigated the ritual. Because we lack more complete sources to measure the population of Mina slaves entering Rio de Janeiro in the early and mid-eighteenth century, turning to ecclesiastical documents is a necessary recourse. One important conclu-sion from these documents is that Mina slaves baptized in the city were usually those who stayed there, while those who passed through Rio un-baptized were sent on to Minas Gerais, where the ritual was performed. In 1718, the crown wrote to the archbishop of Bahia to take umbrage that Mina slaves were being sent from the major port cities of Brazil on to Minas without receiving the sacrament, which, he said, was "against my recom-mendation." "It is enough of an abuse to the service of God and to the souls of these unfortunates that they were taken to Brazil unbaptized, but to then allow them on to Minas and the interior is reprehensible."[35]

Baptisms of adults from Angola, Kongo, or Benguela were rare in the documents. Where they occurred (just as with the Mina baptisms), the sub conditione proceedings were only one layer of the complexity surrounding them. In the first place it needed to be ascertained that the slave was ready to receive the baptism; as two registers phrased it, the slave was "first examined and approved" or "first examined and approved in the Doc-trine." Other religious authorities could be called in for their opinions both on a slave's readiness, and whether he or she had been baptized before. The vicar Ignacio Manoel noted of one adult from Benguela that "she declared to her owner that she had been sold unbaptized"; of another female from Benguela that "she affirmed that she was not baptized when she was taken from her land." He reported of a third, from Angola, who was the property of a freed black, that his owner knew him to be unbap-tized because of the testimony of an Angolan ship's captain who "has known the slave since he was very small." It was the clearest case of an adult slave arriving from the region who was unbaptized. Manoel also noted in the register of an adult Gentio of Guinea that "he declared that he had not been baptized in Luanda because he had been captured and smug-gled on board."[36] In the records of adults who had arrived from Kongo, Angola, or Benguela without having been baptized at some point, it is often possible to intuit something obscure or illicit in the manner by which the slave embarked. The majority of cases suggest that the trade from central-western Africa was done in accord with the norms of resgate, that is, re-demption—the idea that buying the slave ultimately involved the slave's spiritual transformation, not just his or her forced labor, so that the bap-tism should be done before the slave set foot aboard ship. The method for indoctrinating adults before baptism, whether or not they were slaves, is laid out in the *Constituições Primeiras*, but it is difficult to know the degree to which it was followed in the actual situations involving slaves.[37] In the Bishopric of Rio de Janeiro, the bishop D. João da Cruz had a short-lived but notorious episcopate (1741–45) in which he reportedly showed the fiery conviction of a reformer. The historian Julita Scarano reproduced one of Cruz's polemics, transcribed in the *Monumenta Missionária Africana*, that deauthorized the standard practice of baptizing Africans before leaving port for Brazil. He alleged that slaves could only be baptized after they had arrived and learned the Portuguese language sufficiently well to comprehend the doctrine and be able to respond to questions during the baptism ritual.[38]

The port of Rio de Janeiro saw very few vessels that served East Africa during the eighteenth century. According to Antonil, in Minas Gerais there were some slaves "from Mozambique, who had come on ships from India."[39] But it was highly improbable that ships from India, returning to Portugal, had stopped in Rio de Janeiro; Rio was out of the way, and it was buffered by crosswinds that would have made such a voyage almost impossible.[40] Still, between 1720 and 1722, seventeen adult slaves described as being from São Lourenço—by which Madagascar was previously known—were baptized in Sé Parish. These were the only references to that island that I encountered in all the records. Also in those years, the entries appeared of two adult slaves from Mozambique. That nineteen slaves from the eastern coast were baptized within three years does imply the possibility that a ship serving that route had made it to Rio de Janeiro. Of the 17 from São Lourenço, 4 were baptized in 1720, 11 in 1721, and 2 in 1722; the 2 from Mozambique were baptized in 1720. The concentration of rituals around 1720 and 1721 suggests that most of the slave owners were following church guidelines, which stipulated baptizing slaves within six months of arriving on Brazilian soil, or at most within two years.[41]

The segment of baptism records that presents the greatest diversity with respect to proveniences is that of slave mothers having their children baptized. As discussed previously, the principal gentios were Guinea, Angola, and Kongo, but there were other gentios or nations adduced. I found a few cases where the mother was described as an "infidel," but in each of them the mother in question had given birth aboard the slave ship, adrift in the Atlantic.[42]

Of the 6,609 (table 4) registered baptisms of innocents (newborns and infants) during the period under study, 2,952 were brought to the church by mothers described as *gentias* (female heathen). Of that number, 2,680 belonged to the principal three provenience categories—Guinea, Mina, and Angola (table 6). The remaining 272, not mentioned in table 6, were divided among various minority derivations: Benguela (120), Cape Verde (70), Kongo (33), Ganguela (26), Massangano (9), Monjolo (4), Ambaca (3), Coura (2), Rebolo (2), São Lourenço (1), Quissamã (1), Luanda (1). It should be remembered that the data being examined in this study are from the years 1718–60, which was before the slave trade intensified in the later eighteenth century. Among the minority proveniences outside the main Guinea-Mina-Angola circuit, Cape Verde (often written as one word, *cabo-verde*) had a special prominence. Although slaves bearing this designation have long been regarded as an unremarkable fringe in Rio de Janeiro's slave population and overall social life, the baptism records show that they were present in a large enough number to be recognized as a subgroup. That is especially true given that over the 1750s, female Cape Verde slaves were concentrated in the parishes of Sé (10) and Santo José (19).

Among other minority groups—such as the Ambaca, Luanda, and Quissamã—the simple fact that they were named as such at all suggests that there was something significant in the reference for comprehending the slave's identity in colonial Brazil. These examples also indicate that slave identification could be based on place names, and not a purported ethnic group. The ethnic group was one component in the construction of the identity of the *nation*, from the point of view of colonial society, but neither the only nor even the most important one. At the same time, and this is fundamental, once a given reference to an African locale was established as a social identifier in the context of Brazilian society, it took on a new character. The individuals coming from a determined locale or region ultimately were viewed as constituting not merely loose demographic assemblages but coherent social groups composed of members who could recognize each other as such. They could interact at deeper levels, creating new forms of sociability and organization—among them, the lay Catholic brotherhoods.[43]

THE ORGANIZATION OF PROVENIENCE GROUPS

As I said in the Introduction, I use the word "provenience" to speak about the displacement of people from Africa to the Americas in order to give attention not only to their cultural background but also to the social conditions and geographical routes of the displacement. Sometimes it is possible to trace the routes from people's homelands; in other instances we only know markets and ports along their routes and will never know their point of departure or the places and peoples to which they belonged.

Roger Bastide (1898–1974), walking in the footsteps of the first culturalists, and in particular of Melville Herskovits, produced voluminous studies of the "African religions" in Brazil, among them the already-mentioned *Le Candomblé de Bahia (Rite Nagô)* (Mouton, 1958) and *Les Religions Africaines au Brésil. Vers une sociologie des Interpénétrations de Cililization.* (Pressses Universitaires de France, 1960). His attention was addressed to candomblé in Bahia since it was, as he declared, the most African religious practice he could find in Brazil. From my point of view, we should highlight its importance in the opposite direction and see the candomblé as a religious practiced performed by descendants of Africans under an entirely new social context that cannot be close to African practices, since enslavement and forced migration imposed an entirely different status on them. The change of place, the transfer of people to a new set of social circumstances, is not somehow irrelevant or secondary to the study of religion. African religious practices can be, in all apparent aspects, performed in Brazil, but even when a group with a shared prior understanding of this practice unites to pursue it, the surrounding social conditions, perceptions, and attitudes are different from the (itself presumed) integrity of the past. Even when the shared goal is to recuperate or reconstruct the past, this remains an impossibility, although new social meanings are created that should not be downplayed.

In distinction from these authors who have zeroed in on displacements, and established a direct relation between places of displacement and nations or gentios, as Rodrigues, Herskovits, and Bastide I am proposing the idea of provenience groups. This concept acknowledges the potential presence, even the potential power, of a shared provenience underlying a group of people in the New World. But without lingering on what the content of that shared provenience should be in order to be legitimate, I focus more on the group's construction of shared experience in the state of captivity and in the new social circumstance, and on the tension between individual and collective strategies throughout the process of social organization.

Proveniences refer to names of the places or social groups from which African people were taken as slaves by the various agencies involved in the trade. It is an identification attributed by others that might or might not have a relation with local realities, in the form of actual place names, kingdoms, and internally recognized ethnic groups. The concept of provenience groups, on the other hand, takes the proveniences as one attribute of identification, and looks at how people organized themselves around them. There is a process of self-attribution, at the level of the group in the new context, of an identity attributed or imposed from outside. It is also in this sense that there can exist proveniences with a thousand, or a few, representatives, even though a slave can still be called by the name of that "nation." Unlike places of displacement or provenience, then, provenience groups only begin to cohere when people appropriate aspects of that attributed identity and begin to act in society as some reflection of that identity. The term *nação* remains slippery in period documents, because it can easily convey either individual proveniences or provenience groups— but in fact its power is that it conveys both at the same time. Also, the barriers between individuals' proveniences and provenience groups are difficult to establish in a temporally or geographically consistent way, because individuals who may not be in contact with each other but share particular references to provenience in the New World context are able to act to create personal and collective identities in dialogue with that set of places of displacement that could be their homelands or not.

The concept of provenience group has a profoundly organizational character, and is related to what the Norwegian anthropologist Fredrik Barth called ethnic groups—particularly because Barth was preoccupied with how ethnic groups form and express their organization. He noted that although ethnic configurations take into account cultural differences, there is not an equivalence between ethnic groups and culture, because each group selects the components of culture that it considers most meaningful and important.[44] This openness to alternatives gives social actors space— culturally, socially, historically—to create different provenience groups at different times, in different places, even if they share the same background. And we do find that slaves from the Mina Coast who were taken to different places or in different eras to the New World organized themselves in diverse forms, depending on the place and circumstances. In Bahia, they adopted and used different labels (Mina, Nagô, Jêje), but in Rio de Janeiro they were usually under the same provenience group called Mina.

The idea of provenience groups also differs from the analysis of Nina Rodrigues. I emphasize the importance of social arrangements that develop in the state of captivity (or freed from it, but still in its shadow), while Rodrigues's attempts to discern "racial origins" of Africans and their descendants implied a racial ideal and a "pure" past. I also differ from the view of Herskovits and his followers because I privilege these actions as social and collective arrangements that result from people's agency, rather than particular African cultural traits that one might find both in Africa and in different parts of the Americas. Here, culture and ethnicity are among the components more or less deliberately used to construct meaningful social arrangements in the new circumstances that the provenience groups confront. The question of the relation between culture and ethnic identity has been explored far more by historians and anthropologists in the context of Hispanic America, with reference to pre-Columbian indigenous peoples, than in the contexts of African peoples or African descendants in the New World. For this relatively unexplored area, the theoretical approach of the anthropologist Miguel Alberto Bartolomé would seem to offer promising directions. He has stated that although a collective identity tends to reflect cultural norms of a given society, the identity does not depend on those norms to exist. Therefore, the configurations and textures of identity are not joined at the hip with the dominant culture, and can change at different speeds and in different directions from culture. That is, culture is one of the aspects of identity, but not the totality of identity. Culture can change without identity necessarily changing. In that sense— and this is the key point—Bartolomé concludes that even if an ethnic identity is expressed through a past culture, or images of a past culture, in fact that identity is deeply entrenched in the actor's present and always in conversation with it. He observes that the Spanish conquest shows that even societies who were submitted to a wrenching cultural transformation could still maintain their ethnic identity.[45]

In a practical sense, however, attempting to study provenience groups is no simple matter. In the context under discussion, Africans in the city of Rio de Janeiro, one immediate problem is how to define ethnicity. The first matter at hand is to distinguish ethnic groups from nations, because while the historiography often uses either or both words at will, they are not interchangeable. Nation has dimensions of culture and ethnicity, to be sure, but this social unit was defined within the framework of the Portuguese Empire and the Atlantic world, and imposed on slaves by colonial agents. The nation was in essence a box of attributes and references that were presented, aspects of which the formative group could adopt, adapt, re-elaborate, or do their best to ignore. As the different individuals in the group reinterpreted the contours of what nação (nation) meant in their personal and social lives, a creative process occurred through which a shared language and set of common cultural practices developed. Within this complex process of building a new identity and organizing a new group based on common provenience, it should be noted that culture and identity are both present but to a degree dissociable and in dialogue, as Bartolomé proposes.

Because nations and provenience groups are historical phenomena that accompanied the centuries-long slave trade, and even persisted after its abolition in different forms, we can consider them in light of their transformation across space and time in order to get a clearer sense of the ruptures and continuities in the passage from Africa to the Americas. One of the assumptions of an analysis based on provenience groups is that individuals and groups, even in captivity, had before them infinite possibilities of social arrangements and rearrangements. While the importance of slave populations' native social organizations and cultural practices prior to dislocation is not eliminated, the principal focus is on how these elements were placed alongside others to be redistributed and reorganized once in the New World. I believe this method best suits the situations that historians of African slavery confront, in which the new forms of social organization articulated by Africans in the diaspora have more to do with the immediate conditions of captivity than with memories of the past. The past is not effaced but is brought back, as it were, to the degree that present conditions permit. That means, among other things, that the criteria used to determine who belonged to this or that group were defined in the specific locality and social context in which the group organized, and not by some sort of ironclad tradition from Africa that even the disruptions of New World slavery were not enough to unbind.

It should be obvious from the foregoing discussion that I believe the provenience group called Mina in Rio de Janeiro was not identical to the groups called Mina in Bahia, Pernambuco, or Maranhão. The Mina identity was associated with a variety of smaller nations or ethnic groups, such as (in nineteenth-century Rio alone) Mina-Calabar, Mina-Mahi, and Mina-Nagô, all subgroups that included Gbe and Yoruba speakers deriving from different proveniences. Studies have not been done on the diversity of Mina in Bahia, but related research indicates that there the Nagô were seen as distinct. The Jêje nation of Bahia might correspond in broad outline to the peoples called Mina in Rio, but in Rio the Yoruba speakers were classified within Mina identity while in Bahia the Yoruba speakers (Nagô) were separate from the Gbe speakers (Mina and Jêje). Of course, what was described as Mina in nineteenth-century Rio might have been different from the Mina in that city a century before. We know that in the eighteenth century, the group called Mina was predominately Gbe speaking, but during the nineteenth century that changed as Yoruba speakers became more numerous. I am using linguistic difference here for the sake of argument as a sort of grand divider of the ethnic waters, but even this is far too simplistic. Literature on African history demonstrates the pervasive and complex exchanges between Gbe and Yoruba speakers in the region of the Bight of Benin, both in culture and in social relations—not to mention the recorded cases of bilingualism, intermarriage, and collective migrations. And I do not want to give the impression that any and all change in these spheres of identity was a direct consequence of the slave trade. Be it in Africa or in the diaspora, in regions more or less touched by the Atlantic slave trade, in every epoch, such changes arose according to wider logics or strategies of social arrangement that were manifested differently in every situation. Thus, rather than looking at ethnicities in the sense of "pure" origins or lineages with steadfast cultural characteristics, I see the nations and provenience groups as social configurations engaged in permanent processes of reorganization and redefinition.

Following this reasoning it comes to mind that the different possibilities for an ethnic group to appropriate aspects of cultural traditions from other groups within the same overall nation, or even from other nations, makes an isolated definition of ethnicity quite difficult, principally when cultural criteria are used to try to distinguish between groups. And most of the extant literature follows and reiterates that problematic perspective, which means that we have to draw more widely on all the available primary sources and theoretical models. At times the differences between nations and ethnic groups are clear, at other times not, but even when they are clear, their meanings might be diverse. All that said, it remains important to keep in view the distinction, whether one analyzes nations at the macro-level or the micro-level. I view the nation as an assemblage of ethnic groups, engaged in continual historical processes of change, rather than as a constellation of cultural manifestations, traits, or heritage stripped from their social and historical contexts. It is this dynamic, and not only the transfer or diffusion of African cultures around the Atlantic, that underlies the processes of identification and differentiation of the African populations in captivity.

A focus on provenience groups places at least as much significance on circumstantial criteria, such as ports of embarkation, as on cultural aspects such as language. But even cultural components of identity may not be ethnic. For example, the Mina in both Rio de Janeiro and Minas Gerais all spoke what was called in eighteenth-century documents the "general language of Mina."[46] Advanced linguistic studies of this "language" remain to be performed, but evidence suggests that it emerged from the coexistence of several languages, likely of the Gbe family. And when Mina in Rio de Janeiro founded the Brotherhood of Santo Elesbão and Santa Efigênia in 1740, they did so not as a purely "ethnic" exercise but in the company of Africans from Cape Verde, São Tomé, Mozambique, and even more disparate regions. Indeed, the brotherhood was a sort of supra-organizational unit that comprised various African nations. I could find no standard name for this level of social organization in the period documents. The word Africans existed in colonial vocabulary, but it did not enter into daily usage to encapsulate peoples otherwise recognized as diverse until the nineteenth century.[47] During the eighteenth century, the usual expressions were "all nations" and "the assembled nations."

But if what many historians of Latin America and the Caribbean call "ethnic groups" or even "tribes" are, in fact, colonial-era nations and provenience groups, how do we arrive at a coherent definition of an ethnic group? A nation can be recognized within the archives of slave society by a series of distinctive traits—provenience, language, physical markings, rituals, material culture. Proceeding along this line of analysis takes us right back to the methodology of Melville Herskovits. Similarly, most historians explain the existence of an ethnic group by arguing that its members share a "common origin." The problem here is the assumption that cultural traits have the mysterious power to not merely represent but actively produce connections between the past and the present. African slaves in the New World are often portrayed (even by scholars with honorable intentions) as being joined at the hip with an all-powerful past, and even when other cultural influences become absorbed into social life that the African past is still present, whether the Africans and their descendants know it or not. This is the attitude pervading Roger Bastide's arguments in his book *As Religiões Africanas no Brasil*, and it can often seem vaguely condescending since Westerners are implicitly constructed as less dominated by their pasts. There is a corollary to this view, more normative in character, which quietly (sometimes loudly) roots for Africans and their descendants in the New World who chose to adhere to some idea or expression of an authentic African past. But those choices have to be considered in each context. In contrast to those views, the utility of provenience groups as a base for analysis is that they throw into bold relief the processes of constructing connections, exercised directly or indirectly by diverse institutions of slavery in the lives of African slaves in the New World. "Traits" of particular groups have not persisted through the centuries; the cultural backgrounds of ethnic groups are continually reworked and reelaborated through time and space.

I am attempting to move the debate away from focusing on "origins," in terms of an original or ideal culture, to focus on provenience groups and the constantly changing cultural background and processes of complex social change that define them. We might be able to move away from the fretting over cultural loss and degradation or the squabbles over authenticity that are understandable but have been increasingly shown to be unproductive. João Pacheco was writing of change in indigenous groups when he observed: "Social units abandon old cultural forms, receive (and remember) forms from other societies, and beyond that create new and distinct forms."[48] Ethnic groups should be seen as a kind of toolbox from which people may draw to make innovative and practical use of their social organization, politics, kinship, and language, in particular historical contexts. They are in a constant state of transformation, although changes are always complicated and usually do not occur quickly. That is why one can no longer establish a list of particular cultural traits and march off to discover the relics and shadows that have survived of them in the New World, as Herskovits and his followers (such as Bastide) did. Once we understand that ethnic groups cannot be considered outside of specific historical contexts, it is easier to understand that they will produce and negotiate different responses and interjections within their particular historical circumstances. In the case of African slaves in Brazil, one segment of such a generally defined ethnic group from Africa was captured, enslaved, and carried to Brazil, where some of those people ultimately managed to reunite and configure newly meaningful ways to coexist. They reestablished older forms of sociability while reworking them and combining them with others created in the milieu of a Portuguese colonial society. I suggest that this perspective is the most historically defensible way to begin evaluating identity construction amongst Africans in the New World, and I use it in the following section, in which I analyze the Mina provenience group of eighteenth-century Rio de Janeiro in more depth.

THE MINA PROVENIENCE GROUP

The distribution of principal provenience groups in Brazil derived from Portuguese naval routes (which themselves depended on a range of actors, including nautical and shipbuilding skills as well as the winds and tides) and the commercial accords between people in Africa, Portugal, and Portuguese America. In the eighteenth century, Akan slaves from modern Ghana (who were called Fante-Ashante in Brazil) were more commonly traded by the English, and most of them were sent to English colonies, although some were traded into Brazilian ports. Portuguese and Brazilian merchants found their niche in the relatively close-by Bight of Benin. The substantial contingent of Mahi (and other Gbe-speaking) slaves who disembarked in Brazilian ports—making their way to Rio de Janeiro, Bahia, Maranhão, Minas Gerais, and Goiás—were obtained through networks of both African traders and European agents and intermediaries.

In a pioneering study of the Brotherhoods of the Rosário in Minas Gerais, Julita Scarano showed that these associations predominantly considered themselves Mina, followed by groups calling themselves Benguela, Nagô, and Angola. There were also many smaller groups, some with only a handful of representatives, known as "Dagomé (Dahomey), Tapa (Nupe), Kongo-Cabinda, Mozambique, Maqui (Mahi), Sabará (Savalu), Timbu (Tibu?), Cobu, Xambá (Chamba), Malê (Muslims)." The indigenous were also represented, under the name Carijó.[49] In his well-known book *The Golden Age of Brazil*, focused on the eighteenth century, the historian Charles R. Boxer mentioned Mina, Angola, "luangos (Loango), caboverdes (Cape Verde), (Mozambique), creoles of the kingdom (*crioulos do reino*, from Portugal), creoles of Rio, bastards, and some random Chinese."[50] Neither Scarano nor Boxer was concerned with ethnic groups or African provenience, but both helpfully registered the presence of Africans of various nominal identities. Their lists help us comprehend both the diversity of groups articulating an identity, and the multiplicity of criteria that underlay that identity. Scarano was able to probe additional documents in Minas to attain a level of detail that the baptismal records in Rio could not provide, but that are conversant with the documents of Rio's Brotherhood of Santo Elesbão and Santa Efigênia, which demonstrated that Mahi, as well as the Savalu, were present.[51] In the documents of both Rio and Minas, it is clear that these were internal subgroups of the Mina.

The proveniences listed by Boxer are similar to those identified in Rio's baptismal records, while the references Scarano provided are similar to those in the documents of the Mina brotherhood in Rio. Boxer referred to various sources but did not mention documents pertaining to a religious brotherhood, although these might be one the best resources for comprehending the diversity of African ethnic groups in captivity in colonial Brazil. The level of organization attained by the Mina in Brazil was high, even earlier than the late eighteenth century, when the importation of Yoruba speakers (the so-called Nagô of Bahia) began to accelerate.[52]

According to the available baptismal records, the entrance of Mina slaves in Rio was most prominent during the years 1718–26, with a total of 681 adults baptized. The periods of greatest ritual activity were 1722, 1723, and 1724. In the Parish of Sé, the numbers fell dramatically, from a total of 681 adults baptized between 1718 and 1726, inclusive (nine years) to 235 between 1744 and 1750, inclusive (seven years), which shows a drop in

Table 7. Mina Adults Baptized in Rio de Janeiro, 1718–1760

YEAR	PARISH								TOTAL	
	Sé		Candelária		São José		Santa Rita			
	#	%	#	%	#	%	#	%	#	%
1751	23	2.0	35	3.1	9	0.8	0	0	67	5.8
1752	14	1.2	34	3.0	18	1.6	14	1.2	80	7.0
1753	9	0.8	27	2.4	14	1.2	28	2.4	78	6.8
1754	13	1.1	44	3.8	22	1.9	21	1.8	100	8.7
1755	28	2.4	52	4.5	24	2.1	26	2.3	130	11.3
1756	28	2.4	49	4.3	47	4.1	24	2.1	148	12.9
1757	34	3.0	41	3.6	35	3.1	21	1.8	131	11.4
1758	22	1.9	68	5.9	31	2.7	39	3.4	160	13.9
1759	13	1.1	56	4.9	35	3.1	25	2.2	129	11.2
1760	37	3.2	43	3.7	1.8	1.6	26	2.3	124	10.8
Total[a]	221	19.3	449	39.1	253	22.1	224	19.5	1,147	100

Source: ACMRJ, *Livros de Batismo de Escravos, Rio de Janeiro*: Sé, 1718–26, 1744–61;
Candelária, 1745–74; São José, 1751–90; Santa Rita, 1751–99.
[a]Rounding of decimals accounts for discrepancies in some of the totals.

annual rates from 75 to 34. Together, these two nonconsecutive periods in Sé Parish saw a total of 916 adult Mina baptized, or 57 per year. In terms of the numbers of Mina slaves arriving in Rio, there were many more who passed on through the city to Minas Gerais without appearing in the baptismal sources.

Table 7 demonstrates that the Mina were concentrated in the Parish of Candelária (carved out of the original Sé in 1632), with 39.1 percent of the total baptisms performed on adult Mina slaves. Candelária covered the port of Rio, along with a busy commercial district.

Manolo Florentino has argued that the supply of slaves to Brazil was elastic.[53] The commerce linking the Mina Coast to Rio de Janeiro offers a rich case study showing that this elasticity needs to be reassessed within each geographical and historical aspect of the slave trade. Low investment and high risk characterized the Mina trade, carried out by small boats,[54] often through clandestine operations, as opposed to the more broad-based Angola commerce that involved higher investment but relatively stable conditions of supply and demand. In the mid-1750s the number of Mina adult baptisms rose slightly, implying an equivalent increase in imports, but the sources available suggest that Rio's trade with Mina never again reached the levels of the early 1720s, when the most extravagant quantities of Minas gold poured through Rio and Bahia out to the slave markets of the Bight of Benin.

Data on marriage between slaves provide another source of insight into the Mina provenience group. The ecclesiastical compendium *Constituições Primeiras* was in favor of slave marriage, but the eighteenth-century Jesuit Andreoni suggested that slave masters were not enthusiastic proponents of marriages between the men and women they owned.[55] That may be true, but the proportion of slaves who actually went through with the vows was small. It would be safe to say that of the minority of all slaves who married, by far most of them married individuals belonging to the same master. Baptism records of children include the civil status of the mother, since it was necessary to state whether the child was legitimate (conceived in marriage) or natural (conceived out of marriage). Of the 6,609 records of children baptized—some of them children who, as I have specified, might have had the same mother, so that the total number of mothers might be somewhat less than that—only 253 noted that the mother was married.

When slaves married in Rio (much as Andreoni and Schwartz found in Bahia, and Faria reports for Campos), they usually married someone within their provenience group: Guinea with Guinea, Mina with Mina, and so on. This suggests that even if the general values placed on marriage in colonial Brazilian society led it to be encouraged among slaves, the endogamy practiced by members of provenience groups perhaps represented the exploitation of a small but significant space for the strategic alliance of people with some shared social, cultural, and linguistic background. Further study is needed in order to understand the nature of these unions and what new options and constraints marriage may have presented to slaves in Rio. Based on data published by João José Reis in *Rebelião Escrava no Brasil*, the historian Kátia Mattoso cites 16 marriages between Africans, 13 of which were within what Reis termed ethnic groups (9 Nagô couples, 2 Jêje, 1 Hausa, and 1 Bornu), and all of those 26 people involved came from the Mina Coast. Still examining Bahia, Mattoso suggested that some ethnic groups or nations tended to be more endogamous than others, and that both endogamy and free unions (living together in a relationship outside of marriage) are more consistently observed among freed Africans than among slaves, particularly after 1850.[56] I am unaware of the situation in Bahia in the eighteenth century, but the data for that period in Rio do show a strong inclination for endogamy among provenience groups, whether or not the slaves involved had been freed.

Given the risks in drawing comparisons between Bahia and Rio in this context—different geographic locations, holding different commercial relations with Africa, in two different centuries—we can make at least one observation. If in Bahia the groups from the Mina Coast showed the most marked inclination for endogamy—13 cases, versus 3 for Angola—in Rio it was Angola that seemed to pursue endogamy most commonly. But as has been shown, Angola slaves were the dominant African group in Rio at the time, as the Mina were in Bahia later. The critical calculation, then, is the percentage of endogamous people within each provenience group. In Rio in the eighteenth century, 77 percent of Angola women married Angola men; 87 percent of so-called Guinea women married Guinea men; but only 33 percent of Mina women were endogamous. In both cases, the smaller provenience group was less endogamous. The questions for future research then are to investigate in detail why endogamy was more common when the provenience group had a numerically larger population; and why smaller provenience groups tended to be marked by a search for marriage partners beyond their own group. It will also be important (if a particularly difficult task) to understand how people actually sought and evaluated potential partners, within or outside their groups.

I am unable to consider in depth the indices of marriage between freed slaves, or free unions, and the way that provenience group demography might have intersected with them. It is possible to begin such a project by looking at the baptism records for children of natural (unmarried) parents in which the identity of the father is adduced. But as a formal, socially recognized status, marriage provides a particularly helpful perspective into the types of unions and organizations available to provenience groups, and as we have seen these options seem to vary with place, time, and circumstance. The idea of matrimonial strategies being carefully weighed and assessed in each situation faced by slaves does not suggest that the result-

Table 8. Marriages of Female African Slaves in Rio de Janeiro, 1718–1760

MAN'S PROVENIENCE	WOMAN'S PROVENIENCE						TOTAL	
	Guinea		Mina		Angola			
	#	%	#	%	#	%	#	%
Mina	10	4.0	1	0.4	6	2.4	17	6.7
Guinea	1	0.4	85	33.6	0	0.0	86	34.0
Angola	12	4.7	0	0.0	96	37.9	108	42.7
Others	4	1.6	5	2.0	23	9.1	32	12.6
No data	3	1.2	7	2.8	0	0.0	10	4.0
Total[a]	30	11.9	98	38.7	125	49.4	253	100.0

Source: ACMRJ, *Livros de Batismo de Escravos, Rio de Janeiro*: Sé, 1718–26, 1744–61; Candelária, 1745–74; São José, 1751–90; Santa Rita, 1751–99.
[a]Rounding of decimals accounts for discrepancies in some of the totals.

ing patterns of marriages seen in the documents should be shapeless and incoherent. Rather, the tendency for endogamy within the largest provenience groups in eighteenth-century Rio (Angola) and nineteenth-century Bahia (Nagô) indicates that even in distant times and places, and independent of the internal contours of identity construction and social organization adopted by various provenience groups, homologous conditions in Brazil's slave regime could foster equivalent practices and solutions.

The data in table 8 show that in Rio de Janeiro, Mina women represented 12 percent of the total number of married African women. That number itself was small, as noted earlier—of 6,609 births recorded to slave mothers, only 253 of those mothers were married. Obviously, most African women had natural children, and either did not marry or married after giving birth.

The phenomenon of intermarriage between provenience groups, being principally Mina/Angola, is significant not only in itself but because of the wider new social relationships and intermingling of identities that such conjugal groupings could create. The tenor of the coexistence of Mina and Angola groups in lay brotherhoods takes on a new light from this angle. As chapter 5 of this book shows, tensions within the Brotherhood of Santo

Elesbão and Santa Efigênia were attributed to the entrance of "Angola blacks" and "creoles."[57] Mina women tended to marry outside the group more than Mina men, and it was they (Angola women) who were typically accused of provoking conflicts in the brotherhood by bringing in hostile elements from outside.

The changing distribution of Rio's slave population through the 1750s tracks with the growth of the city, which had until recently been concentrated along the coast of Guanabara Bay but was rapidly spreading to the hinterland, taking over the wetlands and smaller hills. The expanding habitations to the north, clinging to the hillsides, became the jurisdiction of the new Parish of Santa Rita in 1751. By 1760, the population of Rio de Janeiro numbered somewhere around 30,000. Urban change can be seen behind the distribution of younger slaves in Rio.

In the 1750s Mina and Angola slaves of child-rearing age, and their children, were concentrated in the new parish districts—80 percent lived in Santa Rita or São José, as opposed to 20 percent in the older parishes of Sé and Candelária. Over the decade, 28.7 percent of baptisms were performed in Santa Rita, while no less than 51.4 percent of the total were registered in São José (table 9), where the most slave owners lived. A significant portion of these mothers from São José must have enjoyed relative freedom of transit, given what sources show was the frequency of attending such churches as Rosário, Santa Efigênia, Lampadosa, São Jorge, and São Domingos, all on the far side of the city. We can also observe that the number of baptisms of Mina children (31.1 percent) versus Angola children (68.9 percent) shows that the Mina still had a substantial presence in the city's slave population, relative to slaves from the central-western African coast, as midcentury progressed. By comparing the baptism records for innocents and adults, it is possible to conclude that adult recent arrivals tended to be concentrated in the Parish of Candelária, but there is a gender component, with women from both the Mina Coast and Angola being more numerous, and men outnumbering women in Candelária (where the port was located, an important location of work for male slaves, especially Mina). Descriptions of daily life from the era lead us to surmise that in the Parish of São José, both Angola and Mina women could be found in the domestic realm but probably more frequently in the street, since female Mina slaves had a recognizable presence as food vendors—so-

Table 9. Distribution of Child Baptisms according to Mother's Proveniences, 1751–1760

PARISH	MOTHER'S PROVENIENCE				TOTAL	
	Mina		Angola			
	#	%	#	%	#	%
Sé, 1751–60	62	5.8	92	8.6	154	14.3
Candelária, 1751–60	34	3.2	26	2.4	60	5.6
Santa Rita, 1751–60	88	8.2	220	20.5	308	28.7
São José, 1751–60	150	14.0	402	37.4	552	51.4
Total[a]	334	31.1	740	68.9	1,074	100.0

Source: ACMRJ, Livros de Batismo de Escravos, Rio de Janeiro: Sé, 1718–26, 1744–61; Candelária, 1745–74; São José, 1751–90; Santa Rita, 1751–99.
[a]Rounding of decimals accounts for discrepancies in some of the totals.

called *escravas do tabuleiro* (tray-bearing female slave venders), who circulated throughout the city carrying their wares.[58] The Parish of Sé, which comprised the oldest parts of the city, was relatively dilapidated and had the fewest numbers of slaves of the four parishes. Although both male and female Mina slaves were spread over the other three parishes, men were concentrated in Candelária and women in São José.

The total of 1,481 baptisms of Mina slaves between 1751 and 1760 (table 10) corresponds to the sum of Mina adult slaves baptized, and the number of Mina mothers who took their children to be baptized. Since there were probably a number of slaves not listed in those books, this is still an imperfect picture of the Mina population of Rio de Janeiro by the 1750s, but there is not a better estimation for the period. There is no reasonable way to estimate the numbers of adults who were not baptized, of women who did not bear children, of women who had their children baptized outside the city limits, or of women who did not baptize their children at all. Of these, Mina women without children were probably the single most significant portion of the demographic that remains invisible in the numbers recorded in this chapter's tables. It was also nearly impossible to identify adult men who had been baptized in parishes outside the city of Rio. Both men and women tended to move around a great deal between the captaincies of Bahia, Rio de Janeiro, and Minas Gerais. Acknowledging these limitations,

Table 10. Distribution of Mina Baptisms by Parish, 1718–1760

BAPTISMS	Sé	Candelária	São José	Santa Rita	TOTAL
		PARISH			
Children	62	34	150	88	334
Adults	221	449	253	224	1,147
Total	283	483	403	312	1,481

Source: ACMRJ, *Livros de Batismo de Escravos*, Rio de Janeiro: Sé, 1718–26, 1744–61; Candelária, 1745–74; São José, 1751–90; Santa Rita, 1751–99.

then, the data we do have show that the greatest concentrations of Mina men were in Candelária, and of Mina women in São José. Together, these two parishes correspond to 60 percent of the Mina slaves in the city of Rio de Janeiro between 1751 and 1760, as can be calculated from table 10.

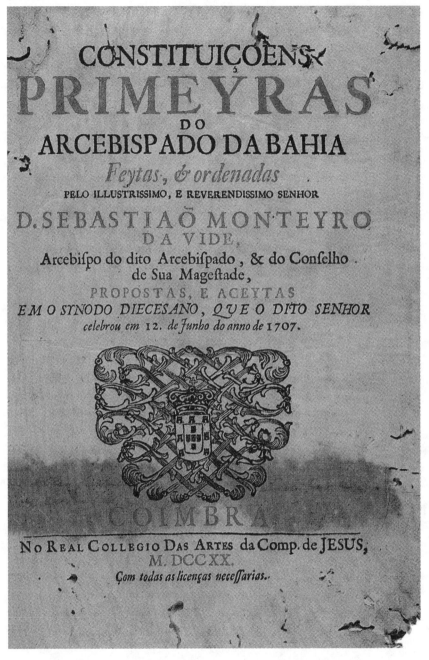

CONSTITUIÇOENS
PRIMEYRAS
DO
ARCEBISPADO DA BAHIA

Feytas, & ordenadas

PELO ILLUSTRISSIMO, E REVERENDISSIMO SENHOR

D. SEBASTIAÕ MONTEYRO
DA VIDE,

Arcebifpo do dito Arcebifpado, & do Confelho
de Sua Mageftade,

PROPOSTAS, E ACEYTAS

*EM O SYNODO DIECESANO, QUE O DITO SENHOR
celebrou em* 12. *de Junho do anno de* 1707.

No REAL COLLEGIO DAS ARTES da Comp. de JESUS,
M. DCC XX.

Com todas as licenças neceſſarias.

Title page of the *Constituições Primeiras do Arcebispado da Bahia* (1707), the first official set of
regulations of the Brazilian Catholic Church. Announced in Bahia in 1707, it was published
in Portugal in 1719/1720. Courtesy of BN, Brazil. Published in a modern edition: Sebastião
Monteiro da Vide (Dom), *Constituições Primeiras do Arcebispado da Bahia* (Brasília: Senado
Federal, 2007).

ETHIOPE
RESGATADO,

EMPENHADO, SUSTENTADO,
Corregido, inftruido, e libertado.

DISCURSO
THEOLOGICO-JURIDICO,

EM QUE SE PROPOEM O MODO
de comerciar, haver, e poffuir validamente, quanto
a hum, e outro foro, os Pretos cativos Africanos,
e as principaes obrigações, que correm a quem
delles fe fervir.

CONSAGRADO
A'

SANTISSIMA VIRGEM
MARIA

NOSSA SENHORA.

Pelo Padre

MANOEL RIBEIRO ROCHA,

Lisbonenfe, Domiciliario da Cidade da Bahia, e nella Advogado, e Bacharel formado na Univerfidade de Coimbra.

LISBOA:
Na Officina Patriarcal de Francifco Luiz Ameno

M. DCC. LVIII.
Com todos as licenças neceffarias.

Title page of Manoel Ribeiro Rocha's *Ethiope Resgatado, Empenhado, Sustentado, Corrigido, Instruído e Libertado*, on the debate about the conversion and indoctrination of African slaves in Brazil, published in Portugal in 1758. Courtesy of BN, Brazil. Published in a modern edition: Manoel Ribeiro Rocha, *Etíope Resgatado, Empenhado, Sustentado, Corrigido, Instruído e Libertado*, presented and transcribed from the original by Silvia Hunold Lara (Campinas: IFCH-UNICAMP, 1991).

Sketches of male Africans slaves from different proveniences (called "nations"), by Jean-Baptiste Debret (ca. 1820). The artist focused here on the detail of tattoos and hairstyles. Debret reproduced many of these sketches in his plates of street porters and dockworkers. Courtesy of BN, Brazil. Reprinted in Jean Baptiste Debret, *O Brasil de Debret*, plate 56.

Sketches of female African slaves from different proveniences (called "nations"), by Jean-Baptiste Debret (ca. 1820). Here, the artist's eye was caught by the hairstyles and the use of European-style clothing among the domestic slaves of elite households. Debret reproduced many of these sketches in his scenes of the home life of Brazilian families. Courtesy of BN, Brazil. Reprinted in Jean Baptiste Debret, *O Brasil de Debret*, plate 44.

Urban Transport in Rio de Janeiro, by Carlos Julião (ca. 1780). Indigenous hammock porters in Rio de Janeiro. Until the second half of the eighteenth century, some indigenous free workers shared with Africans the task of conveying people through the city streets. At the end of the eighteen century most porters were Africans, but Carlos Julião—a soldier serving Portugal— did not miss the few remaining indigenous porters. Courtesy of BN, Brazil. Printed in Carlos Julião, *Riscos Iluminados de Figurinhos de Brancos e Negros dos Uzos do Rio de Janeiro e Serro do Frio*, plate 7.

Poor urban dwelling in Rio de Janeiro, by Jean-Baptiste Debret (ca. 1820). Various architectural developments came to the city of Rio de Janeiro following the installation of the Portuguese court in 1808, although the old part of the city occupied by people of humble means was affected less than other districts. The style and appearance of those poor houses had changed little since the eighteenth century. Courtesy of BN, Brazil. Reprinted in Jean Baptiste Debret, *O Brasil de Debret*, plate 54.

African Women Collecting Donations on the Street, by Carlos Julião (ca. 1780). Notable in this image of African women in the folia of a Catholic Lay Brotherhood is the ornate, festive attire, including that worn by a little girl accompanying the older women. Courtesy of BN, Brazil. Printed in Carlos Julião, *Riscos Iluminados de Figurinhos de Brancos e Negros dos Uzos do Rio de Janeiro e Serro do Frio*, plate 35.

Funeral of the son of an African king of a folia, by Jean-Baptiste Debret (ca. 1820). Although Debret suggested that the folias no longer appeared in public processions on saints' days after the arrival of the Portuguese court (1808), he was able to observe this funeral cortege depicted in detail. Courtesy of BN, Brazil. Reprinted in Jean Baptiste Debret, *O Brasil de Debret*, plate 80.

Collection of Donations in the Church of the Rosário of Rio Grande, by Jean-Baptiste Debret (ca. 1820). This interior scene of a church in Rio Grande, southern Brazil, shows the folia of the Brotherhood of the Rosário. The king and queen lead the ceremonial collection of donations, alongside the *capitão da guarda* (royal bodyguard), musicians, and other members of the court. Courtesy of BN, Brazil. Reprinted in Jean Baptiste Debret, *O Brasil de Debret*, plate 90.

Queen of the Folia, by Carlos Julião (ca. 1780). A cortege featuring the queen, dressed in her regal attire. Parasols, musical instruments, and dancing add to the vibrancy of the event. Courtesy of BN, Brazil. Printed in Carlos Julião, *Riscos Iluminados de Figurinhos de Brancos e Negros dos Uzos do Rio de Janeiro e Serro do Frio*, plate 37.

King and Queen of the Folia, by Carlos Julião (ca. 1780). The king and queen are the focal point of this street procession, which is also distinguished by the presence of a parasol and the standard of their reign. Note the presence of the *capitão da guarda* (royal bodyguard) following the royal couple. Courtesy of BN, Brazil. Printed in Carlos Julião, *Riscos Iluminados de Figurinhos de Brancos e Negros dos Uzos do Rio de Janeiro e Serro do Frio*, plate 38.

African girls dance in the folia, by Carlos Julião (ca. 1780). Note the stylized African costume, a sheet around the waist combined with lace, which is quite unlike the adult attire. Julião's original plate reflects the artist's detailed examination of the markings and tattoos on the girls' arms and chests. Courtesy of BN, Brazil. Printed in Carlos Julião, *Riscos Iluminados de Figurinhos de Brancos e Negros dos Uzos do Rio de Janeiro e Serro do Frio*, plate 26.

PART TWO

By the closing decades of the sixteenth century, the city of Rio de Janeiro began to expand markedly. It strained its older limits at the hills to push restlessly outward toward the fertile lowlands, while the urban core—based on Morro do Castelo (Castle Hill), the Fort of São Sebastião (Saint Sebastian), the Church of São Sebastião (where the saint's image was kept), and the College of the Jesuits—began a progressive slide into decline. One indication of the increased population in the region came in 1634, when the small Chapel of Candelária in the plains was elevated to a parish. In 1640, Rio's assembly acceded to a request articulated by citizens to transform the city's system of natural drainage, which was overwhelmed and unpredictable, into a more efficient network of trenches. Once completed, the aptly named Vala (drainage ditch) carried away city rainwater as well as some waste, and also served as a popular and functional demarcation of Rio's urban space from the surrounding fields.

THE CONSTRUCTION OF URBAN SPACE

The principal social activities that had been centered on the Church of São Sebastião began to change as the city's reach was extended to the newly important lowlands. The residents of Castle Hill, so-called *homens bons* (respectable men), and their families relocated from the older, tightly clustered neighborhoods on the Castle Hill streets in search of fresh air, open space, and enhanced prestige. Meanwhile, they also gradually disappeared from the nocturnal processions that led up the hill from São Sebastião to participate in the activities of the chapels along Rio's plains.[1] The bishop and the priests directly under him stayed behind on the hill, as did two black brotherhoods (Our Lady of the Rosário and São Benedito) and at least one brotherhood of *pardos*. It is unclear when each of these congregations formed, but already in 1639 the two black groups united to form the Black Men's Brotherhood of Our Lady of the Rosário and São Benedito. The association's *compromisso* was approved by Catholic authorities in 1669, but evidence suggests that the two groups may have been in existence for sixty years by then.

The Prelacy of Rio de Janeiro dated to 1576, and in 1659, the Church of São Sebastião was elevated in status to the episcopal See of Rio's prelacy. But because that church was rather the worse for wear, the bishop petitioned the king to transfer the See to the newly built Church of Saint Joseph (São José) on the edge of the city.[2] That idea was immediately rebuffed by the brothers of São José, who had no interest in the bishop's occupation of their church. The religious life of the city center continued to suffer from the slow but constant attrition of its nobler flock. Pope Innocent XI intervened to create the Diocese of Rio de Janeiro in 1676, transforming the prelacy to a bishopric;[3] and in 1685, São Sebastião was reconfigured into a cathedral for the episcopal See. But the problems persisted. The poverty encroaching more and more around the old church was also noticeable within it, as its brotherhoods and lay activities were increasingly being sustained almost entirely by enslaved or freed blacks and small numbers of pardos.

But all spheres of Rio's religious life, including the most humble, absorbed the bustling energy of a growing city in motion. The black brotherhoods were increasingly visible in public parades, carrying images of the saints, colorful banners, and other sacred objects and adornments.[4] As they grew in numbers, the conflicts also were more marked between different brotherhoods—as well as between the brotherhoods and the Catholic hierarchy. By the end of the seventeenth century, the priests of the See resolved to expulse both the Brotherhood of Our Lady of the Rosário and São Benedito (led by Angola Africans and creoles) and the Brotherhood of São Domingos (led by so-called Guinea gentios) from the Church of São Sebastião.[5] In essence, such disputes took two often related forms: on the

one hand, conflict between the brotherhoods and the ecclesiastical authorities; and on the other, conflict between brotherhoods over the use of space
in the church and over the place of each in the local hierarchy. Public
processions were often the clearest manifestation of that ordering (since
sequence equated to status), as well as colorful stages for its (subtle or
direct) contestation.[6] This concern over the order of appearance in processions reflects a pervasive preoccupation with the way hierarchical order
was conceived in colonial society framed by the ancien régime.[7] According
to Schwartz, an ordered society makes viable in practice hierarchies of
grade, privilege, and honor. In such a system it is possible to define the
position of any individual according to his or her insignia, privileges, or
even obligations. In such social conditions, "protocol and order assume
important symbolic significance in public events," serving to reinforce the
"prerogatives of each group."[8]

In June 1702, D. Fr. Francisco de São Jerônimo became the third bishop
of the Bishopric of Rio de Janeiro; his tenure lasted until his death in 1721.
Born in Lisbon, a doctor of theology and censor for the *Santo Oficio* (Holy
Office), D. Fr. Francisco arrived seemingly intent on chafing local sensibilities. Once established in Rio, he fired off a jeremiad to the crown
about the unacceptable condition of the Church of São Sebastião relative to
the disproportionate opulence of the newer churches. Like a sharp blow
to a hornets' nest, this act aggravated the aggression that had been mildly
simmering between Rio's churches (and even after the initial heat wore off,
the peevishness between churches persisted for a century).[9] In his letter,
the bishop unleashed particular invective about the habits of Rio's female
population.[10] Whatever his effects on local women's comportment in general, the bishop did attain permission in 1705 to build a convent, which
later would be called the Convent of Nossa Senhora da Ajuda (Our Lady of
Relief).[11]

The lay brotherhoods of Rio de Janeiro drew inspiration from older Portuguese models, as well as from the local Santa Casa de Misericórdia (Holy
House of Mercy), but they represented diverse sectors of society. In the
eighteenth century, according to the regulations of the Tribunal of Orders,
each parish should have a Brotherhood of the Santíssimo Sacramento.
Since it had the official incentive of the ecclesiastical authorities, this devotion was usually held in high regard locally, a fact which attracted people

and families of greater or lesser means. Still, its members had little autonomy, because the bishop kept close watch over its functions. Throughout eighteenth-century Brazil, these were the most sought-after and exclusive brotherhoods for white men; perhaps only the third orders of Carmo and São Francisco were more competitive.[12] Most churches were constructed through the contributions (financial and otherwise) of groups organized around the devotion to particular saints, such as the lay brotherhoods; their constitution typically reflected other nonreligious social factors, such as common profession, familial ties, or a differentiating identity (the blacks and pardos). A brotherhood that built a church effectively owned it, and could open it to the use of smaller and poorer congregations who might need to promise in their written statutes to perform certain obligations for the more powerful brotherhood. In Rio, the Church of São José, constructed in the lowlands in the seventeenth century, was the domain of the brotherhood of carpenters; as time went on, historical factors and urban change led some of the wealthiest families of the city to worship in that church. Africans, African-descended creoles, and other *pretos* (blacks) were devoted to Saint Benedict and Our Lady of the Rosário, while the pardos united around Our Lady of the Conceição. Each group had a saint, and a charter or set of vows and statutes (the compromisso) binding them to the local church and to the larger Catholic edifice with its roots in Rome. They also displayed the color and insignia associated with their saints on their flags and banners. These colors and insignia referred most directly to saints, but at the same time they were "read" by people in the society as another part of the symbolic universe that inscribed their humble bearers in a discrete social position and rank.

Among the principal public events of the city were the festive or funeral processions organized by lay brotherhoods. In the hierarchy of religious associations, the black and pardo groups were always made to embody their lowly position by appearing in the processions' final ranks. But even here, at the end of the parade, there were finer distinctions to be made. Mulattos and freed blacks enjoyed somewhat higher status, especially if they had served time in the military (in, for instance, the Ordinance Company of Freed Blacks, created in 1698). The lowest of the low were the slaves recently arrived from Africa, referred to as *pretos novos* (new blacks).

Compared to European cities and even to Spanish American cities of the era, it is clear that Rio de Janeiro in the seventeenth century was poor.[13] During the light of day, the city was harsh and unappealing to the eye (and to the nose, as some period documentation emphasizes). One entered Rio's urban core along unpaved and craggy roads, lined with improvised stalls and low houses clustered so densely as to prevent the coastal breezes from ventilating their musty interiors. Malodorous trash was everywhere. Pedestrians did their best to tiptoe and hop through the refuse, as did a remarkable number of ambulatory vendors selling just about anything one might want to eat or drink. Here and there in the plazas, impromptu slave markets offered the spectacle of male and female slaves, in varying states of undress and often still reeling from the middle passage, on display before skeptical and haggling buyers. But at night the fetid gloom deepened to murkiness, and the city took on a macabre aspect. The darkness was nearly total, broken only by the glimpse of an occasional greasy candle burning within a house, or the lamps placed as a gesture of grandeur above the signs for a few private commercial establishments. More often, it was the bobbing lanterns of nocturnal funeral processions that offered a bold but ephemeral challenge to the darkness; their light revealed sinister-looking men and women, idling alone or in small groups along the narrow streets. The reek of the trash seemed to gather its pungency at night, broken every now and then by the sudden rainstorms that emptied the streets of litter but turned them to mud.

Not farther away from the urban core, along the seaside, the situation was different. A few roads were paved with stone, and they were lined with houses (often used simultaneously for residence and commerce). Although the city's freed blacks tended to work in the warrens of central Rio, where they could also afford cheap housing, it was in the less populated areas beyond the Vala trench that the black brotherhoods began to receive small donations of land to build their own chapels in the first half of the eighteenth century. In 1700, the Church of the Rosário began construction near a stretch of the Vala, on its far side.[14] And in 1706, the Chapel of Saint Domingo was inaugurated near the Campo da Cidade (City Field), which came to be called the Campo de São Domingos.

A century and a half after the first French invasion of Rio de Janeiro had been successfully turned back in 1565, French corsairs attacked again, this time more decisively, in 1710 and 1711. They took Rio not for its own sake but for its strategic port, through which so much gold from the mines of Minas Gerais was known to pass.[15] That the city fell so quickly indicates how poorly it was guarded. In fact, the problems were less of a military or tactical nature than with a profoundly ineffective city administration, in which all the wealth was maintained in the hands of a cadre of powerful mill owners and merchants. Perhaps fittingly, it was they who paid the ransom to retrieve the bruised city from the French; the payment accepted by René Duguay-Trouin to sail away from Rio consisted of 600,000 *cruzados*, 100 chests of sugar, and 200 head of cattle (to feed the French sailors).[16]

After this embarrassing and costly episode, more emphasis was placed on keeping the city secure. Plans were debated in 1713 for a protective wall, and construction finally began two years later, only to be halted and finally abandoned at an unknown date. However, the sketches made by João Massé, coordinator of the project, did survive, and they give a view of the city's dimensions as well as some principal features. The sketches also depict the chapels of the Rosário and São Domingos, although these are shown to be outside the wall's zone of protection.[17]

The eighteenth century was marked, throughout the Christian West, by the crisis of Constantine Christianity in parallel with the rise of the modern state. The events analyzed in this book, focusing on the Mina in Rio de Janeiro, occurred within a set of historical circumstances whose connection to the new relations between church and state are complex, multiple, and deserving of more attention than I can provide here.[18] In the Portuguese Empire, the bishops maintained a significant autonomy through the effects of the Padroado, which kept the ecclesiastical administration under the orientation of the Tribunal of Conscience and Orders in Portugal and acted as a buffer against the forces for both secular and religious change. The bishops strove to maintain their stature as the highest authority in the territory of their jurisdiction, and were notorious for evading certain guidelines from the Council of Trent (1564), which stipulated that they should yield to papal authority in questions of ecclesiastical procedure (such as norms for indoctrination, administration of sacraments, and filling out of parish record books).

It may be recalled that in 1707, a synod of the diocese was held in Bahia. The synod was poorly attended, with the bishops of Olinda, Maranhão, and Rio de Janeiro absent. The synod proceeded with its Bahian representatives, and its most enduring result was the publication in 1719 of the *Constituições Primeiras*, the already-mentioned ecclesiastical code and regulation that was first written for Bahia and later applied to Brazil. Given the lack of other interventions to define such guidelines for other bishoprics in the ensuing years, the code from Bahia gradually became adopted into the bishoprics throughout Brazil. The need for these regulatory structures was both urgent and delicate, because Catholic religiosity in eighteenth-century Brazil—what some scholars have aptly termed baroque Catholicism[19]— depended on wide lay participation. The diverse ceremonies that the public instigated, in larger or smaller groups—in their homes, in churches, or in chapels they themselves had built—were important for the church's vitality and reach. These events and practices also became dynamic spaces for sociability in colonial society.[20] In Brazil, researchers exploring the history of the church have tended to see the profusion of lay religious activity as an expression of the distance between ecclesiastical structures and the general population, especially given the sheer scale of the territory that was under the jurisdiction of a few scattered church officials.[21] That factor should not be ignored, but neither should we discount the predisposition among bishops in the eighteenth century to avoid the more stringent mandates of roman clericalism that had been propagated by the Council of Trent.[22] The issue is less one of inaccessible regions, or a lack of religious functionaries dedicated to pastoral work, or a supposed indifference toward the catechism among slaves. The prevailing attitude of local authorities, even in urban centers such as Rio, was to work around the recommendations of the new ecclesiastical model. There were administrative complications too, not least in the filtering of Rome's guidelines through Portugal's Tribunal of Conscience and Orders, with the socially impractical result that they were indiscriminately applied to slaves and free people, black and white, cities and villages, lay congregations and clerics. From the perspective of the Catholicism envisioned by the Council of Trent, the city of Rio de Janeiro in the eighteenth century presented a picture of incomplete Christianity (but then so did most of Brazil).

In 1719, Aires Saldanha e Albuquerque Coutinho Matos e Noronha became governor of the captaincy. Aires Saldanha had a special concern for public works; many roads were improved and paved under his watch, and work on the Carioca Aqueduct was accelerated (at least in part through indigenous labor). It was also during his administration that the highest numbers of baptisms of adult Mina slaves was recorded, suggesting that more slaves were entering the city during this phase of urban development; simultaneously, there were higher levels of Mina slaves entering the mine regions of Minas Gerais. In 1725 there was a new governor, Luís Vahia Monteiro,[23] and a new bishop—D. Fr. Antônio de Guadalupe—became Rio's fourth, replacing D. Francisco de São Jerônimo. Antônio was steeped in more rigorous observation of Catholic traditions than his predecessor, and quickly established the daily celebration of the Liturgy of Hours and of the Holy Mass. Public prayers and catechisms were commonplace in his administration, which was also marked by the broad endorsement of Bahia's *Constituições Primeiras* for Rio de Janeiro.[24] Through the financial assistance and oversight of Monteiro and D. Fr. Antônio, some of the preto and pardo brotherhoods of Rio were able to secure their hold on permanent spaces for their congregations.[25]

Already in 1725, the Church of the Brotherhood of Our Lady of the Rosário and São Benedito of Black Men was inaugurated. This was a genuine advance for the brotherhood, even though their church had to be constructed near an undesirable spot along the Vala trench, where city effluent tended to accumulate in reeking pools until rainstorms would carry it out to the ocean.[26] In 1734, the See cathedral was transferred from the Church of São Sebastião on Castle Hill to the Church of the Santa Cruz of the Militaries; three years later the See was relocated to the newer and increasingly central Church of the Rosário. That meant relocating the Cabido (chapter of the See) as well. But the priests of the Cabido who for four decades had tried to rid the prestigious cathedral of its black brotherhood suddenly found themselves with the blacks once again, although this time in a situation where the priests were the guests and the blacks, the hosts.[27] By this time the city boasted many churches and chapels constructed by lay brotherhoods, including Santa Luzia, São José, São Domingos, and Santa Rita, and Candelária, the holy candle. Of course, not all the lay associations were able to build their own spaces. Many of the Africans arriving from the Mina Coast, for example, maintained their congregations in the consecrated churches for blacks within the city, but it was a period of flux. In 1715, one group of Mina slaves organized the Brotherhood of Santo Antônio da Mouraria (said Glorious Saint Anthony of the Moors) in the backrooms of the Church of Saint Sebastian, alongside the brotherhoods of the Rosário and São Benedito, and of São Domingos. They stayed behind when the other black brotherhoods moved on from the old church to their own newer chapels. Little is known about this association, and about the provenience of the Mina who composed the brotherhood; the reference to Moors suggests that they were converted Muslims, possibly brought from Cacheu and arriving in Rio by way of Cape Verde. In 1737, when the Cabido abandoned the Church of São Sebastiáo for the Church of the Rosário, the brotherhood went with them to find their own space in the newer church. Sometime before 1740, in the Church of São Domingos, another group of Mina formed a congregation around the worship of the Menino (Child) Jesus.[28] In the 1740s, another group of devout Africans organized a congregation at the Church of the Rosário: the Brotherhood of Our Lady of Lampadosa, which comprised Africans of various nations, including Mina.

Thus, in 1740, when the Brotherhood of Santo Elesbão and Santa Efigênia was created (about which more will be said in the following chapter), Rio de Janeiro contained two churches that were owned by black brotherhoods—Rosário and São Domingos—and another church where a brotherhood of pardos, Our Lady of Assunçáo (Assumption) and Boa Morte (Good Death), was organized.[29] Beyond these, there were many smaller brotherhoods and congregations that had formed within the city's less privileged ranks. Many were not officially documented or registered, and they united to worship in whatever space they could find in the urban churches. While most of the devoted in these congregations were slaves, the leaders were almost always freed blacks; some were people of means, and the Mina were prominent in these relatively elevated ranks.[30]

The manner of dressing, down to sartorial details, was read as an expression of one's position in the hierarchy of colonial society. Clerics wore longer robes than laymen. Freed black women used much of their available income in gold jewelry and the bright, ornately embellished *panos da costa* (large pieces of colored cloth originating in the African Atlantic ports, usually worn by women around torsos or over their shoulders) to maintain a distinctive visual impression.[31] The African cloth was used to wrap and carry babies on the mother's back, or to cover the head in the manner of a shawl, which was adopted from the Portuguese habit. Because these cloths were highly valued by both male and female Africans, they were an increasingly prominent component of the trade between Brazil and Africa. Palm oil, cola nuts, certain vegetables, beads, amulets, and soaps were also sent in bulk from Africa to Rio, where they were sold at the marketplace in stands that freed Africans themselves often owned.[32]

Not until a later era did conditions in the city allow for wheeled means of public transport. Elites rode in tasseled hammocks or padded chairs suspended on poles, both carried by slaves; these were the same types of conveyance Rio's nobility had used a century before. Everyone else got around on foot, although here too there was opportunity for the better endowed to demonstrate their greater wealth and respectability than the average pedestrian riffraff. This was of great importance, since the image a person presented on the street for public scrutiny had ramifications for his or her position in the social hierarchy. If one lacked the resources to be carried about by slaves, one could still perhaps be accompanied by a slave, who would often be festooned in elaborate costume and carrying a large parasol to shade the master's respectable head. There was some irony in the hammock: as a way to carry a living person, it connoted deference and material wealth. But when the passenger was dead, observers knew that the deceased was an individual of modest means, since a hammock was the cheapest way to carry the body to the cemetery.

In the early eighteenth century, most houses in Rio were single-story structures. Because houses also served the dual function of residence and place of commerce, they were often structured with the store or office close to the street; the domestic area was in the more private back section, connected to the front by a corridor. A small backyard was common. The walls were built of stone or brick, secured with a mortar with a whale-oil base. In poorer houses the floor might have been bare earth, stamped to a hard evenness; wealthier houses had stone or brick floors. Whitewashing the houses' outer walls was mandatory, but infrequently enforced; many poor people left them plain. Furniture was a rarity for all but the wealthiest residents. A foreigner who passed some time in the city during this era visited a home where, he later wrote, all the women were sitting "Moorish style, on a hard bench." Beside that, the house appeared to contain only one table and chair, which were offered to him to use.[33]

A chronic lack of skilled carpenters meant that nearly all the doors and windows, as well as such furniture as existed, had a rustic look and feel. Still, windows were remarkably uniform in size at around one meter wide by two high. They opened to the inside, and could be locked shut with a simple but sturdy wooden latch. Doors were usually a meter wide also, but often were longer than the windows. They were topped with an awning, or if possible a form of wooden shutter that allowed air to circulate. Peepholes were standard, for the convenience of the residents. Some houses used tightly layered palm fronds for a roof, while other dwellings incorporated rounded shingles of ceramic tile. Smaller houses might have a two-plane roof, with one sloping toward the street, and the other toward the rear of the house. Larger houses grew to the rear, lengthwise, instead of up or laterally; thus, to accommodate a lengthening structure, the roof on such houses would be inverted, with the slopes to the sides. The nature and condition of the roof were assessed by people in colonial society as a direct expression of the resources belonging to inhabitants of the house. A plain or inadequately tiled roof, a double-tiled roof, or a roof bearing yet a third layer of colored tiles visible to passersby—these different roofs related to the ancien régime's hierarchical universe, and to the tiered public display of wealth elsewhere in the city: they likely corresponded to (first) a man who had no slaves to accompany his passage through the streets; (second) a better-off man, probably carried in a hammock by two reasonably dressed slaves; and finally, a rich man, who would ride on a padded sedan hoisted by four slaves attired in velvet, lace, and silk.

With time this standard form of house construction took on new variations, principally from the development of second-story lofts or attics into habitable spaces. These new rooms were often rented out, turning a single house into a multifamily home. With further subdivision into smaller quarters, some houses also became collective habitations for freed blacks or poor whites. One freed slave known to own his own house, Caetano da Costa, died in 1749; he left behind his two-story house and three slaves to his wife.[34] As the city grew, domestic architecture also became more ambitious. Two-story, even three-story, houses became commonplace in some neighborhoods, with elegant wood floors and steep staircases. In the back, low fences demarcated the yards belonging to different houses.[35]

The Parish of Sé, which made up the oldest part of Rio de Janeiro, contained in the 1780s some 1,600 houses (table 11). It is as yet impossible

Table 11. Distribution of Houses by Parish in Rio de Janeiro, 1779–1789

PARISH	HOUSE TYPE						TOTAL	
	1-Story		2-Story		3-Story			
	#	%	#	%	#	%	#	%
Sé	1,600	27.6	457	7.9	15	0.3	2,072	35.7
Candelária	480	8.3	676	11.6	188	3.2	1,344	23.1
São José	860	14.8	338	5.8	26	0.4	1,224	21.1
Santa Rita	646	11.1	450	7.7	71	1.2	1,167	20.1
Total[a]	3,586	61.8	1,921	33.1	300	5.2	5,807	100.0

Source: "Memórias Públicas e Econômicas da Cidade de São Sebastião do Rio de Janeiro para Uso de Vice-rei Luiz de Vasconcellos por Observação Curiosa dos Anos de 1779 até o de 1789," 31.
[a]Rounding of decimals accounts for discrepancies in some of the totals.

to decipher the documents to know how many of these houses kept slaves, or how many slaves.[36] However, if the Parish of São José had the most slaves in the decade of the 1750s,[37] it had only 26 two-story houses in the same period. The parish with the most two-story houses was Candelária, where the prevalent commercial activity in those districts took over the house's bottom floor and the family moved up to the second story. In that sense, these houses should not be thought of as two-story residences, but as commercial buildings in which the owner and his family lived above the business.

Manolo Florentino has compiled 1,067 postmortem inventories of the owners of rural and urban households in Rio de Janeiro from the years 1790–1835. Based on that research, he argues that "almost all the free men inventoried were the masters of at least one slave."[38] We can only wonder how many of those slaves were Mina, recently arrived and cheap in relation to other slaves who would be already acquainted with the Portuguese language (thus making them a likely purchase for free men or freed blacks working up the socioeconomic ladder). The larger problem is to comprehend who had the means to buy slaves at the time, how many they bought, and what the different social ramifications were for owning one slave, or more, or not owning slaves. That is, the wills and testaments of freed Mina suggest that, if they were able to buy their freedom (usually from money made providing services on the street), some among them also saved money and bought one or more African slaves, sometimes by pooling their resources. The value placed on owning a slave seems to have been universal in colonial Brazil's slave society; this is a subject that needs further study.

WHAT WAS DONE WITH THE DEAD

The corpses deriving from well-off families were buried within the churches' walls.[39] For slaves, of course, church floor space was elite real estate, too exclusive socially and physically inadequate anyway to absorb the high volume of defunct slaves. By the seventeenth century, the flow of slave corpses had overwhelmed Rio's existing open-air cemeteries and had led to the establishment of newer, ampler ones. Two of these were the 1613 Cemetery of the Rocio (Dew) of the City, also called the Cemetery of Mulattos, and the 1623 Cemetery of the Santa Casa de Misericórdia (Holy House of Mercy). Convents also increasingly used parts of their grounds for small cemeteries dedicated to the burial of slaves.

The bodies of slaves, as well as poor whites, were often carried to their final resting places in coffins rented for this purpose by the Church of the Santa Casa da Misericórdia, which held a monopoly on this service. In 1687, the Brotherhood of Our Lady of the Rosário and São Benedito of Black Men received a special license to possess their own coffins. That way, they had to pay only for funerals themselves and not for the transportation of the cadaver to the burial site. This privilege was expanded to the Brotherhood of Our Lady of Boa Morte of Pardo Men in 1688, and to the Brotherhood of São Domingos in 1699. This made the process cheap enough for Rio's slaves that many could have an actual burial ceremony, and escape the fate of the anonymous collective pits, owned by the Santa Casa de Misericórdia, where those of the humblest means were interred. The use of hammocks to carry the dead, mentioned previously, was the usual way to make the process less expensive. Since just a few slaves and free blacks were able to gather enough resources to pay for a more proper burial independent of Misericórdia's rental coffins and pits, Misericórdia could still dedicate much of its attention to the less frequent but still lucrative and socially significant funerals of Rio's wealthier residents. The attempts of Miseri-

córdia to control the funeral market derived not only from financial interests but, perhaps more significantly, desire for the prestige and recognition
that such a position would bring.[40]

The Church of São Domingos was inaugurated in 1706, and soon it
was interring slave bodies both inside and outside its walls. In 1709, the
Franciscans there obtained a separate piece of land by the convent that they
dedicated as a cemetery for slaves (the land had already been used as an
informal dumping ground for deceased slaves). In 1722, the brotherhood
of the newly built Church of Santa Rita also built a cemetery on its grounds;
as its name implies, the Cemetery of New Blacks was dedicated to Africans.
The Cemetery of the Rosário was opened at roughly the same time. The pits
at Misericórdia remained the standard option for poor blacks who, for
whatever reason, had not entered into a contractual agreement with one of
the brotherhoods to provide a more dignified end for their earthly remains.
The preferred cemeteries for blacks who had the capacity to choose seem to
have been those alongside the churches of Our Lady of the Rosário and São
Domingos. Others were buried in the cemetery of the Candelária Church,
which was the seat of Candelária Parish. The church had worked out a deal
with slave owners, who could deposit their dead there for prearranged
prices. According to wills, obituary records, and other documents, it seems
that black people in Rio at the time were never buried in coffins. They were
lowered into the grave in a net, usually wrapped in white cloths or a white
sheet. Some blacks did pay extra for special habiliment—freed Mina with
enough disposable income tended to prefer being buried in the characteristic habit of São Francisco—but the body was always transported in a
hammock.

One of the most-cited justifications for the creation of black brotherhoods in colonial Brazil was the observed tendency of masters to abandon
slaves who had become old, sick, or injured. Slaves who died with no
system of support beyond the attentions of their owners typically had their
cadavers tossed unceremoniously on the beaches or in the fields outside
the city, or, in the best possible case, dropped at the door of a church, where
it was asked that they be buried "for the love of God" (i.e., at no charge to
the master). It would not be thought untoward for a slave master of limited
means to present himself to the priests with the slave's corpse, requesting a
charitable burial. But as a 1735 petition from a brotherhood in Salvador to

the crown suggests, this might be distasteful to the master: "Owners prefer to discard the bodies of slaves secretly, rather than endure the priests' drawn-out and embarrassing investigations into their capacity to pay for the ritual. And even if a charitable burial is finally deemed appropriate, enough time has gone by that the remains of the slave are too frightful to handle."[41]

But, in fact, it was not only the ostensibly flint-hearted slave masters who abandoned black cadavers to the weeds and gulls. Even brotherhoods would resort to the practice when they did not have enough funds to provide for a burial. This unpleasant fact was admitted in petitions from brotherhoods in Bahia, and it is reflected in the documentation of the Church of Santo Elesbão and Santa Efigênia in Rio. When reading the petitions, it is important to recall that whenever anyone wrote to the crown asking for special support or privileges, dramatic elaborations of one's unfortunate circumstances was a normal and expected part of the rhetoric. But often, particularly in the case of black brotherhoods, the vivid descriptions of dire straits can be verified by other documents and do not seem to depart greatly from reality.

The preoccupation with death, particularly understandable in a slave regime characterized by high mortality, led many blacks (even those with limited or no property) to record a testament that specified their final wishes and their preferred conditions of interment. In other cases, where there was no testament, the obituary often recorded a few details of the individual's life and how he or she was preparing for death. We see from such sources that, to cite several examples, Tereza de Jesus, a freed Mina slave, married to a freed black man, was dressed in the habit of Santa Rita and buried in the grounds of Santa Efigênia. Antônia de Jesus, another freed Mina, was buried at the Church of the Rosário. João Batista, a freed Mina, married to the freed Mina Ana Maria, was attired in the habit of São Francisco and laid to rest at Santa Efigênia.[42] This apparent mixture of devotions, locations of burial, and funeral garb suggests the diverse options available to blacks as they planned for death, and does away with the idea that there might have been exclusive or consistent practices of devotion for slaves, freed blacks, or ethnic groups. The manner of religiosity was above all flexible, in that it combined the devotion to a given saint with a range of religious services that could be contracted, according to various factors (cost, the spouse's faith, etc.), all of which were administered in a form to maximize each person's salvation within the limits of available resources.

On the day of the event, the burial procession only set out late in the afternoon. Groups of friends, supporters, and brotherhood members would gather early in the morning at the house where the dead lay. African musicians often brought instruments and would keep the music and singing going for hours. The burials of men or women were proclaimed with different bell tolls: one toll on a large bell for men, two on a smaller bell for women. Jean-Baptiste Debret, a French artist who arrived in Rio de Janeiro in 1816, described the burial of a black female from Mozambique at the Church of the Lampadosa. He noted that most of the accompanying mourners were women, who seemed also to be charged with collecting the money to pay for the funeral, and he noted the phrase repeated throughout the wake: "We are weeping for our kin [parente]." The idea of kinship in this context raises the strong possibility that the procession Debret observed was made up, not of one extended family but of the Mozambique provenience group within which these women organized socially and articulated their religious practices. Among Africans, the use of the term kinship commonly applies to wider social groups than in Western, blood-relation cases, and its use in the context of a provenience group in the New World would be consistent. Africans from Mozambique could consider themselves "kin" in Rio de Janeiro, as could Africans from Angola or Africans from the Mina Coast.[43]

In the following section I present a brief survey of the obituaries of slaves from the Parish of Candelária, between the years of 1724 and 1736. Candelária at the time had seventeen official burying grounds: eleven at churches, four discrete cemeteries, and two places (Carmo and Hospício de São Francisco) that are unclear as to their location or affiliation. The vast majority of burial sites were churches, which shows the close proximity even at this late date in Rio's urban milieu between the living, the dead, and the saints.[44]

The drawings by Debret, dated between 1816 and 1830 in Rio de Janeiro, were made a century after the period examined here, but suggest that little had changed in funerary practice. Significantly, Debret mentioned that the grounds most prized by the black lay brotherhoods included the cemetery of the "Old Sé" (most likely in reference to the Church of the Rosário), and the Churches of Our Lady of Lampadosa, Our Lady of Parto (Childbirth), and São Domingos.[45] The absence of separate cemeteries for slaves indicates that such places were not deemed necessary. It is notable that even those eighteenth-century masters who insisted on having their slaves baptized to save their souls showed little preoccupation with the destiny of their human remains. Although official church doctrine mandated that the corpses of converted, baptized heathen should be given Christian burials, colonial society viewed the bodies of their slaves with rather more indifference. That explains the common practice of dumping slave corpses in the fields or on the beach, instead of bothering to bury them properly.

Many obituary records indicate that the bodies were interred in the patio area in the grounds at the front of the church. Given the high numbers of burials, the smaller cemeteries that appeared alongside churches were most likely the necessary lateral extensions of those front burial grounds. Around the Church of Candelária alone in the twelve years of records surveyed, space had to be found for 115 dead slaves. This church was the seat of the parish, and thus well known and distinguished, but perhaps something else helps explain the slaves' affinity for it: the Church of Candelária housed images of Crispim and Crispiniano, the patron saints of shoemakers and the open-minded protectors of underdogs and the victims of discrimination. There was a brotherhood of shoemakers devoted to these two saints there.[46]

In general obituaries were registered in the parish where the deceased resided, but in the case of slaves the record was made where the master resided. The obituary should include the locale of the burial, which could be in any church or cemetery independent of where the record was made. Sometimes a description of funerary attire was made; records tended to become more detailed and standardized with the passing of time. Although I found 623 obituaries, I analyze only those that presented complete information.

In addition to the cemetery at Candelária, most Africans were buried in two other cemeteries—those at the Church of the Rosário and the Church of São Domingos, both on the outskirts of Rio proper (and São Domingos was extra-muros, or beyond the proposed borders of the city's protective wall). Of the 71 burials of Mina slaves, 32 were in the Rosário, 23 in the Candelária, and 8 in the São Domingos cemeteries (table 12). These numbers bolster the argument made in chapter 3 that the Mina coexisted with Angola slaves

Table 12. Distribution of Slave Obituaries from Candelária Parish, by Locale of Burial in the City of Rio de Janeiro, 1724–1736

BURIAL	PROVENIENCE					OTHERS			TOTAL
	Mina	Angola	Guinea	Benguela	Kongo	Cabo Verde	Crioulo	Pardo	
Rosário Church	32	29	24	3	1	2	26	5	122
São Domingos Cemetery	8	28	22	3	2	1	5	4	73
Candelária Church	23	29	9	11	5	4	24	10	115
Santa Rita Church	3	7	3	0	1	0	2	1	17
Bom Jesus Church	0	1	0	0	0	0	1	0	2
Sé Church	3	3	7	1	0	1	2	5	22
Carmo Cemetery	0	0	0	0	0	0	0	12	12
São Pedro Church	0	1	0	0	0	0	0	0	1
São Cristóvão Church	0	2	0	0	0	0	0	0	2
João Dias Cemetery	1	3	0	2	1	0	0	0	7
São Francisco Hospício	0	0	1	0	0	0	0	0	1
Santo Antônio Cemetery	0	1	0	0	0	0	0	1	2
Hospício Church	1	6	0	0	1	0	0	1	9
São Bento Church	0	1	0	0	0	0	0	2	3
N.S.a Outeiro Church	0	0	0	0	0	0	0	1	1
N.S.a do Parto Church	0	0	0	0	0	0	3	0	3
Misericórdia Cemetery	0	4	0	0	0	0	1	0	5
Total	71	115	66	20	11	8	64	42	397

Source: ACMRJ, *Livro de Óbito de Escravos, Freguesia da Candelária, 1724–1736.*
a"N.S." in Portuguese stands for *Nossa Senhora* (Our Lady).

in the Church of the Rosário and the Church of São Domingos, which is not to say that theirs was a harmonious relationship. The numbers also show that Mina were concentrated in Candelária Parish, where the Brotherhood of Santo Elesbão and Santa Efigênia was established in 1740; but despite the limited association of Mina with the Church of São Domingos, that church would provide the meeting place for two congregations of Mina in the 1740s (Menino Jesus, which might have existed as early as the 1720s, and Santo Elesbão and Santa Efigênia). The presence of twenty Benguela slaves should be noted in the data, although only three were buried at the Rosário cemetery. The prominent African demographic in the cemeteries of both

São Domingos and Rosário was the so-called Guinea heathen, probably a part of the group that left the Sé in 1704. Their offspring, a first generation of creoles, would rise to prominence in the Brotherhood of the Rosário not long after the period studied here.[47]

The burial records show that in death as in life, Rio's Africans shared certain spaces in varying combinations, which may help future investigations of their intergroup cooperation and conflicts over time in colonial society. It is a basic premise of this book that even though Africans may have come to Brazil as captives and slaves, they were not entirely stripped of the capacity for self-determination; religious practice and affiliation were a vital aspect of this self-determination, as was the construction and maintenance of provenience groups. Obviously there were constraints on the exercise of those volitions, and researchers confront the echoes of those constraints in the documents. Here, due to the simple scarcity of places available for slave burial, corpses representing diverse provenience groups and local social associations were jostled together in the same cemeteries in a manner that obscures the groups' diversity and modes of organization.[48] We are often limited to painting with a broad brush. Data on the dead and the living Africans in Rio suggest that Angola were the majority in the churches of Rosário and São Domingos. They had departed the See some years before and built those two churches; in the case of Saint Domingos, they had done so together with Africans labeled "Guinea heathen." Other Mina stayed at the See, and had by 1715 started the Brotherhood of Santo Antônio of the Moors (mentioned in chapter 2). This brotherhood left the Church of São Benedito and moved to the Church of the Rosário together with the Cabido in 1737. Another group of Mina united at Rosário within the Brotherhood of Our Lady da Lampadosa. A third segment of Mina organized around the devotion of the Menino Jesus (sometimes called Menino Deus) at the Church of São Domingos. Yet a fourth group founded the Brotherhood of Santo Elesbão and Santa Efigênia, also at São Domingos, in 1740. It is possible to affirm that Santo Antônio of the Moors and Menino Jesus were the first two Mina brotherhoods in Rio de Janeiro. Research suggests that the former was linked with slaves from Cape Verde, whereas all indications suggest that the latter emerged from Africans from the Bight of Benin who, already in the 1720s (seven Mina were buried in 1724), had installed themselves at the Church of São Domingos. Their multiple subdivisions into different congregations might imply that the Mina were a dispersed, diffuse minority. However, they were both a numerically significant sector of Rio's African demographic and, as initial research into their wills and testaments is revealing, their separation into distinct religious fraternities did not dissolve their overarching, mutual social ties. Chapter 6 shows various instances of collaboration between different Mina brotherhoods during the eighteenth century.

It is worth considering the distributions of these burial records from the perspectives of time and gender.[49] Of the 499 records from the period 1724–36 deemed suitable for basic analysis, 251 referred to women and 248 to men (table 13). This is a curious finding given the nearly unanimous scholarly opinion about gender ratios in Atlantic slave commerce: more men were taken from Africa and made it to the New World than women.[50] Of course, these obituaries point to Christian burials, and do not tell us the total number of African deaths. This suggests that if more men than women were brought from Africa, more African women attained the better socioeconomic conditions necessary for a Christian burial than African men did in early eighteenth-century Rio. These conditions involved not merely belonging to a religious organization, but frequent devotional contributions to its charitable fund, as well as to other causes; the personal accumulation of some patrimony that was saved for the funeral; and good relations with the masters. All of these considerations in turn provide an argument that women might have had a notable influence in the administration of the brotherhoods to which they belonged—even though men were prone to limit what they saw as excessive female assertiveness, as chapter 6 shows in more detail.

The feminine profile was especially marked in Mina burials, with thirty-five males recorded versus forty-four women for the period. Luciano Figueiredo has highlighted the substantial proportion of black and pardo women participating in brotherhoods in Minas Gerais (a tendency reversed in the white population), which he explains by characterizing the women as more stable than men in that social milieu.[51] But a broadly similar finding in Rio de Janeiro indicates that some explanation beyond local factors is necessary.

Another way to view the slave population through these figures is by manner of identification; that is, a basic distinction can be made between slaves characterized by their African provenience (described as belonging to a nation), and slaves described in other ways. The first group is dominated by Angola (117), followed by Mina (79) and Guinea (68). The second becomes a catchall, containing creoles (68), pardos (47), and slaves without any qualifying description of provenience or color (47). The gender difference observed above is consistent in this second group, particularly for creoles (19 men vs. 49 women) and pardos (15 vs. 32). This reinforces the idea that women, African or locally born (and birthrates for this generation are equivalent), ultimately had greater access to Christian burial practices than men. It is difficult to evaluate how representative these numbers are of the whole population of enslaved and freed blacks in the city, but we can attempt a tentative projection.

Lacking a population census in the eighteenth century, we have to rely on records of baptisms and obituaries; these provide an imperfect but workable notion of the distribution of births and deaths. Taking the three most significant African nations in colonial Rio, and looking more specifically at the Parish of Sé between 1718 and 1750, documents show the following: 958 baptisms of children of Guinea mothers, compared to 66 obituaries for Guinea men and women; 238 baptisms of children of Angola mothers, compared to 115 total Angola obituaries; and 296 baptisms of children of Mina mothers, compared to 71 obituaries of Mina.[52]

It is possible to conclude from this that only a small contingent of African slaves had access to Christian burials. Given that the cadavers of most slaves were either left at the mercy of the elements outside the city, or dropped in the communal pit at Santa Casa da Misericórdia, or discarded at the door of churches to be disposed of anonymously, it becomes reasonable to imagine that the performance of a burial ritual based on ecclesiastical norms probably accrued almost exclusively to slaves affiliated with a lay Catholic brotherhood. Even for this comparatively elite group, the norms were probably rarely fulfilled in every particular. Having the sacraments administered promptly after death, acquiring appropriate funerary attire for the corpse, providing transport to the cemetery, including a priest in the procession, burning all those candles—these individual expenses added up fast to what could seem a small fortune. Even if a modest hammock, rather than a pricier rented wooden coffin, was used to carry the dead, the costs were still steep.

Table 13. Distribution of Slave Burials by Year and Sex in the City of Rio de Janeiro, 1724–1736

IDENTIFIER	ANNUAL DISTRIBUTION													
	1724		1725		1726		1727		1728		1729		1730	
	m	f	m	f	m	f	m	f	m	f	m	f	m	f
Mina	5	2	1	4	1	1	1		4	2	2	4	2	2
Guinea		2	20	22	11	8	1	2		1				
Angola	4	7							5	6	6	5	3	4
Cabo Verde	1		2									1		
Benguela										1			1	1
São Tomé				1										
Kongo											3			
Ganguela														
Quissamã														
Muxicongo														
Mozambique							1							
Monjolo											1			
Ambaca														1
Cacheo														
São Lourenço														
Massangano														
mulatto											1			
boçal[a]														
Rebelo														
creole		3	6	6		1				5		6	1	1
pardo		4	4	4	1	4	1	1	1	1	2	2		5
slave	1		1					1	1			1		1
cabra				1		1								
ladino[b]					1									
Indian					1									
black							1							
freed														
Total	11	18	35	37	15	15	5	3	11	16	14	18	10	15

Source: ACMRJ, *Livro de Óbito de Escravos, Freguesia da Candelária*, 1724–1736.

[a]"Boçal" refers to recent arrived African slaves who did not know how to behave within the colonial world.

[b]"Ladino" refers to African slaves who had learned Portuguese and had adapted to local habits.

OF BURIALS												TOTAL		
1731		1732		1733		1734		1735		1736		Sex		General
m	f	m	f	m	f	m	f	m	f	m	f	m	f	
4	5	2	7	2	6	7	4	2	4	2	3	35	44	79
			1									33	35	68
9	1	13	9	2	6	3	6	11	3	10	4	66	51	117
			1			1	1			1		7	1	8
2	1			2	1	1		5	1	1	3	12	8	20
	1		1									1	2	3
1				1		3		4	1			12	1	13
							1	1	1			1	2	3
								1				1	0	1
								1				1	0	1
												1	0	1
							1			1	1	3	1	4
												0	1	1
		1										1	0	1
			1									0	1	1
		1										1	0	1
		1						1				3	0	3
											1	0	1	1
										1		1	0	1
2	5	1	5	1	5	4	2	3	3	1	7	19	49	68
1	3	1	2		1	2	1			1	4	15	32	47
1		3	1		1		2	10	8	10	4	29	18	47
1	1										1	1	4	5
												1	0	1
1												2	0	2
												1	0	1
					1							1	0	1
22	17	25	26	8	21	23	16	40	22	28	27	248	251	499

The data for Guinea slaves stand out from the rest: 958 baptisms with a Guinea mother present, while only 35 Christian burials of Guinea women were recorded over the same period (table 13 on pages 134–35). I noted earlier the probability that many of these women were domestic slaves, given their high incidence of marriage. But if even half of them were, or a third, the marginal rate of Christian burials they attained detracts from the common image of the protective, caring mistress who looked out for her slave's interests in the end. Whatever advantages were given a female domestic slave over other types of servitude in eighteenth-century Rio, obtaining a Christian burial was evidently not among them.

For Angola and Mina slaves, the numbers are more balanced, likely an expression of their more active organization into lay brotherhoods throughout the first half of the century. At the same time, the Guinea identity—as discussed in chapter 3—was undergoing a sort of social and conceptual vanishing act. The only substantial reference to forms of association between enslaved and freed Guinea comes from the observation from Vieira Fazenda that Guinea were represented in the Brotherhood of São Domingos. But the rarity of specific information about what Guinea did and where they did it almost undoubtedly derives from the fact that although the so-called Guinea heathen had been bundled under a purportedly geographic and cultural designation, for the convenience of Rio's colonial slaveholding society, these African peoples did not develop the mechanisms for local forms of sociability that other, more prominent provenience groups constructed in the city of Rio de Janeiro.

The diminishing number of obituaries through time corresponds with what a range of other documents makes clear—even brotherhoods, not only poor Africans on their own, faced increasing hardship in paying for the Christian burials. It was common for brotherhoods to carry the corpse of a deceased member to the door of a church, and to try to collect enough charitable contributions there to pay for a ceremony. If sufficient funds were not raised, the corpse would often be left behind to be buried "for the love of God," a tactic identical to that used by poor or miserly slave owners. At one point, the judge of the Brotherhood of São Domingos of the Convent of São Francisco in the city of Salvador petitioned the crown to build a tomb where brothers could be buried. Acknowledging the brotherhood's lack of means, he said the objective in creating their own space was to avoid having to "leave our defunct ones in the entryways of churches to be buried for the love of God."[53] All of this implies that belonging to a brotherhood was perhaps the only resource available to slaves and freed blacks hoping to escape the ignoble anonymity of mass graves for a socially recognized Christian burial. The brotherhoods could attempt various measures to meet this request, from collecting members' contributions, to asking for public donations, to writing a letter to the king; but clearly many times even these efforts were not enough to provide for a funeral for each member.

The testaments show that when freed blacks, and more commonly freed black women, had some money saved at the time of death, they often left most of it to their brotherhoods. If the philanthropic desires expressed in those testaments were common knowledge in advance among other people in the association, it raises the possibility that such individual benefactors might have carried more influence or prestige while alive (as well as ensuring a burial befitting their means). All the brotherhoods depended on charity, from members and nonmembers alike. The Brotherhood of Our Lady of the Rosário was one of the beneficiaries listed in Maria do Rosário's will. Maria, a freed slave, requested to be buried in the cemetery of the Church of the Rosário attired in the habit of São Francisco—"I ask the brothers of my association to accompany my corpse to its final resting place according to custom." Among her possessions were listed four slaves, although one ran away at the first opportunity and she specified that another, a young boy, should be freed upon her death. The will also mentioned several pieces of gold jewelry, most of them chain necklaces, that were to be found with her early master, and a cross adorned with seven diamonds that was in hock. It was noted that she still owed eighteen *patacas* for the purchase of some dressmaking cloth.

By the early 1740s, the Church of the Rosário provided shelter to at least three brotherhoods who counted Mina among their members: that of Our Lady of the Rosário, of the Glorious Santo Antônio of the Moors, and of Our Lady of Lampadosa. This probably explains the high proportion of Mina buried at the cemetery of the Rosary church. Of 79 Mina funerals (table 13), 32 were carried out there, versus only 8 at the cemetery of the Chapel of São Domingos (table 12). In the second half of the century, with the inaugurations of the churches of Santa Efigênia and Lampadosa, many of the Mina who received funerals had them performed at these newer churches. The brotherhoods would also continue to depend on the freed, elite class of Africans represented by Maria do Rosário. Beyond their comparative financial power, these influential individuals could also serve the critical function of mediating between a congregation of blacks—most of them Africans and slaves, on the lowest rung of colonial society—and the colonial church that recognized the congregation's legitimacy.

PROVENIENCE GROUPS AND THEIR PROCESSIONS AND FESTIVITIES

In Lisbon, the Board of the Brotherhood of Our Lady of the Rosário of the Monastery of São Domingos, a group founded in the sixteenth century, was composed of both administrative functionaries, and a court—with a king, duke, count, and other nobles—representing a microcosm of the hierarchical Portuguese royal court. The brotherhoods in Brazil were drawing on this tradition when they elected, from within their own ranks, kings and queens as their own ruling figureheads. Among black brotherhoods, the practice was even more common than among white ones. The principal difference between the Portuguese tradition and its adaptation in Brazil was that in the colony, black brotherhoods had two separate boards: one for executive administration, and one, often called a court, for the *folia* (revelry).

When a brotherhood decided to create a folia, the court was charged with organizing its officials and subjects in a form based on well-known hierarchies. If the court called itself a Reinado (Reign), it elected kings and queens; an Estado Imperial (Empire) elected emperors and empresses. Several times a year, the folia would parade through the city streets, dressed in regal splendor, collecting charitable contributions for the festival of the saint after which their church was named. Just as the regular members of a brotherhood marched in public adorned with special capes and emblems, the nobility of the folia were attired for the event: kings wore crowns and mantles, and carried scepters; the queens wore crowns and elaborate gowns; and the rest of the folia carried walking sticks, banners, flags, and musical instruments (not necessarily of African derivation). The instruments were used, in the case of African brotherhoods, to play for dances and to support the singing of songs in different African languages.

The kings and queens of the folia never walked in the open air without the protection of an enormous parasol, borne by a liveried attendant; this was another nod to the standard markers of prestige in the ancien régime.[54] A brotherhood and its folia bore identical insignia and color schemes on their capes and banners, demonstrating that one pertained to the other. Important processions and festival days reunited folias, marchers, spectators, and often some of colonial society's more distinctive personages. The folklore scholar Luís da Câmara Cascudo noted that the processions of the brotherhoods of São Gonçalo, Divino, and others could typically count on the presence of high city officials.[55]

The folias were considered by government and church authorities to be peaceful organizations. Still, occasional commotion was not unheard of, and this was particularly true for the events associated with the elections of kings and queens. Across colonial Brazil, different black brotherhoods chose kings representing various African nations. For instance, the compromisso of the Brotherhood of Our Lady of the Rosário in Recife mentioned an Angola king,[56] but in 1674 they elected a Kongo king and a Kongo queen. At the Church of the Lampadosa in Rio de Janeiro, kings from different nations were elected at various times: a Rebolo-Tunda king (1760s) and a Cabunda king (1811).[57]

Slave owners were known to enhance the pomp of these parades by loaning jewelry, costumes, and other decorations to the elected kings and queens for their promenade to the church, where the vicar was waiting to crown them. In 1729, the Brotherhood of the Rosário in Salvador was prohibited from participating in public events because of what were termed their excesses. In 1786, they petitioned the crown for permission to parade for a few days with all their nobility, dances, and songs (which, it was specified, were in the "Angola language").[58] As a rule, though, whatever excesses occurred during the parades appeared to take place outside the folia proper. The courts and their retinues took most public events seriously and maintained a solemn comportment. What happened afterward might be a different story, and perhaps that was why many of the brotherhoods agreed in principle in their founding statutes to return from any festive event (including funeral processions) in quiet order. The informal disbanding of a parade could easily lead to bumptious exchanges between different groups, or between marchers and spectators, as well as to noise, music, or dance deemed threatening or improper; confusion; and fights—particularly given that strong drink was nearly always in abundance.

In Rio de Janeiro, the São Domingos Field was a favored route for black folias in the second half of the eighteenth century. In the Chapel of Santana, the folias often paraded with the Portuguese motif of the Império do Divino (Empire of the Divine), while those at the Church of the Lampadosa were known for their festivals for King Baltazar, associated with the King of Kongo. At the Church of Santa Efigênia, the brotherhood's folia had for their theme the Império de Santo Elesbão (Empire of Santo Elesbão), amplifying the tiers of royalty to include several kings serving under an emperor. One notable aspect of the various folias is that they commonly visited each other's churches and paid homage to each other. For many years, during the festival of the Chapel of Santana, the folia from Lampadosa marched to Santana to salute the folia of the Império do Divino. This again suggests that the underlying connections between the members of different brotherhoods, most of them Africans and slaves (or former slaves), were at least as strong as the individual loyalties to particular brotherhoods.[59]

To attempt a rough family tree for these folias, it seems that the brotherhood at Lampadosa was the first to adopt the processional traditions associated with the Church of the Rosário. The folias of Santana and Santo Elesbão were both based at the Church of São Domingos. The brotherhoods of Rosário and São Domingos date back, as noted earlier, to the seventeenth century. They were located at Rio's first See church, São Sebastião, where the increasing ostentation of their folias appears to have been one of the reasons for their expulsion. It is possible that even at that time the Brotherhood of the Rosário elected kings and queens, while the Brotherhood of São Domingos elected emperors and empresses, and these two practices were passed on to the associations that came later.

In 1763, the year that Rio de Janeiro took Salvador's place as the capital of the colony of Brazil, the aforementioned Rebolo-Tunda king waited to assume his office as the leader of the brotherhood's folia at the Church of the Lampadosa. This king was a slave who happened to belong to Count da Cunha, the first viceroy. Notwithstanding several loud voices of opposition raised against the folias in Rio's elite social circles, da Cunha went ahead and authorized the public crowning of his slave, as well as all the "typical celebrations" that would be expected to precede it. But the city's high criminal judge moved against da Cunha and outlawed the ritual, arguing that the folias presented too much risk of physical danger and general chaos to be permitted.[60] The brotherhoods' parades highlighted a murky area of the *Constituições Primeiras*, the ecclesiastical rules written in Bahia and applied throughout Brazil. Those regulations specifically authorized religious processions which were "honest and decent," and made mention of the Império do Divino association as an example to be followed. However, they expressly prohibited "disorder" and "immoral acts," with no further interpretive detail offered. The problem was that in practice, the folias were usually viewed as decent on the way to the church or funeral, but characterized as indecent the moment the parade was over and the members were going home or wandering around. In the absence of a viable principle, the legal status of each event was the product of local negotiations between the group and the officials charged with deciding the matter. The Brazilian historian Martha Abreu, analyzing the festivals of the Divino, found a 1780 document from the Oversea Council that recommended tolerance with the dances of the "blacks," and with the licentiousness that was presumed to be a natural part of those practices.[61]

Although the folias are represented in several colorful images by the eighteenth-century Portuguese artist and draftsman Carlos Julião, they appear not to have been registered by other artists. Later, in the nineteenth century, the French artist Debret wrote a short account of them:

> We do some justice to the history of the black brotherhoods by recalling that, with the arrival of the Portuguese court in Rio de Janeiro, there was a complete prohibition on the blacks' costumed revelries, which were undertaken at certain times of the year to remember their homelands. These entertainments were deemed too clamorous and intemperate. The prohibition applied equally to other festive behaviors, quite tranquil by contrast but still performed in costume, which the blacks had introduced into local Catholic custom. This is why it is only in other provinces of Brazil, but not here in the capital, that one can still observe the election of a king, a queen, a captain of the guard, and other nobles from among a company of blacks.[62]

His statement implies that during his stay in Brazil (1826–31), most of it spent in Rio de Janeiro, Debret never personally witnessed the parades or other festivities. What happened during the commemorations that Debret suggested were celebrations of the black Africans' homelands? There is very little evidence of their cultural background, and much less that could show how such practices and attitudes might have informed the nuances of the folias. The one thing that is clear is that whatever happened "extra-muros," beyond the wall that separated the urban core of Rio from its wilder environs, was not observed by the artists and writers who left accounts of the city's social and cultural life. If Debret had seen any of these events, dedicated and prolific artist that he was, one might assume he would have sketched them.

Another aspect of the festivals and processions that should be emphasized was the distinctive participation of men and women. In a certain sense, the folias brought the differentiated gender roles at work in the internal operations of the brotherhood into the light of day. The brotherhoods were a nominally masculine space in which women's participation was typically viewed as necessary, but simultaneously as a potential threat to men's power that had to be constantly scrutinized and contained. Beyond any material resources that women might provide, a unique dimension of women's identity was their association with witchcraft. Available sources on this theme emerge mostly from inquisitorial records, and until now the evidence does not provide enough information for a persuasive broader analysis of how witchcraft intersected with the organization of ethnic groups and other social associations. But there are suggestive descriptions of festive gatherings called *calundus* or *batuques*, such as the one in this 1780 formal correspondence from Martinho de Mello e Castro to the king of Portugal about tensions over the festival of the Church of the Rosário in Recife:

> I received the notice dated 09 June from Your Majesty in which Your Majesty ordered me to report about the letter from the Holy Office and the Governor of Pernambuco, and to examine the situation in Recife with respect to superstitious dances (a concern of the Holy Office) as well as dances that may not be the most saintly and yet may not be worth punishing (as the Governor maintains). The latter form refers to the celebrations of blacks who are divided into nations, and each group with its own instruments, dances and gambols with harlequins, or writhes about with diverse corporal

movements that are perhaps not as innocent as those characterizing the fandangos of Castela, or the *fofas* and *lunduns* danced by whites and pardos in Portugal. These are regrettable yet do not appear dangerous. But what I am told are the most despicable dances, the ones perhaps needing swift prohibition, are those that the Mina blacks perform in their own spaces, hidden away from the public eye in houses or fields, led by a female black who stands before altars that are covered in idolatrous objects. The people worship live goats, as well as clay likenesses of goats. They rub themselves with diverse oils and blood from a chicken they first slaughter for the purpose, and eat corn cakes over which bizarre blessings have been uttered, phrases which make the rustics believe that eating the cakes will bring good fortune in wealth or romance . . . I believe thus that the Holy Office speaks of certain dances, and the governor of others, and I cannot persuade one authority to disallow what another approves. This is my statement, and Your Majesty, in the shining lights of his wisdom, will resolve the matter to its most just solution.[63]

The rather harried distinction between dances that were "superstitious" versus "not the most saintly" demonstrates the flexibility (and complexity) of the criteria used to determine what was socially legitimate behavior. Houses often received particular attention from authorities because of their capacity to shelter religious practices, not merely dance, from outside observers. The reference in this letter to Mina blacks hiding out among private alters, worshipping goats, and sacrificing chickens presents a deliberately extreme case of the practices that were thought prudent to prohibit. Most of the cases that called for official deliberation lay somewhere between the poles of a public parade and a purportedly pagan ceremony (replete with idols and blood sacrifice).

The city of Rio de Janeiro experienced substantial changes in infrastructure in the 1770s, during the administration of the viceroy Marquês de Lavradio. He implemented substantial projects, such as paving roads, constructing a new slaughterhouse, draining and filling over with earth the lagoon of Pavuna, and the clearing of many new footpaths. One of his initiatives that would affect daily life for many people in Rio was the relocation of the slave market from the Rua Direita, a principal street in the business district, to a distant region of the city commonly referred to as

Valongo.[64] Now, Africans recently arrived at port were no longer kept in the streets in the center of the city awaiting buyers, but were removed to this locale; and slaves sold to work in Minas Gerais or other places outside Rio tended thereafter to gather in Saint Domingos Field—where the Marquês claimed they had "all the comforts"—before they were marched out.[65] It was also during the Marquês's rule that the idea was floated to demolish the small chapels constructed by black brotherhoods in the territories beyond the boundaries of the (unfinished) city walls. Once distant and considered irrelevant, those lands were newly prized in the face of Rio's urban expansion. Documents show that this plan was supported by the viceroy and the bishop, as well as by the black brothers of the Rosário, who stood to benefit. The idea was to simply cut off support for maintaining and reforming those chapels until they deteriorated beyond functional use; the time involved would not be considerable, given their already poor condition. Once effectively condemned, they could be taken over by the church (a provision included in the *Constituições Primeiras*),[66] which was empowered to order their demolition. In such a case the several black brotherhoods would be transferred to the Church of the Rosário, which in turn would receive more generous dispensations and could accumulate funds to pay for its own renovations. The Brothers of the Rosário sent a missive to the king arguing their case:

> Various black brotherhoods occupy undignified and indecent little chapels, which barely qualify for the name, among them the Brotherhoods of Mercês and São Domingos, São Philip, São Tiago, the Menino Jesus, Santa Efigênia and Santo Elesbão, Our Lady of Lampadosa, São Mateus, São Benedito and Santo Antônio, Bom Jesus do Cáliçe, Our Lady of Belém and Santo Antônio of the Moors. It would well serve Your Majesty to annex them, and in demolishing them and their gruesome cemeteries Your Majesty would further be providing a great service to God. The brotherhoods would be welcomed here, and the small sums they can offer to this church will bring to a happy end our desperate need for support to finish the many works to improve this house of God.[67]

In the opinion of the viceroy Marquês de Lavradio, these chapels were the sites of "base and indecent acts," which were eagerly performed by the "depraved, vile people" who composed the congregations. This allegation was adduced as reason enough for the chapels' destruction.[68] But the list of black brotherhoods compiled in the petition above provides a sense of how the fields beyond Rio's Vala trench must have looked after 1750 when the brotherhoods departed the principal churches of the Rosário and of São Domingos to create their own spaces. The region had grown full of small, very poor chapels, surrounded by cemeteries in precarious conditions. It is also possible to conclude from this list that several chapels resisted the pressure and ultimately transformed into more substantial churches (São Domingos, Santa Efigênia, Lampadosa, and Bom Jesus do Cálice). The others seem to have disappeared quickly, and some of these produced no further documentary evidence after being named in the petition for destruction written by brothers of the Rosário. Among these was the Brotherhood of Santo Antônio of the Moors, whose actual physical site I could never locate.

It is increasingly clear from a range of scholarship (not only this book but much recent work in the history of slavery) that the social formations, alliances, and institutions adopted by urban slave populations are far more complicated than have previously been imagined.[1] Research on African slaves, in particular, is showing how prominent and diverse this complexity was across the colonies of the New World. Underlying this scholarship is one basic perception: although society presents established rules and limits for identity construction and group organization, individuals learn to maneuver dynamically within the circumstances of each particular case to create a strategic balance between contestation and acceptance. That is, there exists neither an absolute determinism of social regulation on human action, nor the boundless autonomy of individual volition.[2] On the one hand, colonial slave society imposed rigid constraints on the *pretos*; on the other hand, this same society opened to them a myriad of other, often quite unintended pathways to distinction and dignity across a rich cultural terrain. And as I have argued in the preceding chapters, the principal route to social prominence for African slaves—and particularly for freed African slaves—was membership in a lay religious brotherhood.

Devotional processions and funeral parades offered important opportunities for fraternal orders of pretos and pardos to be represented publicly within the dominant religious hierarchy, even if they were typically left to bring up the rear in Catholic ceremonial parades. The brotherhoods' participation was nonetheless coherent and meaningful despite being relegated to the last ranks. I take the lay brotherhood to be a "modern" institution (very different from the medieval orders), whose internal organization is based on the same models and principles of ancien régime hierarchical societies and European absolutist states. In that sense the "court society" analyzed by Norbert Elias can be understood to embrace not only the state but the church as well. In his discussion of the architecture and social organization of the French court, Elias observed that almost every feature one encounters in majestic scale in the palace of the king, one finds in small scale in the house of the nobleman.[3] The same might be said in relation to church ritual: almost everything one witnesses in the grandeur of Vatican spectacles, one sees in reduced form in Brazil's many local bishoprics striving with fewer resources to convey the full symbolic power of Catholic pomp and pageantry. The poor brotherhoods' exertions to reproduce the ceremonial patterns and gestures of prestigious, better-endowed religious groups—such as the Santíssimo Sacramento—demonstrate this process of hierarchical influence.

It should also be remembered that in eighteenth-century Brazilian society the abolitionist mentality that coalesced in the next century did not yet exist. The concept of liberty was not seen as a universal value that could or should be extended to everyone, and among slaves freedom was more immediately comprehended and desired. Freedom in this context was an individual victory, represented by the definite but often intangible advance of one step up the ladder of the social hierarchy. Even at the moment of buying his or her freedom, the slave, upon presenting the agreed-upon sum to the master, would have to ask the master's permission; and the master was legally and socially understood as "conceding" freedom to the slave. And freed slaves could be reenslaved through a variety of mechanisms in colonial society. Still, a slave who saw no hope of emancipation through broad legislative means or a master's act of beneficence could seek out the small personal freedoms afforded by daily life, in such areas as were permitted or ignored by authorities. In the world of the urban slave, these modest spheres of self-determination typically included the choice of conjugal partners, the chance to work for oneself to build up savings, the ability to frequent recreational gatherings, the possibility to traverse and learn from the city (even to find a place to live outside the purview of the master), and the opportunity to join a lay brotherhood. Within the strictures of slave life, brotherhoods provided special access to the experience of liberty, of social recognition, and of administrative activity. In the city of Rio de Janeiro, the Brotherhood of Santo Elesbão and Santa Efigênia was one of these rare spaces where the Mina slaves could construct their own sociability.

In this era, brotherhoods were at once a locus of the exercise of liberty among black slaves, and a medium of indoctrination for African peoples within Portuguese society. They were among the few venues for association that the Portuguese state tolerated among the pretos, and in fact from the point of view of the church, they had a genuine appeal. Far from being disparaged as misguided vestiges of medieval religiosity, the brotherhoods were understood to offer a congenial space for collective indoctrination as well as for encouraging the arduous sacramental obligations prescribed by the Council of Trent. An examination of the brotherhoods' statutes and other internal documents reveals that in one form or another, all of the groups traced their spiritual and formal lineage back to the Brotherhood of Our Lady of the Rosário of the Monastery of São Domingos, founded in Lisbon in 1565.

The two fundamental pillars that have traditionally supported lay religious fraternities are devotion and charity; or, in the words of Russell-Wood, "propagation of doctrine" and "social philanthropy."[4] Documents suggest that in the Brotherhood of Santo Elesbão and Santa Efigênia, greater emphasis appears to have been given to devotion than to charity. In fact, the scope of charity is interpreted narrowly enough within the documents, addressing primarily the group and its members rather than the larger community around it. This recalls John Bossy's definition of "medieval charity" as a type of beneficence in which giving money is less esteemed than performing "acts of physical charity" such as providing food and clothing, visiting the sick or imprisoned, and participating in funerals.[5] The idea of medieval charity reappears in a highly particular way in the *compromisso* of the Brotherhood of Santo Elesbão and Santa Efigênia: the principal charitable act is to attend the funerals of group members. Even the giving of alms, when the total sum exceeds a stipulated amount, is considered an act of devotion but not of charity.

It is significant that in the compromisso of this Brotherhood, the word *charity* appears only one time. Chap. 11 declares that the brotherhood was to unanimously appear, "incorporated," on the occasion of a funeral of one of the group members.[6] This obligation, almost a contractual agreement in tone, is considered an act of charity. Such a definition of charity stands in stark contrast to the notion that philanthropic acts are practiced to benefit others without the expectation of retribution or quid pro quo. But charity, in the philanthropic sense, could occur between brotherhoods of pretos. In these instances, works of beneficence were administered by a brotherhood to other needy people and not to group members themselves. For example, the Santa Casa de Misericórdia included in its compromisso a summary of fourteen such acts of charity—seven spiritual, seven physical.[7] They are all philanthropic insofar as they are intended to serve the poor. However, the compromisso of Santo Elesbão and Santa Efigênia makes no mention of philanthropy, only of charity—and even then, it is charity tailored to the needs of the group itself. With its stringent, contractual language, the compromisso carries an implicit threat of exclusion from the brotherhood if precepts are broken.

In this document, whose first chapters were composed in 1740, "devotion" is articulated as an individual commitment that each brother needed to make to the group (unlike "charity," which always refers to a group activity). It appears in numerous chapters, always in the context of encouraging a member, "for devotion," to bring even more to the brotherhood's endeavors than is called for in the compromisso. Thus, to show "zeal and devotion," a brother can offer "munificent alms" (chaps. 5, 12, 22, and 5 in the folio). Also for "devotion," white, pardo, and ecclesiastical brothers are accepted into the fraternity (chaps. 10, 11). One chapter (26) suggests a link between devotion and celebrations, but that discussion ends with a remark that the expenses of sacred festivities not be paid from the brotherhood's coffer.

Although it is customary to view the twin ideals of devotion and charity as integral to the constitution of all lay brotherhoods,[8] in the associations studied here these values were subjugated to preoccupations of a practical nature, relative to the internal needs and organization of each group. Faithfulness to the saints, made manifest in acts of devotion (alms), enabled initiates to attain general membership in the brotherhood but did not make them eligible to take on other, more formal responsibilities. Theoretically, a white person could have been accepted as a devotee by a black brotherhood, but his membership would have been limited to the fraternity as a social body. Ethnic groups or provenience groups were a different category, and would have been off limits. In other words, devotion was the necessary point of entry to the brotherhood, but it alone did not create mechanisms of ethnic or group identification within the brotherhood. Devotion per se obviously mattered because it substantiated both the compromisso (the contractual spirit uniting the brothers through the communal enactment of devotional practice) and the institutional profile of the brotherhood. In that sense, numbers were important. The more members, the greater recognition a brotherhood received from religious authorities and from society at large, and for that simple reason the standards or rules for affiliation were often wide. From the perspective of the pretos, either slave or freed—and whatever their religious orientation—participation in lay fraternal orders was desirable on purely secular grounds: such groups presented the only social space in colonial Brazil that was protected from unwarranted interventions by the dominant institutions of society. The state had to respect a brotherhood's organization and activities (since these were presumably sanctioned by the church); similarly, the church had to recognize a brotherhood's legitimacy as a lay association of Catholic faith, as long as its compromisso had been approved. And the brotherhoods of white men, who unproblematically excluded blacks on social grounds, still were bound by the rules of the church to respect black associations.

The goal of this chapter is to lay a framework for understanding how the Brotherhood of Santo Elesbão and Santa Efigênia articulated its identity between two poles: the formal Portuguese Catholic concept of lay religious organizations, and the historical contours of daily life in a colonial city based on slavery, peopled by a diverse composition of Africans and their descendants, as well as by Europeans. (Of particular help to me in this undertaking were documents containing regulations and correspondence exchanged between the brotherhood and the Tribunal of Conscience and Orders in Portugal, which was the sphere of Portuguese administration most directly involved in enforcing the Padroado.) In the second half of the eighteenth century, the Church of Santo Elesbão and Santa Efigênia housed a number of smaller brotherhoods. Some constituted their identity around ethnic or provenience groups, such as the Mahi Congregation or the Mina

Congregation; others, while involving ethnicity and provenience, were based on devotion to particular saints or other entities, such the Almas do Purgatório (Souls of Purgatory) or Our Lady of Remédios (Our Lady of Remedies).[9]

The Brotherhood of Santo Elesbão and Santa Efigênia had a relatively low profile among Rio de Janeiro's black brotherhoods, a condition that persisted into the nineteenth century (and more recent times as well). Travelers or correspondents visiting the city of Rio de Janeiro rarely made mention of it;[10] nor does it appear in the documentation of the Tribunal of Conscience and Orders after 1808, when that institution established its base in Brazil.[11] In general the brotherhood seems to have interacted only minimally with the various official institutions of the era, which reduced the possibility of discovering hidden veins of complementary documentation. In light of the paucity of substantive historical documents from other sources, an analysis of compromissos is arguably the most promising approach for comprehending the discursive development of this brotherhood's identity, as well as the tangible practices (quotidian, festive, or otherwise) involved in negotiating and expressing it.

APPROVAL OF THE BROTHERHOOD OF SANTO ELESBÃO AND SANTA EFIGÊNIA

The ecclesiastical procedures to organize and gain approval for the brotherhood began in 1740. The documentary trail of this process had to be pieced together through persistence and luck, because the brotherhood's name was not uniformly recorded in the beginning. The text of the first proposed compromisso refers merely to a "fraternity of the saints of our brotherhood," also calling them "glorious saints," without specifying which saints these were. Nor was the name of the brotherhood itself included, which would have conveyed the names of the patron saints. It is a separate but related document, prepared by Bishop D. Antônio de Guadalupe to authorize the creation of the "Brotherhood of Santo Elesbão and Santa Efigênia," that makes the connection. Another anonymous document from the period refers to the Brotherhood of the Glorious Saints Elesbão and Efigênia. A further variation was found in the insignia of the brotherhood itself, which bears the inscription "Venerable Brotherhood of

Santo Elesbão and Santa Efigênia."[12] Nowhere was it explained how these two saints came to be paired; usually orders formed around the devotion of a single saint. In other cases of multiple devotions within the same brotherhood, however, such a brotherhood typically emerged from the fusion of several smaller, informal devotional associations that shared some common ground, spiritual or secular.

Early in this process, the vicar of the parish of Candelária, the parish where the group hoped to establish their brotherhood, expressed his support. He viewed it as a noble endeavor that would encourage other local blacks to devote themselves to dark-skinned saints under the purview of the church. The vicar did raise a skeptical eyebrow at what he felt was the surprisingly large number of lay orders in the area associated with Africans of the Mina nation. But he concluded that because this petition for a new brotherhood included a substantial list of supplicants, it deserved the attention and approval of higher authorities.[13] The response by other regional ecclesiastics to a petition from Bahia in 1765 begins to suggest the absence of any overarching guidelines for evaluating the worthiness of proposed black brotherhoods. In that case, church officials opposed the constitution of the Fraternity of Senhor Jesus dos Martírios (Lord Jesus of the Martyrs) of Vila de Cachoeira, which had been formed by Africans of the Jêje nation. The officials did forward the brothers' petition on to the Tribunal of Conscience and Orders in Lisbon, but they appended a note suggesting that the petition be dismissed because the Jêje "are too recently and imperfectly withdrawn from their pagan traditions in Africa, and are tenacious in their superstitions." For this reason, the note continues, it would be more "convenient" to leave this group subject to the oversight and discipline of the local parish.[14]

The two predominant themes of the compromisso of the Brotherhood of Santo Elesbão and Santa Efigênia are the administration of death (and the treatment of the dead), and the management of resources that were dedicated to festivals, funerals, and acts of service or assistance to the brothers. A close reading of the entire document suggests that the first twenty chapters were probably an early version of the complete text, while the ensuing chapters were additions or alterations annexed to the main corpus during the long petition process (1740 to 1764). The first approval notice, in 1740, refers to twenty-four chapters, which indicates that chaps. 21 through 24 must have been composed soon after, or on the occasion of, the brotherhood's formalization in 1740. Of the twenty-four chapters the brotherhood submitted to the Tribunal of Conscience and Orders, twenty-three were approved and one rejected.[15] Over the next ten years, eight more chapters were added by the brothers, and a 1748 correspondence from the bishopric refers to the official acceptance of four more chapters into the compromisso approved in 1740.[16] Monsenhor Pizarro mentioned two provisions of the compromisso, one dated 24 January 1747 and the other 28 August 1754, although he did not describe their contents.[17] In 1764, five more chapters were sent to Lisbon, numbered separately from the earlier chapters and bound together.[18] Soon after, the total of thirty-seven chapters written by the brothers and approved by the local bishop were sent to Portugal for the king's consideration.[19] Included with them was also an undated *acrescentamento*, or addition, probably composed before 1764.[20] Royal approval was granted to the brotherhood in 1767.[21]

The first chapter of the compromisso is a formal introduction to the brotherhood, indicating its judge, scribe, "and other humble brothers" as authors of the document. It states that the group was located in the Church of São Domingos,[22] and justifies its presentation of compromisso as a way to spread the faith and increase its ranks of "loyal Christians." Rather than listing the contents of each of the ensuing chapters, in the following discussion I consider the major subjects and concerns of the whole document. I refer to the original numeration or dates of the chapters when possible to indicate how specific changes in the brothers' arguments developed over time—changes which would have derived, in whole or in part, from the negative reactions of ecclesiastical authorities to particular chapters, ideas, lines, or words in the proposed statutes.

FESTIVALS

The annual festival dedicated to the patron saint or saints of each brotherhood represented the high point of the yearly religious cycle, and was celebrated sumptuously for days, even a week or longer. The inside of the church was decorated with icons, candles, flowers, and bunting, while outside on its grounds a makeshift village of tents and stands sprung up to sell food and drink, and offer raffle giveaways of livestock. Musicians played and sang, and dancers twirled and leapt, all to celebrate the event and attract passersby. The apogee of the festival was the day of the saint, and it was marked by quiet, solemn rituals as well as animated festivities. The Brotherhood of Santo Elesbão and Santa Efigênia wrote in their compromisso that they celebrated their devotion on the day associated with Elesbão, 27 October (although, sometime in the nineteenth century or early twentieth century, they changed to Efigênia's day, 21 September). Well before that time, the brotherhood would begin organizing the festival and gathering funds for its realization. Within the group there were obligatory contributions (specified as charity in the statutes) as well as voluntary ones (given for devotion). Under the former category were membership fees and annual dues, as well as supplemental contributions for specified expenses (these offerings were called *esmolas*, and were considered donations, not alms). Because the operating expenses of a brotherhood often dwarfed the sums collected from within the group, and indeed certain uses of a brotherhood's internal funds (such as the purchase of food to serve during festivals) were prohibited by the church, special processions to beg for donations from the public were authorized by the bishop. These were usually undertaken on city streets, with the image of the saint carried by some of the brothers alongside a platter or sack in which to store the collected donations. A brotherhood that asked for money from the public in this way without the bishop's permission would be severely punished.

Lay brotherhoods begging for money in the streets was already a long-standing tradition in the 1740s. It dates back at least to 1549, when King João III allowed the black brotherhood of the Rosário to collect financial donations on the streets of Lisbon (some sixteen years before the brotherhood had formalized its compromissos). In the *Constituições Primeiras* the practice was deplored and dismissed as an "archaic style" of needy brotherhoods to get help. But the writers of the *Constituições Primeiras* were actually in favor of allowing brotherhoods to beg for money, with the proper permission and regulation. Their foremost preoccupation was the juxtaposition of saintly Roman Catholic images with the African "archaic style" of vigorous dances and syncopated music played on drums and other percussion instruments. They evidently decided that it would be easier to prevent this untoward mingling of traditions by banning the European element, because their work contains a prohibition on taking to the streets the saints, images, or even sacred paintings when a brotherhood was going out to beg.[23] This is rather more surprising because as a historical practice, using music to accompany and enhance the request for charitable donations, was associated with both whites and blacks (i.e., it was not immediately assumed to be some kind of pagan abomination introduced by the Africans). A common theme in Brazilian lithographs from the nineteenth century is a group of white men carrying images of saints and asking for public donations, surrounded by black musicians playing drums and horns. But black brotherhoods, particularly when the majority of members were African, carried more of a cultural threat. They sang their songs in African tongues; played their drums, rasps, marimbas, and other percussion; and dressed in approximations of their native African attire. All of this was legal in the church-sanctioned context and only needed prior authorization from the local authorities.

Elections for positions on the Mesa (brotherhood's board) were usually held in conjunction with the annual festival of the saint. The night before the saint's day, the judge, scribe, procurator, and chaplain would convene the other members at the church for the election. The officials would present the judge with a list of three names of contenders for each position, and "in secret the Judge would ask each of the Brothers which of the three proposed subjects the Brother would elect."[24] Some other brotherhoods carried out elections through voting with fava bean pods. Each elector would select a candidate by depositing a bean pod in the candidate's bag; the candidate who received the highest number of pods was the winner. Whatever the method, whether votes were conveyed by whispers or bean pods, the major judges would tally them and communicate the results to the brotherhood (honestly, it was hoped). In the case of a tie, the judge had the discretion to choose which of the candidates was better suited to the brotherhood's needs.[25]

Within the brotherhood, the ultimate power authorities held to resolve issues important to the group was a characteristic of broader social relations in the ancien régime. The judge and other administrators viewed overt questions from brothers regarding official decisions as a grave threat to order, that is, far more than as insubordination. The brotherhood's board was formed of twelve elected males. Of these, five held offices: judge, procurator, scribe, treasurer, and *andador* (courier). The roster of officials was different in the older Brotherhood of Our Lady of the Rosário of the Monastery of São Domingos in Lisbon. There, all twelve of the elected board members held a position, with six considered higher and six lower. The high positions included judge, procurator, scribe, treasurer, and two administrators. The low positions were king, prince, duke, count, marquis, and cardinal; these did not entirely disappear from Brazilian brotherhoods but were mainly incorporated in the *folias*.

If the saint's festival was the overall responsibility of the judge, it fell to the procurator to plan, organize, and ensure sufficient donations to fund it in many brotherhoods, including that of Elesbão and Efigênia. Through the festival the procurator was to "strive to grow and preserve the Brotherhood," and an important aspect of the arrangements was the visual impact of the decorations inside and entertainments outside the church. Everything needed to look clean, bright, sturdy, well made, and inviting.[26] The rituals leading up to the saint's day festival began earlier, often nine days before, when a *novena* (performance of repeated orations at the same place and time, for nine days) was begun. The novena was followed by the elections, and then the main celebrations on 27 October. During the morning hours a closed mass was held, and the souls of deceased brothers were prayed for. Following that was a Solemn Mass, with the brotherhood dressed in their ritual finery. Once the second mass ended, the group paraded out on a public procession through the streets of the city.

The compromisso does not provide details on the composition or proceedings of the celebratory cortege, perhaps because they are described in detail for the funeral processions. In this the brotherhood may have been following closely the regulations of the *Constituições Primeiras*, which expressed greater interest in the nuance of funeral processions. At any rate, the overall structure was probably similar. In front of the rest of the marchers strode the judge, carrying the tall metal staff symbolizing his office. He would typically be accompanied by the chaplain. Behind them, brothers dressed in their ceremonial cloaks, called *opas*, carried a cross and images of the patron saints.[27] Then came the rest of the procession, with one or two members of greater prestige carrying a banner with the insignia of the brotherhood; there would be several flags, and various additional forms of adornments and *alfaias* (ritual objects and ornaments) used by all brotherhoods in such contexts. In the citywide processions sponsored by the bishop that united multiple brotherhoods, such as the Corpus Christi, each brotherhood would make up one flank of the long parade, carrying again its saints, crosses, and other decorations. According to custom, the black brotherhoods took up the rear, from the richest and most prestigious to the most humble. The existence of internal hierarchical divisions (corresponding to rank or social position) within processions of the Brotherhood of Santo Elesbão and Santa Efigênia is suggested by chap. 13 of the compromisso. At the end of the parade, the cortege would return to the church, replace the saints on the altar, and put away all the other items that had been brought out to enhance the brotherhood's public presentation. Finally, the annual event wound down with a large afternoon meal, and informal activities and camaraderie involving dances, auctions, and lotteries.

A saint's festival was thus long and diverse, with different manifestations occurring both inside and outside the church walls. As a collective event, the festival began inside the church (with the two masses), and passed outward to the church grounds and beyond to the city; it also ended inside the church with the dinner gathering. Were contemporary observers concerned with a black brotherhood apparently taking over part of a church for period of hours or days? Even in the text of the Constituições Primeiras, there is ambiguity over what types of behavior are to be allowed within a church: according to those ecclesiastical guidelines, "indecent" acts were prohibited, while "honest" ones were accepted. At the dinner, food was abundantly supplied and probably voraciously consumed, while diners chatted, sang, played instruments, and danced.[28] Devotion to a saint was the festival's justification, but such activities within a church blurred the lines between the sacred and profane. Occasionally accusations of improper behavior were made, but because the tone of the event was religious and worshipful, such momentary scandals were usually resolved quickly or forgotten and the festival was allowed to proceed as if nothing had happened.

For colonial authorities, one way of trying to minimize such disturbances before they occurred was through scrutinizing and regulating the festival preparations. There was likely some of this strategy in Bishop D. Antônio de Guadalupe's position towards the Brotherhood of Santo Elesbão and Santa Efigênia with respect to what he called "licit" (versus illicit) expenses. Since his arrival in 1725, Guadalupe had fought for more stringent observance of the *Constituições Primeiras* and of Catholic rituals and precepts in general. The bishop wanted the brotherhood's compromisso (he drew special attention to chap. 2) to agree clearly with the regulation that only "licit" purchases could be made with the funds collected within the order. Those resources—based on dues, internal contributions, and so on—were expressly forbidden from going toward "dinners and other such things." In other words, the success of the dinner (indeed, its very existence) depended on the brotherhood's ability to obtain donations from the public to underwrite it, through processions undertaken for this purpose, overseen by the church. A brotherhood with a reputation for disorderly or immoral acts within its church during festival days of previous years would have far less success collecting funds from a suspicious citizenry, not to mention gaining the church's permission to take to the streets to beg in the first place.

MORTUARY RITES

Lay orders and devotional practices associated with death were common in the eighteenth century. A prominent example is the image of Christ deceased, lying in a coffin, that was hidden from view throughout the year except for Holy Week, when it was featured in the Procession of the Senhor Morto. The Brotherhood of Our Lady of the Rosário also engaged themes of death and resurrection, and one derivation of this order was the Brotherhood of Our Lady of Boa Morte (Our Lady of the Good Death). A popular saint throughout colonial Brazil was São Miguel Arcanjo (Saint Michael the Archangel). His role, receiving souls of the departed in heaven, made São Miguel the focus of considerable attention among diverse sectors of the population united in their preoccupation with salvation. Devotions such as these are expressions of the baroque Iberian Catholicism that was rooted in the seventeenth century, but that reached a new level in the next century with the discovery of gold and the lavish ornamentation of churches. For the brotherhoods, this baroque aesthetic and the concern with death that were traits of society as a whole intersected in the practices and rituals associated with caring for dead brothers. It is suggestive that in both the *Constituições Primeiras* and many of the brotherhoods' compromissos from the era, detailed guidelines for the order and texture of public processions are laid out in the context of funerals, but not of festivals.[29]

We might well wonder why slaves, most of them African born, and all of them with a supposedly fragile grasp on Catholic doctrine, would dedicate such time, energy, and resources to the goal of obtaining Catholic burials. This subject was raised in chapter 4, but merits further elaboration here since it was both the paramount objective of the brotherhoods and the most direct way for individual slaves to demonstrate their human equality within the hierarchical confines of colonial society. In 1694, an accord was signed between the governor of the captaincy and the Santa Casa de Misericórdia dealing with slave burials. The price of a burial was set at 960 réis, and it was stipulated that when a master could prove his or her inability to pay, the church would absorb the expense by providing a mortuary cloth (in practice, a white sheet), a coffin (actually a cloth or rope hammock), and the use of two slaves to transport and bury the body. It was not unusual even for masters who obviously had the funds to pay, but lacked the inclination, to rid themselves of the corpse in some secluded spot on the coast or outside the city. Dead slaves secretly abandoned in this way would not be given an obituary register, which funerals provided, as well as the Catholic grave. They were also denied, as Debret quotes some women from Mozambique as observing, a place "under the ground until Judgment Day."[30] But even the funerary services offered for a fee by Santa Casa de Misericórdia would seem to have left much to be desired, according to this nineteenth-century account of them:

The poorer people, and certainly the blacks, are treated with far less ceremony in these rites than others more advantaged. Soon after death, the corpse is sewn into a rough sack, and a message is sent to the cemetery to make room for one more. Two men appear at the house of the deceased. They load the corpse into a hammock, suspending it by a pole running along the hammock from head to feet, and carry it with no noticeable delicacy through the streets. If during this walk they encounter other corpses being likewise trundled off to the same horrible resting place, the bearers will roll up all the bodies into one bulging heap, and carry them in the same hammock, each bearer taking a share of the weight. Arriving at the final destination, the men approach a long hole, some six feet wide and four or five deep. Into that pit the corpses are tossed, with no rites performed. The bodies pile up every which way, bent and twisted. Then when the hole is filled near to the very top with corpses comes the handiwork of the black sacristan, who is apparently devoid of any human thought or feeling. He shuffles about with an empty gaze, shoveling dirt on top of the wretched dead to level out the hole with the surrounding earth.[31]

The fear of having one's corpse left to the elements, or to Santa Casa's unseemly collective graves, motivated the slaves to pursue the only other dignified option—a formal, paid Catholic funeral. The brotherhoods' funeral rites did not merely pay homage to the individual dead person, but in their pomp and exuberance they willfully displayed to the rest of society their commitment to proper care of the dead (for Catholics, a body left unburied or interred without proper rites was a supreme offense).[32] It was imperative that the whole brotherhood turn out to mourn and accompany the corpse to the grave, and if a brother was absent from these events it was considered a serious infraction. The corpse was taken first to the church and placed in front of the altar, where a mass would be held; later, after burial, another mass would be held for the souls of brothers long departed.

It is clear that the brotherhoods took the public dimensions of these rituals very seriously, since it was a way to express their prestige and dignity.[33] But detailed descriptions of the funeral practices of Rio's black brotherhoods do not seem to exist, which makes accounts such as the one above—from the early nineteenth century—so important. Other sources indicate that there was little overall change in funerary practice in Rio de Janeiro from the eighteenth century until around 1850, when new legislation regarding burials was approved. The compromisso of the Brotherhood of Santo Elesbão and Santa Efigênia indicates that a sequence of measures was to be taken upon the death of a member (or a spouse or child). To begin with, the brotherhood needed to be formally informed of the death and convene the assembly to begin the rites. The deceased's final wishes with respect to property needed to be found; typically these would have been recorded in a will. It should be noted that all these proceedings could reinforce the solidarity of a brotherhood, but disputes and jealousies were also to be expected as the private holdings of the brother were disclosed. Brotherhoods hoped to be listed as beneficiaries in the wills of their members, and if the deceased happened to belong to more than one brotherhood, those groups could argue over how much each was owed (in obligatory payments, if not inheritance).

The process started with informing the treasurer of the death. He, in turn, would tell the courier. The courier then told the judge, the chaplain, and the other brothers, walking from house to house announcing the news and advising that, as the compromisso says, "all gather together to accompany the body of the dead." That the courier knew where all the brothers lived suggests that the brotherhood involved close social ties.[34] The judge led the funeral procession from the church (or from the deceased's house, if there were no mass), carrying his staff of office in hand. The brothers followed, carrying the body and walking "in well-composed ranks." If the deceased had belonged to several brotherhoods, these would all be present in order of age and prestige, from the oldest to the newest. Sensitivity to prestige was also conveyed in where the corpse was laid to rest. Prominent members might be buried within the church, with more humble ones buried outside on the church grounds. The members were to return from the burial site in an ordered fashion, just as they had arrived there, and after a final blessing the group would disperse.

One detail that was impossible to derive from the compromisso was the precise location of burials. Until 1754, the brotherhood was located at the Church of São Domingos, which had a cemetery. That year, the brotherhood's own Chapel of Santo Elesbão and Santa Efigênia was inaugurated, and over the second half of the century numerous obituaries specify the cemetery at that chapel as the place of burial.[35] Presumably, in all cases, the mass for the deceased would be held at the church housing the brotherhood; the public procession would therefore start and end at the same church, assuming that the body was buried at the church where the brotherhood met. Another question might be raised about the brotherhood's use of hammocks to carry its corpses, just as was done in the uninspired service offered by Santa Casa de Misericórdia. If the brothers invested so many capital and symbolic resources in the funeral, why wouldn't they have arranged more formal modes of conveyance? Perhaps because death rites had to accomplish several things at once. Beyond the simple issue of getting a body into the ground, the procedure had to be dignified and thorough enough that all the brothers could remain confident that the burial guidelines in their compromisso were being met. But the street procession—with its displays of fancy attire, flowers, and other pomp— offered a moment for the rest of the city to recognize the brotherhood and admire its vivacious devotion. Because resources were always tight, it would have been reasonable to calculate that the appearance of the living counted just a bit more than that of the dead in this context. The more regal the cortege in its entirety looked, the less onlookers might have noticed or dwelled upon the poor aspect of the corpse, swaying along in its hammock amongst the finery.

Beyond the obligations specific to burials, the brotherhood maintained other death-related commitments to its members as put forth in the compromisso. When a brother died, the group would guarantee that his widow (remaining unmarried) and any children younger than fourteen would have "the same privileges they enjoyed during the life of their husbands and fathers, without being asked to make any contributions."[36] The emphasis on widows hints that the brotherhood valued marriage and deemed it appropriate that the brothers be married. At the same time, a widow without children (Mina women seem to have borne fewer children than women of other African groups) or parents living close by—and African slaves usually had no Catholic parents to mention—became the heir to whatever wealth the deceased left behind. From the brotherhood's perspective, there was another reason to take care of her: perhaps she would eventually marry someone from the brotherhood and keep the inheritance in play.

The brotherhood could also choose to waive the annual dues from a longstanding member who had fallen on hard times or become ill. Poverty and infirmity, often acting in concert, afflicted slaves and freed alike. Through small gestures the brotherhood could ameliorate these conditions, but not reverse them, and the life expectancy of this population was notoriously short.

FREED SLAVES

Brotherhoods could also help to free members who were slaves. To consider what freedom meant or brought to a slave in these contexts, we have to keep in mind how society in that era viewed slavery. Scarano's work was the first to demonstrate that the black brotherhoods, composed basically of slaves and freed slaves, themselves owned slaves that they either bought or inherited from members through their wills.[37] However, the meanings and ramifications of slavery go far beyond immediate ownership or the use of slave labor. Stuart Schwartz argued forcefully that in colonial Brazil, slavery created the fundamental facts of life, and indeed no one was truly free in the presence of slavery.[38] In the 165 sets of compromissos from black brotherhoods analyzed by Patricia Mulvey, 11 made reference to the goal of freeing members from slavery: 5 from Rio de Janeiro, 4 from Bahia, and 2 from Minas Gerais, all of them written before 1800.[39] The particular challenge here is to understand the social conditions in which a given brotherhood could buy or inherit a slave, while at the same time create mechanisms to liberate another.

The 1565 compromisso of the Brotherhood of Our Lady of the Rosário of the Monastery of São Domingos prohibited slaves—along with "white moors," mulattos, and Indians—from holding any administrative position. The document recommends that the brotherhood help enslaved members obtain the resources needed to buy their freedom, but also suggests that the application of funds from the brotherhood's coffers for such purposes be limited.[40] The compromisso of the Brotherhood of Santo Elesbão and Santa Efigênia was even less concerned with the processes and transactions involved in attaining freedom. It assumes in its profiles of the model brother a freed African man, who has a wife and children. Such individuals would not have been the numerical majority among the brothers, but one senses from the compromisso and other documents that they were more prominent and occupied more positions of authority than people from the larger population of slaves. And although the rates of marriage associated with the brotherhood were low, a survey still in progress indicates that the preeminent brothers were all married.[41]

It is striking that the theme of obtaining freedom does not appear in any of the thirty-two chapters of the compromisso of the Brotherhood of Santo Elesbão and Santa Efigênia. But this theme was raised by two separate lay brotherhoods of Mina-Mahi Africans who formed out of the Mahi Congregation at the Church of Santo Elesbão and Santa Efigênia in the second half of the eighteenth century: the brotherhoods of the Devotion of the Almas do Purgatório (Souls of Purgatory) and of Our Lady of Remédios.[42] In both cases, the mention in the compromisso includes proposed methods of financing the purchase of freedom. These initiatives might be understood as a form of mutual aid, similar to the emancipation societies of the nineteenth century.[43] But even these systems of financial support had clear limits, being conceded to members of the congregation only in special circumstances. They represented neither a right for every brother nor a contractual act of charity among all brothers, but were a privilege granted to the most illustrious enslaved brothers obligated to repay the organization as soon as possible (and it must have been assumed that they could do so).

POWER AND RESOURCES

However tempting it might be, given the lack of complementary sources and of better contextual information on the black brotherhoods, the compromisso cannot be read as an ironclad script or template for social behavior. Not only is it true that they were the final products (revised and appended) of disputes, alliances, and compromises between different interest groups at the core of the brotherhoods, but in practical terms some of the strength of such documents (which bridged the Catholic Church and organizational provenience groups of Africans) must have resided in their flexibility. Certainly some of what was written was probably not obeyed, or was not always obeyed in the same way. At the same time, we should also try to appreciate the networks of power and social relations in which detailed guidelines such as these were enforced and obeyed. The compromisso of the Brotherhood of Santo Elesbão and Santa Efigênia had the critical dual function of constructing social norms for the group, and of establishing and embodying the authority of those entrusted with guarding the norms through the exercise of power. The delicate relation between these two spheres was often affected by changes in power relations within the group. The compromisso was altered five times between 1740 and 1764, and it is possible to get a sense in each case of the different interests and strategies involved. The most common form of dispute dealt with finances and with administrative positions (their roles, and how they were appointed). Early in the document the administrative functions and the procedures for nominating brothers to them are laid out, but the fact that this information keeps recurring in increasingly detailed form throughout later additions demonstrates that it was a continual source of contention.

The first twenty chapters of the compromisso describe the attributes of the judge, which was the position of greatest importance and highest authority on the brotherhood's board. The judge would care for the images of the saints, look after the financial and other material holdings of the brotherhood, and "observe the demands" (supervise the proceedings of any legal cases in which the brotherhood was a beneficiary). The main judge could be given the responsibility of appointing other judges (the complete board had a total of twelve judges) or could also accept nominations from among the brothers for a general position called *juiz da Mesa* (judge of the board). This seems to have been a ceremonial title that could be open to any prestigious brother with enough money to pay the hefty donation associated with it; the compromisso refers to the "advantageous size" of that sum.[44] The Board's four officials—judge, procurator, treasurer, and scribe—were to meet at the church every Sunday of the year to address internal affairs of the brotherhood. The mandatory meetings were to assure that the board members kept up with the necessary work ("para evitarem os descuidos que podem haver em cada um dos oficiais que servem"). Chap. 22 introduces a striking addition to the original document: ceremonial board positions for women, including a female "judge of the board." These also carried substantial fees, although whether or not they were the same as the men paid, women did not gain equivalent power. The same chapter also states that the board was to be composed of twelve men and twelve women, which, given the limited number of official administrative functions, suggests that the expansion of board titles was intended at least in part to bolster the annual esmola receipts. But another part of the motivation for all those people on the board came from the need to staff the royal hierarchy to organize the folias.

In the original twenty chapters of the compromisso, participation by women in the brotherhood is mentioned only in chap. 10. The intention there had been to limit membership to women from the Mina Coast, Cape Verde, the island of São Tomé, and Mozambique. Membership was denied to creole women (born of Africans in Brazil), *cabras* (mixed-race), and *pretas d'Angola* (women from Angola). In Portugal, most of the brotherhoods allowed only men to join. A particular exception was the black Brotherhood of Our Lady of the Rosário of the Monastery of São Domingos in Lisbon, in which women were permitted membership if they were married to a brother of the order.[45] In Brazil, brotherhoods of white men tended to include women only as dependents of male members; they gained some small benefits but were not permitted to join outright. The black brother-hoods allowed women to join as members (called irmãs, sisters), whether or not they were already married to a member in good standing. But this could be a source of conflict. The sisters paid dues and were theoretically equal to the other brothers, but as a practical matter they were excluded from participating in decision making or holding high administrative posi-tions. The changes made over time to the compromisso's chapters reflect women's progress toward gaining more power inside the brotherhood. This probably derives from their recognized ability to meet the men on equal financial ground—that is, to pay the higher donations associated with authority and prestige. For example, chap. 26 creates the positions of a juiz and juiza (male judge and female judge) for each patron saint, with the donation set at 12,800 réis per person.[46]

According to the compromisso's twenty initial chapters, the main job of the procurator was to organize the festival of the saints. Chaps. 28 and 31 introduce new responsibilities to the position: caring for sick brothers, distributing monetary contributions to needy brothers, and performing religious services for dying brothers.[47] Beyond this, since part of the job was to collect and distribute donations within the order, the procurator found himself caught up in a variety of internal disputes which he was expected to help resolve. These social and financial functions were critical to the well-being of the group, and the procurator, understood to be second only to the main judge in the brotherhood's hierarchy, needed to be a man of patience, wisdom, and influence.

Under the procurator in rank came the treasurer, who, the compro-misso specified, needed to be a white man. This would seem to follow the model established by the Brotherhood of Our Lady of the Rosário of the Monastery of São Domingos in Lisbon, in their 1565 compromisso. Admis-sion into the brotherhood had been open to white people, as well as to pardos, since its founding. I have been unable to identify any whites or pardos affiliated with the Brotherhood of Santo Elesbão and Santa Efigênia, but all the indications from a range of evidence suggest two hypotheses: these people would have been acquainted in one form or another with the founders of the order, and they would probably have been linked to the commerce of slaves in Rio de Janeiro. (That would make the source of their financial contributions to the brotherhood, which must have been significant, somewhat ironic.) The compromisso also states that if a brother capable of handling the position of treasurer was not to be found, someone from outside the order may be chosen if he was meticulous and honorable.

The last of the four board officials was the scribe, a person able to take care of the books and keep them up to date, "benemérito assim no zelo como na inteligência das contas" (distinguished in his zeal and his expertise in arithmetic). He recorded critical information, including money going in and out of the treasury from dues, donations, and payments for masses. The scribe was fourth in rank, but in the judge's absence, he would preside over the assembly. This was to keep the procurator, as second in command, from concentrating too much power, and also to prevent control of the order from passing, even for a moment, to a white man (the treasurer). A common fifth position in rank was that of courier, although in the Brotherhood of Santo Elesbão and Santa Efigênia this position was not part of the board, which was limited to four officials.

The brotherhood made money from essentially two sources: internal dues and contributions, and public donations. Chap. 27 does not precisely mandate, but assumes, that the two female judges of the patron saints were directly responsible for asking for money in the street processions. Collecting public money is not mentioned in a detailed way, but it is well known that this was one of the principal functions of the folias. All of this means that women holding places of prestige within the brotherhood's hierarchy, along with the king of the folia, were responsible for a significant part of the order's income. We are left to wonder how the folias differed in their strategies for gathering money in the earlier years, before a parallel hierarchy of women was established in the brotherhood. It should be remembered that monies collected in this way went to a fund, not authorized by the bishop, to be used for dinners and other special needs. The compromisso does not spell out how these funds would be spent or divided, and I found no documents pertaining to the brotherhood's accounting. But clearly, the control of resources was a growing point of concern for the board, especially after 1746, when plans were laid by the order to construct their own church. Taken together, these points demonstrate the dynamic process by which the need for income intersected with other concerns about gender and the concentration of power.

In the first twenty chapters, the annual donations associated with membership and administrative functions are listed. Among the officials, the judge owed 12,000 réis; if he wished to stay past his mandate, he needed to offer another *esmola avantajada* (distinguished contribution). The scribe owed 10,000 réis. It was notable that the treasurer, procurador, and courier were exempt from paying elevated dues, given the amount of time involved in these positions. Of course, if these office holders chose to contribute to *por sua devoção* (by showing their devotion), their offering would be accepted. Other brothers affiliated with the board in festive, nonadministrative roles owed 2,000 réis a piece. Rank-and-file brothers owed 480 réis. We gain some perspective on these amounts by considering that at the time, cheap slaves could be bought and sold in Rio's markets for 50,000 réis. When new judge positions were created for the patron saints in chap. 26, this represented a significant enhancement to the brotherhood's internal receipts.

The order needed to augment its income, but it was not acquisitive to the point of sacrificing what its officials deemed harmonious social relations. In chap. 30, the compromisso acknowledges that it was not uncommon to encounter an unruly element or two among the sincere and worshipful brothers.[48] To avoid the intrusions of these "enemies of peace," the board (led by the judge) had the obligation to interview new brothers to determine whether they had been expelled from another brotherhood. If a prospective member was discovered to have a history of disobedience, he was to be immediately and forever expelled from the Brotherhood of Santo Elesbão and Santa Efigênia, no matter what amount of money he had agreed to or offered to pay. "We are only interested in quiet, peaceful people here," the compromisso states, "not rabble-rousers."[49]

The compromisso also devotes several chapters to the relations between the brotherhood and the chaplain. Early in the text it is stated that the judge and the other officials would select this person, and his main duty was to lead fifty masses a year, including those for the living and for the dead. He would be paid a donation of 25,000 réis for the year, and needed to arrange his own substitute if he were to miss any of his commitments to the brotherhood. It is instructive to compare the way the compromisso addresses the responsibilities of the chaplain versus those of the board members. The latter are described initially in basic form, although with the passing of time and the growth of the brotherhood's ambitions, somewhat more of the officials' duties and powers (or the limits of those powers) are spelled out. But from the very first, the compromisso is quite specific about what is expected of the chaplain. For one thing, he needed to sign a contract for his term. The contract would list the masses he must lead, and also would require that he be present at all burials and all solemn occasions, whether in the church, on the street, or elsewhere. This formality and precaution reflected the distrust that characterized most interactions between black brotherhoods and ecclesiastical authority.

Chap. 23 directs newly detailed demands and rules to the chaplain. It stipulates that every brother who died during the term had a right to no fewer than ten masses. But more boldly, the matter of payment is now spelled out to remove any ambiguity. The chaplain would be paid at the end of the year, and no longer should expect a fixed sum: for every mass he had performed until then, he would receive the equivalent of one *pataca* (a silver coin worth 320 réis). If for no other reason, this is why the scribe's function of recording all the masses was so critical. Yet even these measures seem to have been insufficient to inspire consistent attention from the chaplain. By chap. 28, the brothers complain about the frequent absence of the chaplain from the bedsides of sick or dying brothers, grumbling that chaplains "mais procuram a sua conveniência que cumprirem com a sua obrigação" (pursue their own convenience more avidly than their obligations). This chapter authorizes the brotherhood to contract another priest whenever the chaplain, or his substitute, fails to appear. The expense for those services would be deducted from the amount payable to the chaplain at the end of the year. The theme of the unreliable chaplain is taken up yet again, in the last chapter of the compromisso, and here the tone is more bitterness than anger. These abuses of the chaplain against his own word and office are an offense "o que Deus não o tal permite" (not permitted by God), because the dead are not to be punished for the squabbles of the living.

The compromisso also reflects change over time in the frequency and distribution of masses called for. The first twenty chapters do not establish a number of masses that every dead brother should receive, and even in the case of death of one of the four officials of the board, the only special assembly called for is one mass at the church with the corpse. Chap. 23, however, requires ten masses for every member of the brotherhood who passes away.[50] The number of masses was not set for an administrator of the order who dies, but one assumes it would have been in accord with the "zealous service" and "advantageous contributions" of those distinguished individuals. Later, in the undated addition to the compromisso, it is declared that upon death judges of either sex should receive 20 masses; scribes and treasurers, 18; couriers, 12; and other nonofficial members of the board, 16. Over time, the gradual entrenchment of the internal hierarchy of the brotherhood is expressed by the increasing privileges accruing to members of the board, and especially to the four officials. The number of masses for a rank-and-file brother stayed at ten, while that of the judge was twice as many. Certainly the judge paid a larger contribution to the order than other brothers did. But the compromisso reveals a marked trend in the concentration of the brotherhood's expenditures among the board members and their families.

The integration of women into the brotherhood seems to have been viewed as a source of both advantages and challenges. As noted earlier, women provided a source of new income, and the statutes are much more upfront about the donations associated with each female board position than they are about the rights and duties that such positions would entail. (For instance, we are left to wonder about the precise responsibilities of the so-called juiza de ramalhete, whose title would seem to indicate caring for flowers and bouquets.) Elsewhere, women are occasionally mentioned as widows in the event of a married brother's death. The text of the compromisso reflects its era, so that the masculine identity of members is assumed throughout. But it is worth remarking that chap. 10, which denies entry in the order to men or women from Angola, as well as to male and female creoles and cabras, justifies that prohibition based on the alleged "bad behavior" of "sisters" from these populations. Despite this attempt to exclude them, women from Angola could take advantage of another way to enter that the statutes made possible: if they were married to a member in good standing. Although there were few marriages between Mina men and Angola women, the possibility of some such unions was always present.[51] On the other hand, creole and cabra women would have been far less likely to marry an African man.

The compromisso is eloquent in its aversion to female Angola, as well as to female creoles and cabras. It is recommended that, when one term of office is ending for a group of board officials, a reckoning should be made of any inappropriate admissions granted to such women, whose identity might have been hidden or unverified. The official responsible for allowing them to become members should be prohibited from ever again "servir cousa alguma na dita Irmandade" (holding an administrative position in the brotherhood)). And the women, their cover blown, would be expelled. They would receive their entry dues back in full (again demonstrating that the brotherhood's interest in income flow could be sharply subjugated to their social concerns). The registers of the women's membership would be revoked with notations placed at the margin of the record book (to "fique de nenhum efeito seus assentos, de que se fará declaração à margem dos livros deles"). Nowhere does the compromisso define what is meant by creole; the Brazilian-born children of Mina in the brotherhood would have fit an objective definition. The compromisso refers to young children orphaned by the death of a father who was a member, but other than that have little to say about children in general.

As the size of the board expanded, finally encompassing a total of 24 people (12 men and 12 women), the potential for internal debate and tension grew along with it. But the brotherhood still had to answer to ecclesiastical and royal authority as well. In 1767, a royal decree sent from the Tribunal of Conscience and Orders in Lisbon to the bishop of Rio de Janeiro requires the revision of chap. 10 of the compromisso, discussed above. All of the groups previously prohibited from membership were now to be allowed to enter.[52] The specific alteration asked for in the name of King D. José was the removal of any reference to "a diferença da naturalidade dos pretos" (a difference in the nature or essence of black people).[53] In light of this directive, the prohibition against membership could not stand. But the board also maneuvered to limit the ramifications of the change by restructuring itself through new wording. The rewritten chapter states that the board would now be composed of twelve people, of whom six must be irmãos criadores (founders)—from Mina Coast, Cape Verde, São Tomé, or Mozambique; and the other six spots would be dedicated to the nonfounders, including people from outros admitidos, the other groups who had just won the right to enter. This allowed the current members and the nations they represented to safeguard half the positions on the board, while also holding out the possibility that some of the remaining positions would go to whites or pardos, who were obviously not founders of the brotherhood but who had still been accepted as members from the beginning. That a white man, possibly a slave merchant, could in the eyes of the order's African founders be preferable to black people from Angola as officials of the board speaks to the complexity of social relations and strategic alliances in this period.

Chap. 29 deals with discipline. It states that the founders and the rest of the board should enjoy the guarantee of *bom regime* (proper comportment) from the brothers, especially with respect to matters of paying contributions and entry dues. Infractions could be punished, up to and including expulsion from the order. This chapter emphasizes what chap. 24 began to make clear: principal decision making in every sphere of the brotherhood's activity was to be left in the hands of the judge and the other officials, as well as the chaplain (who was included through pressure from the church). This solidified the order's internal hierarchy and increased the prestige associated with the founders' African identities. By chap. 31, the graduated ranking of the four board officials was replaced with a single high administrative level; the procurator, treasurer, and scribe, formerly under the judge, were now also to be treated as superiors equal to the judge, under threat of punishment. At the first offense, the guilty party was required to pray on bended knee to the Holy Mother. A second show of disrespect meant the offender would have to carry "uma pedra que haverá na Irmandade," a rock (of undisclosed size and weight), owned by the brotherhood and kept nearby. A third time would lead to chastising in front of the assembled board; after this, only expulsion was left as a reproof for impertinence to authority. Decisions about expulsion were the prerogative of the board, but unfortunately they seem not to have recorded how many times it (as well as disciplinary action in general) was used, or under what conditions.

THE BOUNDARIES OF GROUP IDENTITY

Since the fifteenth century, first in Portugal and then also in Brazil, historical changes led to the creation of a multiplicity of lay Catholic brotherhoods with distinct, even contrasting identities.[54] In Portugal, the expanding population of Africans and their descendants was not welcome in the earlier, "white" brotherhoods; those institutions both excluded the blacks and encouraged them to form their own orders, such as that of Our Lady of Rosário.[55] In the ensuing years, after the first black brotherhoods were established in Portugal, parallel processes of inclusion and exclusion in their own admission procedures (based on a variety of social criteria) helped lead to the proliferation of diverse black brotherhoods, notably in Brazil. In Rio de Janeiro, Mina blacks had been prohibited from attaining positions of any power in the Brotherhood of the Rosário, and they decided to found their own orders. As noted in chapter 4 of this book, from 1715 to 1740 those Mina left the Church of Rosário, separated into three subgroups, and subsequently organized three new brotherhoods: one created the Brotherhood of Santo Antônio da Mouraria (Saint Anthony of the Moors), another the Brotherhood of the Menino Jesus, and the third the Brotherhood of Santo Elesbão and Santa Efigênia. In their own organizations they could hold the positions of authority and prohibit access to creole and Angola blacks, who had been the ones preventing them from advancing in the Brotherhood of Rosário.[56] Beyond these three orders linked to the Mina "nation," there was a related group, the Mahi Congregation (founded 1762). This congregation created two more devotions: one to the Almas (Souls) of deceased Mina, and the other to Our Lady of Remédios (to aid the poor and sick Mina in Rio).

Taken as a whole from diverse sources, the array of documents pertaining to these groups weaves a fundamental ambiguity around the word *nação* (nation). As detailed in earlier chapters, this term could refer to geography, to ethnic networks, or both: it was used to designate the place of provenience of African peoples, and also to identify African peoples' ethnic background. The double meaning of such a common word in period documents complicates any attempt to distinguish the brotherhoods who based membership on provenience groups (such as that of Santo Elesbão and Santa Efigênia, centered on Africans from Mina Coast, Cape Verde, São Tomé, and Mozambique) from those that formed as subgroups within a provenience group (such as the Mina Congregation, a subset of Mina blacks)—and from those that cohered around an ethnic identity within a provenience group (such as the Mahi Congregation and their derivations). In any analysis of African slave identity in Brazil, it is critical to keep in mind the distinction between *nação* as provenience identifier (Angola na-

174 | Chapter Five

tion, Mina nation) and as ethnic identifier (Rebolo-Tunda nation, Mina-Savalu nation, and so on). Both types of nations were involved in the Brotherhood of Santo Elesbão and Santa Efigênia, although the associated identities could be expressed differently in different situations.

The procedure for evaluating potential members is listed in chap. 10 of the compromisso, where it is admonishes that if the candidate is "preto" or "preta" (male or female black, but in the vernacular context, specifically African), "se examinarão com exata diligência a terra e nação donde vieram" (he/she should be closely examined to determine his/her land and nation they came from). Those individuals who seem to be from Mina Coast, Cape Verde, São Tomé, and Mozambique were rushed through the process, since they were from the nations that founded the brotherhood. Once they paid the entry dues, a record was made of their membership ("logo se fará assento nela dando de sua entrada quatro patacas"), and they were brothers. Official positions on the brotherhood's board could only be held by African people of these nations—except for the role of treasurer, which, as noted earlier, presented a special case where even a white man was preferable to Africans of other nations.[57] The fact that Angola women were prohibited (more emphatically than others) from joining the brotherhood did not seem to create or reflect openly antagonistic relations between Mina and Angola in the city of Rio de Janeiro. To the contrary, although there was tension and occasional conflict, these groups interacted regularly. They shared churches, and cemeteries; they united for festivals and funerals. And one suspects that the members of the Brotherhood of Santo Elesbão and Santa Efigênia would not have been so preoccupied with the admission of Angola women if this were not a common infraction.

THE IMPERIAL STATE OF SANTO ELESBÃO

The major theme of the five new chapters added to the compromisso in 1764 was the creation of a folia in the brotherhood, to be called the Imperial State of Santo Elesbão. The name recalls the Catholic kingdom of Elesbão (who had been a prince, son of an Ethiopian king) in the European Middle Ages.[58] The appearance of the folia is a direct expression of the growth of the brotherhood. Adding new positions to the board (even when they were more festive than administrative) was good for the overall organization, discipline, and camaraderie of a large group; the justification offered for the folia was that it would maintain the *ânimos* (good spirits) of the brotherhood. And of course it would be good for the bottom line, since the kings of the folia, of which there were several, would each pay a donation of 15,000 réis. An impressive folia on the streets would also enhance public donations to the brotherhood during the special processions authorized for that purpose. The donations collected from the public were handed by the folia over to the treasurer, who should in turn place them in the *cofre Divino* (divine safe). No record was kept of the use of these funds, although it is reasonably certain that they underwrote most of the costs of the annual festival of the saint. They likely were also drawn upon to help defray the costs of attending to sick and dying brothers, as well as various ritual and festive expenses. These chapters do not specify that such funds could be used toward the purchase of freedom for enslaved brothers, although the Mahi Congregation's compromisso related to folias did mention that possibility.

The hierarchy would be elected for a period of three years, and while the new positions included yet another judge, most titles were royal: emperor, empress, kings, prince, princess, and so on. As with the official positions on the board, an individual's term could be extended if the properly advantageous donations were furnished. It is apparent that the role of emperor needed to go to a man of some prestige and means, and not only because this was the top rank of the folia. The emperor himself would be responsible for providing the rest of the court with suitably regal attire, as well as all the small decorations and alfaias. The kings and queens would pay for their own outfits, but in recognition of the financial burden the emperor in particular was expected to experience, he was exempt from any other personal contributions to the brotherhood during the three years of his term. The fittings and other arrangements for costumes must have taken place soon after elections were held, since the statutes stipulate that the entire court of the folia was to report to the board on the assigned day to take office already wearing their cloaks, crowns, mantles, and other finery. Although not part of the brotherhood's actual administration, the emperor was to be treated with due deference by the rest of the brothers. When he was brought to address the board, the judge needed to offer him the best position at the table. The folia held their assemblies in the church, although access to space was limited in the church and constantly needed to only a position of judge, but a complete parallel board for women—it seems reasonable to conclude that their financial contributions had been substantial.

Construction of the church represented an unusual accomplishment for a black brotherhood, and in general this project had served to unify the diverse sectors of the order. But after 1754, once ensconced in its new church, the brotherhood's various component nations (here understood as both provenience groups and ethnic groups) began to chafe and quarrel over what one faction termed "preferências e maiorias" (preferences and majorities).[59] But with respect neither to gender nor nation were alliances set in stone, because the push and pull of short-term and long-term interests created dynamic, unpredictable subsets of constituents within the order. Women might band together at one juncture to argue a certain cause, while later in a different context some women would join a group of men to argue another point. The plasticity of these alliances is perhaps not what a modern observer would expect, and yet it appears characteristic of how such groups interacted.

Ever since its founding in 1740, the Brotherhood of Santo Elesbão and Santa Efigênia comprised several African nations, and admitted pardos and whites but excluded Angolans and creoles. From within this first order a group of Mina organized, calling themselves the Pretos Minas (Congregation of Mina Blacks) and electing Pedro Costa Mimozo as the King of their folia.[60] By the time of their next election, a subgroup within the new congregation had emerged as opposed to Mimozo. That subgroup exerted itself to get the faction led by Mimozo voted out of office, but they were unsuccessful. The winner of the vote was Clemente Proença, an ally of Mimozo,[61] but the disputes for power within the congregation soon multiplied in complex new forms. Just as the Congregation of Mina Blacks had arisen through the formalization of a split between Mina and other nations within the brotherhood, the very same Congregation of Mina Blacks would soon undergo its own schism based on identities and interests. The subgroup that formed from within it was called the Mahi Congregation, and its first elected leader was Captain Ignacio Gonçalves do Monte, praised as a "true Mahi."[62] It turns out that Monte had enemies in the Congregation of Mina Blacks, and they all happened to be Dahomeans. He rebelled against them and their congregation, taking his followers with him to derive yet another order from the original Brotherhood of Santo Elesbão and Santa Efigênia. This sequence of events indicates that Pedro Costa Mimozo and Clemente Proença were both from Dahomey. Monte's faction was made up of several Mina subgroups—including Savalu, Agonli, and Iano—but Monte's place of honor as leader, and the name of the new order, suggests that the Mahi were the largest. And notably, the very first page of the Mahi Congregation's Manuscript constructs the somewhat embellished image of a "kingdom of Mahi" towering over West Africa, a kingdom described as "one of the most excellent and powerful of the whole Mina Coast," ready at any moment of its choosing to subdue the nearby kingdom of Dahomey.

From the first, the Brotherhood of Santo Elesbão and Santa Efigênia contained various groups whose disputes for power led to a persistent process of segmentation through the creation of strategic alliances. A breakaway and subsequent founding of a new order was the ultimate articulation of this clash of identities, but even within an order a contrasting identity could be asserted. This was the case with the Agonli and Savalu "nations," minority factions in the Mahi Congregation, who finally elected their own "kings" within that order. Smaller groups wanted avenues to greater participation and prestige in the larger assembly. It was in recognition of this basic fact that the Brotherhood of Santo Elesbão and Santa Efigênia ultimately created the Imperial State. The court of this principal folia grew to comprise as many as seven kings, each one the figurative leader of a "nation" within the brotherhood; each king's court in turn was made up of the so-called kin or *parentes* (relatives, actually subjects) of that ethnic or provenience group. Not counting the category of "Mina," eight such provenience or ethnic groups have so far been identified within the Brotherhood of Santo Elesbão and Santa Efigênia: São Tomé, Mozambique, Cape Verde, Dahomey, Mahi, Savalu, Agonli, and Iano. We can speculate, but do not know for sure why, the total number of kings was smaller than the number of nations present within the order. This may be because the Dahomeans of the Mina Congregation already controlled the Imperial State and did not need a king.

Most of the historical literature that mentions the folias treats them as folkloric ensembles, pleasant and colorful but merely festive appendages to the main entity of the lay brotherhood. To the contrary, I propose that the folias were intimately and strategically linked to the brotherhoods; they were a fundamental aspect of the brotherhoods' internal mechanisms of power, social differentiation, and identity construction. They had important roles, and represented important notions of belonging and participation, for all the members of the brotherhoods. But the festival or street procession was their most public, visible face, and it was this dimension of their activities that has endured to animate the folias' offshoots in contemporary Afro-Brazilian culture, from Rio to Minas Gerais to Recife. These cultural manifestations are often pigeonholed as "folklore," in everything from Brazilian state policy to foreign travel guides; but the concept of folklore has been recuperated from its lowly status by the French historian André Burguière, who perceives in its marginality a discreet, unmapped space of power (rather than a lack of meaning or importance). "Long abandoned to the lovers of the picturesque and exotic, folklore should be of interest to the historian," he argues. "Its apparent insignificance in the social realm indicates that in it was invested, and is still preserved, something of value. A characteristic of power is that it is never exactly where it appears to be."[63]

Analyzing the place of the Imperial State in the Brotherhood of Santo Elesbão and Santa Efigênia allows us to see that the exercise of power within the brotherhood was directly linked to the capacity to resolve the tensions and disputes between and among smaller, component groups. Making possible the election of seven kings from seven nations should be understood as an attempt both to minimize conflict and to improve the receipt of donations in the brotherhood's coffer. If we accept Burguière's view of the nature of folklore, perhaps the folias are intriguing to folklorists because, in one form or another, they contain hidden keys to the comprehension of some of Brazil's later religious practices.

NEGOTIATING NORMS AND ROYAL APPROVAL

The first twenty chapters of the compromisso of the Brotherhood of Santo Elesbão and Santa Efigênia treat a range of subjects but in a very general way. The ensuing revisions and additions appeared in response to specific practical problems, and also more clearly spell out the powers and responsibilities of the board.[64] The initial casualness of the document was an expression of the group's smaller and less formal structure; at the time, the brotherhood met in a private house that the compromisso did not identify. After the brotherhood transferred to the Church of São Domingos the number of members increased, and along with it the need for more complete and rigorous rules. The four chapters added in 1740 brought new detail to what had only been outlined before, especially with respect to how money was to be collected and spent, women's participation, masses for the dead, disciplinary measures, and board positions. The eight chapters that appeared later speak to those themes, and others, but noticeably concentrate power and benefits among the board members. The final addition to the compromisso reinforces the brotherhood's hierarchy through the differential distribution of masses. But during this period the kingdoms of the folia had been instituted as new, alternative hierarchies in the order—in part to help alleviate tensions wrought by the growing power of the board.

Interrogated in a slightly different way, the compromisso reveals that the principal difficulties the brotherhood had to confront over the period were these: the role and methods of the treasurer, women's participation, interference or unreliability from the chaplain (or bishop), clashes between subgroups within the order, and the absence from a brother's funeral of his fellows.[65] The series of solutions created for these problems show that over time, the brotherhood transformed into a relatively well-off and confident organization, building its own church, tackling internal discipline, and confronting the ecclesiastical authorities over their obligations to the brotherhood.

In 1740, when the brotherhood initiated the process for formal recognition by the church, it had around seventy members. That total certainly grew over the years, and one indication of how much comes from a reference to the folia. The folia held meetings of the emperor and the multiple kings, each with a court drawn from his nation, and these must have been bustling affairs. They should be held at the church, according to the compromisso, to avoid "convocar tanta gente em sua casa . . . que faz suspeitar entre a vizinhança" (loading so many people into the emperor and king's houses . . . as to create suspicion among the neighbors). The Mahi Manuscript records one reunion of the Mahi Congregation's folia that brought 200 people to the church.[66]

Daily life changed for many in Brazil after 1750, with the progressive implementation of the policies of the Portuguese minister Sebastião José de Carvalho e Mello (later the Marquis of Pombal). The tone of colonial administration grew more interventionist and centralizing. This affected different sectors of the population in different ways, of course, but the black brotherhoods were soon being scrutinized for their alleged spirit of independence. Both ecclesiastical and secular authorities demanded transparency, order, and humility. In the 1760s, many compromissos sent by nascent brotherhoods in Brazil to Lisbon were denied in what seems to have been a demonstration of monarchical control. During this same period the crown also produced various provisions and other legal instruments reaffirming regal authority over the brotherhoods; the two provisions from King D. José for the Brotherhood of Santo Elesbão and Santa Efigênia are examples.[67]

In 1765, a royal letter was sent to all the brotherhoods within the Bishopric of Rio de Janeiro informing them that they were to send their compromissos to Lisbon to be evaluated and confirmed by the Tribunal of Conscience and Orders. When the compromisso of the Brotherhood of Santo Elesbão and Santa Efigênia arrived at the bishop's chambers in Rio, a functionary there, the purveyor of chapels and residuals, found evidence of a previous oversight: the document had not been sent on to Lisbon for royal approval in 1740. It had made it as far as the desk of Rio's Bishop D. Antônio Guadalupe, who had approved it, and there the matter had stopped. This was not an uncommon occurrence; many Brazilian brotherhoods' compromissos had not been placed on board ships to Portugal before the 1760s, even though official procedures mandated that the crown had the final word on a brotherhood's petition for recognition.[68] So in 1765, the revised compromisso—all thirty-two chapters, including the addition and the five chapters describing the folia—embarked across the Atlantic for the first time.[69] They received official approval in a provision signed by King D. José on 11 March 1767; the provision affirmed the brotherhood's creation and revalidated its license, adding one note and several changes to the compromisso.[70]

King D. José's note emphasizes that the crown had full power over this and every other lay brotherhood in Brazil (which was a standard announcement from Lisbon at the time). Comparing the provision's modifications with the version of the compromisso that had been revised to accommodate them, it is clear that the king's changes had been only partially adopted by

In its last five chapters, the *compromisso* of the Brotherhood of Santo Elesbão and Santa Efigênia authorized the election of up to seven kings to compose the court of the Imperial State of Santo Elesbão. The only condition imposed for the selection of kings was that each reign should represent sufficient numbers of members within its own court, who in turn should hold sufficient amounts of personal wealth to support the reign's material needs during the term in office. The document cites the importance of "bens móveis como de raiz," or both portable and stationary property; a good indication of what those terms probably referred to can be found in the wills of freed Mina slaves.[1] Beyond that criterion, those five chapters, added in 1764 to sanction the creation of the *folia* within the brotherhood, did not provide details about how the reigns should be formed or organized. I did not find evidence of the existence of "empires" previous to 1764, only reigns. However, based on a small but rich body of documentation, it is certain that even by the 1740s, the election of kings and queens was common practice in the brotherhood. The Mahi Manuscript mentioned two kings of the Mina Congregation (one of them was Pedro da Costa Mimozo, already a king in 1748, and the other Clemente Proença, who followed Mimozo). The first king of the Mahi Congregation was elected in 1762.

The Mahi Manuscript is perhaps the most important document available to shine light on the lives of slaves who had departed from the Bight of Benin to enter the world of slavery in colonial Brazil. The document was written in or around 1786, in the structure of a dialogue. Its authors were two men identified as Mahi: Francisco Alves de Souza, a freed slave and the leader of the Congregation, and Gonçalo Cordeiro, who held an *alferes* (second lieutenant) in the Black Regiment as well as being Souza's secretary and right-hand man. This Manuscript also transcribes the compromisso of a subgroup of the Mahi Congregation, the Devotion to the Souls of Purgatory, but it is particularly useful for helping us comprehend the presence of small, self-identifying ethnic groups within the Brotherhood of Santo Elesbão and Santa Efigênia. A second document critical to my analysis was the 1788 compromisso of the Fraternity of Our Lady of the Remedies, which was written by the principals of the Devotion to the Souls. Although constituted by the same people, the two organizations had different objectives and rules. The earlier group, the devotion, focused on the salvation of the souls of deceased brothers, as well as praying for ancestors who had not been converted. The later group, the fraternity, was dedicated to caring for any Mina Africans in the city who were poor, aged, or infirm. It may appear odd at first glance, but the creation of parallel, distinct groupings out of a single constituency was part of a strategy by Francisco Alves de Souza and his allies to orient and articulate the Mahi as a formidable faction within the Brotherhood of Santo Elesbão and Santa Efigênia.

Whatever else the devotion and the fraternity had in common, they both explicitly commingled the formulation of official norms with the informality of daily life. In Brazil, according to Schwartz, both government and society are structured according to "two interlinked systems of organization": metropolitan administration (based on bureaucratic norms), and a "web of primary interpersonal relations" that is not officially recognized.[2] The coexistence of established, institutional rules and informal relationships permeates social calculation and social action in Brazil, creating a universe of possibilities in which official versus unofficial, formal versus informal, impersonal versus personal, and collective versus individual circumstances are unpredictably hybridized.

This final chapter focuses on the informal groups that cohered around ethnic criteria inside the Brotherhood of Santo Elesbão and Santa Efigênia. In particular I am concerned with the kingdoms of the folia, seven of which were allowed (and regulated) by the statutes of the brotherhood. I hope to show how the Mahi reconstructed its identity as an ethnic group within the strictures of a milieu dominated by captivity, but in which new options for social organization and cultural expression were also present—largely (and it would seem paradoxically) through the avenue of Catholic religious activity.

Francisco Alves de Souza's narrative of the Mahi Congregation begins with his arrival from Bahia in Rio de Janeiro in 1748, where he found a number of Mina blacks organized in the Mina Congregation.[3] This congregation had already formalized its separation from the other nations that made up the Brotherhood of Santo Elesbão and Santa Efigênia (Mozambique, Cape Verde, São Tomé), which was still based at the Church of São Domingos. The Mina nation gathered Africans from different ethnic groups, with such names in the documents as Savalu, Mahi, Agonli, Dahomey, and Iano, all of whom spoke what colonial observers called the "general tongue of Mina." At the time, the congregation had as its king Pedro da Costa Mimozo; at the end of his term he was followed by his ally, Clemente Proença, in a highly contested election. Proença's time in office was fractious, as the previous chapter shows, with subgroups increasingly jostling for power within the Mina Congregation.[4]

As Souza told it, the troubles within the congregation began to manifest because the Dahomeans, the most powerful subgroup and hence in control of the leadership, began to abuse their majority position at the expense of other subgroups. There were clashes in which, it was alleged, *ditos picantes* (heated words) were uttered by the Dahomey majority. Scandalized by the affronts and excesses of the Dahomeans, Souza wrote, the Mahi and the other smaller subgroups saw no dignified option other than to abandon the Mina Congregation. In 1762 they created their own Mahi Congregation, and elected Ignacio Gonçalves do Monte as their king.[5] Sometime after that, Monte composed a Termo (a written document) that has regrettably been lost, but references to it were made elsewhere because Monte apparently included the bold declaration that he would serve as leader of the Mahi Congregation until his death. These events are the first substantive indication that the later reigns of the folias were constituted according to ethnic groups organized within the Brotherhood of Santo Elesbão and Santa Efigênia. For a while, at least three smaller subgroups—the Savalu, Agonli, and Iano—remained united within the Mahi Congregation, under its Mahi leader. But at a certain moment, the Savalu and Agonli each created their own reigns. Why the Iano seemed not to do so remains unclear.[6] The so-called *alas* (wings or flanks, actually factions) of the funeral corteges and festive processions mentioned in the compromisso of the Brotherhood of Santo Elesbão and Santa Efigênia were probably composed by these groups, which had organized around their shared devotional and ethnic sensibilities. Of these subgroups, the only one for which I encountered significant information was the Mahi, and it is clear that they had not only their congregation but, within it, the two devotions discussed in chapter 5 (Almas do Purgatório and Our Lady of Remédios).

The complex distribution of new titles as part of the folia, the growth in membership of the brotherhood, and the construction of the Church of Santo Elesbão and Santa Efigênia were contemporary and interrelated occurrences. Just as the creation of a separate board for women was intended to resolve some of the brotherhood's growing pains, the creation of the Imperial State also was an attempt to redistribute participation and prestige to ameliorate conflicts within the brotherhood. In that sense the inclusion of the folia and its titles in the compromisso in 1764 gave formal recognition to the presence of the (or at least seven of the) subgroups, giving each of them the guarantee of an election for their own king. But it would seem that the first election of the folia's emperor and kings took place before ecclesiastical authorities gave their approval to the Imperial State in 1764. The election of the Mahi king in 1762 was most likely an expression of this new configuration of power in the brotherhood, suggesting that other kings would also have been elected at the same time.

Negotiations between the brotherhood and church officials over the content and phrasing of their compromisso were obviously important for arriving at a document that would serve as a point of reference for the future. But as I have argued, many of the particularities of the compromisso were included after the fact—that is, once new needs and problems had already arisen, demanding the implementation of solutions that only later would be written down as a prescriptive set of regulations. The Imperial State offered solutions to many immediate internal conflicts in which different groups sought material and symbolic advantage: roles and titles, space in the church, access to donation funds, the ordering of public processions, and so on. In their increasingly fine segmentation, the reigns accompanied the processes of social organization of Africans in the city of Rio de Janeiro over the years: initially composed of Africans from diverse regions (but excluding Angola), as the brotherhood grew its members articulated and reinforced more restrictive boundaries of identity and incorporation; finally the folia, with its separate kingdoms, embodied the assertion of ethnic difference.

Given that the Dahomeans were prominent enough in the brotherhood for the rest of the subgroups to unite against them, it is reasonable to suspect that they had first held the position of king when there was only one such title available. The other subgroups would have had to dispute the hierarchy of lower ranks (counts, dukes, etc.) among them. With the institution of the Imperial State, the majority Dahomeans would have reserved the privilege to elect the emperor, and the title of king was distributed as a gesture of equivalence among the other subgroups. Unfortunately, little is known about the kings in general, or about how each subgroup might have used the Imperial State differently to communicate an ethnic identity. Perhaps more research will uncover new sources, but at present the only king whose story can begin to be told is the Mahi Congregation's first king, Ignacio Gonçalves do Monte.

THE REIGN OF THE "MINA MAHI"

Monte was elected in 1762 amid praise of his "true Mahi" character, and the Manuscript suggests that he was responsible for not merely inspiring but growing the congregation. The Manuscript also establishes lines of continuity between the Mahi Congregation and its two devotions, and presents Francisco Alves de Souza as Monte's heir as the political, material, and symbolic leader of the group.[7] More specifically, we learn that the two kings who led before Monte had spoken Portuguese with difficulty, and had governed bocalmente—that is, orally—without producing written documentation of their priorities and mechanisms of governance. Monte had written a declaration of his term and a brief outline of regulations for the congregation. But Souza had produced a more complete set of vows and statutes, in a manner that effectively displayed his capacity with the Portuguese language. Souza had been involved with the Mina Congregation since 1748, and by 1762 (when the Mahi Congregation was created) he was obviously a prominent member since he had been chosen as an imediato, or adjunct, of King Monte.[8]

At a date that was not recorded in the Manuscript, Monte fell mortally ill. On his deathbed, he summoned Souza and placed in his hands the leadership of the congregation. This transfer of power was carried out in the presence of witnesses, said *pessoas de crédito* (with reputations for honesty) and considered appropriate company for the spectacle of a king's death.[9] Souza accepted Monte's wishes and served, with the title of substitute, as the congregation's leader until Monte's death on 25 December 1783. The Mahi Manuscript indicates that the passing of Monte opened up a series of conflicts within the Mahi Congregation that persisted until 1788, and probably later.

Unlike many other compromissos or statutes that merely state rules, and thus camouflage the tensions that gave rise to them, the dialogues of the Mahi Manuscript more openly address the concerns and disputes that pervaded the congregation. Of course, we must keep in mind that Souza and Gonçalo Cordeiro—his co-author, secretary, and confidante—might not have applied the strictest standards of objectivity to their presentation of these subjects. The two men were old friends; Souza referred to Cordeiro as "my dear and loyal comrade, to whom I have given the most loyal friendship since infancy."[10] This statement raises immediate questions. When was this infancy? How long was it understood to last, and how and where was it passed (Africa or Bahia)? There is also no mention of time spent in captivity, and whether this separated the two men or how it otherwise affected them. Cordeiro stayed close to Souza during the troubled years after Monte died and the succession to Souza was challenged; he took on other powers as well, being elected secretary of the Devotion of Almas and was involved in initiating the composition of statutes for the Fraternity of Nossa Senhora dos Remédios.

WHO SHOULD HAVE THE KEYS TO THE SAFE?

A critical source of conflict was control of the congregation's coffers. When Monte died, this control passed to his widow. The safe held the king's own donation as well as other contributions toward the expenses associated with the king's responsibilities to the brothers. Unlike the Brotherhood of Santo Elesbão and Santa Efigênia, in which these internal funds derived from contributions from individual brothers according to the obligatory donations whose amounts were specified in the compromisso, gathering funds for the Imperial State and the kingdoms were largely the responsibility of the emperor and the kings themselves. That is why the five chapters dedicated to the folia in the brotherhood's compromisso make clear that those brothers elected to these high positions in the folia should have access to patrimony sufficient to sustain the activities of the offices. In the Mahi Congregation, looking after the safe was the responsibility of the queen; Monte's wife was therefore probably in charge of the safe during the whole twenty years of his royal tenure. When he died, she refused to turn it over to the congregation. The circumstances of that conflict encapsulate the tension between personal and group allegiances when property of both financial and symbolic value was at stake.

Her opponents pointed out that with the king's death, her own term as queen ended, and therefore the safe and its key should be returned to the group. At play in this dispute was not only the safe, although it was the fundamental object of interest; there were other items, including books, a cloth purchased in the store of one Antonio Ramalho Lisboa, and a large African *pano da costa* (left to the congregation in the will of Ignacio da Silva Roza, it was used to cover the table of the church consistory on the days the members paid their donations).[11] For her part, Monte's widow countered that all the source of all those items (and most of the money) was *dinheiro da finta*, or voluntary contributions, during the time of Monte's reign. She argued that since she was the heir of King Monte, she stood to inherit the products of voluntary contributions made to him or in his name.

In the compromisso of the Brotherhood of Santo Elesbão and Santa Efigênia, chapter 5 of the folia section refers in explicit terms only to the king's donation but not to any such obligatory payment from other members, and that is why a donation from a brother was considered *finta*, or voluntary. This case shows the growing centralization of power in the hands of the king (and his queen), but also reveals the absence, from both the larger brotherhood and for that matter the church, of formal mechanisms of control over the congregations or reigns. The informality of norms with respect to the kings' responsibility and accountability provided Monte's widow with the space to maneuver against the congregation who elected him. But she was too smart to merely argue. Soon after Monte's death, Souza removed himself from the congregation for a period of fourteen days, due to his own bout with a disease: *erizipela*.[12] Taking advantage of his absence, the queen convened an assembly of the congregation in the consistory of the Church of Santo Elesbão and Santa Efigênia. Helped, it seems, by a few loyal operatives, she managed to bring others to the reunion from outside the congregation—representatives of the Mina and other nations. The outcome of this meeting was her election as queen of the Mahi Congregation, in substitution of the king. In 1762, she had been crowned because her husband was elected; now, she was elected queen herself with no king alongside.[13]

The diversity of nations present shows that the dispute for succession among the Mahi was of interest to Mina and other sectors of the Brotherhood of Santo Elesbão and Santa Efigênia. The queen apparently counted representatives from various nations among her allies too, not just some of the Mahi. Souza was careful to allege that she had called the meeting under false pretenses, which might have gone far to explain its high attendance: to collect donations for the soul of the fallen king. Once all the brothers were present, she turned the tables and proposed her own election. He noted that many of those present quickly perceived what was happening and distanced themselves from her socially ("fugiram dela no mesmo dia"), although one man unnamed in the sources (a creole from Bahia) assisted her with the plan and ultimately lived with her.[14]

The fact that prominent individuals such as the queen, and Souza, had networks of alliances reaching beyond the Mahi Congregation suggests that members of the brotherhood organized themselves not only in formal groupings (ethnically based reigns) but also in political factions that could cut across the lines of ethnicity or nation. The dispute over the safe reveals that, in this occasion, the Mahi were divided into at least two factions— those supporting the king's widow as queen, and those more aligned with Souza, still serving as director but representing a legitimate and complete change in leadership. Each faction sought support outside the circle of Mahi in the larger brotherhood. The tumult was probably substantial. Although the Manuscript does not record the number of people in attendance at the assembly called by the queen, Souza (author of the Manuscript) did later write that at his own election 200 members of the Mahi Congregation were present, along with people from other nations in the brotherhood.[15]

The Manuscript presents a dialogue between Souza and Cordeiro that depicts Souza as reluctant to assume the promise he made to Monte on the king's deathbed to take over leadership of the congregation. He is shown as wanting to avoid confronting Monte's widow, who is portrayed as an "obstreperous enemy of peace and success" responsible for the earlier schism between the Mahi and the Savalu and Agonli. Despite Cordeiro's pleas, Souza insisted on remaining the director and not pursuing the crown of the king of the congregation. Souza maintained that while he respected Monte's wishes, he also knew that the queen had many supporters in the congregation; and of these, many were involved in "abuses and superstitions." Although this startling accusation is not pursued in the text, it would seem that Souza did not want to confront the queen precisely because he feared the effects of what in context referred to witchcraft. If Souza tended to believe in witchcraft or curses, his own sudden sickness once he became Monte's successor might have given him cause to worry about his fate if he confronted political opponents too directly.[16] But he would have to avoid making too pointed an accusation in this respect. By accusing the queen of witchcraft (or any other "heathen" practices and beliefs), he would in effect be implicating a number of her closest allies as well, and that could invite problems for not only the congregation but the entire brotherhood. Instead, he took the subtle approach of raising the subject in a different way: he declared in the Manuscript that all Mina are God fearing, and claimed it was the Angola who, by insisting on carrying out their primitive pagan practices, led the white community in Rio de Janeiro to think that all *pretos* (Africans) were given over to superstitious, backward nonsense.[17]

As the dialogue proceeds, Souza proposed that the congregation should select another person from within its ranks to serve as king. Cordeiro lamented his friend's demurral, and warned that the queen could draw on her allies to help her take control of the congregation. Significantly, he argued that a woman had never occupied such a lofty position; this confirms the notion that the queen wanted to govern in the place of the king, and not merely at the side of a successor to her husband. Cordeiro went on to explain that women were permitted to hold the office of judge, because of their number within the group and their ability to pay the substantial donation, but that this contained no guarantee that they could ever govern the congregation. Drawing on a story of the origins of the church itself to back up his claim, Cordeiro said that women lack the *robusteza* (robustness) of men for high leadership.[18] Souza countered that Cordeiro may as well dispense with the arguments, because he would not pursue the kingship.

Not sitting idly back, other members of the congregation got involved. Frustrated with both the coronation of the queen and the continued refusals of the director to confront her, a group of brothers calling themselves the Notables (maiores) sent a solicitation to the highest colonial court in Rio de Janeiro, the Tribunal da Relação (High Court), with two petitions: first, that Souza be obliged to assume leadership of the congregation; and second, that the queen return the safe and the other disputed items to the congregation.[19] The court was amenable to the Notables' request, or at least the first part of it. On 9 March 1784, less than three months after Monte's death, a lower official from the court (the meirinho das cadeias) appeared before Souza to notify him of the proceeding initiated by the Notables, and to inform him that a minister of the court had ordered Souza to report to him in person to resolve the matter. Souza then agreed to accept the kingship, which prevented the indignity of his being brought by force to the High Court. The court official also informed Souza that the queen had sent her own solicitation for a hearing, and the matter was pending.

Lest we infer that the Notables were simply admirers of Souza within the congregation, a sort of fan base anxious to see him ensconced in power, a small conflict would soon arise between them and Souza himself that revealed their interests in the matter. But first, Souza affirmed to his loyal friend Cordeiro that he would take the leadership of the congregation; he also stated that he wanted to address the assembled brothers, to discuss the "poor style" and "malice" to which recent events had exposed him.[20] This seems not to have been an allusion to the queen (whom he deeply feared) but to his own supporters, who had grown increasingly strident and even threatening toward him as his reluctance to accept the leadership had persisted. Just before taking power, Souza stunned the Notables—who had brought him into office—by announcing that he accepted his new official responsibilities but intended to refuse the title of king and stay with the less formal charge and title of regente (regent), or associate king. Cordeiro, aware of the Notables' ardent disapproval of this idea, tried to reason with Souza by pointing out that the use of the title of king was a tradition extending to dos primeiros fundadores (the founders of the brotherhood).

Souza countered that he preferred another title, one more consonant with his "profession" (which, regrettably, remains unknown to us). And he made the remarkable argument that the kingly title "perturbs good harmony and devotion." But it emerges from the Manuscript that the Notables were far less interested in Souza the individual than in having a king in front of the congregation. Without a king, the entire hierarchy of royal titles in the folia (princes, counts, dukes, marquis, generals, and so forth) had no basis for existence. The court structure descended from the king as the major title and authority—and not from the queen. Without the king (as the head) and his court (the body), a critical mechanism of social distinction within the congregation and the brotherhood would disappear. The Notables asserted that the whole purpose of the hierarchy of *postos e nomes* (positions and titles) in the court was to "distinguish the large from the small, the greater from the lesser, the exalted nobleman from the lowly mechanic; and to maintain the proper respect between them all." Souza and the Notables were formidable opponents. The crisis was finally resolved with the official extinction of the title "king," which was replaced by "regent," but it was clarified that all the aspects of the king's position would be maintained—including the court. The Notables were satisfied with this compromise since they did not lose, as they put it, "any of the rights and small regal privileges we have enjoyed for so long."[21]

According to the Mahi Congregation's hierarchy, just beneath the regent was his substitute. These two high officials were followed by brothers who held titles or duties; after them came brothers who carried only "names." Finally, at the bottom was the large group of brothers who lacked any of the congregation's formal social distinctions. Titles and duties were, as the terms suggest, rather different. A duty was a function or position that was awarded by election and evaluated according to regulations, such as judge or secretary. A title was an honorary distinction conferred upon individuals deemed worthy by someone holding a superior rank; worthiness was a quality typically measured in personal wealth and prestige. The actual titles used drew from the ranks of European nobility ("como se dá cá na terra dos brancos"), but sometimes added an African element as well. In contrast, duties and names were usually given in the general tongue of Mina "à imitação dos fidalgos de nosso reino de Mahi" (in imitation of the nobles of our Mahi Kingdom).[22] Altogether the combination of titles, duties, names, and languages created an intricate hierarchy, part of which, from around the time of Souza's acceptance of leadership, is reproduced here.[23] Note that the same person could hold several attributes at once; and one person, Boaventura Fernandes Braga (6, 12), held attributes corresponding to two different ranks. Rita Sebastiana was Souza's wife.

NAME	RANK
1. Francisco Alves de Souza	Regente (Regent)
2. Rita Sebastiana	Regenta (Female Regent)
3. João Figueiredo	Vice Regente (Vice Regent)
4. Antônio da Costa Falcão	2° Vice Regente (2nd Vice Regent)
5. Gonçalo Cordeiro	Secretário (Secretary)
6. Boaventura Fernandes Braga	2° Secretário (Secretary)
	4° do Conselho (4th Counsel)
7. Luiz Rodrigues Silva	Procurador (Procurator)
	Aggau (General)
8. José da Silva	Aggau (General)
9. José Antônio dos Santos	1° do Conselho (1st Counsel)
	1° Chave (1st Key)
10. Alexandre de Carvalho	2° do Conselho (2nd Counsel)
	2° Chave (2nd Key)
	Eiçuûm Valûm (Duke)
11. Marçal Soares	3° do Conselho (3rd Counsel)
	3° Chave (4th Key)
	Aleolû Belppôn Lifoto (Duke)
12. Boaventura Fernandes Braga	Chave de Dentro (Inner Key)
	Aeolû Cocoti de Daçâ (Duke)
13. José Luiz	5° do Conselho (5th Counsel)
	Ajacôto Chaul de Za (Marquis)
14. Luiz da Silva	6° do Conselho (6th Counsel)
	Ledô (Count)

In the company of Cordeiro and another brother,[24] Francisco Alves de Souza reported to the consistory of the Church of Santo Elesbão and Santa Efigênia on 13 March 1786 for the ceremony marking his rise to the highest office of the Mahi Congregation. Seeing so many people gathered there, including the Notables, he feigned surprise. His modesty was disingenuous, given his involvement in the intense mediations behind the scenes to arrive at this juncture. As secretary of the congregation Cordeiro went so far as to highlight four of the Notables' names in his account of the occasion, noting respectfully that all were freed men. (Their names appear as seventh, eighth, ninth, and tenth in rank in the list above.) The names of Souza and his wife were registered as Regents in the record book of the Brotherhood of Santo Elesbão and Santa Efigênia, and some forty of the brothers in attendance signed the inscription. Before signing the book himself, Souza delivered some brief remarks on the original motivations for the founding of the congregation.

> From the beginning, this land has brought very many African blacks from the Mina Coast and Angola. But because of the cruelty and inhumanity of some of the men who bought and owned them, when the slaves became wounded or sick or elderly, they could do nothing but lie on the ground naked and unprotected to await a death from hunger and the cold. They had no one to bury them. If the owners refused to call on the Santa Casa da Misericórdia, with its well-known zeal and charity, to collect and bury these unfortunates[,] their cadavers remained exposed and illegitimate. For this reason the blacks themselves entered into a group or corporation with the intention to properly serve their compatriots at such a time. That is, when one of our nation dies, his *parentes* will collect money to bury him properly, and arrange for masses for his soul.[25]

The usual translation for "parentes" would be relatives, but in the context the word means people of the same nation, indicating that burials were under the responsibility of the provenience group. Although inflected with sarcasm in its description of the interment practices of Santa Casa da Misericórdia, in its overall themes Souza's speech was a standard one for the occasion of taking high office in a black lay brotherhood at the time.[26] Souza also was communicating his personal intention to focus attention and resources on the brothers in greatest need. Once in office Souza spent his spare time outlining statutes, not only for the Mahi Congregation but for the two groups about to be created within the congregation—the Devotion to the Almas do Purgatório (1786), and the Fraternity of Our Lady of Remédios (1788). As noted at the beginning of this chapter, the former group was concerned with the souls in particular of deceased Mahi brothers, while the latter hoped to ameliorate the effects of poverty among all Mina in the city of Rio de Janeiro. There is no way to know whether these two groups were Souza's innovation, or whether they had been a vision of King Monte's that Souza was now striving to fulfill. Because the groups were within the umbrella Mahi Congregation, both sets of statutes would refer to its larger organizational structure; they were careful to affirm that the congregation's safe should possess three locks with three different keys, to be distributed among members of the congregation's board (to ensure that only in the presence of all three people could the safe be opened). The current safe, held by the widow, had only one lock and key.

The fate of that safe had still been hanging in the deliberations of the High Court with respect to the petition of the former queen, Monte's widow. The court had taken longer on this problem than on Souza's responsibilities to the congregation. Finally, the Mahi Congregation's representative informed Souza that the court hearings were about to be concluded and that a judgment was expected soon. Several days later the representative appeared again before Souza, this time much distressed. The court in its wisdom had sided with the widow, he reported. She would stay in possession of the safe and the other associated items, and there was no possibility of appeal. Delighted and inspired with her victory, the widow let it be known that she was interested in the position of empress of the Mina Coast, the highest position a woman could attain in the Imperial State of Santo Elesbão. She also made a copy of the High Court judge's verdict and delivered it to the viceroy, alleging that the decision was being disrespected by allies of Souza in the Mahi Congregation who were improperly withholding the delivery to her of donations that had been piling up since Monte's death. This statement suggests that the widow had ambitions to control not only the safe, which ostensibly contained gifts to her husband, but the congregation's new income—and hence its capacity for any financial transactions—as well. She went further, accusing Souza of being the *cabeça de motim* (head of an insurrectionary movement) to foist himself on the majority of the Mahi Congregation, who in fact wanted her as regent. That was a gravely serious accusation, one of the most serious that could be made against someone within not only the Mahi Congregation, or the Brotherhood of Santo Elesbão and Santa Efigênia, but the political imaginary of Portuguese colonial society itself. According to the brotherhood's compromisso, a member accused and found to be guilty of mutiny was immediately subject to a range of disciplinary measures from the board (from public reprimand, to the humiliation of carrying the rock back and forth, to expulsion). The viceroy was sufficiently persuaded by the widow of Souza's malfeasance for him to prohibit Souza from appearing with the rest of his folia during the street processions of both the Church of Santo Elesbão and Santa Efigênia and the Church of Our Lady of Rosário. Souza's absence stunned his supporters and seems to have been a blow unprecedented within any folia in the brotherhood. It effectively prohibited his folia, the Mahi court of the Imperial State of Santo Elesbão, from carrying out the traditional collection of public donations during the processions.

It should be noted that Souza had recently clashed with his superiors on the brotherhood's board precisely on the issue of public donations, or how they were collected. One of his declarations soon after accepting the position of regent of the Mahi Congregation was that the standard practice of collecting donations on the street to the *por toque de tambores* (rhythmic accompaniment of drumming) should be done away with. But this contradicted the compromisso of the brotherhood, which specified that acquiring donations from the public should be carried out in the *estilo antigo* (early style), that is, with the drums—and under the direction of women. Souza's instructions to his folia meant that he was publicly opposing the board of the brotherhood, making him theoretically subject to official reproof.[27] Adding to the complexity of this situation is the ethnic dimension, since the Mahi had originally broken away from the Mina Congregation some twenty years before to get away from what they regarded as the domineering behavior of the Dahomeans, and now, the Dahomeans were still extremely influential in the brotherhood and seem to have been the most formidable faction of support for the widow. Souza's attempts to introduce changes in the Mahi Congregation that went against the norms of the Brotherhood of Santo Elesbão and Santa Efigênia may have been, as he maintained, in the name of a more rigorous Catholic orientation for the congregation. But those attempts, and the responses they received from the brotherhood at large, cannot be analyzed without keeping in mind ethnic identities as one factor.[28]

Even after prohibiting Souza from appearing with his folia, the viceroy expressed a persistent interest in the case. He ordered both Souza and the king of the Brotherhood of Our Lady of Rosário to appear before him to explore the matter further. Souza took the opportunity to ask for pity because of his own *pouquidade* (unimportance) and *inocência* (in this case, lack of familiarity with subtle codes of behavior) instead of punishment for the baseless contrivances of the widow. His self-description was figurative. Souza was certainly a prominent man in his community, he held a prestigious position in the congregation, and we see from the documents that he was intimately aware of his corresponding rights and responsibilities. Some time after this meeting, in the face of the viceroy's continuing skepticism, Cordeiro made a shrewd and unexpected tactical maneuver to get his friend off the hook. He explained that the sentence was invalid because the "congregation is a devotion that all participate in of their own choice, with no obligation, because we have no statutes"—in other words, the group was informal and unrecognized in the eyes of secular or church law, hence not subject to this type of intervention. This elegant argument took advantage of the fact that even though the Mahi Congregation had internally approved the statutes of the Devotion to the Souls (on 31 January 1786), the document had never been sent on to the ecclesiastical authorities. The Mahi Congregation had no official recognition. And the compromisso of the Brotherhood of Santo Elesbão and Santa Efigênia, which provided for the creation of the Imperial State and by extension the Mahi court, was of little help to the viceroy in nailing down Souza's status and obligations in this nuanced conflict.

One notable aspect of social life within the brotherhood that this long dispute helps bring to light is the strength and influence that women could exert within a milieu where power was officially concentrated among men. In the Mahi Manuscript women were described as "vain connivers, disruptors of peace and tranquility" (orgulhosas, amigas de enredos, perturbadoras da paz e do sossego) to be endured as a source of donations. But women brought diverse strategies to bear on the limited space for participation that men allowed them, and could make significant waves. These strategies might involve collective mobilization, or for individual women the playing on men's fear of witchcraft; the widow probably leveraged that against Souza, as well as her own strong personality and ambitions.[29]

In 1788 Souza and his allies decided to complete the statutes for the

Fraternity of Nossa Senhora dos Remédios. This second smaller group drawn from within the Mahi Congregation was dedicated to assisting those poor, sick, and aged Mina blacks who had no system of support beyond wandering the streets begging. Once completed, the statutes were sent directly to Dona Maria I, Queen of Portugal and Brazil, for her approval. This document, like the one drawn up earlier for the Devotion to the Souls, took pains to state that the Mahi Congregation should have a safe requiring three different keys to be opened (to prevent the "inconveniences" brought to the congregation by individual access).[30] But unusually, the statutes also go on to mention the conflict over the present safe, which was still held by Monte's widow. This was done in a careful manner, in language that, if the compromisso were accepted, would get the safe back from the widow once and for all, with royal approval.

Chap. 12 described the safe that Souza and his supporters intend to have. Its three keys would be divided among the congregation's regent, secretary, and procurator. Chap. 13 outlined the conflict with the widow and asked for its resolution through whatever legitimate steps were necessary. The widow had gained unjust control over the congregations' finances, the chapter states, and the situation was the more grievous because she was a woman and hence naturally incapable of fulfilling such a function (one must wonder what the queen of Portugal thought upon reading that). More to the point, chap. 13 argues that Monte's widow had no claim or right to the inheritance of the king of the Mahi Congregation, only to the personal effects of her husband.[31] Given these terms, if the queen approved the statutes of the fraternity, the widow's hold on the safe would be automatically rendered illegitimate and it would have to be returned to the leaders of the congregation, namely Souza and his allies.

The statute emphasizes that stewardship of the safe was an attribute of the congregation's queen, a privilege that Souza as regent wanted to pass on to his wife. But the crisis of succession, unprecedented in twenty years of the Mahi Congregation's existence, focused on the ambiguity of the social regulations of the brotherhood regarding the queen's personal rights and her responsibilities to the congregation independent of the presence of a king. Chap. 13 was also phrased to raise the suspicion that since Monte's widow had used external means to maintain her hold on the safe against the will of the congregation's leadership (and she possessed the only key), the contents of the safe might be at risk. While the safe belonged to the Mahi Congregation, and all the members' donations should be paid into it, each smaller organization associated with the congregation would have its own funds and objects of value which would have been placed there as well. That made the oversight and administration of the safe especially complicated, since different groups would pool their property within it. Thus whatever its other objectives, the creation of the Fraternity of Our Lady of Remedies in 1788 seems to have represented a strategy to increase the number of organizations relying on shared access to the safe, adding weight to the argument that the safe belonged not with Monte's widow but with Souza's wife, the female regent of the Mahi Congregation. As can be verified from the signatures of the authors and directors included at the end of the statutes, the fraternity was led by some of Souza's key allies and was designed to enhance his power in the Mahi Congregation against the widow's supporters. The new fraternity was undoubtedly a response to the plight of Mina blacks who scraped out an existence begging on the streets of Rio de Janeiro, but it was no less a rejoinder to the (equally sophisticated) machinations of the widow and her victory in the High Court two years earlier.

It is unclear whether these statutes, and their built-in appeal for royal intervention, were sent to Lisbon before or after the widow sought out the viceroy in Rio de Janeiro. According to standard procedures at the time, the crown should be the last recourse in any dispute. This conflict had passed through several levels of authority: beginning within the congregation, it was carried to Rio's High Court (by supporters of Souza); then to the viceroy (by the widow and her supporters); and finally to the queen of Portugal and Brazil (again by Souza and his people). The safe was at the heart of the dispute, but much more than a small box of money and cloth was at stake: the safe was the symbol of the social structure, accomplishments, and ambitions of the congregation itself. Souza and Monte's widow, ably assisted by their operatives, were wrangling over control of power within the Mahi Congregation—but also, and more fundamentally, over the nature of that power.[32]

THE STATUTES OF THE DEVOTION TO
THE SOULS OF PURGATORY

The founding statutes for this subgroup of the Mahi Congregation consisted of sixteen chapters. It was written by Souza and Cordeiro, formalized within the Mahi Congregation on 31 January 1786, and transcribed in the Mahi Manuscript.[33] In tone, the rules and regulations for this devotion drew inspiration from the compromisso of the Brotherhood of Santo Elesbão and Santa Efigênia, but there were divergences; these owed largely to how the devotion fit into the larger organizational structure of the congregation and the brotherhood.

According to the brotherhood's compromisso, the election of an emperor was associated with the folia (the Imperial State of Santo Elesbão). It is implied that every new emperor should establish a congregation of some sort that would have its own complete board of officials, although the emperor would still be the dominant authority in political, symbolic, and financial terms for that congregation.[34] The rank of king, one step below emperor, was a position with different priorities; kings were responsible for payment of a substantial donation, but were not obligated to organize a congregation.[35] The five chapters of the compromisso describing the folia and the duties of the royal titles were approved in 1764, but the Mina Congregation dates back at least to 1748 and perhaps even to 1740, the year of the founding of the brotherhood. The statutes thus were written to formally incorporate a preexisting organization within the brotherhood, not to mandate its creation.

The appearance of the statutes of the Devotion to the Souls of Purgatory in 1786 represented a means of institutionally recognizing the Mahi Congregation, similar to the way the Mina Congregation had been. The Mahi Congregation would have its own folia, which over time asserted increasing independence from the Imperial State of Santo Elesbão (including holding street processions at different times). The Mahi Congregation dedicated itself in general terms to "charity for the living and prayers for the souls of the dead" (fazer caridade com os vivos e sufragar as almas dos mortos), but in practice it was more inwardly focused on its ancestors and it ethnic network, whether enslaved or freed. In special cases it would even loan money to an enslaved member for the purchase of freedom, but again only Mahi could hope to take advantage of this resource.

Recall that although the compromisso of the Brotherhood of Santo Elesbão and Santa Efigênia indicated that a king was not required to organize a congregation, it did permit up to seven kings, compared to one emperor for the whole brotherhood. This meant that the man elected king would typically be a prominent member of one of the eight or so component nations (ethnic group or provenience group) within the brotherhood; but internal conflicts were inevitable, since the members of a given nation did not hold identical beliefs and values. Souza, elected the king and later using the title of regent of the Mahi Congregation, was an unusually energetic proponent of Catholic doctrine and ritual. It is instructive to compare the statutes he helped write for the devotion with the compromisso of the brotherhood. The latter document makes no reference to heathen practice or superstitions, but Souza was determined in his statutes to cleanse the improper elements ("tirar o mau estilo," as he put it) he saw in the norms of the brotherhood. The tenor of the dialogue between Souza and Cordeiro exemplifies this preoccupation. Cordeiro suggested that it causes him great suffering to see his parentes still behaving as pagans, resisting Catholicism, and fleeing the salvation that was their proper destiny ("fim para o que fomos nascidos"). Souza responded by praising the wonders they had received from the generous hand ("liberal mão") of God. He stressed that patience was necessary because "from the very birth of the World [these wonders] are slow in arriving," and he affirmed his faith that one day all of them would be Christians.[36]

For Souza, the underlying objective of the devotion, and by extension the larger Mahi Congregation, was the displacement of any hint of paganism and its substitution with Catholicism. Two points need to be made here. First, Souza's deep Christian sensibilities (and his willingness to enshrine them in statutes) likely explain some of the vigorous opposition he faced within the congregation. The fact that the compromisso of the Brotherhood of Santo Elesbão and Santa Efigênia carefully avoid any reference to paganism, primitive practice, or superstition is another indication that the issue was polemical and needed to be negotiated carefully. Second, Souza's overt Christianity sat oddly with his overriding fear of the dark powers of Monte's widow. But again, Souza's particular manner of expressing his opposition to superstitions and witchcraft was not incompatible with believing in their force.

There were other differences between the statutes of this devotion and the compromisso of the brotherhood. For instance, while only in chap. 10 of the statutes of the brotherhood's compromisso are criteria for membership outlined, this subject is addressed early and directly in the statutes of the devotion. Chap. 2 of the devotion's statutes emphasize that only Mahi can serve on the board, while chap. 3 prohibits people from Angola from joining the Mahi Congregation of which the devotion was a subset. These statutes date from 1786, nearly twenty years after the royal request had been received to alter chap. 10 of the brotherhood's compromisso and remove the prohibition of Angola and creoles.[37] The Brotherhood of Santo Elesbão and Santa Efigênia had needed to make the change in their regulations, becoming officially more inclusive, in order to receive approval of their compromisso from the Tribunal of Conscience and Orders and the Portuguese Crown. Despite having no clear documentary evidence, one can assume that the early prohibition against Angola was not merely copied over from the compromisso to the devotion's statutes. Its reappearance in the statutes years afterward suggests that the social exclusivity impossible to maintain at the formal level of the brotherhood had quietly been transferred to the separate congregations which made up the brotherhood (and which did not require royal approval of their statutes). The result was the same in any case, since Angola blacks would still have trouble joining any of the ethnic congregations based at the Church of Santo Elesbão and Santa Efigênia.[38]

Souza was reluctant even to enter in contact with Angolans, claiming that they were incorrigibly mired in heathenism, indecency, and sorcery. At one point he leveled a specific accusation:

> The Angola blacks have the abominable habit of removing the cadavers of their dead kin from the tombs of the Santa Casa da Misericórdia, laying them about the entryways of churches, and serenading them with pagan chants. The Angola go on to exploit the deplorable spectacle of their dead to beg money from passing churchgoers, claiming that the money is needed to provide a proper burial. This is so common in the city that white men accuse all blacks, whether Mina or Angola, of the same offense, and that is why I strive to properly govern and protect my people.[39]

Elsewhere in the Manuscript he repeated the charge, highlighting the Angola blacks' duplicity and sacrilege while adding that an official had ordered them to be apprehended and punished. The discrimination against Angola blacks came to be applied to other African nations from the central-western coast; Souza's secretary Cordeiro admonished brothers for merely "socializing with Benguela people."[40]

Although the writers of the Mahi Manuscript commonly used the words *abuso* (profanity or indecency), *gentilismo* (paganism), and *superstição* (super-stition), they expended much greater effort in detailing the punishments such practices deserved than in actually explaining what those practices were or how they could be recognized. But this was characteristic of texts from the era. The compilation of regulations from Brazilian bishops in the *Constituições Primeiras* also made use of the terms without defining them. Reading these documents, one infers an implicit urging from the authors that there was a broad public consensus or shared common-sense under-standing of what was meant, rendering explanations unnecessary. There was consistency in their usage: the context was always accusatory, and involved circumstances in which ecclesiastical norms had been broken, mocked, or otherwise deviated from.[41] But their persistent ambiguity in the very documents that were intended to provide rules for social behavior left a wide margin for the flexible interpretation and negotiation of individual cases. And it remains unclear, despite the ominous tones, how often such practices were identified and punished.[42] The Inquisition was more vexed by heresy and Judaism than by paganism. Even still, many in Rio de Janeiro in the 1780s would have remembered how Bishop D. Francisco de São Jer-ônimo had mobilized against the New Christians (converted Jews and their descendants) throughout the captaincy.[43] In the first volume of the *Consti-tuições Primeiras*, the discussion of paganism conveys less a call for persecut-ing than for indoctrinating the guilty parties. Souza (who was a devout Catholic, regent of the Mahi Congregation, and de facto leader of its two derivative orders), appears to have treated allegations of paganism among the brothers under him in a way similar to how other authorities in colonial society handled allegations of apostasy among the New Christians in Bra-zil. Expulsion (or excommunication) should be the last recourse, turned to only if the infraction against the church was too severe or if all reasonable efforts to instruct the accused in Christian doctrine should fail.[44]

The compromisso of the Brotherhood of Santo Elesbão and Santa Efi-gênia was written almost fifty years before the statutes of the Devotion to the Souls of Purgatory and included no reference at all to paganism or superstition. That fact, when considered in light of the internal controversies sparked by Souza's espoused efforts to "remove the bad elements" from the devotion in 1786, reinforces the idea that Souza himself, not the brotherhood at large, was responsible for bringing the issue to the forefront. The profile of these "bad elements" emerges from Souza's writings —drums in the public processions, witchcraft and sorcery, consorting with Africans from certain nations (Angola, Benguela), desecration of crypts, and pagan rituals involving dead bodies. One set of practices Souza did not describe, but with which he was likely familiar, were the religious rituals involving music, dance, and animal sacrifice (often called by the general name *calundu*). These were very common in West Africa, especially among the peoples around the Bight of Benin who provided significant numbers of slaves to Brazil, but they have not been adequately explored in the historiography of colonial Brazil.[45] Of the prominent cases known to scholars of such practices in Brazil, few were in Rio de Janeiro. A famous narrative from Nuno Marques Pereira (1625–1733) describes his visit to a large rural property in Minas Gerais, where the singing, drumming, and dancing emanating at a slaves' calundu kept the tired traveler awake all night. An intriguing case of a calundu in Bahia in 1785 involved Africans of different nations—Dahomey, Mahi, and Tapa/Nupe. Police records refer to similar practices in Pernambuco.[46]

That the calundus were a feature of life in Rio de Janeiro can hardly be doubted, and it is suggestive that the (occasional) persecution promoted by civil and religious authorities was internalized within the Mahi Congregation and its derivative groups. The congregation itself took on the obligation to identify such behavior among potential members, and prohibit their membership if found guilty. Chap. 3 of the devotion's statutes describes the procedure: "Everyone who wishes to enter this adjunct or congregation (except blacks from Angola) will be examined by the secretary and the *aggau* [general], who is also the procurator. These officials will verify whether or not the candidates, men or women, are involved with heathen customs, paganism or superstition. Discovering that they are, they will not be received here."[47] Again, what remains unclear is precisely what would be prohibited, and the circumstances under which a brother (potential or active) might be denounced for such behavior.

Recent research into the interactions of the Inquisition with lay brotherhoods has not been of significant help. We see from the records that whatever the Inquisition's concern with specific expressions of heresy or profanity, when dealing with the brotherhoods its accusations tended to be diffuse—so vague even that crimes went undescribed, and the guilty unidentified.[48] These delicate matters were usually resolved among the officials of the brotherhoods. Details of expulsions, if they occurred, were kept secret, and accusations within the brotherhoods were rare (Monte's widow was never accused of such practices, despite the certainty of Souza and Cordeiro). Social and political considerations could increase one's reluctance to accuse a fellow brother of engaging in pagan practices, but the consistency with which indications of guilt were allowed to discreetly disappear also suggests that the brotherhood as a whole preferred to distance itself from the whole subject in its documents. This could be equally true for practitioners, and for those who feared them; Souza's attitude toward the widow of the deceased king reflected his belief in witchcraft, and although he desired to win the case he did not want to risk evoking what he feared might be her full wrath in doing so.

Francisco Alves de Souza publicly challenged witchcraft and pagan ritual in the name of Christian faith, but he did so in part because inwardly he trembled at their power. Souza stood at the intersection of several social experiences, perspectives, and values that influenced his attitude. He was an African, had been a slave, had attained his freedom, and had come to serve the highest position of authority in the Mahi Congregation. Clearly he was among the elite sector of Mina Africans in Rio de Janeiro in the eighteenth century. He possessed personal wealth, was literate in Portuguese (often demurring that he wrote poorly), knew arithmetic, and adorned his speech with biblical citations in Latin. In one of his dialogues with Cordeiro in the Mahi Manuscript, the topic under discussion was geography. Cordeiro asked him to define the concept of a *zona* (zone) in this context, and his answer is impressive: "It is a space on the known terrestrial globe between two parallel circles . . . The globe contains diverse climates, and geographers divide them into five zones or bands, drawn according to their temperature. There are one torrid, two temperate, and two cold or glacial zones."[49] When asked about the conquest of Africa, he offered an expansive response.

Already during the reign of Senhor Dom Afonso V, the most faithful monarch of Portugal, there was commerce along the coasts of Africa in Guinea for ivory and gold . . . The discoverer of these riches was another Portuguese, Senhor Infante Dom Henrique, or Henry the Navigator, third son of the first King João. It was the desire of Dom Henrique to convert the infidels and spread the sacred faith of Catholicism, as well as extend the reach of the Portuguese crown. He was an astute geographer and mathematician, and revealed the ignorance of many other scientists by showing the existence of antipodes on the earth, and also showing that the torrid zone of the globe was inhabited. When he went to Ceuta, Dom Henrique learned from the Moors of a great desert region in Africa they called Caharâ or Sahara, and of people there the Moors called azenegues. Those people, and blacks called Ialof, marked the end of the territory of the Moors and the beginning of a place the Moors called Guinacolo, or in the Portuguese tongue Guinea, whose name comes from its principal city Genna which was famous among traders and craftsmen for its fine gold. It sat just inland from the coast in a part of Africa that was very remote from the kingdoms of Fez and Morocco.[50]

The dialogues provided Souza with an opportunity to demonstrate the scope of his knowledge in a range of subjects. At one point he mentioned that he had a friend who was a helmsman, well acquainted with the waterways of western Africa, and this friend had taught him many details about the Mina Coast; he went on to share a vivid description of the Volta River.[51] Souza showed himself to be familiar with *Ilustração* (Illustration), a Portuguese version of Enlightenment that combines the new European thinking with Portuguese holy fervor. He reflected on his own conversion:

Your Merciful awoke in me the potential of the soul, with the recollection of death, that is the ultimate end we all face. Consider the wisdom of São Basílio, the bishop of Capadocia, who was asked by the gentio philosopher Eubolo for the definition of philosophy. São Basílio replied that its basic principle was the thought of death. Eubolo was so taken with this response that he soon converted to the faith of Jesus Christ our Lord. There is much to learn from the way these few words could affect a heathen, and it is a lesson for me, a miserable sinner that still in my infancy came to know the faith of Your Holiness and am a Christian by the grace of God. And none of the light I now see was revealed to me by my father or my mother.[52]

This excerpt still leaves some doubt about Souza's early life. Both he and Cordeiro stated in the Manuscript that they spent their infancy together, but it is never stated where. Souza's reference to a conversion at such a tender age encourages the interpretation that he and Cordeiro were shipped to Bahia when still quite young, and Souza would have been converted there. Souza arrived in Rio de Janeiro later, in 1748, but there is no hint that Cordeiro arrived with him or even spent much time in Bahia. Nonetheless, we see in Souza's account of his own faith a reflection of the rigor with which the statutes of the Devotion to the Souls of Purgatory speak to enforcing Christian doctrine among the brothers. The statutes are expressly concerned with fostering the spirituality of the devotion's members in positive terms, but there is a steely undertone: disciplinary measures and punishments for those whose commitment was irresolute are included throughout. Chap. 4 determined that all members should be devoted to God, the Virgin Mary, and all the saints, especially the saints associated with their names and guardian angels. The saints of the souls in Purgatory deserved special attention, and masses would be held daily for them with special services held on Monday, the day dedicated to them. For members who could not attend mass—and these would mostly have been slaves, with generally inflexible demands on their time—it was recommended to pray on bended knee before an image of the crucified Christ and recite "six Our-Fathers, six Ave-Marias, with Gloria Patris included for the Souls of Purgatory."[53] Freed slaves were held to another standard. Chap. 10 declares that freed members who were absent "without just motive" from a funeral procession for a deceased brother would have to pay a penalty (euphemistically called a donation) of 120 réis into the safe to compensate their *rebeldia e frouxidão* (insubordination and weakness). Those who could justify their absence from the all-important funeral procession by showing "legitimate cause," such as a commitment related to work, needed to recite "the Our Father and Ave Maria with the Gloria Patris, offered to the sacred passion of God for the soul of our fallen kin." A freed member of the devotion who did accompany the procession to the cemetery needed to offer special prayers to "the Sacred Death and Passion of our Lord, for the soul of the dead" at graveside. In accordance with chap. 14, every member of the devotion, excepting only laborers and the elderly, should fast on the Mondays of Lent, and attend masses. Those who were literate were required to read the nine prayers of São Gregório (Saint Gregory), which were collo-quially called the Novena of Souls, while members unable to read were instructed to recite nine each of Our Fathers, Ave Marias, and Gloria Patris for the souls in Purgatory.

As with the discussion they introduced of paganism and superstition, the statutes of the Devotion to the Souls of Purgatory also depart from the model of the compromisso of the Brotherhood of Santo Elesbão and Santa Efigênia in their detailed focus on Catholic doctrine, practices, and obliga-tions. Even though the Constituições Primeiras had recommended the consis-tent regulation of Catholic doctrine within all levels of the lay brotherhoods, the Brotherhood of Santo Elesbão and Santa Efigênia did not address the subject in their founding documents. So once again Souza's innovation, this time in emphasizing religious instruction, would seem to derive from his own personal preoccupations and initiative. But we must not assume that the absence of explicit ecclesiastical norms from the brotherhood's statutes meant that the brotherhood was trying to ignore them or keep them out. (According to the Ordenações Filipinas, in fact, indoctrination of slaves was the sole responsibility of their owners.) Their appearance in the statutes written by Souza for the devotion raises the possibility that one of the functions of such smaller groups within the brotherhood was precisely to reinforce the ecclesiastical norms, while the brotherhood's compro-misso established the overarching structures of organization and pro-cedure. The absence of norms from any one document must not be given too much weight, since eighteenth-century Rio de Janeiro was a baroque society, with all its spheres of social life pervaded by an intricate profusion of norms. Rather, it is more important to note how the norms were articu-lated, how different norms interacted, and, when broken, how they were reformulated or reinforced.

The Mahi Congregation's statutes do adhere somewhat more closely to the tone of practical regulations characterizing the compromisso of the brotherhood. Chap. 1 determines that the congregation should be led by a regent and vice-regent elected by vote; chap. 2 limits eligibility for those positions to "natives of the Mina Coast and of the kingdom of Mahi." The regent was to work in the best interests of the congregants and meet with the Notables, or the council of prestigious brothers holding bureaucratic positions and royal titles, whenever necessary for the resolution of problems or decisions. The following chapters address other topics, but chap. 10 returns to the regent and the proper veneration he is due from other congregants; his authority included the right to determine how to punish a member who showed disrespect to his position. The guilty member would be "chastised according to the judgment of the regent," who would need to confer with his companion "the female regent, and others who hold positions of authority in the same Congregation." This centralization of decision making among the small group of congregation leaders may have been modeled on similar provisions in the compromisso of the Brotherhood of Santo Elesbão and Santa Efigênia. Chap. 31 of that earlier document had stipulated that the judge, procurator, and treasurer must be treated as "superiors" (although here, unlike in the congregation's statutes, specific punishments were also outlined for disobedience to authority).[54]

The procurator received special attention in the Souza's statutes for the Mahi Congregation. The duties of this position were to stay abreast of any legal proceedings involving the devotion; keep track of the members (especially the old, sick, or poor) and report news of their condition to the regent; visit the sick or dying; and mediate internal disputes. This last function was seen as perhaps the most critical of the position, "because many times, from a small spark a roaring flame is created" (porque muitas vezes, por um pequeno incêndio se levanta uma grande labareda). According to chap. 15, another responsibility of the representative was to look after the four books the congregation was to maintain: one each for the membership registry, for income and expenses, for the statutes, and for lists of masses performed. Keeping accurate records of the masses realized by the congregation was less an expression of spiritual probity than of necessary accounting, since the chaplain contracted by the Brotherhood of Santo Elesbão and Santa Efigênia was paid annually for the number of masses he performed during the year.[55]

Like all lay religious organizations at the time, the Mahi Congregation had an institutional preoccupation with death and the fate of the dead. Its creation of a separate devotion to address the needs of the dead was not without precedent among Brazil's lay brotherhoods; groups similar to its own Devotion to the Souls of Purgatory are to be found within various other brotherhoods. It was unusual, however, in focusing its activity strictly among deceased brothers of the Mahi nation. This ethnic exclusivity promoted comradeship with other congregations, as chap. 5 of the statutes suggests: even if the deceased in question had identified himself or herself principally as a member of a separate brotherhood in the city, and was only secondarily a member of the Mahi Congregation, the Devotion to the Souls of Purgatory within the Mahi Congregation was required to accompany the funeral procession led by the other brotherhood. The regent had the obligation to collect donations within the devotion to pay for masses for the *irmão falecido* (deceased brother).

The subtle distinctions in responsibilities and priorities between the Brotherhood of Santo Elesbão and Santa Efigênia and the Mahi Congregation permit us to observe that the sphere of charity was much more the jurisdiction of the congregation than of the brotherhood. This was true in the contexts of both funerals and freedom. In the former case, the congregation had a privileged place alongside the chaplain, whose various services for the dead were incorporated more clearly and fully into the statutes of the congregation than of the brotherhood. The chaplain was to hear the confession of the sick and dying, give the Holy Sacrament, and assist in the preparation of the will and the distribution of the bequests; he would ready the sinner to "die of the present life," as the *Constituições Primeiras* put it. The congregation was intimately associated with these rituals and services through its statutes, which formally called for them; through the solicitous actions of its officials to assist the chaplain; and through the presence and support of its members.[56]

Members of the Mahi Congregation could, under special conditions, turn to the congregation's coffers for financial help in buying their freedom (completing the *ajuste de sua alforria*). A congregant making use of that service would have to formally accept the obligation to repay the amount borrowed.[57] Although the privilege was not accessible to every member— whether because of intrinsic limits to the congregation's purse, or (also) because it was provided only selectively to members meeting unwritten qualifications—its prominent appearance here and in other congregations within the brotherhood suggests that it was viewed as a special responsibility of the smaller ethnic organizations.

Visiting Brazil in the first half of the nineteenth century, the French artist Debret recorded the following observations of sociability, social differentiation, and the acquisition of freedom among slaves. His depiction corresponds closely with what the eighteenth-century documents imply about social relations within the ethnic reigns of the black lay brotherhoods.

> When two blacks of unequal rank encounter each other on the street during the performance of their errands, the vassal will respectfully salute the sovereign of his caste, kiss his hand, and ask for his blessing. Dedicated to his king, trusting in his superior knowledge, it is to him the subject turns for consultation during difficult circumstances. And the noble slaves, thanks to their lofty position, can obtain from their subjects the means sufficient to buy their freedom. Once freed, the noble blacks will then scrupulously direct all their activity towards the repayment of that sacred debt.[58]

The mention of "noble slaves" with royal titles seems a clear reference to the nobility of the folias. The description of how the nobles bought their freedom with money borrowed from their "subjects" also likely refers to the brotherhoods, since these were the only institutions that commonly engaged in such transactions.[59] If the specificity and emphasis demonstrated by the Mahi Congregation's statutes are any indication, the purchasing of freedom with money borrowed from a pool of contributions was taken extremely seriously and created formidable bonds between the freed slave and the congregation. Among the Mina Africans who gathered at the Church of Santo Elesbão and Santa Efigênia, this special distribution of resources was limited to the tighter network within the provenience group (those they called *parentes*).

The social category of parente was something altogether different from *irmão* (brother). Everyone belonging to the brotherhood was a "brother." Their conception of *parente*, or "kin," is a more fundamental and exclusive quality of identity. Belonging to a lay brotherhood implied the immediate but abstract sense of joining a religious group, in the context of the rules and rituals of a Catholic fraternity of brothers. The collective phrase "brothers by compromisso" was commonly used in all brotherhoods, whether of blacks, *pardos*, or whites, and nicely connotes the formality upon which membership in this religious "family" was predicated. For blacks, and most especially Africans, *parente* could be used in any situation, not only in a religious context. The word suggested social links rooted in shared identities (ethnic or provenience) that were built from the active reconstruction of a common past that had nothing to do with genetic kinship or blood ties. It addressed a social grouping conceived with historical qualities, whose parameters were refined through socioreligious organization in the present. For example, the Devotion to the Alms of Purgatory accepted members from various African nations, but the assertion of its core identity was Mahi, reflected in the regulation that only a Mahi could lead it (and reflected also in the devotion's overarching concern for deceased Mahi). The folia should be understood as, among other things, an expression of ethnic identity that highlighted the brotherhood's diversity. But each flank of the folia was also a mechanism to attract more parentes to the congregation and catalyze their indoctrination; at least that is how the Catholic Church saw the matter. The *Constituições Primeiras* understood the folia to be useful for conversion and squarely within the missionary tradition, and that is why they kept it off their list of "very indecent actions" to be prohibited.[60] This perception was echoed in chap. 13 of the statutes of the Devotion to the Souls of Purgatory, which argued for the creation of a folia because, the writers stated, "experience has shown us" that folias are advantageous for "exercitar os ânimos dos pretos" (raising the spirits of the blacks) and attracting new members.[61] Those statutes also recommend that the folia of the Mahis should march to the Church of the Rosário in a show of support whenever the Brotherhood of the Rosário there elected a Mina king.

> The *folia* of our Mahi nation should proceed to Church of Our Lady of the Rosário on the day of that saint to celebrate when the King who has been chosen there is from the Mina Coast. The Mahi folia will accompany him (but if the King is of any nation but Mina, our folia will not accompany him) to the palace of His Illustrious Excellency the Viceroy of this State; and after the festivities every member of the folia will return to his house in the peaceful and orderly manner such occasions require.[62]

This show of solidarity with the Mina from another brotherhood is not surprising. Indeed the forceful insistence on Mahi primacy in their own congregation (and its associated groups) might lead one to the impression that fraternizing with orders of Africans of other nations would have been viewed as untoward, even deviant behavior.[63] But not only did it undoubtedly occur; in this case it was explicitly encouraged, perhaps to help maintain the bonds of the Mina provenience group across the city. Angola people were the majority in the Brotherhood of the Rosário, and typically dominated its leadership, but Mina were present in considerable numbers (and many of them also belonged to the Brotherhood of Santo Elesbão and Santa Efigênia). Similar to the marriage practices discussed earlier in this book, despite very straight notions of belonging there were intermarriage and intergroup cooperation among different provenience groups, suggesting how social norms were continually reconstructed and reenacted through the testing of their limits.

Documents pertaining to the Mahi Congregation are an especially rich resource for helping us understand the complex relations between social norms and the exercise of power in daily life. The various conflicts that developed within the Brotherhood of Santo Elesbão and Santa Efigênia often led to changes at the formal level of the association and its regulations, but the tensions would persist in new forms and call for new solutions. Women progressively gained more and more space to participate in the brotherhood, but their presence was contested all along the way. Angola won the right to enter the brotherhood through a royal provision, but were consistently excluded both from positions of power and from the quotidian activities of the lay community at the church, which were segmented and organized according to ethnic group. The Mahi Congregation reproduced many of these characteristics of the larger brotherhood, but it also asserted its autonomy—whether in terms of a separate ethnic identity, or in the direct engagement with paganism and superstition implemented by Souza.[64] Even within these smaller organizations, there were disputes of diverse forms; the story of the Mahi Congregation's safe indicates how unpredictable and serious they could become. A look at the statutes of the Fraternity of Nossa Senhora dos Remédios will also show how conflicts within the Mahi Congregation could lead to transformations of the organization and profile of the association itself.

THE RECONSTRUCTION OF IDENTITY

On 4 June 1788, two years after the emergence of the Devotion to the Almas do Purgatório, but still during the period of legal tussling over possession of the Mahi Congregation's safe, Francisco Alves de Souza and a group of elite congregants in his circle completed the statutes for the Fraternity of Our Lady of Remédios. The statutes were promptly sent to Lisbon for approval, which was granted in October by a royal procurator. It is difficult to miss the connection between this new association and the Devotion to the Almas do Purgatório, at least if one looks at the individual brothers' signatures that appear on the statutes (alongside those of Souza; his wife, Rita Sebastiana; and the secretary Gonçalo Cordeiro). Of the nine brothers who helped found the new fraternity, five also held positions of authority in the devotion;[65] and of those five, two had been present at the deathbed of King Monte when leadership was passed to Souza back in December 1783.[66] This continuity is an indication of the unity Souza had managed to maintain among a segment of the Mahi elite throughout the course of the conflict over the safe. (Given the lack of complementary documentation, it is difficult to measure the impact of that conflict over time on the rank-and-file brothers.)

The statutes of the new fraternity insist on strict observance of Catholic doctrine. They recommend that the group enlist the services of a "capelão instruído e de bons costumes" (learned and honorable chaplain), which might also be a subtle acknowledgment of the erratic performance of the chaplain contracted by the Brotherhood of Santo Elesbão and Santa Efigênia. Funds are allocated for the purchase of wine, as well as flour for the holy bread and even "an iron of excellent make" for shaping the consecrated host. Chap. 4 is especially emphatic in its account of how the behavior of members was to be evaluated; it was left to the officials to hear accusations, weigh evidence, and determine the fate of the accused.

> Any person who wishes to join the Fraternity shall agree to an annual contribution of six hundred and forty . . . and will present himself to the Procurator, who will welcome him and enter the membership in the Book of Brothers. However, if the new brother makes it known that he is a black of offensive habits, given to vice or villainy, or to witchcraft and superstitions, the Procurator will report to the Board, who will then decide based on the information about the brother's conduct whether or not to exclude him from the Fraternity.[67]

The fraternity would have its own folia, which, being under Souza's direction, was more explicitly linked to Catholic rituals than was the folia of the Brotherhood of Santo Elesbão and Santa Efigênia. It should participate in the festival of the Rosário, as well as carrying out its own festivities on the day of the Holy Spirit.[68] Still, the basic premise of the fraternity was charity, and its choice of patron saint clearly communicated its priorities. As stated in the petition accompanying the statutes that were sent to Queen Maria I, the fraternity's mission was to improve the health and dignity of the poor Mina Africans in Rio de Janeiro by providing "remedies, nursing, food, and even funeral shrouds." Beyond this, the fraternity would pray for the souls of dead brothers, which was an objective common to all lay religious associations.[69]

When Souza officially took over as Regent of the Mahi Congregation in 1786, he stated before the assembled brothers his own priorities as leader and Catholic: burying the dead and caring for the poor—or, in a word, charity.[70] The two smaller groups within the congregation that Souza helped found undertook charity in distinct ways. As practiced by the Devotion to the Souls of Purgatory, charitable acts were directed inward, to members of the group; but the Fraternity of Our Lady of Remédios would reach out to all the Mina in the city. While the first group focused on souls of the dead, the second looked after the living who were sick or hungry, and even provided shelter to the neediest. And while the devotion assisted its members (primarily the noble ranks of the folia) in buying their freedom, the fraternity used its funds to hire legal mediation when an enslaved member raised a just complaint against his or her master.[71] Over this same period, the number of positions of authority on the board of the Mahi Congregation was clearly increasing, which indicates that the congregation was expanding its membership and its influence among the Mina of the Church of Santo Elesbão and Santa Efigênia. I am not suggesting that the charitable work of the Mahi Congregation was solely responsible for its growing stature (assuming the work was effectively carried out), or even that the types of activities assumed by the devotion and fraternity had not already been occurring in other forms. Rather, there was a shift or reorientation at the very basic level of identity conceptualization and articulation—what might be called the norms of identity construction.[72]

As they narrate the rise of the Mahi Congregation within the Mina Congregation of the Brotherhood of Santo Elesbão and Santa Efigênia, Souza and his secretary, Gonçalo Cordeiro, depicted a winnowing process catalyzed by intergroup conflict. That is, a series of what the Manuscript treats as "us versus them" conflicts involving two sets of antagonists (first the Dahomeans, then the widow and her allies, all of them portrayed as superstitious malcontents) helped produce a particular sense of Mahi identity that Souza and Cordeiro traced all the way back to a purportedly glorious Mahi Kingdom, whose dominion was supposed to have stretched across the whole Mina Coast. The regent and his secretary drew a continuous line between this powerful representation of an African kingdom and themselves, the legitimate and humble heirs of their ancestors, for whose salvation they now prayed to God.

Ultimately, control over the Mahi Congregation, not just in terms of money and procedure but the power to articulate its very identity, was at stake in the dispute between Souza and the widow. The two smaller associations were created, at least in part, to formalize Souza's status as leader. That is why, for example, chap. 3 of the statutes of the Fraternity of Our Lady of Remédios includes the affirmation that the congregation—the larger Mahi Congregation, not merely the fraternity—wished to keep Souza as their regent. And within the statutes of the fraternity were two requests regarding matters of great importance to the congregation as a whole: first, that widow be forced to turn over the safe and other valuable items to the congregation;[73] and second, that the fraternity be exempted from paying taxes on processions and funerals.[74] An exemption granted to a small fraternity could quickly be used as a precedent to argue for similar exemptions, not only for the Mahi Congregation but for all the associations based at the Church of Santo Elesbão and Santa Efigênia.

The Mahi Manuscript was not a passive record of the struggles between Souza and the widow (and their cadres of operatives) for control over the organization and identity of the Mahi Congregation. Rather, it was a tactic in the fray, intended by Souza and Cordeiro to further their cause by recasting the terms of the dispute. Nowhere is that more evident than in the final part of the Manuscript, when the dialogue turns to a description of the Mina Coast provided by Souza at Cordeiro's request.[75]

Both of these men had been taken to Brazil at a very young age from regions located well inland from the Bight of Benin, so they would have had extremely little personal familiarity with the coast. Souza alleged that everything he knew had been told to him by his friend the unnamed helmsman, who had reportedly accrued impressive practical knowledge of the area. But what strikes the reader is that in its historical and social dimensions, Souza's narrative reproduces the perspective of fifteenth-century and sixteenth-century Portuguese writings in which a Christian Mina Coast (anchored by the Mina Castle) was framed in opposition to the heathen kingdom of Benin. At no time did Souza or Cordeiro mention their own African pasts, the slave trade that carried them across the Atlantic, or their experiences in captivity. Rather, Souza dwelled on the conversion of heathens, which was usually carried out in the environs of the Portuguese castle. He then turned to a description of the coast as one travels from the castle to the kingdom of Benin. In general form, his account—replete with references to geographic features, prominent European forts, and native villages—is indistinguishable from those of the scribes who were approving witnesses to a conquest 200 years before.

Souza's depiction of Benin, which again is supposed to derive from the direct observations of his friend the pilot, accentuates the fantastic. Benin was a mysterious territory permeated with rivers, lagoons, and bogs, where ferocious beasts large and small, of types unknown in Brazil, lurked in hiding to attack the unwary. Even the similar bore a touch of the strange: sheep there "grew hair instead of wool." But there were valuable discoveries to be made as well, Souza noted, such as the peppers, cotton, and palm oil that attracted Dutch traders. The kingdom had as its capital a "beautiful and grandiose city," also called Benin, that "é do tamanho de uma légua sem muros, mas está cercada de uma grande cava" (is a league across, encircled not with walls but with a deep trench). Its king, who was called Bâ Benin by the deferential natives, captured untold numbers of people to be traded as slaves "for bracelets and other things."[76] Souza described the natives of Benin as daring and generous, as well as zealously loyal to the king: "para mostrarem que o são fazem em seus corpos umas cicatrizes, ou marcas" (to show their identity and allegiance, they cut scars and marks into their bodies). The natives displayed other elaborate but curious customs. The men could only wear garments given to them by the king, and young women were restricted to the use of clothing given to them from their future husbands, so "não se vê pela rua senão ranchos de homens e mulheres nus" (the street corteges were full of naked men and women). The king appeared in public only once a year, in an enormous festival whose grim centerpiece was the sacrifice of over one hundred slaves ("mais de cem pessoas, todos escravos"). Human sacrifice was an integral part of funerals, as well, and when the funeral was for a king there was an especially *cerimônia bárbara* (barbarous ceremony):

> When a king dies, the nobles of his court, who are called Ômon, slaughter 16 slaves, then carry them to the crypt to be buried along with the king and the king's robes and personal property. Some of these same princes and nobles may also be killed at the gravesite to accompany the corpse of the fallen king, under the notion that they will serve him in the other world. Seven days later yet another sacrifice of slaves who are called Ovem is carried out; there is dancing atop the sepulcher of the king to the throbbing of drums, and celebrations spring up all around the grave, the people exulting in their grief and apparitions. It is said in this place that God, being good and pure by nature, does not require human sacrifice; so they devote their sacrifices to the Devil, to please him, while at the same time they worship their idols.[77]

Souza and Cordeiro were emphatic in denying any similarity between these savage customs and the habits of the Mahi, although such practices were common among all the Yoruba and Fon speakers of the region (including the Mahi). The objective of this second dialogue is to reconstruct the identity of the Mahi within the Christian universe, as a small bright light of Catholicism surrounded by the darkness of the kingdom of Benin and other heathen groups. Profane practices were left out of their discussion of the Mahi, except insofar as the Mahi were shown confronting these offenses with compassion and the word of God.

A more tangible example of this reelaboration of the past is perceptible in the way that the *pano da costa* was put to new use by the Mahi Congregation. The particular cloth in question was probably from the Mina Coast, since it had been offered to the congregation by a brother. It was kept with the congregation's safe not only because of its symbolic connection to a homeland across the Atlantic, but because of the important role accorded it within the proceedings of the congregation: this cloth was used to cover the table in the consistory of the Church of Santo Elesbão and Santa Efigênia on the day each year that brothers approached the table to contribute their annual donation. It was used instead of the customary white lace cloth of Portuguese make.[78] In this context, meaning on the church table, the African cloth represented a new use of the pano da costa in the Christian universe. The pano da costa, and other African objects and memories were brought to the scene to link their lives and social practices with their African past. As the Mahi Manuscript shows, this is the same feeling that made them strongly concerned about registering and telling the history of the Mina Coast, in particular of the Mina Castle, and of conversions and a growing Christian presence there. No one denied that there were ancestors who had never been converted, and lived as heathens; and the souls of these ancestors received prayers for redemption in the Devotion to the Almas do Purgatório, where they assumed would be their heathen and Catholic ancestors and all deceased people.

This Catholic Mahi identity was constructed in opposition to a heathen Benin, where naked people wandered the streets and human life had little value other than to provide bloody sacrifice to idols (Souza's more direct treatment of the theme of human sacrifice in his writing suggests it was more heinous to him than witchcraft—or more containable). In Souza's account of the Mahi, the fight between good and evil, between God and the devil, began in Africa but persisted into the Church of Santo Elesbão and Santa Efigênia, where they were so "scandalized and affronted" by the Dahomeans that the Mahi broke away to form a new congregation. It remains unclear whether the "heated words" of the Dahomeans involved witchcraft, or perhaps accusations of black magic against the Mahi. But with Souza as regent of the Mahi Congregation, the Mahi identity was increasingly refined through the negation of heathen elements in their African past, and the development of a Christianized identity based on redemption and Catholic doctrine in the new setting of Brazil's colonial slave society.

I could find no documents dating after 1788 to provide a hint of how these stories continued to play out. Souza's personal zeal and popularity, as well as his intellectual attributes, probably helped maintain his influence for some time in the Mahi Congregation, and even in the larger Brotherhood of Santo Elesbão and Santa Efigênia. It is curious to note that across Rio de Janeiro, however, the Mina Africans as a group were increasingly associated with witchcraft and boisterous pagan rituals. In 1835, the city's chief of police led a lengthy investigation of several Mina, including one "a quem muitos outros rendem o maior respeito, e que ali vão iniciar-se em princípios religiosos (to whom many others show the greatest deference, and who apparently initiates them in religious principles).[79] Such initiation ceremonies would have been carried out like the early calundus, later called "houses that offer good fortune" (casas de dar fortuna), where it was alleged that the festivities were accompanied by fantastical visions and apparitions. In referring specifically to *visagens* (apparitions), the police record echoes Souza's description, given fifty years earlier, of the death rites performed at the sepulcher of the kings of Benin. Additional period documentation shows that these houses of good fortune in Rio de Janeiro were notorious sites of dancing, chanting, and animal sacrifice, all carried out to the pulsing rhythms of the drums. But this part of the story must be told another day. . . .

POSTSCRIPT

The writing phase of the work involved in transforming my doctoral dissertation into a book was completed in 1997. Much has changed since then. Not only have many exciting new works been published (or others brought to my attention) that contribute much-needed context, nuance, or counterpoint to my arguments in the book, but my own research has continued as well—motivated by the desire to learn more about the Mahi, and inspired by new sources as well as new conversations. I have two goals in this essay: first, to introduce more detail to the book's sketch of the daily life of Mina Africans in the Brotherhood of Santo Elesbão and Santa Efigênia (a subject with increasingly evident links to the history of Africa and the slave trade); and second, to offer some final reflections on what this case tells us about culture and ethnicity.

As the book went to press, I was particularly interested in trying to discover connections between the scenario I had found in Rio de Janeiro and the circumstances in Minas Gerais and Bahia. It was something of a surprise to discover that very few of the studies based in those places dealt in a sustained way with the question of African slave proveniences in the eighteenth century. But drawing from them, and from many of the primary sources on which they were based, I could conclude with some certainty that Minas Gerais was the dominant destination of the slave trade between Brazil and the Bight of Benin in the first half of the eighteenth century. In other words, although the slave trade to Rio and Bahia differed in volume and composition, its primary objective was the same in each city—to feed the gold mines of Minas. And notwithstanding the demographic differences in the trade to Rio and Bahia, I was more struck by the distinct forms of identification of slave proveniences, often with completely different names for the same nations, utilized by the primary sources (and historians) affiliated with each place. Still, the data provided specific insights, such as the fact that between 1700 and 1750 slaves arriving from the Mina Coast represented up to 10 percent of Rio's slave population, while over 30 percent of the slaves in Minas Gerais were Mina.[1]

The eighteenth-century (1737–1800) slave inventories analyzed by Pierre Verger included 140 slaves from the Mina Coast: 121 Jêje, 16 Mina, 1 Lada,[2] 1 Mahi, and 1 Savalu.[3] Such small numbers are suggestive but not statistically meaningful. But in Rio de Janeiro and Minas Gerais, there was more consistency in the designation of slave proveniences. Beyond the Mina category, there were prominent references in the documents in each of these places to Mahi,[4] Savalu,[5] Chamba,[6] and Nagô. In Minas Gerais mention was also occasionally made to Lada and Jaquem slaves;[7] Coura and Cobu were more common there, but less common in Rio de Janeiro.[8] I have not yet been able to identify the slaves called Craberá (possibly the Kabre?) or Fuam.

It should be noted that especially for Rio de Janeiro, the nature of the evidence complicates the conclusion that one group appeared more frequently than another, because certain types of documents foreground particular groups. Wills, manumission records, and marriage records all contain more Coura than Mahi, but in the Mahi Manuscript Mahis are predominant (perhaps predictably) over the Coura. And I want to emphasize the fact that a group bearing the same designation—that is, purportedly of the same "nation"—could assume, in different places and circumstances, different configurations of social and ethnic identity.

The richest vein of evidence I encountered was in the Arquivo da Cúria Metropolitana do Rio de Janeiro (ACMRJ), where I could find new documents, in particular the *Livro de Batismo de Escravos, Freguesia da Sé, 1726–33,* and more than one hundred wills transcribed in the books for registering the burials of deceased people (*Livro de Óbito*). Many Mina were able to buy their freedom and accumulate personal property, which would have been listed in wills. Prominent individuals are relatively easier for the historian to trace this way because the date of their death would have been recorded elsewhere, and indeed the first will I could locate was that of Ignacio

Monte, Souza's predecessor as king of the Mahi Congregation. After that, I began to scour the archives of obituaries, as well as participate with networks of colleagues (especially Sheila de Castro Faria). With time I was able to accumulate over 100 wills of Mina Africans in Rio de Janeiro dating from the eighteenth century. Information about their husbands or wives led to marriage records as another useful source. Working backward from the freed slaves' manumission letters, I could learn about their owners, who were often Mina as well, and whose wills listed their slaves as property. By compiling the names of witnesses, small business partners, and other people who appeared tangentially in the wills, the social universe of these Mina expanded even more; I am presently compiling all of this material into one database.[9]

A Mina would typically identify himself or herself as such on legal documents, where the declaration of provenience was required. Although some of the freed slaves would instead refer to themselves as *pretos forros* (freed blacks), in most cases the presence of complementary documentation permitted me to ascertain whether or not they would otherwise have used the term Mina. Most of the freed Mina were members of a lay brotherhood (or of more than one), such as that of Santo Elesbão and Santa Efigênia, Our Lady of Rosário, São Domingos, or Santo Antônio da Mouraria. Few of these people declared a profession, but among them the principal occupations were barbers, shoemakers, and street venders.

It was perhaps inevitable that my research would lead me to the history of Africa, but I could not have imagined how much I would learn in that area, from both archival material and scholarly exchange, through trips to the United States and Canada between 2000 and 2007. It quickly became obvious that my approach to studying the Mahi should be expanded, because they presented a special opportunity to comprehend the historical connections drawn by a people between an African past and the new milieu of slavery and a colonial slave economy. Recent works that locate Brazil within the African diaspora were a critical part of this process. But I also read carefully the work of Robin Law, which focuses on African coastal kingdoms, and the work of Robert Cornevin on the history of Benin and Togo. Cornevin's intimate knowledge of French colonial Africa brings a distinctive nuance to his writing. If Law helped me understand the Atlantic slave trade based at the Bight of Benin, Cornevin contributed both historical perspective on the Mahi and frameworks for understanding their relations with neighboring peoples of the hinterland in the eighteenth century. In broad terms, the goal of my present research is to follow the Mahi (and the groups often united with them, such as the Cobu and Coura) from Africa to Minas Gerais, exploring the transformations in lifestyle, social practices, and organizational strategies that they underwent in this long journey. I am also interested in how the Mahi, once in Brazil, may have used aspects of that colonial society to their own advantage.

Still, looking closely at the Cobu, Coura, and other groups is important, and not only for their interactions with the Mahi.[10] Their stories provide additional insight into the complex processes of identity construction and identity ascription that occurred as Africans and non-Africans interacted in the New World. Their stories also further highlight the utility of a research perspective based on provenience groups rather than a vaguely defined ethnicity. When a slave self-identified as "Mina-Mahi" or "Mina-Coura," such designations combined the general name of a *nação* (nation) with the more specific name of a *terra* (homeland). These are categories or levels of identity that have nothing inherently to do with some kind of frozen and immutable ethnicity.[11] The allusion to a homeland was meaningful not only in the strict geographical sense, but more fundamentally as a reference to a localized past that was shared with others and which thus could serve as the basis for the construction (or reconstruction) of a group memory and social organization. I perceived from studying the Mahi that there may have been other small groups coexisting within the umbrella Mina provenience group—socializing, collaborating, and struggling with each other in diverse ways, for many reasons, but principally over questions of power and identity. Although colonial documents reinforce the idea that all the Mina spoke the so-called general tongue of Mina, there was a pronounced linguistic diversity among them, and even bilingualism or multilingualism, just as there was among Africans all around the Bight of Benin and its hinterlands.[12] It is increasingly clear that a "Mina identity" in Rio de Janeiro was complex and dynamic, continually absorbing different social aspects (including linguistics) from both Africa and Brazil.

Perhaps the most promising way to get a handle on these large questions is through history at the microlevel. Biographies, to the degree that we can reconstitute them, reveal much about how the affirmation of a nation or homeland intersected with self-determination, sociability, and survival strategies in the complex push and pull of identity construction. Based on ongoing research, I have begun to assemble biographies of several freed Mina slaves; as much as possible, I follow these individuals' social networks to trace the nature of the ties—religious, professional, financial, kinship, or otherwise—that link them to others across the city. I am especially interested in how these people articulated a sense of both nation and homeland, and in what circumstances such identities were expressed. Below I present three of these biographies, spanning three Mina subgroups: Ignacio Monte, king of the Mahi Congregation (Mina-Mahi); his wife, and later widow, Victoria Correa da Conceição (Mina-Coura), and Antônio Luiz Soares (Mina-Cobu).

Earlier literature on these groups is scarce. The first and most detailed account of the Mahi was written in 1920 by French colonial administrator J. A. M. A. R. Bergé. This writer observed that the Mahi territory was a preferred "hunting ground" for the Dahomeans in search of captives. A second important work came from Robert Cornevin, another French colonial administrator, whose Histoire du Dahomey (1962) offers systematic data on the Benin region. Cornevin averred that the Mahi had migrated northward from areas closer to the coast, coming to occupy a mountainous territory north of the kingdom of Dahomey alongside Yoruba speakers who had arrived from the east.[13] The only academic work on the Mahi is a doctoral dissertation that remains unpublished (and that only briefly treats the years before 1770).

None of the Africanist literature I encountered dealt at any length with the Coura or Cobu. Pierre Verger linked the word Courano/Coirano to a lake called Curamo near the city of Lagos (or Onim, in modern Nigeria). Verger transcribed the description of an attack by Dahomeans on the Fort of Ouidah (Ajudá in Portuguese) that ended with the imprisonment of the fort's director, João Basílio, in 1743; the presence of Couranos in the fort is noted, along with the observation that they were "enemies of the King of Dahomey."[14] Another document cited by Verger announced in 1767 that Ouidah was being invaded by "coiranos." Verger implied that the Coura were a coastal people, centered around the lake region, but the lack of corroborating evidence (in his work or elsewhere) casts doubt on this notion. I suspect that the place called the "land of the Coura" by the Coura, or Couranos, lay to the north of the Mahi territory, in modern Benin. And based on African cartography and Brazilian slave trade data, I hypothesize that the region of the Cobu lay even farther to the north.

Documentation from Minas Gerais includes references to the Mahi, Coura, and Cobu by the 1720s, if not earlier.[15] Ignacio Monte and Victoria Correa must have embarked on the Middle Passage after that, probably around 1740. Both were baptized in 1742—Ignacio in Rio de Janeiro and Victoria in Vila Rica, Minas Gerais—in their midtwenties. Antônio Luiz's arrival in Brazil in the hold of a slaver must have been before theirs, however, because he died an elderly man in 1755.

THE "NATIONS" IN THE CONTEXT OF RIO DE JANEIRO

Victoria Correa was approximately twenty-five years old,[16] and the property of Domingos Correa Campos, when she was baptized in the Church of Our Lady of the Conception in Vila Rica, Minas Gerais, on 27 January 1742. Her ceremony was recorded by the vicar Leão Sá, who made a point to comment that the slave "had her face cut, in the style of her land; she was short, and comely of figure."[17] We know nothing about her during the years between that date and 13 December, 1755, when in Rio de Janeiro she bought her freedom from her master at the time, Domingues Rabello de Almeida, for 180,000 réis.[18] Monte's baptism notice was succinct in comparison to Correa's, but priests in Rio who recorded baptisms demonstrated a characteristic taste for brevity. It was observed only that two adult slaves owned by Domingos Gonçalves do Monte, Ignacio Mina and José Mina, were baptized. Serving as Ignacio Monte's godfather was another José, a slave owned by Antônio Gonçalves; and his godmother was Tereza, slave of Domingos Francisco.[19] In 1757, Antônio Gonçalves da Costa (the same person who owned Ignacio's godfather?) paid Domingos Gonçalves do Monte the substantial sum of 350,000 réis to buy Ignacio's freedom.[20] His price was high because Ignacio was a barber and a bleeder, and probably a dentist as well, according to his letter of freedom.[21] I do not know why Costa would have been willing to pay this amount of money to free Ignacio, but I did determine that Antônio Gonçalves da Costa was also a barber.

The marriage of Ignacio Monte and Victoria Correa was announced in the Parish of Candelária in early 1759, and the ceremony itself took place on the 27 February that year, at eight o'clock in the evening.[22] They would spend the next quarter century together, in Rio. Ignacio died on 27 December, 1783. Victoria served as principal executor of his will.[23] Although some of her activities in the ensuing period can be traced through other documents, I have not yet found a will or obituary record under her name.

For some time, Monte had cultivated close relations with members of his extended ethnic group (people he called *patrícios*), first in the Mina Congregation and later in the Mahi Congregation.[24] That would help him rise to prominence in the Church of Santo Elesbão and Santa Efigênia in the early 1760s. In 1762, the brotherhood wrote to Lisbon, requesting permission from the Tribunal of Conscience and Orders to amend their statutes to create a *folia* called the Imperial State of Santo Elesbão (see chapter 5 of this book). Permission was granted in 1764, and the folia began to hold annual elections for an emperor and empress, seven kings and queens, and various dukes, counts, and other ranks. In 1763, soon after Monte had been elected king of the Mahi within the brotherhood (and while the proposed changes to the statutes, including the postulate that emperors and kings should be able to demonstrate the possession of personal patrimony, were being mulled over in Portugal), he sat down to write a will.[25] He named three executors: his wife, Victoria; Francisco do Couto Suzano (a "Mina black" and member of the brotherhood); and José dos Santos Martins (another Mina brother, as well as fellow barber).[26] The will is quite detailed, but given what we may speculate were Monte's ambitions within the brotherhood, it should be interpreted with care. Here, in fact, Ignacio made no mention of Antonio Gonçalves—his godfather and the man who paid for Ignacio's freedom (whether or not this was the same man remains unclear), asserting instead that he bought his own freedom.

The will was written twenty years before Monte's death, and seems not to have been updated, so we cannot know the state of his personal fortunes in 1783.[27] We do have the will of José dos Santos Martins, who died in 1800, to provide a general idea; he had served as one of Monte's three executors. Martins was the owner of no fewer than eleven slaves, valued in total at 934,000 réis, as well as a collection of instruments from his profession.[28] The wills and other personal documents provide insight into how the members of the Brotherhood of Santo Elesbão and Santa Efigênia created diverse networks of connections and relationships. Beyond the formal hierarchies of the brotherhood itself, there were many informal relations between individuals or groups involving loans, or the paying of debt through a mix of money and services. There were trade associations (such as among barbers or greengrocers) and smaller groups organized around particular devotions. The wills of members of the Mahi Congregation clearly reveal that some were creditors, and others borrowers, in transactions internal to the group. Ignacio Monte made many small loans, and engaged in the renegotiation and servicing of debts to others, creating an intricate web of debts, favors, and obligations that were carefully recorded in a small book to which (according to his will) his wife, Victoria, had access.[29] The recording of these transactions helps us perceive how resources flowed back and forth between group members: elite brothers channeled their funds into the congregation by making loans to buy the freedom of brothers, or investing in small businesses, as well as providing small loans or contributions on an individual basis for emergencies (such as sickness).

All this activity took place under the watchful eyes of the leaders of the Brotherhood of Santo Elesbão and Santa Efigênia, who often appeared in the wills of prestigious brothers as executors, witnesses, or editors (most brothers, even the better off, were illiterate). José dos Santos Martins, the successful barber who died in 1800, was an executor of Monte's will and a witness to the will of Luiz Francisco do Couto, a Mina member of the brotherhood and barber who died in 1777. In his will Couto stated that he had been freed upon his master's death saying "I was a slave of João Francisco do Couto, who did me the goodness of liberating me when he died." It is unlikely that Luiz would have been able to save or borrow enough money to pay for his own freedom. When he died, he left behind a long list of debts, most of them to other members of the brotherhood or the Mahi Congregation. These creditors included Rosa da Cruz, wife of Manoel Lobo dos Santos, both of the brotherhood; and Alexandre de Carvalho, Luiz's godson, and Boaventura Fernandes Braga, his godfather, both noted members of the Mahi Congregation.[30]

The Mina population in Rio de Janeiro I studied was a prominent part of the city's African workforce in the eighteenth century. An African with a trade or vocation enjoyed advantages, even if he or she were a slave, that a freed but unemployed African did not. A trade offered sociability and the potential for financial gain, as well as differing degrees of recognition and prestige; influence outside the brotherhood was often reflected by influence within it. I have been able to identify with certainty four barbers and bleeders within the Mahi Congregation: Ignacio Gonçalves do Monte, José dos Santos Martins, Gonçalo Cordeiro, and Luiz Francisoo do Couto. It hardly seems coincidental that all four would sign their names to the statutes that created the Fraternity of Our Lady of Remédios, a devotion dedicated to improving the physical condition of Rio's poor and sick Mina blacks through medicine, botanicals, and other treatments. The barbers may have represented a core power group within the Mahi Congregation, since of these four, two held high positions (Monte was king, and Cordeiro secretary) and Martins was a close ally of Monte (and also served as an executor of Monte's will). These three were also literate.

Merchants were another important professional sector within the brotherhood. The will of Luiz Fagundes, who died in 1751, shows that he had acquired substantial patrimony: two small houses near the Church of São Domingos. Fagundes was also a member of the brotherhood there and asked to be buried at that church. His houses would seem to be a measure of his success as a vendor in the market in front of the part of the city port known at Praia do Peixe.[31] A second Mina entrepreneur in the brotherhood was Antônio Vieira da Costa, who had been baptized in Portugal, in the Parish of São João da Foz in Porto, on his circuitous trajectory to Brazil. Until his death in 1800, he worked at his own stand in the market in front of the part of the city port known as Praia dos Mineiros.[32]

A different activity that could also foster enduring social bonds was military service. We know that Ignacio Monte held the rank of captain in the Regimento de Homens Pretos (Black Men's Regiment), and his old friend and confidante Gonçalo Cordeiro was a *alferes* (second lieutenant) there. Many other members of the brotherhood can be identified as having served in the regiment, which was popularly known as the Henriques Regiment in reference to Henrique Dias (a hero of the seventeenth-century war against the Dutch in Pernambuco). Although it lacked the financial promise of other trades, participating in the regiment brought recognition not only internally but from wider society; it should not appear extraordinary that Monte, who held high rank in the Mahi Congregation, would also attain a position of prominence in the regiment.

THE "LANDS" IN THE CONTEXT OF RIO DE JANEIRO

It was standard procedure of the era to specify provenience in wills, and ex-slaves needed to be able to prove that they had been freed in order to leave a will at all. To satisfy those requirements, former slaves hoping to create a will were often intensely questioned for details on both subjects, even when a manumission letter could be helpfully produced (for instance, it was important for authorities to know whether freedom had been bestowed as a gift or had been purchased). Of the wills I surveyed, nearly every one declared the provenience as "natural of the Mina Coast." Despite their legal formality and the pragmatic lists of possessions, executors, heirs, witnesses, and so forth, wills could display a significantly individualized character because they permitted the inclusion of personal statements or autobiographical information.

Antônio Luiz Soares, who had survived the ownership of multiple masters before gaining his freedom, was a member of the Brotherhood of Santo Elesbão and Santa Efigênia, although he considered the Brotherhood of São Domingos his primary order. He asked to be buried at the Chapel of São Domingos. Still, when he died an old man in 1755, Soares left 3,400 réis toward the construction of the Church of Santo Elesbão and Santa Efigênia, which had broken ground a year before. In his will, the story is told—in awkward but confident prose—of his life, from birth in Africa to freedom in Rio de Janeiro.

> I declare that I was born in a brutish land of heathens as was the Mina Coast . . . I am of the Cobu nation, and left that kingdom from there when the Lord remembered me . . . around seven years, a little more or less, to be sold. I went to the City of Bahia [Salvador], where I was sold to the first master I had in that city, by name Antônio de Bastos Mendes, who instructed me in the Holy Doctrine and wished to have me baptized. So I was baptized at the Church of Nossa Senhora da Conceição da Praia of Salvador. I left to be sold in this City of Rio de Janeiro and was bought by the dead man, in his life called Antônio Soares, who was a foreigner and apothecary who lived with his wife behind the Convent of Nossa Senhora on Carmo Hill. I freed myself from that slavery of the dead man for two hundred and some thousands of réis that were given to the Reverend Father Teodósio de Souza, who was his executor and who passed to me the Manumission Letter for the above-

mentioned price, and everything was done with the approval and consent and goodwill of the woman who was the widow of the above-mentioned dead man.[33]

For his part, Soares had served as the executor of at least two other people's wills; it is worth mentioning them because they help illustrate his wider social circle, which included some elite Mina. One of them was Tereza Gomes da Silva, who died in 1752 and was buried at São Domingos's cemetery in an extravagant funeral.[34] The second executor of Tereza's will, along with Soares, was Antônio Pires dos Santos. One of the founders of the Brotherhood of Santo Elesbão and Santa Efigênia, Santos helped to purchase the land for the brotherhood's church in 1744.[35] And the other will Soares was named to execute was that of Luiz Fagundes, the vender mentioned above. In his will, Fagundes asserted: "I am of the Mina nation, and came from my land to this little America; I was baptized in the city of Bahia, and was the slave of various masters."[36] He supposedly came from Clará, a region unidentified in the transcript or elsewhere. We are left to wonder precisely what "land" it was that he had come from, as well as to puzzle over the balance of African social identities and local relationships that united Fagundes with Soares, Silva, and Santos.

The existence of such connections between individuals is an intriguing fact that raises more questions than it answers. What sorts of relations did prominent Mina such as Antônio Luiz Soares, or Ignacio Monte, maintain with their *parentes* (also called *patrícios*)? How did participation in the brotherhood with other Mina affect one's multiple dimensions of daily life and sociability? Soares died in 1755, while Monte was still a member of the Mina Congregation but before he would be elected king of the Mahi Congregation; at the time, the Brotherhood of Santo Elesbão and Santa Efigênia was based at the Church of São Domingos. Evidence suggests that they knew each other for at least ten years, outside as well as inside the brotherhood. Perhaps Monte, younger and ambitious, spent some time with Soares, whose business acumen and social sensibilities had established him in Rio's community of freed Mina. Monte's will, like Soares's, furnished an autobiographical sketch:

I declare that I am a freed African, born in the Mina Coast. As a slave I was owned by Domingos Gonçalves do Monte, to whom I gave in exchange for my liberty three hundred and fifty thousand reis, as my Manumission Letter states. I declare that I am married to Victoria Correa da Conceição, freed black, and until the writing of this my will we have not had children; nor do I have children with any other woman, when I was single or since I was married. I further declare that my wife is also my blood kin, three steps removed, because she was the daughter of my grandfather [Eseú] Agoa, a renowned king of the heathen on the coast of the Kingdom of May, or Maqui.[37]

Of note here is Monte's reference to his grandfather as a Mahi king, as well as his remark that he and his wife were blood relations. The study of kinship is an especially demanding specialization of anthropology, and it is even more difficult in a historical case with limited data. However, if the kinship of Monte (of Mahi derivation) and Conceição (of Coura derivation) was based on several generations of intermarriage, we can hypothesize that an exchange of women between the Mahi and Coura might not have been uncommon. This would be in accordance with the idea that Mahi and Coura were actually lands that were neighboring or close to one another, whereby the locals had regular interchange (based on war, slaving, marriage, or other activities). At the same time, Monte's allusion to a Mahi Kingdom—similar to Soares's reference to a Cobu Kingdom—deserves particular attention.

The notion that identity was based on the coexistence and interaction of peoples and villages in a given territory conflicts with the practice of centralized political authority and political borders—and with kingship and kingdoms, such as those of Allada, Dahomey, and Hueda.[38] Indeed, the assertion of a longstanding Mahi Kingdom seems not to hold up to historical analysis: the first attempt to unify a Mahi people under the centralized political power of a king seems to have occurred only in the last quarter of the eighteenth century (and it was due largely to the continued pressure from nearby Dahomey). Monte's evocation of a Mahi Kingdom, articulated when he was in Rio de Janeiro, happened before those events and seems more than anything else to be a response to his immediate circumstances. In the Portuguese Catholic tradition, which underlay colonial Brazilian society, so-called African nations had been organizing into brotherhoods and electing their kings and queens since at least the fifteenth century.[39] References to Mahi or Cobu Kingdoms in the wills demonstrate that these Mina Africans were reinterpreting their past according to the terms and modalities they had learned from the Portuguese absolutist worldview. That is, using the term *kingdom* for the Land of the Mahi, or *king* for one's grandfather in Africa, was a translation of the past that recast it in meaningful terms in the present. Without a doubt, the "ethnic" reigns of the folias in the black brotherhoods were important spheres of political reorganization for Africans in captivity, but when they spoke (or wrote) about ethnic reigns, this does not mean they were necessarily organized under kingdoms in Africa—even when they referred to their homelands as kingdoms. It should be noted that Monte himself penned his own will,[40] and the word Agoa was the best way he found to convey the name, or title or position, of his grandfather in Portuguese. Agoa immediately recalls the narrative of the founding of the Mahi as a people, which we know from the work of Cornevin. That author shows that in the seventeenth century, the Bight of Benin and its immediate hinterland were crosscut with migrations; some of these movements of people provided the origins of the kingdom of Dahomey. During these movements, a group under the leadership of a man named Agoua-Guédé was dislocated from the coastal lagoons and pushed northward. The group settled in Ouakin, where members mixed with local peoples as well as with Yoruba-speaking groups arriving from the east (among them was a group that established itself in Dassa, a place cited by the secretary of the Mahi Congregation as the homeland of the notable brother Boaventura Braga).[41] In Portuguese there is a notable phonetic similarity between Monte's Agoa and the historical Agoua.

The unavoidable conclusion from all this is that the name of a *terra* (land or place), and not necessarily the name of an ethnic group, provided the necessary reference around which to construct and reconstruct identities in the new setting of colonial Brazil. In what seems a play of words, geographic location and ethnic group (here again I follow Fredrik Barth's analysis of ethnicity) are not the same thing, yet they interweave and articulate each other in the process of formulating identities. There is little reason to doubt that this was already occurring before the crossing of the Atlantic, due to the frequent migrations within Africa. Certainly it occurred afterward in the reconstruction of identities in the New World—now with reference to a past much more distant in space, if not (also) in time. Such a spatial reference to the past is underscored in the use of such ancestral phrases as "her brutish land," "when I came from my land," and "the god of her land," which run through the colonial documentation I consulted in Rio de Janeiro. But this terminology was also common among native Portuguese speakers of the era, as with the priest who wrote of Victoria Correa da Conceição that she bore facial markings "in the style of her land." Without a substantial ethnic or cultural reference—bolstered by the memories, evocations, and myths of an actual African place where a given people was said to be "from"—ethnic nations could neither consolidate nor perpetuate themselves in the New World.[42] Both references were necessary. When the last generation of Mina Africans died out in Rio, their African nations died out with them.[43]

It should be emphasized that whatever the myriad challenges and transformations experienced by the Mina Africans brought to Brazil as slaves, the documents that some of them left in Rio de Janeiro make clear that they identified themselves and interacted as Dahomeans, or Mahi, Coura, Cobu, or Savalu. Nonetheless, the strong link with their African past should not mislead us into believing that their discourses and social practices in Rio were somehow a direct reproduction of African social organization or territorial politics. Subsets of Mina could claim to come from the kingdom of the Mahi, or the land of the Coura, or of the Cobu, but this manner of defining their proveniences was reshaped into larger nations through a colonial worldview. Certainly some of the places they mentioned—such as Savalu, Dassa, and Za—did exist (and still do); we need to better understand these places, the historical relations between them, and their insertion in the circuitous routes of the slave trade. The important point, however, is that in colonial Brazil, the ethnic identity of these Africans was principally designated according to territoriality, by names that referred to their homelands. All the personal identification documents an African could hope to attain in colonial society—baptism and marriage records, a manumission letter, a will—required a declaration of provenience. The Portuguese word used in that formal context, naturalidade, or birthplace, left no room for ambiguity.

This line of study has ramifications for the concept of African "nations" more broadly. The meanings, markers, and discourses that identified a given nation could not be gathered and passed down, like a bag of valuables, to the later generations of African descendants born in Brazil. Only Africans brought to Brazil could belong to a nation, because the whole premise of the nation—which was an aspect of Portuguese Imperial power —depended on one's place of birth in the colonial universe, not on lineage. At the same time, as we saw with the term *naturalidade*, the colonial concept of "nation" carried the built-in implication that something, some inherent ethnic quality linked to the homeland, could be inherited. But the argument for an unchanging ethnic heritage is complicated, both theoretically and historically, by the emergence of African-descended creoles in Brazil who developed other social practices.

The institutionalized aversion to creoles in the Mahi Congregation (as well as the larger Brotherhood of Santo Elesbão and Santa Efigênia) should be understood in light of the strong links created among Africans who survived both the Middle Passage and the travails of slavery to reconstruct their lives in Brazil. The base of shared identity among the Mahi took on geographical dimensions as well as temporal ones, embodied in the notion of a land known to them but left behind. The two devotions created within the Mahi Congregation were concerned with the well-being of Mina Africans, whether in Africa (the Devotion to the Almas do Purgatório was, among other things, an ancestral cult) or in Rio de Janeiro (the Fraternity of Our Lady of Remédios featured the skills of barbers, bleeders, dentists, and other healers). The Brotherhood of Santo Elesbão and Santa Efigênia recreated some Mina traditions and references, and lost or transformed many others, in the effort to reinforce their own ties of sociability. It is ironic that when the Mina in Rio had children—and they, particularly the Mahi, had few—these children would be part of the very demographic of creoles that the Brotherhood strove to exclude in order to maintain its own identity.

If the blanket identity of the Mina nation was capable of obscuring the identities of its various component groups, it also provided new forms and avenues for those identities to be expressed. The Mahi engaged in reconstructing their African past as part of a dialogic process that involved the expansion of their presence and participation in the brotherhood. The boundaries between past and present could dissolve a bit through the elaboration of the folia—with its Western royalty, solemn rituals, festivals, and ornate processions. The folia represented nothing less than a new dynasty, recasting the indeterminate land of the Mahi as a powerful kingdom and its *gentios* as charitable Christians. This crossing of temporal lines is obvious in the title of the Mahi Congregation's founding document:

Rules or statutes in the form of a dialogue, where are announced the vows
and charitable functions of the Mina blacks and their compatriots in Brazil,
especially in Rio de Janeiro, where they must conduct and organize themselves without the disgraces of heathen superstition; composed by Francisco
Alves de Souza, black, of the kingdom of Mahi, one of the most excellent and
powerful of the Mina Coast.[44]

Taken together, the various documents I encountered in Brazil and
Portugal demonstrate that the Mahi, Coura, Cobu, and other Mina subgroups reinvented earlier forms of sociability—and devised new ones—in
Rio de Janeiro. They developed ties within their groups and across groups,
from the relatively permanent (marriage, religious affiliation) to the relatively mercurial (political factions and strategic alliances, a characteristic of
the Brotherhood of Santo Elesbão and Santa Efigênia's internal dynamics).
The memory of an African past that these groups constructed enabled them
all to be identified as "Mina blacks," as their colonial slave society categorized them, but also as Mahi, or Coura, and so on, when it better suited
their individual and collective needs and interests.

The research that led to my doctoral dissertation, and later this book,
continues today down paths unforeseeable to me a decade ago. It reveals in
increasingly nuanced terms that African "nations" were the result of colonial processes of representation and organization of both places and people; the category drew from ethnic configurations without being themselves actual ethnic groups. While the cultural heritage of a group or
individual is vital to the construction of identities and memories, that
cultural heritage is not frozen in timeless purity but is in a constant state of
adaptation and transformation. Going back and forth between narrower
and wider historical frames (as in this postscript, from individual biogra-
phy to African history) has underscored that the techniques and perspectives of microhistory are fundamental to the comprehension of historical
processes at the macrolevel, while the reverse is also necessarily true.

One of the most promising developments in the study of Atlantic commerce and the African diaspora is the *Trans-Atlantic Slave Trade Database*,
which allows researchers to estimate with unprecedented precision the
number of slaves sent to different parts of the Americas, as well as to
determine the ports used by the ships carrying them.[45] But those data must
be incorporated into studies of colonial documents from the Americas and

the Caribbean, as well as African sources, in order to arrive at a more complete understanding of from where in Africa particular slaves came, and where they actually went in the New World. Only then can work of the sort I have attempted in this book—to analyze sociability, organization, and identity construction among captive and freed Africans—be undertaken with more grace and cohesion. This is beyond the reach of any one historian, and I hope that like-minded scholars will collaborate in research groups across specializations (and national borders) to write what might be called the microhistory of the African diaspora.

The following tables provide general demographic data for the city of Rio de Janeiro and for each parish, based in the collection of *Livros de Batismo de Escravos* housed by the ACMRJ. They show the total of 9,578 records collected (table 14) and the 9,269 records used for further calculations (table 15), according to parish. Until the seventeenth century the city of Rio de Janeiro had only one parish. In 1632 it was subdivided in two parishes: Sé (See) and Candelária. For decades between 1718 and 1750 the only available volumes were those of the Parish of Sé; those of Candelária were lost or destroyed (tables 16 and 17). In 1751 the city was subdivided into four parishes: Sé, Candelária, São José, and Santa Rita. For the decade of 1751–60 I worked on the four urban parishes (tables 18, 19, 20, 21).

Table 14. Total Slave Baptisms in Rio de Janeiro, 1718–1760

PARISHES	BAPTISMS					TOTAL
	With mother	Without mother	Adults	No age given	No information	
Sé, 1718–26	983	21	127	728	50	1,909
Sé, 1744–60	1,381	0	274	9	49	1,713
Sé, 1751–60	893	7	311	13	67	1,291
Candelária, 1751–60	1,648	5	571	15	15	2,254
São José, 1751–60	1,117	3	315	6	49	1,490
Santa Rita, 1751–60	587	11	288	3	32	921
Total	6,609	47	1,886	774	262	9,578

Source: ACMRJ, *Livros de Batismo de Escravos*, Rio de Janeiro: Sé, 1718–26, 1744–60, 1751–90; Candelária, 1745–74; São José, 1751–90; Santa Rita, 1751–60.

Table 15. Total Slave Baptisms Valid for Analysis, 1718–1760

PARISHES	BAPTISMS		TOTAL
	Baptism with mother	Baptism of adults	
Sé (1), 1718–26	983	855	1,838
Sé (2), 1744–60	1,381	283	1,664
Sé (3), 1751–60	893	324	1,217
Candelária, 1751–60	1,648	586	2,234
São José, 1751–60	1,117	321	1,438
Santa Rita, 1751–60	587	291	878
Total	6,609	2,660	9,269

Source: ACMRJ, *Livros de Batismo de Escravos*, Rio de Janeiro: Sé, 1718–26, 1744–60, 1751–90; Candelária, 1745–74; São José, 1751–90; Santa Rita, 1751–60.

Table 16. Slave Baptisms in Sé Parish, Rio de Janeiro, 1718–1726

YEAR	BAPTISMS										TOTAL	
	With mother		Infants		Adults		No age given		No information			
	#	%	#	%	#	%	#	%	#	%	#	%
1718	108	5.7	1	0.1	21	1.1	42	2.2	7	0.4	179	9.4
1719	111	5.8	1	0.1	12	0.6	66	3.5	5	0.3	195	10.2
1720	106	5.6	4	0.2	5	0.3	63	3.3	7	0.4	185	9.7
1721	116	6.1	0	0.0	10	0.5	114	6.0	7	0.4	247	12.9
1722	136	7.1	2	0.1	9	0.5	111	5.8	5	0.3	263	13.8
1723	115	6.0	0	0.0	0	0.0	87	4.6	3	0.2	205	10.7
1724	119	6.2	12	0.6	28	1.5	143	7.5	5	0.3	307	16.1
1725	136	7.1	1	0.1	36	1.9	76	4.0	5	0.3	254	13.3
1726	36	1.9	0	0.0	6	0.3	26	1.4	6	0.3	74	3.9
Total[a]	983	51.5	21	1.1	127	6.7	728	38.1	50	2.6	1,909	100

Source: ACMRJ, *Livro de Batismo de Escravos*, Rio de Janeiro: Sé, 1718–26.
[a]Rounding of decimals accounts for discrepancies in some of the totals.

Table 17. Slave Baptisms in Sé Parish, Rio de Janeiro, 1744–1750

YEAR	BAPTISMS										TOTAL	
	With mother		Infants		Adults		No age given		No information			
	#	%	#	%	#	%	#	%	#	%	#	%
1744	171	10.0	1	0.1	16	0.9	5	0.3	10	0.6	203	11.9
1745	220	12.8	0	0.0	15	0.9	0	0.0	10	0.6	245	14.3
1746	187	10.9	0	0.0	40	2.3	0	0.0	6	0.4	233	13.6
1747	208	12.1	0	0.0	27	1.6	1	0.1	4	0.2	240	14.0
1748	192	11.2	0	0.0	44	2.6	0	0.0	5	0.3	241	14.1
1749	182	10.6	0	0.0	57	3.3	0	0.0	10	0.6	249	14.5
1750	220	12.8	2	0.1	75	4.4	3	0.2	2	0.1	302	17.6
Total[a]	1,380	80.6	3	0.2	274	16.0	9	0.5	47	2.7	1,713	100.0

Source: ACMRJ, *Livro de Batismo de Escravos*, Rio de Janeiro: Sé, 1744–60.
[a]Rounding of decimals accounts for discrepancies in some of the totals.

Table 18. Slave Baptisms in Sé Parish, Rio de Janeiro, 1751–1760

YEAR	BAPTISMS										TOTAL	
	With mother		Infants		Adults		No age given		No infor- mation			
	#	%	#	%	#	%	#	%	#	%	#	%
1751	92	7.1	1	0.1	28	2.2	4	0.3	20	1.5	145	11.2
1752	80	6.2	0	0.0	27	2.1	0	0.0	6	0.5	113	8.8
1753	104	8.1	2	0.2	23	1.8	0	0.0	7	0.5	136	10.5
1754	94	7.3	0	0.0	20	1.5	0	0.0	1	0.1	115	8.9
1755	76	5.9	3	0.2	42	3.3	2	0.2	7	0.5	130	10.1
1756	93	7.2	1	0.1	43	3.3	1	0.1	9	0.7	147	11.4
1757	96	7.4	1	0.1	42	3.3	3	0.2	3	0.2	145	11.2
1758	96	7.4	0	0.0	26	2.0	1	0.1	4	0.3	127	9.8
1759	76	5.9	0	0.0	22	1.7	0	0.0	9	0.7	107	8.3
1760	86	6.7	0	0.0	38	2.9	1	0.1	1	0.1	126	9.8
Total[a]	893	69.2	8	0.6	311	16.0	12	0.9	67	5.2	1,291	100.0

Source: ACMRJ, Livro de Batismo de Escravos, Rio de Janeiro: Sé, 1751–60.
[a]Rounding of decimals accounts for discrepancies in some of the totals.

Table 19. Slave Baptisms in Candelária Parish, Rio de Janeiro, 1751–1760

YEAR	BAPTISMS										TOTAL	
	With mother		Infants		Adults		No age given		No infor- mation			
	#	%	#	%	#	%	#	%	#	%	#	%
1751	194	7.8	0	0.0	60	2.4	1	0.0	2	0.1	257	10.4
1752	181	7.3	0	0.0	57	2.3	0	0.0	1	0.0	239	9.6
1753	214	8.6	0	0.0	52	2.1	3	0.1	2	0.1	271	10.9
1754	182	7.3	1	0.0	56	2.3	2	0.1	1	0.0	242	9.8
1755	177	7.1	2	0.1	64	2.6	4	0.2	2	0.1	249	10.0
1756	165	6.7	0	0.0	71	2.9	1	0.0	2	0.1	239	9.6
1757	179	7.2	0	0.0	60	2.4	3	0.1	3	0.1	245	9.2
1758	161	6.5	2	0.1	83	3.3	1	0.0	1	0.0	248	10.0
1759	195	7.9	0	0.0	68	2.7	0	0.0	1	0.7	107	8.3
1760	175	7.1	0	0.0	49	2.0	2	0.1	0	0.0	226	9.1
Total[a]	1,823	73.5	5	0.2	620	25.0	17	0.7	15	0.6	2,480	100

Source: ACMRJ, *Livro de Batismo de Escravos*, Rio de Janeiro: Candelária, 1751–60.

[a]Rounding of decimals accounts for discrepancies in some of the totals.

Table 20. Slave Baptisms in São José Parish, Rio de Janeiro, 1751–1760

YEAR	BAPTISMS										TOTAL	
	With mother		Infants		Adults		No age given		No information			
	#	%	#	%	#	%	#	%	#	%	#	%
1751	101	6.8	1	0.1	12	0.8	0	0.0	2	0.1	116	7.8
1752	105	7.0	1	0.1	24	1.6	0	0.0	0	0.0	130	8.7
1753	127	8.5	0	0.0	26	1.7	0	0.0	1	0.1	154	10.3
1754	115	7.7	1	0.1	29	1.9	3	0.2	4	0.3	152	10.2
1755	121	8.1	0	0.0	30	2.0	0	0.0	5	0.3	156	10.5
1756	101	6.8	1	0.1	52	3.5	2	0.1	3	0.2	159	10.7
1757	121	8.1	2	0.1	40	2.7	1	0.1	4	0.3	168	11.3
1758	111	7.4	1	0.1	36	2.4	0	0.0	8	0.5	156	10.5
1759	109	7.3	2	0.1	43	2.9	0	0.0	7	0.5	161	10.8
1760	106	7.1	0	0.0	23	1.5	0	0.0	9	0.6	138	9.3
Total[a]	1,117	75.0	9	0.6	315	21.1	6	0.4	43	2.9	1,490	100

Source: ACMRJ, Livro de Batismo de Escravos, Rio de Janeiro: São José, 1751–60.

[a]Rounding of decimals accounts for discrepancies in some of the totals.

Table 21. Slave Baptisms in Santa Rita Parish, Rio de Janeiro, 1751–1760

YEAR	BAPTISMS										TOTAL	
	With mother		Infants		Adults		No age given		No infor-mation			
	#	%	#	%	#	%	#	%	#	%	#	%
1751	0	0.0	0	0.0	0	0.0	0	0.0	0	0.0	0	0.0
1752	25	2.7	0	0.0	17	1.8	0	0.0	5	0.5	47	5.1
1753	72	7.8	1	0.1	36	3.9	0	0.0	7	0.8	116	12.6
1754	60	6.5	1	0.1	28	3.0	1	0.1	3	0.3	93	10.1
1755	73	7.9	5	0.5	37	4.0	0	0.0	7	0.8	122	13.2
1756	78	8.5	3	0.3	41	4.5	2	0.2	2	0.2	126	13.7
1757	63	6.8	0	0.0	25	2.7	0	0.1	4	0.4	92	10.0
1758	73	7.9	1	0.1	41	4.5	0	0.0	1	0.1	116	12.6
1759	64	6.9	0	0.0	31	3.4	0	0.0	0	0.0	95	10.3
1760	79	8.6	0	0.0	32	3.5	0	0.0	3	0.3	114	12.4
Total[a]	587	63.7	11	1.2	288	31.3	3	0.3	32	3.5	921	100.0

Source: ACMRJ, *Livro de Batismo de Escravos, Rio de Janeiro: Santa Rita, 1751–60*.

[a]Rounding of decimals accounts for discrepancies in some of the totals.

INTRODUCTION

1 The classic work on the subject is Bastide, *O Candomblé da Bahia*.

2 Arquivo Nacional, Rio de Janeiro, "Estatutos da Congregação dos Pretos Minas Makii no RJ (1786). Cópia de documento da Biblioteca Nacional (1907)."

3 Biblioteca Nacional, Rio de Janeiro, "Regra ou estatuto por modo de um diálogo onde, se dá notícia das Caridades e Sufragações das Almas que usam os pretos Minas, com seus Nacionais no Estado do Brazil, especialmente no Rio de Janeiro, por onde se hão de regerem e governarem for a de todo o abuzo gentílico e supersticioso; composto por Francisco Alves de Souza preto e natural do Reino de Makim, um dos mais excelentes e potentados daquela oriunda Costa da Mina." (Rules or statutes in the form of a dialogue, where are announced the vows and charitable functions of the Mina blacks and their compatriots in Brazil, especially in Rio de Janeiro, where they must conduct and organize themselves without the disgraces of heathen superstition; composed by Francisco Alves de Souza, black, of the kingdom of Mahi, one of the most excellent and powerful of the Mina Coast.)

4 *Catálogo da Exposição de História do Brasil* (1882). The exhibition, organized by the National Library, was launched in December 1881.

5 The full citation to the manuscript is "Estatutos da Congregação dos Pretos Minas Maki no Rio de Janeiro (1786)," Biblioteca Nacional, Rio de Janeiro. I will refer to it simply as the Mahi Manuscript.

6 The modern definition of the Portuguese word *derrota* is "defeat" or "overthrow," but the word also has a nautical usage, referring to a ship's route, and in this sense *derrota* is a written account of a voyage.

7 C. Ginzburg, "Sinais."

8 The Mahi appear in Brazilian documents as Maki, Makim, Maqui, Maquim, and Maí, and are different from the Mahim, a group located on the coast of modern Nigeria.

9 On the Nagô in Bahia, see Juana Elbein dos Santos, *Os Nagô e a Morte*; and Maria Inês Cortes de Oliveira, "Quem Eram os 'Negros da Guiné'?"

10 The former indicates a union in Brazil of two linguistic and cultural traditions, while the latter is a subgroup of the Jêje. But it should be emphasized that these terms usually derive from the anthropological studies of candomblé, and not from the historiography of slavery.

11 Verger, *Os Orixás*.

12 I. A. Akinjogbin, *Dahomey and Its Neighbours, 1708–1818* (I first encountered this in João José Reis, "Identidade e Diversidade Étnica nas Irmandades Negras no Tempo da Escravidão"); Karl Polanyi, *Dahomey and the Slave Trade*.

13 Verger, *Fluxo e Refluxo do Tráfico de Escravos entre o Golfo do Benin e a Bahia de Todos os Santos dos Séculos XVIII a XIX*, 9, 91. The Mahi are included among the slave groups that were known as "Mina" in Rio de Janeiro and Minas Gerais.

14 On the *língua geral* (general tongue), see Antonio da Costa Peixoto, *Obra Nova de Lingua Geral da Mina*.

15 Jêje is a Bahian nation for African slaves who spoke Gbe languages, at the time usually called Ewe or Eves in Portuguese.

16 Rodrigues, *Os Africanos no Brasil*, 105–6.

17 Translator's note: The most basic definition of *compromisso*, the standard Portuguese term in this context, is "commitment" (whether publicly or privately assumed). Its applicability to the organizing principles of a religious brotherhood resides in the word's formal connotations of structure, ritual, and authority, as well as in a separate spiritual or devotional sensibility. Clearly, the formal statutes or laws that established a brotherhood were understood to derive their meaning from their underlying relationship to Catholic beliefs and hierarchy. An English translation might be "statutes and vows," although the actual term *compromisso* is preferable in the text.

18 The first is in Fitzler and Enes, *A Seção Ultramarina da Biblioteca Nacional*; the second, is "Inventário de códices e de documentos avulsos do A H U referentes ao Rio de Janeiro—316 códices abrangendo milhares de documentos com datas entre 1548 e 183.—326 caixas com 27.446 documentos avulsos de 1614–1853." I thank Francisco Silva Gomes for bringing this to my attention. He is also cited in Mulvey, *The Black Lay Brotherhoods of Colonial Brazil*, 297.

19 The catalog of the Conselho Ultramarino informs: "Compromisso da Irmandade de Nossa Senhora dos Remédios dos homens pretos de Minas (1788), a qual se acha colocada na capela de Santa Efigênia no Rio de Janeiro. 1 vol.; 21 x 35, 5 cm; 26 fls. (13 fls. Br.) enc. Int. veludo: b. est. (16 imagens) A H U / CU-cód.1300." There is an error in the description when it mentions that the request came from "pretos de Minas," that is, blacks from the captaincy of Minas Gerais in Brazil," instead of "pretos da Mina," that is, blacks from the Mina Coast.

20 For the concept of an "ethnic text," I relied on Joutard, "Un Projet Régional de

Recherche sur les Ethnotextes." I have continued to work with Joutard's essay; some of my more recent reflections are included in this book's postscript.

21 For more on this archive, see Antônio Alves Ferreira (Monsenhor) Santos, *Arquidiocese de São Sebastião do Rio de Janeiro*; and José Carlos de Macedo Soares, "Fontes da História da Igreja Católica no Brasil." According to the treaty between the Catholic Church and Portugal, baptismal records were regarded as official documents of the kingdom. For more on this point, see Maria Eulália Lahmeyer Lobo, "Historiografia do Rio de Janeiro," 45.

22 On commemoration and memory, see Pierre Nora, "Entre Mémoire et Histoire." Of course, Nora focused on national sites of memory in France, and never delved into African slavery.

23 The full citation for the Portuguese general regulation promoted by Felipe I is *Código Philipino ou Ordenações e Leis do Reino de Portugal recompiladas por mando D'El Rey D. Philipe I*.

24 *Constituições Primeiras do Arcebispado da Bahia*.

25 By "register" I mean the individual biographical information. A record in the baptism book can refer to one or more registers. Each page of a book contains anywhere from four to twelve records, depending on the size of the script and the size of the folio.

26 Debret, *Viagem Pitoresca e Histórica ao Brasil*, plate 35: "Negras cozinheiras, vendedoras de angu"; Agassiz and Agassiz, *Viagem ao Brasil*, 68.

27 Schwartz, *Segredos Internos*; Russell-Wood, *The Black Man in Slavery and Freedom in Colonial Brazil*; Karasch, *Slave Life in Rio de Janeiro, 1808–1850*; Verger, *Fluxo e Refluxo do Tráfico de Escravos entre o Golfo do Benin e a Bahia de Todos os Santos dos séculos XVIII a XIX*; Reis, *Rebelião Escrava no Brasil*.

28 Scarano, *Devoção e Escravidão*; Boschi, *Os Leigos e o Poder*.

29 According to Braudel, certain structures resist change: "I reflected on the difficulty of breaking certain geographical frames, certain biological realities, certain productivity limits, even this or that spiritual coercion: mental frames can also be long-term prisons." Braudel, *Escritos sobre a História*, 50.

30 Still according to Braudel, "a history with brief, rapid, nervous oscillations. By definition ultra-sensitive, the smallest step throws into alert all its gauges and instruments. As such, it is more passionate and rich in humanity, but more dangerous as well." Braudel, *Escritos sobre a História*, 14.

31 Oliveira, *Identidade, Etnia e Estrutura Social*; Oliveira, "Os Instrumentos de Bordo"; Bartolomé, *Gente de Costumbre y Gente de Razón*, 75–98. See also Yvonne Maggie, *Medo do Feitiço*.

32 Elias, *A Sociedade de Corte*.

33 As Marc Bloch remarks: "The question, in a word, is not to know whether or not Jesus Christ was crucified and came to life again. What we are trying to learn at this point is how there come to be so many people who believe in the Crucifixion and the Resurrection." Bloch, *Introdução à História*, 33.

34 The notion of the "historical situation" was utilized by João Pacheco de Oliveira in his analysis of the insertion of indigenous communities into national society. Oliveira, "O Nosso Governo," 54–59.

35 Fundamental reading on these issues includes Charles Boxer, A Idade de Ouro do Brasil; Schwartz, Burocracia e Sociedade no Brasil Colonial, and Segredos Internos; and Alfredo Bosi, Dialética da Colonização.

36 Boschi, Os Leigos e o Poder, 59–60.

37 I gained some insight on extant sources and bibliographies for this topic from Eulália Lobo, História do Rio de Janeiro, and "Historiografia do Rio de Janeiro."

38 João Lúcio de Azevedo, Épocas de Portugal Económico; Maurício Goulart, A Escravidão Africana no Brasil; Verger, Fluxo e Refluxo; Manolo Garcia Florentino, Em Costas Negras; Luis Felipe Alencastro, "La Traite Négrière et l'Unité Nationale Brésilienne"; Klein, "The Portuguese Trade from Angola in the 18th Century"; Corcino Medeiros dos Santos, O Rio de Janeiro e a Conjuntura Atlântica.

39 Castro, Das Cores do Silêncio.

40 Maurício, Templos Históricos do Rio de Janeiro; Coaracy, Memórias da Cidade do Rio de Janeiro; José de Souza Azevedo Pizarro Araújo, Memórias Históricas do Rio de Janeiro; Moreira de Azevedo, O Rio de Janeiro; Luiz Gonçalves dos Santos, Memórias para Servir à História do Reino do Brasil; Fazenda, Antiqualhas e Memórias do Rio de Janeiro.

41 This is probably the moment to observe that the origin of this book, my doctoral dissertation, was written side by side (and perhaps in some intertextual argument) with two very important dissertations on the history of Rio de Janeiro: Maria Fernanda Bicalho, "A Cidade e o Império: O Rio de Janeiro na Dinâmica Colonial Portuguesa, Séculos XVII e XVIII" (Ph.D. diss., University of São Paulo, 1997); and Nireu Oliveira Cavalcanti, "A Cidade do Rio de Janeiro: As Muralhas, Sua Gente, os Construtores (1710–1810)" (Ph.D. diss., Federal University of Rio de Janeiro, 1998). As both were defended after my own, they could not be included here in the formal sense.

42 Ferrez, O Rio de Janeiro e a Defesa do seu Porto; and As Cidades do Salvador e Rio de Janeiro no Século XVIII; Barreiros, Atlas da Evolução Urbana da Cidade do Rio de Janeiro; Julião, Riscos Iluminados de Figurinhos de Brancos e Negros dos Uzos do Rio de Janeiro e Serro do Frio; two editions of Debret, Viagem Pitoresca e Histórica ao Brasil and O Brasil de Debret (the first is the complete text and images in black and white, and the second contains selected colored plates).

43 Reis, Rebelião Escrava no Brasil.

44 On paleography, see Euripedes Franklin Leal and Ana Regina Berwanger, Noções de Paleografia e Diplomática.

45 When I had finished the dissertation in 1997, I read Jeux d'Échelles, edited by Jacques Revel. This book provided theoretical insights that I had been lacking and, although it is not cited in the body of the text, has shaped subsequent revisions of my work.

1 | FROM ETHIOPIA TO GUINEA

1 This sketch of early visions of Africa is adapted from the documents and commentary in Catherine Coquery-Vidrovitch, A Descoberta da África, 19–28.

2 Vitorino Magalhães Godinho, Ensaios II, 117–26.

3 Both gold and slaves were highly valued merchandise in African trade long before the Portuguese arrived. Claude Meillassoux, Antropologia da Escravidão.

4 The fifteenth parallel crosses the coast of what is today Senegal, and the Equator is close to the island of São Tomé. A. Teixeira Mota, Topónimos de Origem Portuguesa na Costa Ocidental de África.

5 The historiography of slave commerce in Portuguese domains has often referred to Zurara. See João Lúcio de Azevedo, Épocas de Portugal Económico; and Maurício Goulart, A Escravidão Africana no Brasil.

6 Luis Felipe Barreto, Descobrimentos e Renascimento, 67. The initial publication was by J. P. Aillaud. I draw from a commemorative edition published 150 years after Denis located Zurara's manuscript. J. Bragança, "Introdução."

7 Zurara, Crônicas de Guiné, 46–47.

8 The idea of ransom was also linked to the salvation of pagans. The Portuguese would buy Africans supposedly condemned to death, offering them their lives and the possibility of saving their souls. Suess, Paulo, "Introdução Crítica," in A Conquista Espiritual da América Espanhola.

9 Azevedo, Épocas de Portugal Económico, 173.

10 Blake, European Beginnings in West Africa, 1454–1578, 22.

11 Zurara, Crônicas de Guiné, 146.

12 The symbol of the two palms is a recurring motif in letters from the period. João de Barros Asia, 1ª. Década referred to them as marking the transition between the lands of the azenegues (southern moors) and of the negroes. They also are drawn festooning the grounds of Mina Castle in some sixteenth-century maps.

13 Zurara, Crônicas de Guiné, 256.

14 According to him, after 1448 "we dedicated our efforts to merchandizing, not to the responsible safeguarding and defense of our holdings." This phrase was highlighted by Pierre Chaunu in Expansão Européia do Século XIII ao XV, 113n134.

15 This affirmation, and what historians have made of it, takes on new meanings in light of the debates around the formation of the modern Portuguese state. Antônio Manoel Espanha, Às Vésperas do Leviathan, 22–36.

16 Kenneth Baxter Wolf, "The 'Moors' of West Africa and the Beginnings of the Portuguese Slave Trade," 449–69.

17 Suess, A Conquista Espiritual da América Espanhola, 225–32.

18 Luis Felipe Barreto, Descobrimentos e Renascimento, 65–66.

19 According to Bragança, the Romanus Pontifex of Nicholas V reflects a familiarity with the first edition of the Chronicles of Guinea. Bragança, "Do Título desta Crônica." See also Godinho, Ensaios II, 122–26.

20 Zurara, *Crônicas de Guiné*, 86.

21 Ibid., 124.

22 Pina, *Crônicas de Rui de Pina*; Pereira, *Esmeraldo de Situ Orbis*; Barros, *Ásia*, 88–89.

23 Cadamosto, a Venetian merchant, went there on an expedition sponsored by Henry the Navigator. See excerpts from the *Relation de Voyages à la Côte Occidentale d'Afrique* in Coquery-Vidrovitch, *A Descoberta da África*, 70–78.

24 Barros, *Ásia*.

25 Pereira, *Esmeraldo de Situ Orbis*, 68, 64.

26 Ibid., 69–70.

27 Barros, *Ásia*, 88–89. It seems that the next organized efforts to convert natives in the region were not until the second half of the sixteenth century, when missionaries were sent to the kingdom of Warri in present-day Nigeria. J. Cuvelier and L. Jadin, *L'Ancien Congo d'après les Archives Romaines (1518–1640)*, 73.

28 Boxer highlights two factors for this—first, that the program for conversion set up in Kongo was unsubstantial and weakly pursued, and second, that the peoples of Angola were seen by the Portuguese as too poorly developed to benefit from such ministrations. Boxer, *Relações Raciais no Império Colonial Português (1415–1825)*, 27.

29 Pina, *Crônicas de Rui de Pina*, 992.

30 "É porém pelas Doações, e concessões Apostólicas, que os Reis seus antecessors tinham do dito Senhorio, com é legitamente se poderam dele também intitular; mas porque em seus dias, e até no tempo d'El Rei, foi Guiné coisa mui pequena, e de pouca estima para Reis dela se intitularam, o deixaram por ventura de fazer." Pina, *Crônicas de Rui de Pina*, 934.

31 D. Afonso I wrote a letter of obedience to D. Manoel, king of Portugal in 1512. Coquery-Vidrovitch, *A Descoberta da África*, 93–94.

32 Boxer, *Relações Raciais no Império Colonial Português (1415–1825)*, 52.

33 Chaunu, *Expansão Européia do Século XIII ao XV*, 117.

34 Among many publications, Martellus's and Cantino's maps are in Max Justo Guedes and Gerald Lombardi, *Portugal Brazil*. Pages 88–89 for Martellus's; and 147 for Cantino's.

35 Goulart, *A Escravidão Africana no Brasil*, 98–99. For more on the trading of slaves from Kongo through São Tomé, see Jean Nsondé, "Les Relations Culturelles et Commerciales entre Populations de Langue Kongo et Européens du XVIe au XVIIIe Siècle dans la Région du Bas-Congo"; and Isabel de Castro Henriques, "L'Invention Sociale de São Tomé et Principe au XVIe Siècle."

36 Goulart, *A Escravidão Africana no Brasil*, 101. See also Boxer, *A Idade de Ouro do Brasil*, 29.

37 Azevedo, *Épocas de Portugal Económico*, 81.

38 Goulart, *A Escravidão Africana no Brasil*, 115–16.

39 He wrote, "One can say that the importation of black colonial strongbacks [colonos] to Brazil involved members of all the nations." Later, he clarified: "The

best known in Brazil were those from Guinea (in whose number were Berbers, Jalofos, Felupos, and Mandingas), Kongo, Mozambique, and the Mina Coast, whence came the majority of slaves entering Bahia. The easy mode of travel between Mina and Bahia led to the curious fact that slaves there rarely bothered learning Portuguese and communicated with each other in *nagô*." Varnhagen, *História Geral do Brasil*, 1:224.

40 A. J. R. Russell-Wood, "United States Scholarly Contributions to the Historiography of Colonial Brazil."

41 Rodrigues's *Os Africanos no Brasil* was his last work of dozens. He died, in 1906, before completing it; it was not published until 1933.

42 Romero, "O Brasil Social," transcribed in Arthur Ramos, *As Culturas Negras no Novo Mundo*, 185. The same passage with small alterations appears in Romero, *História da Literatura Brasileira*, 199–200.

43 Azevedo, *Épocas do Portugal Económico*, 71.

44 Sérgio Buarque de Holanda, "Prefácio."

45 Goulart, *A Escravidão Africana no Brasil*, 185.

46 This and other maps from the era are in *Mapas Históricos Brasileiros*.

47 In his book about race relations, Boxer considered the Portuguese presence in northwest Africa (from Morocco to Mina) but dwelled on the analysis of Kongo and Angola. Boxer, *Relações Raciais no Império Colonial Português*, 16–43.

48 Mauro, *Le Portugal et l'Atlantique au XVII Siècle (1570–1670)*, 158.

49 There is yet to be written a book about African and Bahian history that comes close to what José Roberto do Amaral Lapa attained with respect to India in *A Bahia e a Carreira da Índia*.

50 There were no studies about Africans from the Mina Coast in the rest of the captaincy of Rio de Janeiro at the time this volume was first published. For further information, see Soares, *Rotas Atlânticas da Diáspora Africana*.

51 This terminology, characteristic of the cultural school of anthropology, will be analyzed more closely in the pages that follow in this chapter. The first edition of this work by Ramos appeared in 1937; that makes it a contemporary of the publications of Herskovits's group, whose style it approximated. According to Ramos, the term Mina referred specifically to the Fanti-Ashanti. See Ramos, *As Culturas Negras no Novo Mundo*, 181, 185–87.

52 Herskovits, *Antropologia Cultural*.

53 Polanyi, *Dahomey and the Slave Trade*, ix.

54 I could not find reliable information as to whether the books were written separately or in conjunction, but the fact that they appeared only two years apart suggests that they were produced more or less contemporaneously.

55 Bastide echoed Nina Rodrigues on the extension of Guinea from Senegal to Orange. Bastide's analysis of the seventeenth century is curiously limited to the assertion that most slaves *deviam ser* (should be) Bantus.

56 I take in account here the explorations and conquests of Henry the Navigator

(1434–60). Dom Afonso V was the first to incorporate the African possessions into the titles of the Portuguese Crown

57 The island of Príncipe was named in 1470 in homage to the young prince and future king Dom João II, who began his rule in 1481.

58 Rodrigues, *Os Africanos no Brasil*, 23.

59 Bastide, *As Religiões Africanas no Brasil*, 68.

2 | COMMERCE WITH THE MINA COAST

1 In Brazil, the subject of Indian labor and religious education has intrigued both historians and anthropologists. See Manuela Carneiro da Cunha, *História dos Índios no Brasil*; and John M. Monteiro, *Negros da Terra*.

2 Coaracy, *O Rio de Janeiro no Século Dezessete*, 33–34, 44.

3 Delgado de Carvalho, *História da Cidade do Rio de Janeiro*, 32.

4 Pizarro alleged that the contracts for slave imports to Brazil, and specifically to the captaincy of Rio de Janeiro, represented the first official Portuguese trans-actions for slaves in Mina Coast. But at one point Pizarro seemed confused about the dates for the 1615 permit and the contract that followed it, suggesting that they emerged on the same date. Araújo, *Memórias Históricas do Rio de Janeiro*, 239.

5 Coaracy observed that this was the beginning of regular stowage service, in the soon-familiar figure of the black Brazilian stevedore. Coaracy, *O Rio de Janeiro no Século Dezessete*, 46.

6 Ibid., 66.

7 According to Mauro, the durations of Atlantic trips from Angola were usually as follows: 35 days to Pernambuco; 40 days to Bahia; 50 days to Rio de Janeiro. Mauro, *Le Portugal et l'Atlantique au XVII siècle (1570–1670)*, 171.

8 On the relations between Rio de Janeiro and Angola, see Boxer, *Salvador de Sá e a Luta pelo Brasil e Angola (1602–1686)*.

9 Coaracy, *O Rio de Janeiro no Século Dezessete*, 72.

10 Boxer, *Salvador de Sá e a Luta pelo Brasil e Angola (1602–1686)*.

11 Schwartz, *Segredos Internos*, 162.

12 *ABN*, vol. XXXIX, doc. 245, 28.

13 The *capitão-mór* was an administrative position beneath, and typically preced-ing, that of governor. As a captaincy grew in population and developed greater political and commercial complexity, a governor would be named; captain-majors usually saw themselves as the most suitable candidates for that role. The position was common in Portuguese territories in Brazil, Angola, and the Atlantic islands.

14 Boxer, *Salvador de Sá e a Luta pelo Brasil e Angola (1602–1686)*, 202.

15 Coaracy, *O Rio de Janeiro no Século Dezessete*, 121.

16 The allegations against him are heated, and perhaps because of this are occa-

sionally oddly worded: "And proof of all this is that when Salvador Correia came to this realm to buy the post of *capitão-mór*, he had nothing of his own, and in fact was owing, as his own mouth confessed, many times 38,000 *cruzados*, and he had more than 300, but in salary less than 200,000 réis, to serve 5 years." *A B N*, vol. XXXIX, doc. 268, 30.

17 Boxer, *Salvador de Sá e a Luta pelo Brasil e Angola (1602–1686)*, 224; Schwartz, *Segredos Internos*, 160.

18 Polanyi, *Dahomey and the Slave Trade*, 101.

19 Ibid., 102.

20 The Dutch stayed at Mina Coast until 1872, when they sold to England the forts still under their power. These included Mina Castle, Fort Komenda (Vredenburg), and Fort Saint Anthony (which the Portuguese had called Axim when they built it in 1515). From that point, the Cape Coast colony acquired boundaries approximating modern Ghana.

21 Coquery-Vidrovitch, *A Descoberta da África*, 130, 111.

22 Fynn, *Asante and Its Neighbours*, 1700–1807.

23 The patacho was a common commercial vessel, if not as large as some. *Documentos Históricos—1681–1686* (collection of documents published by the B N / R J, vol. XXVIII, 1934); António Carreira, *As Companhias Pombalinas de Navegação*, 140.

24 Florentino, *Em Costas Negras*, 123–29.

25 Arquivo Público do Estado da Bahia, 7, 108. Cited by Verger, *Fluxo e Refluxo do Tráfico de Escravos entre o Golfo do Benin e a Bahia de Todos os Santos dos séculos XVIII a XIX*, 39–40.

26 Boxer, *A Idade de Ouro do Brasil*, 68.

27 Palanquim or liteira refers to a sedan chair, typically curtained, suspended on two sturdy poles, the four handles of which slaves would hoist on their shoulders in order to carry the chair through the streets. It was a form of conveyance for the elite in colonial times and can be seen in drawings from the period.

28 *A B N*, vol. XXXIX, doc. 2.815, 295–96.

29 *A B N*, vol. XXXIX, doc. 2.917, annexed doc. 2.913, 302–4.

30 Manolo Florentino suggests that there was regular trade between Mina Coast and Rio de Janeiro early in the eighteenth century, carried out by resident merchants: "To attend the stupendous demand for captives caused by the discoveries at the mines, they used the gold to buy slaves from diverse parts of Africa. They often bought from the Dutch and English, using gold dust or gold bars, outside of official control." He believes this trade no longer existed after 1816. Florentino, *Em Costas Negras*, 123, 86.

31 We know in one case that the wealthy Portuguese trader Francisco Pinheiro operated concerns in both Angola and Mina Coast, but his relations with traders in Rio remains mostly unknown.

32 Statement dated 1 September, 1706. *A B N*, vol. XXXIX, doc. 2.913, 301–2.

33 João António Andreoni, *Cultura e Opulência do Brasil*; Goulart, *A Escravidão Africana no Brasil*, 165; "Diário da Jornada que fez o Exmo. Senhor Dom Pedro desde o Rio de Janeiro até a cidade de São Paulo, e desta até as Minas ano de 1717," *Revista do Serviço do Patrimônio Histórico e Artístico Nacional* no. 3 (1939): 295–316.

34 Goulart, *A Escravidão Africana no Brasil*, 153, 217.

35 This might be explained by the fact that in Angola, group baptisms were commonly performed on slaves in the barracks before boarding ship. See Boxer, *Salvador de Sá e a Luta pelo Brasil e Angola (1602–1686)*.

36 This point receives more detailed argument in Polanyi, *Dahomey and the Slave Trade*, 134.

37 The reference to Akinjogbin and his book *Dahomey and Its Neighbours* is in Reis, "Identidade e Diversidade Étnica nas Irmandades Negras no Tempo de Escravidão," 18.

38 Verger, *Fluxo e Refluxo do Tráfico de Escravos entre o Golfo do Benin e a Bahia de Todos os Santos dos séculos XVIII a XIX*, 669.

39 Schwartz, *Segredos Internos*, 282. After that time, the Portuguese continued to hang on to the fort (often at great cost) until the twentieth century.

40 Polanyi, *Dahomey and the Slave Trade*, 138.

41 "Contrato novo dos direitos que pagam os escravos que entram no Rio de Janeiro, vindos da Costa da Mina e Cabo Verde, arrematado a Jerônimo Lobo Guimarães por tempo de 3 anos e por preço em cada um deles de 50.00 cruzados. Lisboa, 9 de fevereiro de 1725."; icabn, vol. XXXIX, doc. 5.325, 465.

42 "Contrato novo dos direitos dos escravos, que vão para as Minas do Porto do Rio de Janeiro, que se fez no Conselho Ultramarino com Jerônimo Lobo Guimarães, por tempo de três anos e por preço em cada um deles de 36.000 cruzados e 300,000 réis. para a Fazenda. Lisboa, 28 de março de 1725." *ABN*, vol. XXXIX, doc. 5.460, annexed to 5.459, 474.

43 *ABN*, vol. XXXIX, doc. 4.212, 397.

44 "Informação do Provedor da Fazenda em que expõe as suas dúvidas sobre a execução do contrato de Jerônimo Lobo Guimarães e os direitos que deveriam pagar os escravos. Rio de Janeiro, 03.07.1725." *ABN*, vol. XXXIX, doc. 4.941, annexed to 4.932, 441.

45 "Ata da Junta," 5 July 1725. *ABN*, vol. XXXIX, doc. 4.942, 441.

46 The petitions are available in *ABN*, vol. XXXIX, doc. 4.932–4.937, 441.

47 "Termo de fiança em que os referidos comerciantes se responsabilizaram pelo contrato dos direitos dos escravos, se o renunciasse Jerônimo Lobo Guimarães. Rio de Janeiro, 14.07.1725." *ABN*, vol. XXXIX, doc. 4.940, 441; "Representação dos comerciantes da Praça do Rio de Janeiro Domingos Martins Breto, Bernardo Alves da Silva e Domingos Gonçalves Barreiros sobre os direitos dos escravos que exigia o contratador Jerônimo Lobo Guimarães, de 24.07.1725." *ABN*, vol. XXXIX, doc. 4.939, annexed to 4.932, 441.

48 There were two official decrees to that effect, issued on 13 October 1725 and 20 May 1726. *ABN*, vol. XXXIX, docs. 5.326 and 5.327, annexed to 5.324, 465.

49 *ABN*, vol. XXXIX, doc. 5.234, 459.

50 Boxer referred to this tension in "Brazilian Gold and British Traders in the First Half of the Eighteenth Century," 460.

51 *ABN*, vol. XXXI, doc. 347, 29–30.

52 Goulart, *A Escravidão Africana no Brasil*, 168.

53 As Schwartz noted, "The impact of the magistracy on colonial society should be seen not only in terms of its professional attitudes but, also, in light of the lifestyles and personal motivations of the magistrates and of the reactions or initiatives of certain elements of the colonial population." Schwartz, *Burocracia e Sociedade no Brasil Colonial*, 251.

54 Verger, *Fluxo Refluxo do Tráfico de Escravos entre o Golfo do Benin e a Bahia de Todos os Santos dos séculos XVIII a XIX*, 28–29. The designation "Portuguese" here is uncertain; does it include ships from Rio that might not have had contracts or licenses from the Ultramarine Council?

55 "With the discovery of gold in Minas Gerais in the final decade of the seventeenth century, it became urgently necessary to obtain slaves that were stronger and more capable for mining work and mine conditions than the Bantus of Angola and Kongo. This was resolved by reopening the commerce of slaves between Brazilian ports and the 'Mina Coast,' as the Portuguese called Lower Guinea." Boxer, *Relações Raciais no Império Colonial Português (1415–1825)*, 22.

56 He cited a letter from the viceroy to the secretary of state to that effect. Arquivo Público do Estado da Bahia, ordens régias, vol. 34, doc. 15. Russell-Wood, *Fidalgos e Filantropos*, 33.

57 Boxer, *A Idade de Ouro do Brasil*, 68.

58 Manuscript from the Municipal Library of Porto, apud Scarano, *Devoção e Escravidão*, 107.

59 Boxer, "Brazilian Gold and British Traders in the First Half of the Eighteenth Century," 461.

60 In 1734, the kingdom of Dahomey prohibited the transport of gold outside the borders of the dominion. See Fynn, *Asante and Its Neighbours, 1700–1807*, 15.

61 Consultation of the Oversea Council about a petition from Cristóvão Pereira de Abreu, tobacco contractor residing in the city of Rio de Janeiro, 10 March 1716. *ABN*, vol. XXXIX, doc. 3.474, 351. Florentino, compiling a list of slave traders active between 1811 and 1830, includes the name of Joaquim José Pereira de Abreu. Florentino, *Em Costas Negras*, 281.

62 Not all the tobacco was exported. Bahian tobacco was again most prized by colonial consumers, especially when it had been treated with a sweet paste derived from sugar cane.

63 Translator's note: An *arroba* was a unit of weight that is estimated today at 15 kilograms.

64 Verger, *Fluxo e Refluxo do Tráfico de Escravos entre o Golfo do Benin e a Bahia de Todos os Santos dos séculos XVIII a XIX*, 26. Rio's role as a broker of tobacco from elsewhere in Brazil seems to have begun officially in 1695. In 1700, its 7,750 cruzados of

earnings put it in third place on the list of the captaincy's most valuable contracts, behind the royal tenth and whaling. Jean Baptiste Nardi, *O Fumo Brasileiro no Período Colonial*, 286–94.

65 *ABN*, XXXIX, annex 5.975, 513. This information also appears in Fazenda, "Antiqualhas e Memórias do Rio de Janeiro." *RIHGB*, book 89, vol. 143, 490.

66 "Capitania do Rio de Janeiro—correspondência de várias autoridades e avulsos—ano de 1757." *RIHGB*, book 65, pt. 1 (1902), 88. Monsenhor Pizarro dated the opening of the contract at 1757. Araújo (Monsenhor Pizarro), *Memórias Históricas do Rio de Janeiro*, 2:247.

67 The 1794 almanac mentions the arrival of slaves from "Angola, Benguela, and the Mina Coast," but the 1798 edition does not include the Mina Coast as a site of provenience for slave imports into the city. Nunes, "Almanaque histórico da cidade de S. Sebastião do Rio de Janeiro, 1799" *RIHGB*, vol. 267 , 1965: 93–214.

68 "Sempre é preciso e justo que V.M. faça contribuição annual pelos mesmos 4 anos para a edificação da nova Sé, principalmente desta, cujos dízimos cobra a fazenda real; e atendendo à conjuntura presente em que tem a Real fazenda tantas despesas, se me representa que será boa e suficiente a aplicação de 30.000 cruzados nos ditos 4 anos. Para que as rendas atuais de V.M. não recebem desta contribuição prejuízo algum, basta que V.M. conceda licença para os contratadores de tabaco desta cidade poderem tirar da Bahia mais 700 arrobas de tabaco de fumo, além das que pelo contrato tiram, porque esta licença importará mais que aquela contribuição e será muito conveniente e justa, porque o tabaco, que tiram por contrato, não basta para o gasto que tem na cidade e está muitos meses o estanco sem ele com grande prejuízo dos brancos e maior parte dos pretos, que no fumo do tabaco se sustentam e vivem." Letter dated 3 February 1709. *ABN*, vol. XXXIX, doc. 3238, annexed to 3.236, 326–27.

69 The tobacco contract in the city of Rio de Janeiro during this period allotted 1 percent of profits for *obras pias*, or church-run charities. Nardi, *O Fumo Brasileiro no Período Colonial*, 290.

70 Workers involved in the tobacco contract were divided into three categories: slaves, soldiers, and laborers. Most were paid by the day. Nardi, *O Fumo Brasileiro no Período Colonial*, 296–98.

71 There were other brotherhoods composed of Mina blacks in the churches of São Domingos and Our Lady of the Rosário, but very little information has been found about them. I will return to them in chapter 4.

72 Silveira, "Conferência," 4 (photocopy); Verger, *Fluxo e Refluxo do Tráfico de Escravos entre o Golfo do Benin e a Bahia de Todos os Santos dos séculos XVIII a XIX*, 191.

73 On 12 January 1752, the High Court judge João Eliseu de Souza began an inquiry commanded by royal decree into the connections between Teodósio Rodrigues and João Dias Cunha, both administrators of tobacco, and the

viceroy Conde de Athouguia, who was accused of having undisclosed personal interests in the tobacco trade. Through the mediation of Teodósio, Conde de Athouguia received presents from the king of Dahomey. *ABN*, vol. XXXI, doc. 730, annexed to doc. 729, 57; doc. 794, 60.

74 Campos, *Procissões Tradicionais da Bahia*, 78.
75 At an unknown later date the other two brotherhoods, Menino Jesus and Santo Antônio of the Moors, also constructed chapels.
76 Maurício, *Templos Históricos do Rio de Janeiro*.
77 Polanyi, *Dahomey and the Slave Trade*, 107.
78 Some of them also spoke Yoruba.

3 | AFRICAN "NATIONS" AND PROVENIENCE GROUPS

1 Dating from the twelfth century, when it called for a common authority for religious and military orders, the *Padroado* was conceded to the Order of Christ in the papal bull *Inter Coetera* (1456). Leadership of the Order passed to the king of Portugal, rather than a religious official, starting with the reign of D. Manoel (1469–1521), which established a link between ecclesiastical and temporal powers. In 1522, King João III became the head of both the Order of Christ and the church administration in Portugal; when he attained the leadership of the religious orders thirty years later, the consolidation of religious and civil power in the Portuguese throne was effectively complete. The crown's dual functions were especially apparent in the colonies and occupations. After 1822, the *Padroado* continued nominally in the person of the emperor of Brazil. It was abolished in 1890 with the proclamation of the republic. For more details, see Graça Salgado, *Fiscais e Meirinhos*, 113–21.
2 Depending on many circumstantial factors, more or less information might have been recorded. Sometimes the entry for an adult slave includes a description of the slave's religious character and doctrinal preparedness for the event.
3 I recall here what Schwartz called "metropolitan administration" versus "webs of primary interpersonal relations." Schwartz, *Burocracia e Sociedade no Brasil Colonial*, xi–xii.
4 I am aware of the argument that the Portuguese state perceived Brazil as a complete whole, while the perspective from the Brazilian colony of itself was one of fragmentation in which all manner of connections had to be imagined and created. For another look at this idea, see Afonso Carlos Marques dos Santos, *No Rascunho da Nação*, 23.
5 In 1707, through the efforts of the archbishop of Bahia, a synod of the archdiocese was convened with the goal of adapting the determinations of the Council of Trent to Brazil. The meeting was downgraded to a synod of the diocese when so many bishops failed to turn out, including the bishop from the Diocese of Rio de Janeiro. The results of this meeting were compiled in the

Constituições Primeiras do Arcebispado da Bahia, a work subsequently used to regulate ecclesiastical proceedings in the colony.

6 This point is also raised by Sheila Siqueira de Castro Faria, "A Colônia em Movimento," 283–339.

7 Variations in the form of taking down information seem rarely to have bothered church authorities. Only once (in the ACMRJ, *Livro de Batismo de Escravos, Freguesia da Sé*, 1718–26) did I see a written reprimand; it was placed alongside a record of a group baptism in which the individual registers were jumbled and difficult to interpret.

8 According to Schwartz in Bahia, a varied terminology was used to identify children older than infants but younger than adults: *cria de peito* (still breastfeeding); *cria de pé* (already walks); *menino/menina* (until around age two); *moleque/moleca* (until age fourteen); *moleque grande* (until age twenty); and *rapaz/rapariga* (undetermined age, depending on appearance). Schwartz, *Segredos Internos*, 288. In the baptism records from Rio de Janeiro, almost all children were identified by reference to the mother, and called *inocente*. This makes it essentially impossible to determine the age of a given child, although most were between newborn and seven. In Sé Parish, starting in 1751, the curate began to regularly include the child's date of birth. Almost all of the records he wrote were for ceremonies performed when the child was around a month old, so that all of them were called "inocentes."

9 There is not a reliable estimate for childbearing among female slaves in Rio de Janeiro in the eighteenth century. For Salvador in the nineteenth century, Katia Mattoso derived an average of two children per mother. Katia M. Mattoso, *Bahia, Século XIX*, 168.

10 According to Mary Karasch, in Rio de Janeiro in the nineteenth century "the term *negro* alone often implied African slave." Karasch, *Slave Life in Rio de Janeiro, 1808–1850*, 5. I could not verify this claim for the eighteenth century. In table 13, I included the "preto" (black, in this case man or woman) among the non-Africans. The terms *negro* (negro man) and *negra* (negro woman) do not appear in baptism records of this era.

11 ACMRJ, *Livro de Batismo de Escravos, Freguesia da Sé*, 1718–26. The two cases of freed women were maintained to show that emancipation was not enough to qualify being recorded in the book of freed blacks, rather than the book of captive blacks.

12 ACMRJ, *Livro de Batismo de Escravos, Freguesia da Sé*, 1744–61, 5 May 1745.

13 The Brotherhood of Santana was created in 1735 by a group of creoles, but by the nineteenth century it was identified as an association of soldiers. The story of that relationship, or transformation, remains to be told.

14 In 1871, with the Lei do Ventre Livre (Law of the Free Womb), children born to slave mothers were legally free.

15 ACMRJ, *Livro de Batismo de Escravos, Freguesia da Candelária*, 1745–74, fols. 99v, 100.

16 I was unable to perform a careful survey of the Books of Baptisms of Whites to know how many children of slaves were recorded there.

17 "In the bustling ports of Recife, Salvador, and Rio de Janeiro, as well as in the immediate interior of these centers, negros and mulattos predominated, with pure whites in second place, and Indians and *caboclos* in the third." Boxer, *A Idade de Ouro do Brasil*, 6.

18 Schwartz, *Segredos Internos*, 288.

19 Law dated 1 April 1680. See also the Regimento das Missões do Estado do Maranhão e Pará, 1 December 1686; and Soares, "O Missionário e o Rei."

20 Antonio Moraes e Silva, *Dicionário de Língua Portuguesa*.

21 Paul Augé, *Larousse du XXème Siècle*.

22 Carreira, *Notas sobre o Tráfico Português de Escravos*, 22.

23 Mota, *Topónimos de Origem Portuguesa na Costa Ocidental de África*, 23. Mota also noted that French cartography, the most prevalent in the eighteenth century, made use of Portuguese toponymy.

24 The theme is present in the writings of Padre Antônio Vieira and João Francisco Lisboa. In the recent historiography, see Schwartz, *Segredos Internos*, 58.

25 According to Schwartz, in Bahia the expression "native negro" (*negro da terra*) was used by both Jesuits and colonists, but fell into disuse in the sixteenth century as indigenous slavery waned and the number of Africans in the area increased. Ibid. The expression lived on in Rio de Janeiro and São Paulo until the eighteenth century. Monteiro, *Negros da Terra*.

26 The 1849 city census, the earliest reliable source for local demographics, revealed that Africans made up 66.4 percent of the total slave population. Karasch, *Slave Life in Rio de Janeiro, 1808–1850*, 8.

27 Page 275 of the 1718–26 book contains five entries. Two, referring to "gentio from Guinea," are by Barbosa. The other three are from Rodrigues Cruz: two *pardos* and one "Mina," in place of Barbosa's "*gentio* from Mina." I could not compare these registers with those of Candelária from the same time period because they are described as lost by the ACMRJ.

28 Mina, Angola, and Guinea slaves were responsible for 796 births recorded between 1718 and 1726; only 62, or 8 percent, were legitimate. The census of 1872, the first official census of the Brazilian population, indicated that 10 percent of slaves were married or widowed. Mattoso, *Ser Escravo no Brasil*, 126.

29 However, there was an unusual register worth mentioning in 1754 for the baptism of Ignacia: she was the legitimate child of João and Suzana, "ambos de Guiné, nação benguela" (both of Guinea, Benguela nation). ACMRJ, *Livro de Batismo de Escravos, Freguesia de São José, 1754*.

30 S. M. Baldé, "L'Esclavage et la Guerre Sainte au Funta-Jalon," 192.

31 One eighteenth-century Coura woman, Rosa Egipcíaca—who went from being a prostitute to a devout—is the subject of Luiz Mott's *Rosa Egipcíaca*. The same author also mentions Coura slaves in Minas Gerais in his article "Acotundá."

The four Coura identified in Rio de Janeiro's baptism records were adults undergoing baptism between 1751 and 1760; in the same period, two children were born to a Coura woman.

32 Most of the records used the term "Mina" without further qualification, although the occasional reference to a Mina subgroup demonstrated the growing perception of diversity. On the other hand, the central part of the West Coast is represented by a grand variety of names of ports, locales, or communities, which correlates with the more intense scale of commerce there.

33 To explore behind these names a bit more, Loanda (Luanda) was a Portuguese city, founded in 1575. Kongo and Kasanje were kingdoms. Cabinda was a port. Massangano and Ambaca were locations of seventeenth-century Portuguese forts that fought off the Dutch. Boxer, *Salvador de Sá e a Luta pelo Brasil e Angola*, 182. Both Luanda and Massangano had a Santa Casa da Misericórdia. Russell-Wood, *Fidalgos e Filantropos*, 28. On the variety of African groups in nineteenth-century Rio de Janeiro, see Karasch, *Slave Life in Rio de Janeiro, 1808–1850* (including map on 16); and Boxer, *O Império Colonial Português (1415–1825)* (especially maps 3 and 6). Spelling of these names is not consistent in the documents, although there are some standard variations: the letters *e* and *a* can be switched, as in Embaca/Ambaca or Benguela/Banguela. Similarly, *o* and *u* can alternate, as in Loanda/Luanda or Cacheo/Cacheu.

34 The wording of such registers was generally like this one: "On the 26th of August of 1753, in the Church of São José in this city I baptized and placed the Holy water on Maria, adult, baptized *sub conditione*, as she had requested of her master (Senhor So-and-So) to arrange her baptism, because she had not had that sacrament and could not remember having it, although her master suspected that she had . . . and it being asked that I examine said slave on the matter, I did so and determined that she should be baptized *sub conditione*, which I performed. The godparents were—" ACMRJ, *Livro de Batismo de Escravos, Freguesia de São José*, 1751–90.

35 Patricia Ann Mulvey, *The Black Lay Brotherhoods of Colonial Brazil*, 112.

36 See *Livro de Batismo de Escravos, Freguesia da Candelária*, 1745–74, pp. 99, 118v, 154v, 109v. At the time the bishop of Rio de Janeiro was D. Frei Antônio do Desterro Malheiros O.S.B. [Ordem de São Bento] (1746–73). His episcopate marked a new phase in the religious life of Rio de Janeiro. The new bishop was a Benedictine doctor of theology from Coimbra. He visited Rio briefly in 1740 en route to Luanda, where he was the bishop of Kongo and Angola. He returned to the city in 1747, and was responsible for creating the two new parishes, of São José and Santa Rita. He renewed and reinvigorated the commitments of parish priests to centrally defined rules and standards, including the norms for writing baptismal records.

37 *Constituições Primeiras do Arcebispado da Bahia*, Livro 1°, III, 6, 8; and Livro 1°, XIV, 47, 50, 53, 57.

38 Boxer, *A Idade de Ouro do Brasil*, 29. Elsewhere Boxer described the typical baptismal proceedings for slaves in seventeenth-century Luanda: "The slaves waiting to be exported had been packed into large sheds . . . When the morning broke of the day they were to set sail, they were taken to a nearby church, or to some other adequate place, where a priest would baptize them in bunches, several hundred at a time. The ceremony was quick. Each captive appeared briefly before the priest, who said to him} 'Your name is Pedro,' or 'João,' or 'Francisco,' and so forth, and who handed each one a scrap of paper with the name written on it before quickly tossing a pinch of salt in the captive's mouth. That part finished, the priest then flung holy water on the crowd, and a negro interpreter cried out the message 'Alright, you are all now children of God, setting out on the path to Portuguese (or Spanish) lands where you will learn all about the faith. Forget everything having to do with where you come from; stop eating dogs, rats, or horses. Now you may go, and be happy.'" Boxer, *Salvador de Sá e a Luta pelo Brasil e Angola*, 243.

39 Andreoni, *Cultura e Opulência do Brasil*.

40 About India, see Lapa, *A Bahia e a Carreira da Índia*.

41 ACMRJ, *Livro de Batismo de Escravos, Freguesia de Candelária*, 1718–26.

42 ACMRJ, *Livro de Batismo de Escravos, Freguesia da Candelária*, 1745–74, fols. 49v, 69v. In the *Constituições Primeiras do Arcebispado da Bahia*, Livro 1°, XIV, item 53 specifically addresses the baptism of children of so-called infidel mothers.

43 In 1740, the Brotherhood of Santo Elesbão and Santa Efigênia was founded by peoples deriving from four "nations": Mina, São Tomé, Mozambique, and Cabo Verde.

44 Fredrik Barth, *Ethnic Groups and Boundaries*, 26n5.

45 Bartolomé, "Bases Culturales de la Identidad Étnica."

46 The idea of the general language became particularly widespread after a written vocabulary was compiled in the mid-eighteenth century. Peixoto, *Obra Nova de Língua Geral da Mina*. Luiz Carlos Villalta appears to have been unaware of the existence of purported general African languages in "O Que Se Fala e O Que Se Lê."

47 To be precise, use of the word African to refer all the peoples who had come to Brazil from Africa became more common practice after 1830 and was associated with new legislation that dealt with so-called free Africans. For more on this period, see Leslie Bethell, *A Abolição do Tráfico de Escravos no Brasil*.

48 Oliveira, "Os Instrumentos de Bordo," 118.

49 Scarano, *Devoção e Escravidão*, 108.

50 Boxer also suggested that most Mina slaves were Yoruba speakers, an error in light of recent research. Yoruba speakers began to be trafficked as slaves near the end of the eighteenth century. Boxer, *A Idade de Ouro do Brasil*, 195–96.

51 In the Rio documents, *maki* and *sabaru* are mentioned; in the Minas documents, *maqui* and *sabará*.

52 See Verger, *Fluxo e Refluxo do Tráfico de Escravos entre o Golfo do Benin e a Bahia de Todos os Santos dos séculos XVIII a XIX*. The stereotype of the Mina woman as statuesque and noble, reproduced by both Elizabeth Agassiz and Christiano Jr. in the second half of the nineteenth century, is due more to the internal trafficking of Mina slaves within Brazil at the time (especially between Bahia and Rio) than to Rio's commerce with the Mina Coast, already moribund by this point. Agassiz and Agassiz, *Viagem ao Brasil: 1865–1866*; Azevedo and Mauricio Lissovsky, *Escravos Brasileiros do Século XIX na Fotografia de Christiano Jr.*

53 "The supply of African arms and backs had to be elastic, and cheap." Florentino, *Em Costas Negras*, 85.

54 Several types of vessels were specified throughout the sources on Rio's small-scale naval commerce—*patachos*, *sumacas*, and *galeras*—although official fleets would utilize larger ships. Between 1726 and 1728, I found reference to eleven different departures from Rio de Janeiro to Lisbon: four *naus*, six *navios*, and one *galera*. *ABN*, XXXIX, 469–517.

55 "Some slave masters were in favor of marriage, and not only did not prevent it but openly suggested it to couples they observed, saying in essence 'You, slave, should marry that one in good time.' They would treat such slave couples as if they had been received in Brazil thus, as husband and wife. But they were reluctant to impose marriage, fearing that the slaves would ultimately become annoyed and despondent within the bonds of the institution and might try to kill each other through hexes, spells, or stronger measures." Andreoni, *Cultura e Opulência do Brasil*, 160–61.

56 See Mattoso, Kátia M. de Queiróz. *Bahia, Século XIX: Uma Província no Império*. Rio de Janeiro: Editora Nova Fronteira, 1992: 161–169. For the analysis based on Reis' data see in particular pages 164–165.

57 These were the terms used in the statutes addressed in chapter 5.

58 In 1505, King D. Manoel I gave permission to the freed or "redeemed" black women of the Brotherhood of Rosário in Lisbon to sell herbs and other goods in the markets, alongside white women. In 1515 they were also allowed to work as vendors in the plazas. Mulvey, "The Black Lay Brotherhoods of Colonial Brazil," 22. As Luciano Raposo has shown in *O avesso da Memória*, the "black women of the tray" were a common category in the official documents of the colonial administration; they sold a variety of items, including tarts, cakes, sweets, honey, bread, bananas, tobacco, and beverages. See Luciano Figueiredo, *O Avesso da Memória*, 33–34, 41–42.

4 | URBAN LIFE AND BROTHERHOODS IN THE CITY

1 Among the most popular and upscale churches here were the Santa Casa da Misericórdia, the Brotherhood of São José, and the Third Order of Carmo.

2 The See included the religious functionaries that lived and worked with the *Cabido* (bishop). Sé (See) refers to a bishop's episcopal jurisdiction.

3 According to Monsenhor Pizarro, the bishopric encompassed all the area occupied by Portuguese from Espírito Santo to Prata, and it was answerable to the archbishop of Bahia. It was a creation of the papal bull *Romani Pontificus Pastoralis Solicitudo* of 22 November 1676. That year also saw the commencement in the See of the "Third Book of the Dead—Book and Notations of White People Expired in this city . . ." (*Livro 3° dos Falecidos—Livro e cadernos das pessoas brancas falecidas nesta cidade* . . .), whose title suggests that already the parish records separated whites and blacks. Araújo, *Memórias Históricas do Rio de Janeiro*, 2:217n27. I could not find the books from the eighteenth century in the ACMRJ.

4 A group devoted to Carmo found space in the Chapel of Nossa Senhora do Ó in 1590 (and is still present in the city today). In 1607, Franciscans constructed a convent on a nearby hill for the Carmelites; that hill was first called Morro do Carmo, and later referred to as the Morro of Santo Antônio (Saint Anthony). The Benedictines, present in the Chapel of Nossa Senhora do Ó in 1589, left that Chapel to the Carmelites to found a convent just outside the city on a hill that would be called Morro de São Bento. The churches of São Sebastião and Santa Luzia date from the sixteenth century. In the seventeenth century the churches of São José and Candelária arrived, as well as the chapels of Our Lady of the Conceicão, Our Lady of Parto, and Our Lady of Bonsucesso.

5 Fazenda, "Antiqualhas e Memórias do Rio de Janeiro," tomo 86, 348. If it were not for the quick aside by Vieira Fazenda referring to Guinea blacks associated with Saint Domingos, that connection might not have come to light, because I did not find mention of it anywhere else.

6 Conflicts between brotherhoods and the local Catholic authorities were analyzed with admirable rigor by Carlos Boschi. An understanding of the tensions between brotherhoods is best obtained through the period chroniclers, such as Vieira Fazenda and Padre Perereca, who colorfully described the pugilistic encounters, theft of ceremonial objects, and processions interrupted, along with other incidents. See Boschi, *Os Leigos e o Poder*; and Fazenda, *Antiqualhas e Memórias do Rio de Janeiro*, 5 volumes.

7 Sabotage and delays in the processions led to accords being signed between groups, as well as to the mandatory signing of documents by leaders before the procession began that signified their acceptance of the place given to each brotherhood. Coaracy, *O Rio de Janeiro no Século Dezessete*, 85.

8 Schwartz, *Segredos Internos*, 210. The pomp and ostentation of each brotherhood also served as a form of propaganda to attract new adherents. Russell-Wood, *Fidalgos e Filantropos*, 157.

9 D. Francisco wrote the letter in 1709 cited in chapter 2 of this book.

10 On this polemic, see Silvia Hunold Lara, "Sob o Signo da Cor."

11 Leila Mezan Algranti, *Honradas e Devotas*.

12 According to Scarano, the congregations were to be of the "most esteemed

people . . . not being permitted the entrance, without prior investigation of a white person born in Brazil, since the status of pure blood was required." Julita Scarano, *Devoção e Escravidão*. In Portugal, the Brotherhoods of the Santíssimo Sacramento were perhaps the most numerous of all the lay associations, alongside the Confrarias das Almas.

13 Holanda, "O Semeador e o Ladrilhador"; Angel Rama, "La Ciudad Letrada."

14 It is unclear when the Brotherhood of the Rosário left São Benedito for the new church. The building was inaugurated in 1725, but the transfer took place before that date.

15 But the French were persecuting the Portuguese all along the route to India, on land and at sea, at the time. They burnt Benguela in 1705, and sacked the Islands of Príncipe (1706), São Tomé (1709), and Cape Verde (1712). Whatever their immediate concern for gold in Rio, taken as a whole these actions were part of larger disputes surrounding the War of Spanish Succession between 1702 and 1714. Fernando Novais, *Portugal e Brasil na Crise do Antigo Sistema Colonial*, 26, 40.

16 Mello Barreto Filho and Hermeto Lima, *História da Polícia do Rio de Janeiro*, 65.

17 Fazenda, "Antiqualhas e Memórias do Rio de Janeiro," tomo 86, 367–72. Expressions referring to locations in the city as *extra-muros* (outside the walls) and *dentro dos muros* (within the walls) are common in documents from the era in which the protective wall was a matter of public awareness and debate.

18 In his pioneering work, Caio Boschi explored one aspect of this question—the relations of lay worshippers with the church. Boschi, *Os Leigos e o Poder*.

19 See Boschi, *Os Leigos e o Poder*, 178; and João José Reis, *A Morte é uma Festa*, 49.

20 My view of sociability has been influenced by Roger Chartier and D. Roche, "Social (História)," 573.

21 See in particular the 1977 work by Hoonaert et al., *História da Igreja no Brasil*.

22 Boschi, *Os Leigos e o Poder*, 64–65.

23 Known as Onça (Panther), Monteiro was deposed in 1732 and died a year later.

24 Rupert, *A Igreja no Brasil III*, 3:44.

25 The governor helped finance the last stages of construction of the Church of the Rosário, and brokered an arrangement for the Brotherhood of Our Lady of the Conception of Pardo Men to congregate in the See (Saint Benedict), even though this was against the wishes of the priests.

26 An act established by the judge of the captaincy, Dr. Agostinho Pacheco Teles, prohibited any person, free or slave, from throwing "trash, rubbish, or filth" there, but the act was weakly enforced. João da Costa Ferreira, "A Cidade do Rio de Janeiro e seu Termo."

27 There were many tense years of coexistence until 1808, when the See cathedral was transferred to the Largo do Paço on the occasion of the transfer of the Portuguese Crown to Rio de Janeiro.

28 Maurício, *Templos Históricos do Rio de Janeiro*, 109, 215.

29 If the Cabido priests directed a formidable degree of animosity toward the black brotherhoods located in the See cathedral, the brotherhood of pardos also based there (first dedicated only to Our Lady of the Conception) was not spared the priests' ire. They stayed at Castle Hill until 1729, when Governor Monteiro deemed it proper that they should move to the Church of the Hospício; this was a chapel belonging to the Third Order of São Francisco da Penitência, which had on its grounds a cemetery for slaves. In 1734, that group united with the congregation of the Boa Morte to form the Brotherhood of Nossa Senhora da Conceição e Boa Morte dos Homens Pardos.

30 The last wills and testaments of some of these freed Mina slaves, listing their material patrimony, are transcribed in the funerary books of the parishes, which are today held in the ACMRJ.

31 Various wills include detailed descriptions of gold jewelry, while the pano de costa is visible in many of the drawings from the period.

32 For more on the African goods traded in Rio de Janeiro, see Carreira, As Companhias Pombalinas de Navegação, Comércio e Tráfico de Escravos entre a Costa Africana e o Nordeste Brasileiro, 190–242.

33 "Diário Anônimo de uma Viagem à Costa d'África e as Índias Espanholas." The report was prepared for publication by Gilberto Ferrez.

34 ACMRJ, Livro de Óbitos e Testamentos, Freguesia da Sé, 1746–58, 3 July 1749, 135.

35 A. M. Rios Filho, "Evolução Urbana e Arquitetônica do Rio de Janeiro nos Séculos XVI e XVII (1567–1699)." The work presents a series of photographs of historic houses to illustrate the developments detailed by the author.

36 We can still try to apply the sources on houses to the parish records to get an idea about the occupation of dwellings, patterns of commerce, and distribution of the slave population. Helpful data are available in "Memórias Públicas e Econômicas da Cidade de São Sebastião do Rio de Janeiro para Uso de Vice-rei Luiz de Vasconcellos por Observação Curiosa dos Anos de 1779 até 1789." RIHGB, book 47, pt. 1, 1884, 25–51.

37 Many of the female slaves living there might have worked as ambulatory vendors, the so-called escravas de tabuleiro. See Figueiredo, O Avesso da Memória, 60–71.

38 Manolo Garcia Florentino, Em Costas Negras, 82–83.

39 The available obituary records are much less complete than the baptismal records for early eighteenth-century Rio de Janeiro, although reading them provides a useful portrait of the conditions and options for burial at the time. Could it be that these circumstances were roughly the same as those studied by Katia Mattoso and João Reis in Salvador? Mattoso, Ser Escravo no Brasil; Reis, A Morte é uma Festa.

40 Russell-Wood, Fidalgos e Filantropos, 174.

41 Extract of a petition to the crown from the Brotherhood of São Domingos of the Convent of São Francisco, in the city of Salvador, Bahia. AHU, Bahia, 1735,

transcribed by Mulvey, in "The Black Lay Brotherhoods of Colonial Brazil: A History," 197–99.

42 ACMRJ, *Livro de Óbitos de Livres, Freguesia de Candelária*, 1797–1809, registers from March 1798, 5 June 1799, and 2 August 1799.

43 Chapter 6 of this book provides a case study of how an African kinship group was organized in the Brotherhood of Santo Elesbão and Santa Efigênia. The term *parentes* also appears in the nineteenth century, when Antônio Ferreira, a freed slave of the Benguela nation, petitioned for authorization to perform "together with his kin [*parentes*] the customs and pastimes of that nation." See Martha Campos Abreu, "O Império do Divino"; and Reis, *A Morte é uma Festa*, 55.

44 For a thoughtful analysis of the theme(s) of death that is useful to the present discussion, see Philipp Ariès, *O Homem Diante da Morte*. The close relationship between churches and sepulchral practice continued in Brazil, especially in Rio, until 1850. That year, decree number 583 established the creation of public cemeteries and prohibited burials in or next to churches. See Cláudia Rodrigues, "Lugares dos Mortos na Cidade dos Vivos" (esp. chap. 3).

45 Debret, *Viagem Pitoresca e Histórica ao Brasil*, tomo 2, 3:186. Judging by his sketches, Debret seemed to have been intrigued by the variety of coffins he saw on the streets, from the most splendid to the well worn and rough hewn. The use of hammocks and inexpensive coffins are understood here as the inversion of what Michel Vovelle had in mind with respect to "funerary art," but they are just as eloquent on a given people's social conditions and death practices. Chapter "Iconografia e História das Mentalidades." In Vovelle, *Ideologias e Mentalidades*.

46 According to Vieira Fazenda, the frequently expressed idea that the Church of the Lampadosa contained the images of São Crispim and São Crispiniano was a misconception. I encountered one 1667 testament from a black shoemaker who was a member of both the Brotherhood of the Rosário and of São Crispim and São Crispiniano.

47 See Padre Perereca's comments to that effect in Luiz Gonçalves dos Santos, *Memórias para Servir à História do Reino do Brasil*, 42.

48 In the nineteenth century, the Parish of the Santíssimo Sacramento absorbed the old São Domingos Field and the nearby chapels built by black brotherhoods during the previous century. Cláudia Rodrigues analyzes the records of all 584 burials of Africans in the parish between 1812 and 1885 and found the following distribution of interment at different churches: 17.3 percent were buried at the Church of São Domingos, 16.4 percent at Lampadosa, 12.5 percent at Rosário, 10.1 percent at Santo Elesbão and Santa Efigênia, 9.8 percent at Santíssimo Sacramento, 2.9 percent at Lord Bom Jesus do Calvário, 2.6 percent at São Gonçalo Garcia, 2 percent at Our Lady of Boa Morte (Good Death), and less than 1 percent at diverse locations. Rodrigues, *Lugares dos Mortos*, 220, table

21. The churches of Lampadosa and Santa Efigênia were constructed in the 1750s.

49 The first table (table 12) of obituaries contains 397 cases, while the second table (table 13) contains 499; the higher number includes records that did not specify the locale of burial. When obituaries recorded that the deceased was buried without the sacraments, which was quite frequent, the cause of death was usually an unidentifiable sudden event.

50 Sheila Castro Faria provocatively revisits this theme in light of important early works by Manning and Klein. Faria, "A Colônia em Movimento," 269–70.

51 Figueiredo, *O Avesso da Memória*, 164.

52 The number of baptisms is derived from adding the data from the first two periods of baptisms in Sé Parish; see chapter 3, table 5.

53 Mulvey, "The Black Lay Brotherhoods of Colonial Brazil," 198.

54 This leaves aside the use of parasols as royal symbols in African kingdoms, notably the kingdom of Kongo. Detailed study is needed of the relations between the cultural and political practices associated with African kings, and those with the kings of African folias in colonial Brazil. Regrettably, this fascinating topic is beyond the scope of this book.

55 Descriptions of the festivals are included under the headings "Divino" and "São Gonçalo" in Cascudo, *Dicionário do Folclore Brasileiro*, 356–57, 432–36.

56 Mulvey, "The Black Lay Brotherhoods of Colonial Brazil," 104–5, 122.

57 Maurício, *Templos Históricos do Rio de Janeiro*, 112–13.

58 Mulvey, "The Black Lay Brotherhoods of Colonial Brazil," 114–15.

59 About Lampadosa, see Vieira Fazenda, "Antiqualhas e Memórias do Rio de Janeiro," tomo 95, 149:123–27; and Maurício, *Templos Históricos do Rio de Janeiro*, 109–17. About the festivities of Império do Divino in the Church of Santana, see Abreu, "O Império do Divino"; and Henrique José do Carmo Neto, "Recordações e Aspectos do Culto de Sangt'Anna."

60 Fazenda, "Antiqualhas e Memórias do Rio de Janeiro," tomo 95, 149:123–27.

61 Abreu, "O Império do Divino," tomo 1, chap. 2, note 56. The relative tolerance that characterized Portuguese administration in these contexts differs greatly from the stance of the English in their African colonies, where anything assumed to be related to witchcraft was discouraged or punished. The 1890 penal code of Brazil distinguished between so-called black magic, which was prohibited and punishable, and white magic, which was held to be beneficial, particularly as a supplement to other cures in matters of physical and mental health. For a comparison of the nineteenth-century penal systems in Brazil and English Africa, see Maggie, *Medo do Feitiço*, 24–30.

62 Debret, *Viagem Pitoresca e Histórica ao Brasil*, tomo 2, 225.

63 The full Portuguese text goes on to greater lengths than the translated extract, which focuses on the dances themselves:

"Recebi o aviso de Vossa Excelência de 9 de Junho em que Sua Majestade ordena dê o meu parecer a vista das Cartas do Santo Ofício e do Governador de Pernambuco, do Santo Ofício vejo tartar de danças que ainda não sejam as mais santas não as considero dignas de uma total reprovação; estas considero eu e pela carta do Governador, vejo serem as mesmas aquelas que os pretos divididas em nações e com instrumentos próprios de cada uma dançam e fazem voltas como arlequins, e outros dançam com diversos movimentos do corpo, que ainda que não sejam as mais inocentes são como os fandangos de Castela, e fofas de Portugal, e os lunduns dos broncos e pardos daquele país; os bailes que entendo serem uma total reprovação são aqueles que os pretos da Costa da Mina fazem às escondidas, ou em casas ou roças com uma preta mestra com altar dos ídolos adorando bodes vivos, e outros feitos de barro, untando seus corpos com diversos óleos, sangue de galo, dando a comer bolos de milho depois de diversas bençãos supersticiosas, fazendo crer os rústicos que naquelas unções de pão dão fortuna, fazem querer bem mulheres a homens, e homens a mulheres, e chega tanto a credulidade de algumas pessoas, ainda daquelas que pareciam não serem rústicos como frades e clérigos, que chegaram a vir presos a minha presença, em os cercos que mandava botar a estas casas, que querendo-os desmaginar me foi preciso em as suas presenças lhes fazer confessar o embuste aos pretos donos das casas; e depois remetê-los aos seus prelados para que este os corrigissem como mereciam, e aos negros fazia castigar com vigorosos açoites, e obrigava aos senhores que os vendessem para fora. Estas são as duas castas de bailes que vi naquela capitania em o tempo que a governei e me persuado que o Santo Ofício fala de uns e o Governador fala de outros, pois não me posso persuadir que o Santo Ofício reprove uns, nem que o Governador desculpe outros. Este é meu parecer, e Sua Majestade com mais claras luzes resolverá o mais justo."

"Deus Guarde a Vossa Excelência ms. ans. Lisboa 10 de Junho de 1780. Conde de Povolide Ilmo. e Exmo. Senhor Martinho de Mello e Castro." BEP, letter manuscript in "Correspondência da Corte, 1780–1781," fol.23r–v.

64 The name Valongo was given to several places in Portugal. It seems to derive from the phrase *vale longo* (long valley), which would be consistent with its application in Rio to a place that was best reached through the curving plain between two hills, Conceição and Livramento. The first recorded reference to the name in Rio de Janeiro seems to be in 1701. I thank Maurício Abreu for this information.

65 Mascarenhas, "Relatório."

66 *Constituições Primeiras do Arcebispado da Bahia*, Livro 4°, Tit. 19, 692.

67 "Várias irmandades de pretos com igrejinhas indignas e indecentes que nem devem ter este nome como são a Irmandade das Mercês e São Domingos, São Felipe, São Tiago, o Menino Jesus, Santa Efigênia e S. Elesbão, Nossa Senhora da Lampadosa, São Mateus, outra de São Benedito em Santo Antônio, o Senhor Jesus do Calix, Nossa Senhora de Belém e Santo Antônio da Mouraria, as quais

sendo vm servido ficarem anexas, e recolhidas a esta Igreja demolindo-se os alpendres em que existem para cemitérios faria vm um grande serviço a Deus, e grande aumento desta Igreja, e irmandades, pois as dispersas despesas que fazem, reunidas, e incorporadas nela ficaria cessando a sua grande necessidade para a conclusão da obra." ahu, Petition from the Brotherhood of the Rosário to the king, 27 July 1774. I thank Fernanda Bicalho for a copy of this correspondence.

68 ahu, Response from Marquês de Lavradio to the king's request for further information on the matters raised by the petition of the Brothers of the Rosário (cited above), dated 17 July 1775.

5 | CONSTRUCTING A RELIGIOUS NORM

1 Even colonial legislation at the time was mostly preoccupied with devising solutions to immediate problems, and not with the establishment of an integrated juridical framework. See Salgado, *Fiscais e Meirinhos*.

2 For a pioneering work regarding this approach in the history of slavery in Brazil, see João José Reis and Eduardo Silva, *Negociação e Conflito*. For more on the brotherhoods in Brazilian colonial society, see Russell-Wood, *The Black Man in Slavery and Freedom in Colonial Brazil*.

3 Norbert Elias, *A Sociedade de Corte*.

4 Russell-Wood, *Fidalgos e Filantropos*, 154.

5 John Bossy, *A Cristandade no Ocidente, 1400–1700*. The notion of charity among family members or ethnic groups is taken up again in chapter 6.

6 The term *incorporated* was common in period ecclesiastical documentation and carried a double meaning. It called for the group to be present as a whole, but beyond that, the brothers should all be dressed in the brotherhood's formal attire and carrying all the flags, staffs, and other objects that represent the brotherhood's overall identity as well as the different roles of the individuals within it. In festive processions, the icons of the protective saints were carried along, but during funerals these were left at the church.

7 The seven spiritual acts: instruct the ignorant, give good counsel, punish transgressors, console the sorrowful, forgive personal affronts, accept human imperfections, pray for the living and the dead. The seven physical acts: liberate captives and visit the imprisoned, care for the sick, clothe the naked, feed the hungry, give drink to the thirsty, give shelter to travelers and the poor, bury the dead. Russell-Wood, *Fidalgos e Filantropos*, 14–15.

8 Anderson José Machado de Oliveira, "Devoção e Caridade."

9 Principal documents relating to these organizations are as follows: Compromisso of the Brotherhood of Santo Elesbão and Santa Efigênia, copy located in the archives of the brotherhood; proposed statutes for the Devotion of the Almas do Purgatório, transcribed in the Mahi Manuscript; and proposed stat-

utes for the Devotion of Our Lady of Remédios, document located in the Arquivo Histórico Ultramarino.

10 Before the completion of my doctoral dissertation, two other works about the Church of Santo Elesbão and Santa Efigênia had been written (but still remain unpublished). The first, Vânia Penha Lopes's "À Venerável Irmandade de Santo Elesbão e Santa Efigênia, ou uma Tentativa de Entendimento da Questão Étnica no Brasil," is a present-day study of the brotherhood devoted to the church's patron saints. The second, Oliveira's "Devoção e Caridade," offers a historical account of the church in the nineteenth century. Together, these works provided a provocative starting point from which to formulate my own project.

11 The Tribunal of Conscience and Orders was transferred to Rio de Janeiro along with the royal family in 1808 and was dissolved in 1822, when Brazil was declared independent. Its documentation from these years (today held at the National Archive) refers to four distinct brotherhoods of Santo Elesbão and Santa Efigênia in Brazil, but does not specify a brotherhood of that name in Rio de Janeiro. Nor, for that matter, does it mention the existence of any brotherhood based in Rio's Church of Santo Elesbão and Santa Efigênia. See Sérgio Chahon, "Aos Pés do Altar e do Trono."

12 For more on how various types of cases were processed by the Tribunal of Conscience and Orders, see Guilherme Pereira Neves, "E Receberá Mercê." Although the author primarily addresses the nineteenth century, at times he considers the eighteenth. And there seems to have been little change in the evaluative methods or bureaucratic nature of these processes from the earlier period to the later one.

13 AISESE, doc. 1. My analysis throughout this chapter draws on the compromisso of the Brotherhood of Santo Elesbão and Santa Efigênia, included in the covenenant book belonging to the archives of the Church of Santo Elesbão and Santa Efigênia (AISESE). This book contains fifteen other documents to which I refer in sequential order as AISESE docs. 1, 2, and so on.

14 Maurício, Templos Históricos do Rio de Janeiro, 215; Mulvey, "The Black Lay Brotherhoods of Colonial Brazil," 113.

15 AISESE, doc. 2.

16 AISESE, doc. 3.

17 I could not find these two provisions, and it was not entirely clear what Monsenhor Pizarro was referring to. It is possible that the so-called 1747 provision was actually the complete collection of documents sent to reformulate the statutes in 1748. Pizarro's second provision, dated 1754, might refer to the inauguration of the Church of Santo Elesbão and Santa Efigênia that year.

18 AISESE, doc. 5.

19 AISESE, doc. 9.

20 AISESE, doc. 16.

21 AISESE, docs. 11 and 12.

22 Chap. 6 of the compromisso mentions that the brotherhood owned some furniture and decorations housed in the church, and recommends against loaning out items belonging to the group. This would suggest, among other things, that several associations shared the same space in the church.

23 *Constituições Primeiras do Arcebispado da Bahia*, Livro 40. , LXIV, 882. Today it is a common sight to see people, especially women, traversing the streets of Rio de Janeiro begging for money with one hand and holding an image of their saint in the other. It is common too among devotees of candomblé, who, upon initiation, ask for donations for their "saints" or protecting deities.

24 Alfredo Mendes de Gouveia, "Relação dos Compromissos de Irmandades, Confrarias e Misericórdias do Brasil."

25 Of course, even a vote based on the palpable transfer of *fava* beans was susceptible to rigging. From this custom derives the modern Brazilian expression "são favas contadas" (the beans are already counted), used when it is assumed that a dispute will secretly be resolved in a premeditated manner.

26 Peter Burke, *A Fabricação do Rei*, 13–25.

27 The ceremonial cloaks were roughly standard across the brotherhoods, but their colors differed in accordance with the particular saint. The cloak of Santo Elesbão is red, and that of Santa Efigênia violet. Each cloak also bore the insignia of the brotherhood to which it pertained. A simpler white cotton cloak could be worn by brothers outside festive or other ritual occasions.

28 A detailed description of this aspect of the festival, known as *comilança*, is to be found in Campos, *Procissões Tradicionais da Bahia*.

29 On death and death rituals, see Ariès, *O Homem Diante da Morte*. For the Brazilian case, see José de Souza Martins, *A Morte e os Mortos na Sociedade Brasileira*; and Reis, *A Morte é uma Festa*.

30 Debret, *Viagem Pitoresca e Histórica ao Brasil*, tomo 2:184.

31 John Luccock, *Notas sobre o Rio de Janeiro e Partes Meridionais do Brasil*, 39.

32 I recall here the preoccupations of Guilherme Marechal with his own death. Georges Duby, *Guilherme Marechal ou o Melhor Cavaleiro do Mundo*.

33 Scarano, *Devoção e Escravidão*, 55.

34 It was not possible to locate the habitations of the brothers in the eighteenth century. I found many hints, but nothing definitive. In the brotherhood's books from the nineteenth century, available in their archive, these data are more easily obtained. According to a survey by Anderson Oliveira, the 298 registers of members between 1843 and 1930 indicate that 69 lived on the same street as the church and 49 on an adjacent street. Oliveira, "Devoção e Caridade," 162. In the eighteenth century, the courier must have had farther to walk. Even though the city was smaller, slaves were dispersed throughout, as most likely were members of the brotherhood.

35 The cemetery was closed in 1850 when new laws mandated burial in public cemeteries. Rodrigues, "Os Lugares dos Mortos na Cidade dos Vivos."

36 AISESE, C.

37 Scarano, *Devoção e Escravidão*, 73.

38 Schwartz pointed out that colonial Brazil deserves to be called a "slave society" due not only to its wide reliance on forced captive labor, but also to the other related social hierarchies that expanded and rigidified through and with slavery there. He also explored the juridical distinctions created between free and slave, and the hierarchies associated with slavery, race, and class. Schwartz, *Segredos Internos*, 209–15.

39 Mulvey, "The Black Lay Brotherhoods of Colonial Brazil," 92.

40 The document contains these lines: "Acordaram que os irmãos desta confraria são muito importunados de muitos escravos que ficam meio forros, e assim escravas que lhe dêem para se acabarem de forrar, em tal caso a Confraria não será obrigada a mais que a favorecer os ditos escravos a falar por eles, e não a demandas, salvo alguma pessoa a que a Confraria tiver muita obrigação, e quiserem tirar pelos irmãos algumas esmolas para isso, mas a custa da Confraria querendo lhe fazer alguma esmola será até a quantia de quinhentos réis e isto porque a Confraria não fique desfraldada." Quoted ibid., 258–61.

41 From research underway at the ACMRJ, I can draw the still-tentative conclusion that most (if not all) the marriages took place after freedom was achieved. And although having children was prized in the abstract, I have not found evidence of children for the majority of married brothers.

42 For sources, see note 9 of this chapter.

43 See Kátia Mattoso's discussion of the Sociedade Protetora dos Desvalidos da Bahia, for whom ethnic identity was part of the criteria involved in accessing support for the purchase of freedom. Mattoso, *Ser Escravo no Brasil*, 151, 163.

44 The statutes say of worthy candidates for this position, "por seu zelo e devoção"; they could be expected to offer "esmola de grandeza avantajada."

45 Mulvey, "The Black Lay Brotherhoods of Colonial Brazil," 27.

46 A royal decree had mandated reductions in the esmolas paid within lay brotherhoods, but this seems to have been ignored with respect to several positions described in the statutes, including the king of the folia. AISESE, doc. 11.

47 Among other groups, notably the Brotherhood of the Rosário do Mosteiro de São Domingos shared this preoccupation with assisting poor and sick members.

48 "É costume haver nas Irmandades principalmente na dos pretos, Irmãos revoltosos inimigos da paz," the statute affirms, adding that such people make themselves known by using "palavras descompostas."

49 "Só se cuida nesta [irmandade] que haja paz e quietação e não distúrbios."

50 Considering all the black brotherhoods of colonial Brazil, the number of masses for dead brothers varied by era and differed from order to order. The Brotherhood of Nossa Senhora do Rosário do Serro in Minas Gerais stipulated six masses per brother (Scarano, *Devoção e Escravidão*, 53), while the Jêje Broth-

erhood of Bom Jesus dos Martírios da Vila de Cachoeira in Bahia held twenty-five for any brother. Reis, *A Morte é uma Festa*, 207.

51 As chapter 3, table 8, of this book shows, only six Mina men married Angola women during the period under study, while twelve Mina women married Angola men.

52 "Que suposto no capítulo 10° recuse não sejam admitidos pretos e pretas de Angola, crioulos e mestiços e cabras. Contudo agora é contente em toda a Irmandade se admitam por Irmãos todos estes recusados."

53 AISESE, docs. 11 and 12.

54 I refer to the notion of contrasting identity developed by Oliveira in *Identidade, Etnia e Estrutura Social*.

55 The 1618 statutes of the Brotherhood of Misericórdia in Salvador established seven conditions for admission; one of them was to be *limpo de sangue* (of clean blood). According to Russell-Wood, the period expression *sangue religioso* (religious blood) derived from usage in Portugal, where it referred to Moors and Jews. Russell-Wood, *Fidalgos e Filantropos*, 93, 108, 40.

56 It is possible to identify three brotherhoods in Bahia constructed around a base of ethnic identity from which Angola blacks had been excluded: two were groups of Jêje Africans, and the third was a group of Nagô-Yoruba Africans. The Brotherhood of Senhor Bom Jesus das Necessidades e Redenção dos Homens Pretos was established in the Chapel of the Corpo Santo in Salvador (1752); the Brotherhood of Lord Bom Jesus, Lord of Martírios dos Homens Pretos was in the Convent of Our Lady of Monte do Carmo, in Cachoeira (1765); and the Brotherhood of Our Lady of Boa Morte was founded in the Church of Barroquinha, in Salvador (date unknown). Mulvey, "The Black Lay Brotherhoods of Colonial Brazil," 296.

57 Other brotherhoods present variations as to the identity of officials, as Mulvey showed. For example, the board of the Brotherhood of Nossa Senhora do Rosário of the Monastery of São Domingos had, among their six highest elected officers, five from Kongo and one from Bahia. On the other hand, the Brotherhood of Nossa Senhora do Terço, which was founded by creoles at the Church of the Rosário in Recife, established that certain groups from West Africa were to compose the board, while the kings of the folia would be Kongo or Angola. Mulvey, "The Black Lay Brotherhoods of Colonial Brazil," 27, 86.

58 Oliveira, "Devoção e Caridade."

59 Mahi Manuscript, 22.

60 According to the baptism register for this man, first called Pedro Mina (and later Pedro Costa), his owner was the chief judge of Rio de Janeiro, Manoel da Costa Mimozo. ACMRJ, *Livro de Batismo de Escravos, Freguesia da Sé*, 1726–33, 38. This book was lost at the ACMRJ and I found it after the Brazilian editon of the book. For this reason it is not mentioned in the tables.

61 Mahi Manuscript, 22.

62 Ibid.

63 André Burguière, "A Antropologia Histórica," 43.

64 Russell-Wood reported a similar phenomenon in the statutes of the Brotherhood of Santa Casa de Misericórdia. The early version of that document, from 1516, seems stubbornly vague. But by 1618 the revised statutes are characterized by "particularity and the absence of ambiguity." Russell-Wood, *Fidalgos e Filantropos*, 75.

65 In the Brotherhood of Santa Casa de Misericórdia, the penalties for missing a funeral were severe, but brothers still displayed resistance to accompanying the funeral processions. Russell-Wood, *Fidalgos e Filantropos*.

66 Mahi Manuscript, 14. According to a survey performed for Viceroy D. Luiz de Vasconcellos, Rio de Janeiro's slave population in the 1780s was around 9,700 men and 7,100 women.

Vasconcellos, "Memórias Públicas Económicas," 27. A note indicates that this was the population within the walls of the city, which would have left a substantial part of São Domingos Field and some of the new developments south of the city proper. The drawings made by Francisco João Roscio in 1769 provide a good sense of this expansion.

67 AISESE, docs. 11 and 12.

68 For a more detailed look at this phenomenon, see Mulvey, "The Black Lay Brotherhoods of Colonial Brazil," especially appendix E, 289–303.

69 AISESE, doc. 10.

70 AISESE, docs. 11 and 12. In 1767 at least eleven more brotherhoods in Brazil had their statutes confirmed in Portugal. Scarano, *Devoção e Escravidão*, 21–22.

71 Provision from D. Antônio do Desterro, dated 18 August 1767. The copy of this approval notice archived in the Church of Santa Efigênia bears the incorrect date 1797; Desterro arrived in Rio de Janeiro in 1747 and died in 1773. AISESE, doc. 15.

6 | CONFLICT AND ETHNIC IDENTITY AMONG MAHI

1 AISESE, compromisso of the Brotherhood of Santo Elesbão and Santa Efigênia, chap. 5 of the section sanctioning creation of the folia. The most common form of portable property in the wills was human property, or slaves. Women's wills might also include gold jewelry. Stationary property was far more rare, and typically took the form of small houses that had been used either as residences or rentals.

2 Schwartz, *Burocracia e Sociedade no Brasil Colonial*, xi–xii.

3 Coincidentally or no, the date Souza provided for his arrival, 1748, corresponds with the year of the first reformulation of the compromisso of the Brotherhood of Santo Elesbão and Santa Efigênia.

4 "Começaram os pretos a zingar as nações umas com as outras, buscando preferências de maiorias." Mahi Manuscript, 22.

5 "Ao que deu ocasião a que as nações Mahi, Agolin, Iano, Savalu saírem do jugo Dagomé escandalizados e afrontados de alguns ditos picantes que os Dagomés lhes diziam, procuraram fazer o seu Rei e com efeito o fizeram, na pessoa do Capitão Ignacio Gonçalves do Monte no ano de 1762 por ser verdadeiro Mahi e este foi o primeiro que fez termo e endireitou e aumentou esta congregação." Mahi Manuscript, 22.

6 Ibid., 22.

7 Ibid., 21–22.

8 The term *imediato* had the connotations of a military position, and perhaps it was applied to Souza because Monte seems to have been a colonel in a local black regiment. I found references to Monte's rank as such but no official evidence of it.

9 These included Luiz Roiz Silva, Antonio da Costa Falcão, and Roza de Souza de Andrade. Ibid., 13.

10 "Meu muito fiel e prezado amigo, a quem professei desde a minha infância, a mais intima e cordial, amizade." Mahi Manuscript, 2.

11 Ibid., 27–28. This is an additional use of the already described pano da costa.

12 Erizipela was a common but poorly diagnosed disease at the time. Symptoms included high fever, generalized pain, and redness and swelling of the legs. It seems to have been a bacterial infection due to germs attacking wounds that were poorly treated, and (now as then) was associated with poor hygiene. Slaves—even freed ones—often lived in deplorable conditions of hygiene, sleeping in dirt-floor houses or yards. A belief among some in contemporary Brazil is that the disease has no medicinal cure, and is linked to curses or black magic, making prayers the most effective remedy.

13 According to Souza, the widow "fez por uma coroa na cabeça dizendo que era a rainha." The expression "fez por" indicates that she was crowned by others. Mahi Manuscript, 13.

14 The compromisso of the Brotherhood of Santo Elesbão and Santa Efigênia still prohibited creoles from entering; this was before chap. 10 was rewritten by royal mandate. Thus Souza's comments are especially critical of the morality of the queen.

15 Mahi Manuscript, 14.

16 As Yvonne Maggie has shown, a combative posture against black magic is one of the possible responses that characterize believers, not unbelievers. Maggie, *Medo do Feitiço*, 22.

17 Souza wrote, "Tudo poderei fazer, visto a desculpa dos prudentes, sábios exceto ser regente . . . Tenho teimado que não quero, porque conheço que a viúva não faz gosto que eu seja sem o seu consentimento." The polemical situation between him and the queen is visible in various parts of the Mahi Manuscript, e.g., 2, 7, 14, 38.

18 The text reads that women may serve as judges "por razão de seu número e por contribuírem com suas esmolas e não a mais servem." Ibid., 14, 39.

19 As with the case of the unreliable chaplain mentioned in chap. 32 of the compromisso of the Brotherhood of Santo Elesbão and Santa Efigênia, a serious impasse within the order could be resolved by resorting to external authority.

20 Mahi Manuscript, 15.

21 Ibid., 23. This language recalls the hierarchy of posts in the Brotherhood of the Santa Casa de Misericórdia, which were divided among *irmãos de maior condição* (better-off brothers), which in Portugal would all have been nobles; and *irmãos de menor condição* (poorer brothers), also called mechanics or mechanical workers. Russell-Wood, *Fidalgos e Filantropos*, 15. The efforts by the maiores to protect their positions of prestige is reminiscent of the French nobles described by Saint-Simon. Elias, *A Sociedade de Corte*.

22 Mahi Manuscript, 23.

23 Adding to the complexity of this organization, there were some titles and positions awarded on the occasion of Souza's election, according to the Manuscript—but those names do not match up with the list that the Manuscript includes soon afterward. It should also be noted that there may be errors in orthography in the transcription of non-Portuguese words.

24 By custom, the king or master should never walk alone; at least two of his fellows should always be present. But this was another tradition which Souza chose not to uphold consistently. On one occasion, a group of brothers insisted on accompanying him, stating "we are here to go with you because it is our duty" (*estamos prontos para o acompanhar pois temos de obrigação*), but Souza dismissed them: "Thank you for such an honor, but the secretary is enough company" (*Obrigado a Vossas Mercês por tanta honra . . . basta que venha o secretário*).

25 "Desde o princípio desta terra em que entraram a conduzir os pretos de África que vem da Costa da Mina e de Angola, e pela desumanidade de alguns senhores que os compravam, todas as vezes que adoeciam de moléstias incuráveis e envelheciam, os deitavam fora para morrer de fome e frio nus por estas praias sem ter quem os mandasse enterrar. Se a Santa Casa da Misericórdia os não mandasse buscar para os enterrar com aquele zelo e caridades que costuma, aí ficariam os cadáveres com o seu invalidez. E por esta razão introduziram os pretos entre si a fazerem este adjunto ou Corporação a fim de fazerem bem aos seus nacionais, a saber, que a Nação que morrer seus parentes tirar esmola para es sepultar e mandar-lhe dizer missas por sua alma." Mahi Manuscript, 20–21.

26 It was common for documents produced by black lay brotherhoods to include language about the suffering of slaves as the basic justification for the creation of brotherhoods. Of course, such suffering did exist, in multitudinous forms. What is notable is the rhetorical utilization of that suffering by brotherhoods in the argument for recognition and benefits.

27 Chap. 27 of the brotherhood's statute reads as follows: "Aos irmãos que assim

forem eleitos serão obrigados a tirar esmolas pelos cantos das ruas onde melhor lhe estiver aos domingos e dias santos como se costuma nas mais Irmandades por estilo antigo . . . Recusando estes tais Irmãos assim nomeados fazê-los serão admoestados." See also the Mahi Manuscript, 22.

28 It should be clarified that the playing of drums in general in this context was not considered a heathen practice. Brotherhoods of white men took to the streets in public processions to collect esmolas accompanied by drumming and wind instruments, always played by blacks. The difference seems to lie in the type of instruments used by black versus white brotherhoods, the rhythms played on them (their nature and origin), and the dances that went along with them. Many such small distinctions are clear if one compares the available drawings and paintings of white brotherhoods with those of black brotherhoods.

29 Mahi Manuscript, 34. Luciano Figueiredo has shown that in Minas Gerais, women were always the minority in lay brotherhoods, due largely to discrimination. Based on his research he hypothesizes that *batuques* (informal recreational gatherings with music and dance) were more important spaces of sociability and power for them. Figueiredo, *O Avesso da Memória*, 164, 171–81.

30 Chap. 12 of the statutes of the Fraternity of Our Lady of Remedies includes the following line: "Haverá um cofre com três chaves, terá a Regente uma, o Secretário outra, e o Procurador outra, mas nunca o cofre se abrirá para coisa alguma, sem estarem presentes todos três pelos inconvenientes, que do contrário se podem seguir." AHU/CU-cód 1300, Estatuto da Confraria de Nossa Senhora dos Remédios, chaps. 12 and 13.

31 Chap. 13: "Mas porque atualmente está . . . de tesoureira das esmolas uma senhora que o fora do Regente passado, hoje falecido, por se ter valido da posse do cofre recorrendo à Justiça para ser conservada naquela mesma posse, como se a administração de semelhantes bens fosse compatível com aquele sexo, ou como, se esta poderá passar por morte do marido à mulher, como herança: Por evitar semelhante abuso, em conseqüência da Graça Régia suplicada será tirado o cofre do poder da depositária." Ibid.

32 Despite its fractious origins, the Fraternity of Our Lady of Remédios existed within the Brotherhood of Santo Elesbão and Santa Efigênia for many years. Today, elder members of the brotherhood recall that the Mahi were associated with mutiny and witchcraft, and prefer not to speak of them.

33 Mahi Manuscript, 30–36.

34 AISESE, *Compromisso* of the Brotherhood of Santo Elesbão and Santa Efigênia, chap. 1 of the *Folia*.

35 The kings and their courts were often referred to as *adjuntos* (adjuncts) at the time, underscoring their informality relative to the emperor.

36 *Cordeiro*: "Não se enfade com as minhas importunações porque a maior paixão que tenho, é de não ver os nossos nacionais todos católicos fazendo serviços a Deus que é o fim a que fomos nascidos."

Souza: "Algum dia nos fará Deus essa vontade, porque ele sabe muito bem o que faz, melhor do que imaginamos; . . . todas as maravilhas que temos recebido e recebemos da sua Onipotência e liberal mão, desde o princípio do Mundo sempre foram devagar. Pois virá tempo, que Vossa mercê veja cumprido este seu gosto."

Mahi Manuscript, 45 (65). This exchange is reminiscent of the Letter of Obedience sent by the heir to the throne of Kongo, D. Afonso I, to the pope in 1512 (cited in chapter 1 of this book).

37 AISESE, doc. 11.

38 Provision dated 11 March 1767, AISESE, doc. 11. The statutes of the Fraternity of Nossa Senhora dos Remédios specifies that members should be "Mina blacks," but does not overtly restrict other nations.

39 "Os de Angola tem por costume tomarem da tumba da Santa Casa da Misericórdia os cadáveres de seus parentes para os porem nas portas das Igrejas com cantigas gentílicas, e supersticiosas tirando esmola dos fiéis para os enterrarem, o que é constante nesta cidade, e por esta razão, os senhores brancos, entenderam que todos os pretos usavam do mesmo, quer que seja Mina, ou de Angola, e essa é a razão porque me eximo de reger e proteger os meus parentes." Mahi Manuscript, 7.

40 Ibid., 21, 44.

41 On the question of sources for the study of deviant behavior in the colonial period, see Ronaldo Vainfas, "Moralidades Brasílicas"; and Mott, "Cotidiano e Vivência Religiosa."

42 It is worth mentioning the case of police repression in the village of Cachoeira, Bahia, which as João Reis showed, represented a strategy by officers to guarantee good relations with ecclesiastical and other authorities. Reis, "Magia Jêje na Bahia."

43 On this movement, and especially the *autos-da-fé* that incorporated city residents, see Azevedo, "Judaísmo no Brasil."

44 Ecclesiastical regulations tended to dwell on the extreme cases, involving excommunication. But the *Constituições Primeiras* also acknowledges that smaller cases of individual infractions would be responded to with attempts to instruct in the Christian faith—even in heathen languages, if need be (Saint Paul and his epistle to the Corinthians are cited). The second book of the *Constituições Primeiras* portrays a continuum: there are many "nations and diverse tongues, that range from heathenism to this State" of spiritual enlightenment; and it was incumbent on religious authorities to make every effort to bring the light of God to the blind. In title 1 of the fifth book, persecution is discussed in the context of "heresy and Judaism."

45 The practice of animal sacrifice still occurs in Brazil today (notably in *candomblé* and *umbanda*), influenced by traditional culture as well as more recent contact with African religions.

46 Pereira, Nuno Marques. *Compêndio Narrativo do Peregrino da América* (1728); Reis, "Magia Jêje na Bahia"; Mott, "Acotundá"; State Library of Pernambuco, "Correspondência a Corte (1780–1781)."

47 "Que todos as pessoas que quiseram entrar nesse adjunto ou congregação (exceto pretos de Angola) sejam examinados pelo secretário deste adjunto e pelo *aggau* que é o Procurador Geral. Vejam que não sejam, pretos ou pretas, que usem de abusos e gentilismos ou superstição. E que em achando, ou tendo notícias que usam, não os podem receber." Mahi Manuscript, 31.

48 For another perspective on this issue, see Vainfas, *A Heresia dos Índios*.

49 "É o espaço do globo terrestre compreendido, entre os dois circulos paralelos entre si . . . Este espaço é como uma banda ou faixa, que contém muitos climas que os geógrafos dividem em cinco zonas ou partes, considerando segundo os diferentes graus de frio ou de calor, estas zonas são a tórrida, duas temperadas e duas frias ou glaciais." Mahi Manuscript, 49.

50 "Já no tempo do Reinado do Senhor Dom Afonso V fidelíssimo monarca de Portugal, havia comércio nas costas de África em Guiné de marfim e o ouro como adiante se mostrará, sendo autor destes descobrimentos o Senhor Infante Dom Henriques, filho 3° de El Rei Dom João, o primeiro, também de Portugal, que com o desejo que tinha da conversão dos infiéis e propagação da Santa Fé católica e do cresentamento da coroa deste Reino, e como bom geógrafo e matemático, que era alcançou tanto desta ciência que mediante a sua profunda erudição mostrou ao Mundo que havia Antípodas, e que, a Zona Tórrida era habitada, cousas naqueles tempos ignorada de todos os matemáticos e cosmógrafos. Contra os que trazem autoridades de Santo Agostinho e Latâncio Firmino que nega em muitos lugares haver Antípodas que são os habitadores das terras que o Infante queria descobrir. E informando-se o dito Infante dos Mouros de Ceuta quando lá esteve, veio a ter notícias dos desertos, de África a que eles chamam Cahará e dos povos que eles chamam azenegues, que confinam com o pretos Ialof aonde se começa a região que os Mouros, chamam Guinacolo, e em português quer dizer Guiné, tomada o seu distintivo da cidade Genna, que pelo muito bem ouro que tem é celebrado o seu Comércio; situada não muito longe do mar daquelas partes mui remotas em África aos Reinos de Fez a Marrocos." Mahi Manuscript, 49–50.

51 Souza went on to describe the size and "fury" of the Volta River, which he called Voltas: "Este rio é muito largo na entrada mas corre com tanta força que se conhece a sua corrente estando 3 léguas do mar, trás tantas árvores de dentro do sertão arrancadas que detendo-se e embarcando-se umas com as outras; causam na boca do rio grandes ariciros, de sorte que senão pode passar em uma canoa, mas que duas vezes no ano que é ordinariamente desde o mês de abril até o de novembro, mas deste mês por diante em que começam as chuvas cresce muito o rio, e corre com muita fúria, quem partir da Mina para o Rio das Voltas ponha-se 3 ou 4 léguas ao mar e faça o caminho de les nordeste,

e irá dar na aldeia deste rio e haverá na derrota quarenta e seis léguas pouco mais ou menos."

52 "Espertou-me Vossa Mercê agora as potências desta alma, com a lembrança da morte, que é o último fim em que havemos parar, e se não veja o que diz São Bazílio bispo da Capadócia pelo filósofo gentio Eubolo, qual era a definição da filosofia: respondeu que a primeira era o pensamento da morte e ficou tão convencido o filósofo, com esta resposta que logo se converteu à fé de Jesus Cristo Senhor Nosso, e é muito para considerar fazer uma só palavra tanto abalo em um gentio, que farei eu miserável pecador que desde minha infância conheço a Sua Santíssima fé e sou cristão pela graça de Deus. E não tendo eu merecimentos nem de meu pai nem de minha mãe." Mahi Manuscript, 57.

53 Ibid., 31.

54 This was the only area in which punishments were clearly prescribed in the statutes. They ranged from praying on bended knee to Our Lady, to carrying a large rock back and forth, to (upon the third offense) expulsion from the brotherhood as an *amotinador* (agitator). AISESE, *Compromisso* of the Brotherhood of Santo Elesbão and Santa Efigênia, chap. 31.

55 Masses were very expensive. It is not uncommon to find masses included in wills prepared by members of lay brotherhoods; in such cases, the person writing the will would commit to having the masses paid for out of his or her private funds upon death.

56 Mahi Manuscript, 32.

57 Ibid.

58 "É comum, quando dois pretos se encontram a serviço na rua, o súdito saudar respeitosamente o soberano de sua casta, beijar-lhe a mão e pedir-lhe a bênção. Dedicado, confiando nos conhecimentos de seu rei consulta-o nas circunstâncias difíceis. Quanto aos escravos nobres, graças à sua posição, conseguem de seus súditos os meios suficientes para comprar a própria liberdade; e desde então empregam escrupulosamente toda a sua atividade no reembolso da dívida sagrada." Debret, *Viagem Pitoresca e Histórica ao Brasil*, 185.

59 Along with the purchase of freedom came a certificate, called a "letter of enfranchisement," that described in florid prose the meanings of freedom. The letter presented to Feliciana Antonia do Desterro when she bought her freedom from Bishop D. Antônio do Desterro was composed well within the conventions of the era: "You can now go wherever you well choose, as master of yourself, as if you had been born free and autonomous from the womb of your mother," and so forth. (It goes on " . . . Lhe damos de hoje e para sempre liberdade para que fique sendo forra, e vá para onde muito bem quiser, como senhora, que ficou sendo de sí, como se livre e liberta nascesse do ventre da sua mãe.") ACMRJ, *Livro das Portarias e Ordens Episcopais*, 1779–1830, bk. 3, fol. 43v.

60 The writers of the *Constituições Primeiras* explained that they saw no reason to interfere, even when there was dancing on church grounds, as long as the

folias were "honest" and "decent." *Constituições Primeiras do Arcebispado da Bahia*, Livro 4, XXX, 742.

61 "Por quanto vemos que a experiência nos tem mostrado, que um estado de folias, nas irmandades pretas [seria] de muita utilidade assim de exercitar os ânimos dos pretos, como para acudirem de novo muitos de fora, assentarem pé na Congregação, a fim de os ir atraindo com aquela suavidade, para os por prontos para as caridades e tudo quanto for de serviço de Deus, nosso Senhor." Mahi Manuscript, 35.

62 "Queremos que no dia de Nossa Senhora do Rosário, haja um Estado de Folias desta nação Mahi, que acompanharão ao rei de Nossa Senhora do Rosário sendo da Costa da Mina e não o sendo, o não acompanharão, somente se permita as suas saídas, para o palácio do Ilustríssimo Excelentíssimo Senhor Vice-Rei deste Estado, e depois de brincarem, recolher-se cada um para sua casa, com toda quietação, e sossego, que se requer em semelhantes funções." Ibid., 35.

63 A provocative analysis of deviance in this context comes from Erving Goffman's exploration of "intergroup deviances" in Erving Goffman, *Estigma*, esp. chaps. 4 and 5.

64 See the discussion of negotiation and conflict in Reis and Silva, *Negociação e Conflito*.

65 The five were Boaventura Fernandes Braga (6, 12), Marçal Soares (11), Antônio da Costa Falcão (4), Luiz Rodrigues Silva (7), and Alexandre de Carvalho (10). The numbers in parentheses refer to the roster of ranks in the section "Who Should Have the Keys to the Safe?" of this chapter.

66 These two were Luiz Rodrigues Silva and Antônio da Costa Falcão.

67 "Toda a pessoa que quiser entrar para a Confraria dará de entrada seiscentos e quarenta de annual . . . , e apresentando-se ao Irmão Procurador ele o aceitará, e fará assinar nos Livros dos Irmãos. Porém se o novo Irmão notoriamente constar que é Preto de péssimos costumes, vicioso, infame, ou que usa de feitiçarias e superstições de nenhuma sorte o aceitará o Procurador, ficando . . . excluído de se queixar à Mesa, a qual informando-se também de sua conduta, ou o excluíra ou o aprovará, conforme o que lhe constar pela informação tomada." AHU/CU-cód. 1300, Estatuto da Confraria de Nossa Senhora do Remédios. *fol.* 7v.

68 Ibid., chap. 10.

69 "Com botica, enfermeiro, comida e até mortalha." Ibid., 5.

70 "Como apresente Irmandade se dedique por seu principal Instituto ao exercitar atos de caridade." Ibid., chap. 14.

71 Ibid., chaps. 9 and 23.

72 Here I depart somewhat from the very useful framework of Reis and Silva in *Negociação e Conflito*, which is concerned with negotiations of the exercise of power in daily life. I argue (particularly in chapter 5 of this book) that such

negotiations are also part of, and expressed in, the institutional sphere of rules and hierarchies

73 Estatuto da Confraria de Nossa Senhora do Remédios. Fol. 10v, 11; Estatuto da Confraria de Nossa Senhora do Remédios. Chap. 13: "But because presently the Treasurer of *Esmolas* is a lady who was the wife of the previous leader, now deceased, who used the secular courts to maintain herself in that position, as if the administration of such things was compatible with that sex, or as if such things could pass from husband to wife, as an inheritance. To avoid such abuse, Her Royal Grace is begged to remove the safe from the person who holds it for its right return to the house of the present leader, or another Brother of the board."

> "Mas porque atualmente estão . . . de Tesoureira das Esmolas uma senhora que o for a do Regente passado, hoje falecido, por se ter valido da posse do cofre recorrendo a Justiça para ser conservada naquela mesma posse, como se a administração de semelhantes bens fosse compatível com aquele sexo, ou como, se esta poderá passar por morte do marido à mulher, como herança: Por evitar semelhante abuso, em conseqüência da Graça Régia suplicada será tirado o cofre do poder da depositária onde se acha para a casa do Regente atual, ou de outro Irmão da Mesa."

74 Estatuto da Confraria de Nossa Senhora do Remédios. Fols. 10v, 15, chap. 24: "The Brotherhood of Mercy in this city has won a privilege, that does not have legal standing, to tax every other brotherhood a sum of four thousand reis each time that they appear on the street, whether for a festive procession or a funeral, in fulfillment of their own statutes. This is a severe and unjust burden to pay. We ask that, if the present statutes are granted royal permission, our Fraternity will not have to pay the Brotherhood of Mercy any penalty whatsoever in order to perform the functions prescribed in these statutes." (A Irmandade da Misericórdia desta Cidade tem advogado o privilégio, que não tem para Lei alguma ou Graça Régia, de multar todas as mais confrarias em quarto mil réis, cada vez que elas saem por conseqüência dos seus mesmos Estatutos a exercitar qualquer ato, ou seja de Procissão, ou de enterro, Quando . . . por gravames pecuniários, é um Direito inerente à Pessoa dos Príncipes Soberanos, e por isso em virtude da Aprovação Régia dos presentes Estatutos pretende a Confraria ficar isenta de contribuir à da Misericórdia multa alguma por exercitar todas e quaisquer funções prescritas neste Compromisso.)

75 The title of this section is "Second dialogue, in which are offered details regarding the founding of the grand fort of São Jorge of the Mina Coast, constructed on the African coast of Guinea, and its ports; and of the Kingdom of Benin; and other curious facts, by Francisco Alves de Souza, black, native of the Kingdom of Mahi—one of the most excellent and powerful of the Mina Coast." (Diálogo segundo em que se dá notícias da fundação da grandiosa

fortaleza de São Jorge da Costa da Mina edificada nas costas de África em
Guiné e dos seus portos e o reino de Benin, e outras notícias curiosas, por
Francisco Alves de Sousa, preto e natural do reino de Mahi um dos mais
excelentes e potentados daquela oriunda costa da Mina.) Mahi Manuscript, 47.

76 Ibid., 60.

77 "Já disse acima que o Rei que presentemente governa se chamava a Dâlicâ, e
estes quando morrem, lhe fazem os fidalgos da sua Corte, a que eles chamam
Ômon, um sacrifício matando 16 mais escravos, e partes dos mesmos fidalgos
e príncipes o acompanham à sepultura aonde se enterram com o cadaver do Rei
defunto, com grande número de seus trastes e vestidos, matando muita gente,
e com elas o sepultam dizendo que é para ele se servir no outro Mundo. E cousa
de sete dias lhes fazem outro sacrifício, matando tantos escravos a que chamam Ovem, dançando em cima do sepulcro do dito Rei a toques de tambores,
saltando ao redor dele fazendo muitas festas e visagens. E dizem que sendo o
Deus por natureza bom não necessitava de sacrifícios porem [o fazem] ao
diabo, para o aplacar adorando ao mesmo tempo a Ídolos." Ibid., 60–61.

78 Ibid., 28.

79 National Archive, códice 334 (1833–40), "Correspondência reservada recebida
pela Repartição de Polícia." Apud Abreu, *O Império do Divino*, bk. 1, n. 58, 220.

POSTSCRIPT

1 Adalgasia Arantes Campos et al., "O Banco de Dados Relativo ao Acervo da
Freguesia da Nossa Senhora do Pilar do Ouro Preto," 24.

2 Lada probably referred to Allada, an important kingdom on the coast. Documentation from the seventeenth century in Brazil called the natives of this place
Arda.

3 Verger, *Fluxo e Refluxo do Tráfico de Escravos entre o Golfo do Benin e a Bahia de Todos os
Santos dos Séculos XVIII a XIX*, 669–75.

4 According to Robin Law, the Mahi people were located north of Dahomey; they
derived from a fusion of Gbe speakers who came from the south and Yoruba
speakers from the east. Law, *The Slave Coast of West Africa, 1550–1750*, 19, 23–26.
There is not a discrete place called Mahi, and the territory of the Mahi people
included specific locales that were associated primarily with the Gbe language
(Savalu) and the Yoruba language (Dassa). For more on the Mahi language, see
Gbéto, *Le Maxi du Centre-Bénin et Centre-Togo*.

5 Savalu was a location within the Mahi territory. See Law, *The Slave Coast of West
Africa, 1550–1750*, 19.

6 Chamba was a place within modern Togo, but the term was often used for Gur
speakers as a group. Law, *The Slave Coast of West Africa, 1550–1750*, 189.

7 Jaquem, also called Jakin and Jeken, was one of the slave ports in the Bay of
Benin.

8 Earlier, I suggested that perhaps the slaves called Cobu (or Cabu) referred to the Kaabu of Senegambia, but present research indicates that these peoples may have come from the north of modern Benin.

9 This is a project in collaboration with Mauricio Abreu, with support from the Fundação de Amparo a Pesquisa do Estado do Rio de Janeiro (FAPERJ), 2007–9.

10 The Cobu have yet to receive significant attention from scholars. Work has begun on the Coura, however, with the completion of an important thesis on the presence of Couras in the Brotherhood of Nossa Senhora do Rosário in the town of Mariana, Minas Gerais, in the second half of the eighteenth century. Pinheiro, "Confrades do Rosário."

11 With a perspective of identity construction that is quite close to what I have called provenience groups, the historian Paul Lovejoy has suggested that the forced migration of millions of Africans to the Americas might have resulted in more inclusive ethnic identities. New forms of solidarity may have emerged in the New World between groups that had previously been separated by social, cultural, or geographic distance. Lovejoy, "Identifying Enslaved Africans in the African Diaspora."

12 Law, "Ethnicity and the Slave Trade."

13 On the Mahi, see J. A. M. A. R. Bergé, "Étude sur le Pays Mahi"; Robert Cornevin, *Histoire du Dahomey avec 10 cartes, 1 croquis et 35 photographies*; I. A. Akinjogbin, *Dahomey and Its Neighbours, 1708–1818*; Jessie Gaston Mulira, *A History of the Mahi Peoples from 1774–1920*; Law, *The Slave Coast of West Africa, 1550–1750*; and Edna G. Bay, *Wives of the Leopard*.

14 "E se seguiu pretender o mesmo Cabo que se lhe entregassem uns negros Couranos inimigos do Rey Daumê, que se dizia estarem na dita Fortaleza . . ." The Cabo here was an *agau* (a general of the Dahomean army). Verger, *Fluxo e Refluxo do Tráfico de Escravos entre o Golfo do Benin e a Bahia de Todos os Santos dos séculos XVIII a XIX*, 204–9.

15 Moacir Rodrigo de Castro Maia, "Quem Tem Padrinho Não Morre Pagão."

16 *Database of the Parish of Pilar*, cited by Patrícia Porto de Oliveira in "Batismo de Escravos Adultos e o Parentesco Espiritual nas Minas Setecentistas," 11.

17 "Rosto coartado à moda de sua terra, era baixa e refeita de corpo." *Coartado* is an archaic Portuguese word that meant "cut or divided in parts," but was also used for simply "cut" or "scarified."

18 I have yet to find an indication from the documents of how, when, or why Victoria wound up in Rio de Janeiro, or of how she obtained the funds to buy her letter of manumission. Her marriage record listed (or should have listed) all of the names she had used up to that moment: at baptism, Victoria Courana, slave of Domingos Correa Campos; upon buying her freedom, Victoria Correa Campos. Victoria does not appear in the list of freed black and *parda* women meticulously studied by Sheila de Castro Faria in *Sinhás Pretas, Damas Mercadoras*.

19 ACMRJ, *Livro de Batismo de Escravos da Freguesia de Nossa Senhora da Candelária*, 1745–74, from where the record dated 22 September 1742 was reproduced in the Habilitações Matrimoniais: Ignacio Monte e Victoria Correa, doc. 22119, caixa 1648.

20 Even more curious than the uncertain identity of Antônio Gonçalves and Antônio Gonçalves da Costa is Ignacio's assertion, thirty years later in his will, that he himself paid his master to purchase his freedom. ACMRJ, *Livro de Óbitos e Testamentos da Freguesia da Sé*, 1776–84, fols. 442v–44.

21 This price seems high, and yet it corresponds to the price paid in 1753 for another slave who was trained as a barber. This slave, Antônio, was freed by his wife, Rita da Silva, who delivered 256,000 réis to his owner with the promise to pay the remaining 94,000 réis in monthly installments of 4,000 réis. For his part, Ignacio had his freedom purchased with a combination of paper currency and gold and silver coins. Antônio's manumission letter was registered in the 1° Ofício de Notas do Rio de Janeiro, *Livro de Notas* 123, p. 130 (12 January 1753). Ignacio's was registered in the 2° Ofício de Notas do Rio de Janeiro, *Livro de Notas* 76, fol. 17v (12 January 1757). Both Ignacio and Antônio appear in the database of freed slaves compiled by Sheila de Castro Faria, whom I thank for the information.

22 ACMRJ, Habilitações Matrimoniais: Ignacio Monte e Victoria Correa, doc. 22119, caixa 1648.

23 ACMRJ, *Livro de Óbitos e Testamentos da Freguesia da Sé*, 1776–84, will of Ignacio Gonçalves do Monte, fols. 442v–444.

24 *Patrício* was used in his will to convey the same meanings as *parente*, a term that became more widespread in the nineteenth century. The notion of kin that both words connote is one of social group rather than family ties per se. This is particularly clear in the later documentation in Rio, as well as in Bahia; see João José Reis, *A Morte É uma Festa*, 55.

25 In accordance with ecclesiastical norms, Ignacio Monte's 1763 will was annexed to his death record. ACMRJ, *Livro de Óbitos e Testamentos da Freguesia da Sé*, 1776–84, will of Ignacio Gonçalves do Monte, fols. 442v–44.

26 Based on the names, it may be that José dos Santos Martins and Manoel dos Santos Martins—a freed Mina slave and a partner in the trio of freed brothers who bought the land for the Church of Santo Elesbão and Santa Efigênia—had both been owned by the same master.

27 Ignacio Monte was bedridden for a period of days before death; seemingly, he had time to rewrite his will. The stakes were even higher in 1783 than in 1763, not least because it was clear that his health was failing. It is curious that the parish death registry shows that he died on 27 December, but an official declaration of the Mahi Congregation specifies that it was the twenty-fifth. Given this, and the lack of a new will, one suspects that the death had been kept secret from the church authorities (and even from the Brotherhood of Santo

Elesbão and Santa Efigênia?) for a couple of days in order to get a handle on the ensuing conflicts regarding the future of the Mahi Congregation.

28 Six slaves were men; of these, two were working barbers and one was an apprentice. The tonsorial implements were evaluated at 8,000 réis and included the following: three used razor sharpeners of Bahian stone, mounted on rollers (900 réis each); three shaving basins (500 réis each); two other worn basins (250 réis each); one small anvil and iron hammer (800 réis); twelve well-used shaving razors (60 réis apiece); two sets of tongs for pulling teeth, and a small pincer (1,400 réis); one wooden razor sharpener (400 réis); and two leather razor cases (160 réis). AN, Inventário de José dos Santos Martins, doc. 7129, caixa 628, galleria A, Juízo dos Orfãos.

29 "I record these transactions in a little book that I keep in my drawer of valuables; my wife has complete knowledge of what is in there. The book has seventy-five pages, each marked with my name or nickname. Everything and anything written there by me is the absolute truth. I keep these records in the same manner as any businessman." (Cujos assentos e declarações faço em um livrinho que tenho na minha gaveta, aonde trago as mais cousas de valor de que minha mulher tem perfeito conhecimento e o dito livrinho tem setenta e cinco folhas, rubricados com o meu nome ou apelido, Monte. Tudo quanto estiver assentado e declarado nele por minha letra, é a mesma verdade. Os ditos assentos e declarações de dívidas, os faço em uma página conforme o número das folhas e as saídas em fronte como livros de deve, e o de haver dos homens de negócio.)

ACMRJ, Livro de Óbitos e Testamentos da Freguesia da Sé, 1776–84, will of Ignacio Gonçalves do Monte, fols. 442v–44.

30 Ibid., fols. 42v and 391. Carvalho and Braga and mentioned in the Mahi Manuscript as well as other documents from the Mahi Congregation.

31 ACMRJ, Livro de Óbitos e Testamentos da Freguesia da Sé, 1746–58, fols. 211–12.

32 ACMRJ, Livro de Óbitos e Testamentos da Freguesia da Sé, 1797–1809, fol. 90v.

33 Declaro que fui nascido em terras de brutos e de gentilidade como foi, [...] a Costa da Mina e sou da nação Cobu e por [...] o Senhor se querer lembrar de mim, passei daquele reino, dele [...] há sete anos pouco mais ou menos a vender [...] da Cidade da Bahia onde fui vendido ao primeiro senhor que tive na dita [terra cidade] por nome Antônio de Bastos Mendes, o que me ensinou a Santa Doutrina e me mandou batizar e, com efeito, fui batizado na Igreja de Nossa Senhora da Conceição da Praia da dita cidade qual parti também a vender nesta Cidade do Rio de Janeiro e fui comprado pelo defunto em sua vida Antônio Soares homem estrangeiro e boticário que foi e morou com sua mulher detrás do Convento da Nossa Senhora do Monte do Carmo e desta escravidão me libertei depois do dito defunto por duzentos e tantos mil réis que dei pela minha pessoa ao defunto o Reverendo Padre Teodósio de Souza como testamenteiro do mesmo defunto o qual

testamenteiro me passou Carta da Liberdade em notas pelo sobredito preço tudo feito a beneplácito e consentimento e vontade da mulher viúva do sobredito defunto.

ACMRJ, Livro de Óbitos e Testamentos da Freguesia da Sé, 1746–58, will of Antônio Luiz Soares, deceased 27 January 1755, fols. 298v–301.

34 Silva's wealth is indicated in her request that her corpse be dressed in the habit of São Francisco, and that her funeral procession be accompanied by twelve priests.

35 The price was 233,330 réis. AN, "Escritura de venda de chãos que faz Maria Correia de Abreu, viúva de Bernardo Tavares, aos irmãos de Santo Elesbão e Santa Efigênia Manoel dos Santos Martins, Antonio Pires dos Santos e Francisco Gonçalves Nunes, pretos forros . . ." 4° Offício de Notas. Livro de Notas: 24/2/1744–7/9/1744. N 36, p. 109.

36 ACMRJ, Livro de Óbitos e Testamentos da Freguesia da Sé, 1746–58, fls. 211–12.

37 Declaro que sou natural da Costa da Mina preto forro, e liberto, e fui escravo de Domingos Gonçalves do Monte, a quem dei por minha liberdade trezentos, e cinqüenta mil réis como constará da minha Carta de Alforria. Declaro que sou casado com Vitória Correa da Conceição, preta forra, e até o fazer deste meu testamento não temos tido filhos, e nem os tenho de outra qualquer mulher em solteiro, e nem depois de casado. Declaro que a dita minha mulher é minha parenta por sangüinidade [sic] em terceiro grau, por ser ela filha do meu avô [Eseú] Agoa; bem conhecido rei que foi entre os gentios daquela costa do Reino de May, ou Maqui.

ACMRJ, Livro de Óbitos e Testamentos da Freguesia da Sé, 1776–84, will of Ignacio Gonçalves Monte, fols. 422v–44.

38 Slippage between the concepts of territory/region/land on the one hand, and country on the other, is common not only in the assertions in these wills but also in the documents of Portuguese and French colonial administrations. See, for example, the title of the work by Bergé—"Étude sur le Pays Mahi"—where the word pays (country) is used instead of the more common, and theoretically distinct, terre (land).

39 Soares, "O Império de Santo Elesbão na Cidade do Rio de Janeiro, século XVIII."

40 He specifies: "O qual testamento por assim o querer, o fiz da minha letra e Sinal, hoje Cidade de São Sebastião do Rio de Janeiro dia mes e ano ao principio declarado. Ignacio Gonçalves do Monte." ACMRJ, Livro de Óbitos e Testamentos da Freguesia da Sé, 1776–84, will of Ignacio Gonçalves Monte, fols. 422v–444.

41 See the roster of directors of the Mahi Congregation in chapter 6, where Braga is identified as a duke, or "aeolû cocoti de daçâ" The suffix de daçâ likely meant "from Dassa." Also, José Luiz, a marquis, was called ajacôto chaul de za," and Za was the name of a city west of Dahomey. For more on these cities see Law, The Slave Coast of West Africa, 1550–1750.

42 The "god of her land" phrase mentioned above emerged from a court hearing against one Josepha Coura, which has been analyzed by Luiz Mott. According to the official narrative of the case, Josepha engaged in something called the *Acotundá* (Dance of Tunda), uttered chants in the Coura language, and offered sacrifices to the god of her land, which was represented by an idol: "A clay figure with its facial features clearly in imitation of the Devil, wearing a white black cape, impaled on an iron stake. This pagan doll was placed on a rug in the middle of her house, surrounded by clay pots of water and metal pans containing offerings such as cooked and raw herbs, shells, African money, a dead chicken, beans, et cetera. Luiz Mott, "Acotundá."

43 On the lands and nations most prominent in eighteenth-century discourse, see Soares, "A 'Nação' que Se Tem." For more on the disappearance of the Mina nation in Rio de Janeiro, see Soares, "From Gbe to Yoruba."

44 As said before, the full title of the Mahi Manuscript at the overture of the document is "Regra ou estatuto por modo de um diálogo onde, se dá notícia das Caridades e Sufragações das Almas que usam os pretos Minas, com seus Nacionais no Estado do Brazil, especialmente no Rio de Janeiro, por onde se hão de regerem e governarem for a de todo o abuzo gentílico e supersticioso; composto por Francisco Alves de Souza preto e natural do Reino de Makim, um dos mais excelentes e potentados daquela oriunda Costa da Mina."

45 David Eltis, Stephen D. Behrendt, David Richardson, and Herbert Klein, *The Trans-Atlantic Slave Trade: A Database*.

BIBLIOGRAPHY

ABBREVIATIONS

ABN—Anais da Biblioteca Nacional
ACMRJ—Arquivo da Cúria Metropolitana do Rio de Janeiro
AHU/CU—Arquivo Histórico Ultramarino/Coleção Ultramarina
AISESE—Arquivo da Irmandade de Santo Elesbão e Santa Efigênia
AN—Arquivo Nacional
APEB—Arquivo Público do Estado da Bahia
BEP—Biblioteca do Estado de Pernambuco
BN(RJ)—Biblioteca Nacional do Rio de Janeiro
CNSR—Confraria de Nossa Senhora dos Remédios
IHGB—Instituto Histórico e Geográfico Brasileiro
RIHGB—Revista do Instituto Histórico e Geográfico Brasileiro

ARCHIVES AND MANUSCRIPTS CONSULTED

Arquivo da Cúria Metropolitana do Rio de Janeiro (ACMRJ)

Habilitações Matrimoniais: Ignacio Monte e Victoria Correa, doc. 22119, caixa 1648
Livro de Batismo de Escravos, Freguesia da Sé, 1718–26
Livro de Batismo de Escravos, Freguesia da Sé, 1744–61
Livro de Batismo de Escravos, Freguesia da Candelária, 1745–74
Livro de Batismo de Escravos, Freguesia de São José, 1751–90
Livro de Batismo de Escravos, Freguesia de Santa Rita, 1751–99
Livro de Óbito de Escravos, Freguesia da Candelária, 1724–36
Livro de Óbito de Escravos, Freguesia da Candelária, 1793–33
Livro de Óbito e Testamentos, Freguesia de Santa Rita, 1751–17[?]
Livro de Óbitos e Testamentos da Freguesia da Sé, 1746–1758

Livro de Óbitos e Testamentos da Freguesia da Sé, 1776–1784
Livro de Óbitos e Testamentos da Freguesia de Nossa Senhora da Candelária, 1797–1809
Livro de Portarias Episcopais, #3, 1779–1830

Arquivo Histórico Ultramarino, Lisbon

"Estatuto da Irmandade de Nossa Senhora dos Remédios," AHU/CU-cód. 1300
"Representação da Irmandade do Rosário," AHU, Rio de Janeiro, caixa 107, doc. 31

Biblioteca do Estado de Pernambuco

"Correspondência da Corte (1780–81)"

Biblioteca Nacional, Rio de Janeiro (BN [RJ])

"Regra ou estatuto por modo de um diálogo onde, se dá notícia das Caridades e Sufragações das Almas que usam os pretos Minas, com seus Nacionais no Estado do Brazil, especialmente no Rio de Janeiro, por onde se hão de regerem e governarem for a de todo o abuzo gentílico e supersticioso; composto por Francisco Alves de Souza preto e natural do Reino de Makim, um dos mais excelentes e potentados daquela oriunda Costa da Mina. (1787)"

Museu do Negro: Arquivo da Irmandade de Santo Elesbão e Santa Efigênia (AISESE)

"Compromisso da Irmandade de Santo Elesbão e Santa Efigênia" (copy, including ecclesiastical correspondence pertaining to the compromisso's approval)
"Estatutos da Congregação dos Pretos Minas Maki no RJ (1786)"

PUBLISHED SOURCES, BOOKS, AND ARTICLES

Abreu, Martha Campos. "O Império do Divino: Festas Religiosas e Cultura Popular no Rio de Janeiro (1830–1900)." Ph.D. diss., Universidade de Campinas, 1996.
Abreu, Maurício. *Evolução Urbana do Rio de Janeiro.* Rio de Janeiro: IPLANRIO, 1988.
Agassiz, Luiz, and Elizabeth Cary Agassiz. *Viagem ao Brasil: 1865–1866.* Belo Horizonte, 1975.
Akinjogbin, I. A. *Dahomey and Its Neighbors, 1708–1818.* Cambridge: Cambridge University Press, 1967.
Alden, Dauril. "The Population of Brazil in the Late Eighteenth Century: A Preliminary Study." *Hispanic American Historical Review* 43 (May 1963): 175–205.

Alencastro, Luis Felipe. "La Traite Négrière et l'Unité Nationale Brésilienne." *Revue Française d'Histoire d'Outre-Mer* 66 (1979): 244–45.

Algranti, Leila Mezan. *Honradas e Devotas: Mulheres da Colônia. Estudo sobre a Condição Feminina nos Conventos e Recolhimentos do Sudeste do Brasil (1750–1822)*. Rio de Janeiro: José Olympio Ed., 1993.

Almeida, Eduardo de Castro, ed. "Inventário dos Documentos Relativos ao Brasil Existentes no Archivo da Marinha e Ultramar Organizado por Eduardo de Castro Almeida: Bahia 1613–1762." *Annaes da Biblioteca Nacional do Rio de Janeiro*. Vol. 31 (1909). Rio de Janeiro: Officinas Graphicas da Bibliotheca Nacional, 1913.

——. "Inventário dos Documentos Relativos ao Brasil Existentes no Archivo da Marinha e Ultramar Organizado por Eduardo de Castro Almeida: Bahia 1613–1762." *Annaes da Biblioteca Nacional do Rio de Janeiro*, vol. 34 (1917). Rio de Janeiro: Officinas Graphicas da Bibliotheca Nacional, 1921.

Andreoni, João António (André João Antonil). *Cultura e Opulência do Brasil: Introdução e Vocabulário por A. P. Canabrava*. São Paulo: Companhia Editora Nacional, 1967.

Araújo, José de Souza Azevedo Pizarro (Monsenhor Pizarro). *Memórias Históricas do Rio de Janeiro*. 10 vols. Rio de Janeiro: Imprensa Nacional, 1948.

Ariès, Philipp. *O Homem Diante da Morte*. 2 vols. Rio de Janeiro: Francisco Alves, 1989.

Augé, Paul. *Larousse du XXème Siècle*. 6 vols. Paris: Larousse, 1930.

Azevedo, João Lúcio de. *Épocas de Portugal Económico: Esboços de História*. Lisbon: Livraria Clássica Editora, 1929.

——. "Judaísmo no Brasil." *Revista do Instituto Histórico e Geográfico Brasileiro* 91, no. 682.

Azevedo, Moreira de. *O Rio de Janeiro: Sua História, Monumentos, Homens Notáveis, Usos e Curiosidades*. 2 vols. Rio de Janeiro: Livraria Brasiliana Editora, 1969.

Azevedo, Paulo Cesar, and Mauricio Lissovsky, eds. *Escravos Brasileiros do Século XIX na Fotografia de Christiano Jr.* Essays by Jacob Gorender, and Manuela Carneiro da Cunha e Muniz Sodré. São Paulo: Editora Ex Libris, 1988.

Baldé, S. M. "L'Esclavage et la Guerre Sainte au Fuuta-Jalon (Maccugaaku au Funta-Jaloo)." In *L'Esclavage en Afrique Précoloniale*, edited by Claude Meillassoux. Paris: Françoise Maspero, 1975.

Barreiros, Eduardo Canabrava. *Atlas da Evolução Urbana da Cidade do Rio de Janeiro: Ensaio—1565–1965*. Rio de Janeiro: IHGB, 1965.

Barreto Filho, Mello, and Hermeto Lima. *História da Polícia do Rio de Janeiro: Aspectos da Vida Carioca 1565–1831*. 3 vols. Rio de Janeiro: Editora A Noite, 1939.

Barreto, Luis Felipe. *Descobrimentos e Renascimento: Formas de Ser e de Pensar nos Séculos XV e XVI*. Lisbon: Imprensa Nacional, Casa da Moeda, 1982.

Barros, João de. *Ásia: Dos Feitos Que os Portugueses Fizeram no Descobrimento e Conquista dos Mares e Terras do Oriente. 1° Década*. 6th ed. Lisbon: Agência Geral das Colônias, 1945.

Barth, Fredrik. "Introduction." In *Ethnic Groups and Boundaries: The Social Organization of Culture Difference*, edited by Fredrik Barth. Boston: Little, Brown, 1969.

Bartolomé, Miguel Alberto. "Bases Culturales de la Identidad Étnica." In *Gente de Costumbre y Gente de Razón: Las Identidades Étnicas en México*, edited by Miguel Alberto Bartolomé. Mexico City: Siglo Vientiuno Editores, 1997.

Bastide, Roger. *As Religiões Africanas no Brasil: Contribuição a uma Sociologia das Interpenetrações de Civilizações*. São Paulo: Livraria Pioneira Editora, 1989.

——. *O Candomblé da Bahia*. São Paulo: Companhia Editora Nacional, 1978.

Bay, Edna G. *Wives of the Leopard: Gender, Politics, and Culture in the Kingdom of Dahomey*. Charlottesville: University of Virginia Press, 1998.

Bergé, J. A. M. A. R. "Étude sur le Pays Mahi." *Bulletin du Comité d'Études Historiques et Scientifiques de l'A O F II* (1928).

Berger, Paulo. *Bibliografia do Rio de Janeiro de Viajantes e Autores Estrangeiros, 1531–1900*. Rio de Janeiro: Livraria São José, 1964.

Bethell, Leslie. *A Abolição do Tráfico de Escravos no Brasil: A Grã-Bretanha, o Brasil e a Questão do Tráfico de Escravos, 1807–1869*. Rio de Janeiro: Expressão e Cultura, 1976.

Biblioteca Nacional. *Anais da Biblioteca Nacional do Rio de Janeiro*. Vol. 31. Rio de Janeiro: Biblioteca Nacional, 1909.

——. *Anais da Biblioteca Nacional do Rio de Janeiro*. Vol. 34. Rio de Janeiro: Biblioteca Nacional, 1910.

Bicalho, Maria Fernanda, "A Cidade e o Império: O Rio de Janeiro na Dinâmica Colonial Portuguesa, Séculos XVII e XVIII." Ph.D. diss., University of São Paulo, 1997.

Blake, John William. *European Beginnings in West Africa, 1454–1578: A Survey of the First Century of White Enterprise in West Africa, with Special Emphasis upon the Rivalry of the Great Powers*. Westport, Conn.: Greenwood Press, 1937.

Bloch, Marc. *Introdução à História*. Publicações Europa-América, n.d.

Boschi, Caio César. *Os Leigos e o Poder: Irmandades Leigas e Política em Minas Gerais*. São Paulo: Editora Ática, 1986.

Bosi, Alfredo. *Dialética da Colonização*. São Paulo: Companhia das Letras, 1992.

Bossy, John. *A Cristandade no Ocidente, 1400–1700*. Lisbon: Edições 70, 1990.

Bott, Elizabeth. *Família e Rede Social: Papéis, Normas e Relacionamentos Externos em Famílias Urbanas Comuns*. Preface by Max Gluckman. Rio de Janeiro: Francisco Alves, 1976.

Boxer, C. R. "Brazilian Gold and British Traders in the First Half of the Eighteenth Century." *Hispanic American Historical Review* 19, no. 3 (1969): 455–72.

——. *A Idade de Ouro do Brasil: Dores de Crescimento de uma Sociedade Colonial*. São Paulo: Companhia Editora Nacional, 1969.

——. *O Império Colonial Português (1415–1825)*. Lisbon: Edições 70, 1981.

———. *Relações Raciais no Império Colonial Português (1415–1825)*. Porto, Portugal: Afrontamento, 1988.

———. *Salvador de Sá e a Luta pelo Brasil e Angola (1602–1686)*. São Paulo: Editora Nacional, 1973.

Bragança, J. "Introdução" and "Do Título desta Crônica." In *Crónicas de Guiné*, by Gomes Eanes Zurara. Barcelos, Portugal: Livraria Civilização Editora, 1973.

Braudel, Fernand. *Escritos sobre a História*. São Paulo: Editora Perspectiva, 1992.

Burguière, André. "A Antropologia Histórica." In *A Nova História*, edited by Jacques Le Goff. Coimbra: Almedina, 1990.

Burke, Peter. *A Fabricação do Rei: A Construção da Imagem Pública de Luis XIV*. Rio de Janeiro: Jorge Zahar Editor, 1994.

Campos, Adalgasia Arantes, et al. "O Banco de Dados Relativo ao Acervo da Freguesia da Nossa Senhora do Pilar de Ouro Preto: Registros Paroquiais e as Possibilidades de Pesquisa." Proceedings of the 10th Seminar on the Economy of Minas Gerais. Diamantina, Brazil. 2002

Campos, S. J. *Procissões Tradicionais da Bahia*. [Published posthumously.] Preface by Arnaldo Pimenta da Cunha. Salvador: Museu da Bahia: Secretaria de Educação e Saúde, 1941.

Carmo Neto, Henrique José do. "Recordações e Aspectos do Culto de Sangt'Anna." *Revista do Instituto Histórico e Geográfico Brasileiro* 94, no. 142, pt. 2 (1927).

Carreira, António. *As Companhias Pombalinas de Navegação, Comércio e Tráfico de Escravos entre a Costa Africana e o Nordeste Brasileiro*. Porto, Portugal: Centro de Estudos da Guiné Portuguesa, 1969.

———. *Notas sobre o Tráfico Português de Escravos, Circunscritos à Costa Ocidental Africana*. Lisbon: Universidade Nova de Lisboa, 1978.

Carvalho, Delgado de. *História da Cidade do Rio de Janeiro*. Rio de Janeiro: Secretaria Municipal da Cultura, 1994.

Cascudo, Luís da Câmara. *Dicionário do Folclore Brasileiro*. Rio de Janeiro: Ediouro, n.d.

Castro, Hebe Maria Mattos de. *Das Cores do Silêncio: Os Significados da Liberdade no Sudeste Escravista—Brasil, Século XIX*. Rio de Janeiro: Arquivo Nacional, 1995.

Castro, Therezinha de. *História Documental do Brasil*. Rio de Janeiro: Record, n.d.

Catálogo da Exposição de História do Brasil. Realizada pela Biblioteca Nacional do Rio de Janeiro a 2 de Dezembro de 1881. Rio de Janeiro: Typographia G. Leuzinger and Filhos, 1881. (3 volumes)

Cavalcanti, Nireu Oliveira, "A Cidade do Rio de Janeiro: As Muralhas, Sua Gente, os Construtores (1710–1810)." Ph.D. diss., Federal University of Rio de Janeiro, 1998.

Chahon, Sérgio. "Aos Pés do Altar e do Trono: As Irmandades e o Poder Régio no Brasil (1808–1822)." M.A. thesis, Universidade de São Paulo, 1996.

Chartier, Roger. "Textos, Impressões, Leituras." In *A Nova História Cultural*, edited by Lynn Hunt. São Paulo: Martins Fontes, 1992.

Chartier, Roger, and D. Roche. "Social (História)." In *A Nova História*, edited by Jacques Le Goff. Coimbra: Almedina, 1990.

Chaunu, Pierre. *Conquista e Exploração dos Novos Mundos: Século XVI*. São Paulo: EduSP, 1984.

———. *Expansão Européia do Século XIII ao XV*. São Paulo: Pioneira, 1978.

Coaracy, Vivaldo. *Memórias da Cidade do Rio de Janeiro*. Belo Horizonte: Itatiaia, 1988.

———. *O Rio de Janeiro no Século Dezessete*. Rio de Janeiro: Livraria José Olympio Editora, 1965.

Código Philipino ou Ordenações e Leis do Reino de Portugal recompiladas por mando D'El Rey D. Philipe I. Facsimile 1603 and 1821. Brasília, Senado Federal. 2004.

Constituições Primeiras do Arcebispado da Bahia. Feitas e Ordenados pelo Illustrissimo e Reverendissimo Senhor D. Sebastião Monteiro da Vide 5° Arcebispo da dito Arcebispado, e do Conselho de sua Magestade: Propostas, e Aceitas em o Sinodo Diocesano, Que o dito senhor celebrou em 12 de junho do anno 1707. São Paulo: Typographia 2 de Dezembro de Antonio Louzada Antunes, 1853.

Coquery-Vidrovitch, Catherine, ed. *A Descoberta da África*. Lisbon: Edições 70, 1981.

Cornevin, Robert. *Histoire du Dahomey avec 10 Cartes, 1 Aroquis et 35 Photographies*. Paris: Éditions Berger-Levrault, 1962.

Cunha, Manuela Carneiro da. *Antropologia do Brasil. Mito–História–Etnicidade*. São Paulo: Brasiliense, 1987.

———, ed. *História dos Índios no Brasil*. São Paulo: FAPESP, 1992.

Cuvelier, J., and L. Jadin. *L'Ancien Congo d'après les Archives Romaines (1518–1640)*. MIRCB, XXXV I, 2. Brussels, 1954.

Debret, Jean-Baptiste. *O Brasil de Debret*. Essay by Sérgio Milliet, Rubens Borba de Morais, and Antônio Carlos Villaça. Belo Horizonte: Editora Vila Rica, 1993.

———. *Viagem Pitoresca e Histórica ao Brasil*. Essay by Sérgio Millet. São Paulo. Livraria Martins, 1940.

———. *Viagem Pitoresca e Histórica ao Brasil*. Preface by Antônio Carlos Villaça. Belo Horizonte: Itatiaia, 1989.

Delumeau, Jean. *A Civilização do Renascimento*. Lisbon: Editorial Estampa, 1984.

Devisse, Jean, ed. *Les Assises du Pouvoir: Temps Médiévaux, Territoires Africains*. Saint-Denis, France: Presses Universitaires de Vincennes, 1994.

Duby, Georges. *Guilherme Marechal ou o Melhor Cavaleiro do Mundo*. Rio de Janeiro: Graal, 1988.

Elias, Norbert. *A Sociedade de Corte*. Lisbon: Editorial Estampa, 1987.

Eltis, David, Stephen D. Behrendt, David Richardson, and Herbert Klein. *The Trans-Atlantic Slave Trade: A Database on CD-ROM*. New York: Cambridge University Press, 1999.

Espanha, Antônio Manoel. *Às Vésperas do Leviathan: Instituições e Poder Político, Portugal—séc. XVII*. Coimbra, Portugal: Livraria Almedina, 1994.

Faria, Sheila de Castro. "Sinhás Pretas, 'Damas Mercadoras.' As pretas minas nas cidades do Rio de Janeiro e de São João Del Rei (1700–1850)." Manuscript, 2004. In author's possession.

Faria, Sheila Siqueira de Castro. "A Colônia em Movimento: Fortuna e Família no Cotidiano Colonial (Sudeste, Século XVIII)." Ph.D. diss., Universidade Federal Fluminense, Niterói, 1994.

Fazenda, Vieira. "Antiqualhas e Memórias do Rio de Janeiro." Revista do Instituto Histórico e Geográfico Brasileiro 86, no. 140 (1919), 1921.

———. "Antiqualhas e Memórias do Rio de Janeiro." Revista do Instituto Histórico e Geográfico Brasileiro 89, no. 143 (1921), 1924.

———. "Antiqualhas e Memórias do Rio de Janeiro." Revista do Instituto Histórico e Geográfico Brasileiro 93, 147 (1923), 1927.

———. "Antiqualhas e Memórias do Rio de Janeiro." Revista do Instituto Histórico e Geográfico Brasileiro 88, 142 (2nd ed.), 1940.

———. "Antiqualhas e Memórias do Rio de Janeiro." Revista do Instituto Histórico e Geográfico Brasileiro 95, 149 (2nd ed.), 1943.

Ferreira, Aurélio Buarque de Holanda. Dicionário da Língua Portuguesa. Rio de Janeiro: Nova Fronteira, 1975.

Ferreira, João da Costa. "A Cidade do Rio de Janeiro e Seu Termo." Revista do Instituto Histórico e Geográfico Brasileiro 164 (1931). Offprint.

Ferrez, Gilberto. As Cidades do Salvador e Rio de Janeiro no Século XVIII: Álbum Iconográfico Comemorativo do Bicentenário da Transferência da Sede do Govêrno do Brasil. Rio de Janeiro: IHGB, 1963.

———. "Diário Anônimo de uma Viagem às Costas d'África e às Índias Espanholas." Revista do Instituto Histórico e Geográfico Brasileiro 267 (April–July 1965).

———. "O Rio de Janeiro." Revista do Instituto Histórico e Geográfico Brasileiro 288 (July–September 1970). Published in 1971.

———. O Rio de Janeiro e a Defesa do Seu Porto—1555–1800. Rio de Janeiro: Serviço de Documentação Geral da Marinha, 1972.

Figueiredo, Luciano. O Avesso da Memória: Cotidiano e Trabalho da Mulher em Minas Gerais no Século XVIII. Preface by Laura de Mello e Souza. Brasília: EdUnB, 1993.

Fitzler, M. A. Hedwig, and Ernesto Enes. A Seção Ultramarina da Biblioteca Nacional: Inventários. Lisbon: Biblioteca Nacional. 1928.

Florentino, Manolo Garcia. "Alforrias e Etnicidade no Rio de Janeiro Oitocentista: Notas de Pesquisa." Topoi 5, 2002.

———. Em Costas Negras: Uma História do Tráfico Atlântico de Escravos entre a África e o Rio de Janeiro (Séculos XVIII e XIX). Rio de Janeiro: Arquivo Nacional, 1995.

Fynn, J. K. Asante and Its Neighbours, 1700–1807. Evanston: Northwestern University Press, 1971.

Gbéto, Flavien. Le Maxi du Centre-Bénin et du Centre-Togo: Une approche Autosegmentale et Dialectologique d'un Parler Gbe de la Section Fon. Cologne: Köppe, 1997.

Ginzburg, C. "Sinais: Raízes de um Paradigma Indiciário." In Mitos, Emblemas, Sinais: Morfologia e História. São Paulo: Companhia das Letras, 1989.

Godinho, Vitorino Magalhães. *Ensaios II: Sobre a História de Portugal*. Lisbon: Livraria Sá da Costa Editora, 1968.

Goffman, Erving. *Estigma: Notas sobre a Manipulação da Identidade Deteriorada*. Rio de Janeiro: Editora Guanabara, n.d.

Goulart, Maurício. *A Escravidão Africana no Brasil: Das Origens à Extinção do Tráfico*. Preface by Sérgio Buarque de Holanda. São Paulo: Editora Alfa-Omega, 1975.

Gouveia, Alfredo Mendes de. "Relação dos Compromissos de Irmandades, Confrarias e Misericórdias do Brasil: Existentes no Arquivo Histórico Colonial de Lisboa, Que Pertenceram ao Cartório do Extinto Conselho Ultramarino 1716–1807." *Anais do IV Congresso de História Nacional* 7 (1949): 201–38.

Gudeman, Stephen, and Stuart Schwartz. "Purgando o Pecado Original: Compadrio e Batismo na Bahia no Século XVIII." In *Escravidão e Invenção da Liberdade*, edited by João José Reis. São Paulo: CNPq, 1988.

Guedes, Max Justo, and Gerald Lombardi, eds. *Portugal Brazil: The Age of Atlantic Discoveries*. Lisbon: Bertrand Editora, 1990.

Guia Brasileiro de Fontes para a História da África, da Escravidão Negra e do Negro na Sociedade Atual. Vol. 2: *Rio de Janeiro-Sergipe*. Rio de Janeiro: Arquivo Nacional, 1988.

Henriques, Isabel de Castro. "L'Invention Sociale de São Tomé et Principe au XVIe siècle." In *Les Assises du Pouvoir: Temps Médiévaux, Territoires Africains*. Saint-Denis, France: Presses Universitaires de Vincennes, 1994.

Herskovits, Melville J. *Antropologia Cultural*. São Paulo: Editora Mestre Jou, 1973.

———. "On the Provenience of New World Negroes." *Social Forces* 12 (1933): 247-62.

Holanda, Sérgio Buarque de. "Prefácio." In *A Escravidão Africana no Brasil: Das Origens à Extinção do Tráfico*. São Paulo: Editora Alfa-Omega, 1975.

———. "O Semeador e o Ladrilhador." In *Raizes do Brasil*. Rio de Janeiro: José Olympio Editora, 1993.

Hoornaert, Eduardo, Riolando Azzi, Klaus van der Grijp, and Benno Brod. *História da Igreja no Brasil: Ensaio de Interpretação a Partir do Povo. Primeira Época*. Petrópolis: Edições Paulinas, 1992.

Jancsó, István. *Cronologia de História do Brasil Colonial (1500–1831)*. São Paulo: Departamento de História, 1994.

Joutard, Philippe. "Un Projet Régional de Recherche sur les Ethnotextes." In *Annales: Économie Sociétés Civilisations* 35, no. 1 (January–February 1980): 176–82.

Julião, Carlos. *Riscos Iluminados de Figurinhos de Brancos e Negros dos Uzos do Rio de Janeiro e Serro do Frio*. Historical introduction and descriptive catalogue by Lygia da Fonseca Fernandes Cunha. Rio de Janeiro: Biblioteca Nacional, 1960.

Karasch, Mary. *Slave Life in Rio de Janeiro, 1808–1850*. Princeton: Princeton University Press, 1987.

Klein, Herbert S. "The Portuguese Trade from Angola in the 18th Century." In *The Middle Passage: Comparative Studies in the Atlantic Slave Trade*. Princeton: Princeton University Press, 1978.

Lacerda, José Maria de Almeida e Araújo Correa de. *Diccionario Enciclopédico*. 2 vols. Lisbon: Escritório de Francisco Arthur da Silva, 1879.

Lapa, José Roberto do Amaral. *A Bahia e a Carreira da Índia*. São Paulo: Companhia Editora Nacional, 1968.

Lara, Silvia Hunold, ed. *Revista Brasileira de História*, 16, file "Escravidão." São Paulo: ANPUH, 1988.

——. "Sob o Signo da Cor: Trajes Femininos e Relações Raciais nas Cidades de Salvador e do Rio de Janeiro, ca. 1750–1815." Paper presented at the Latin American Studies Association, 1974.

Law, Robin. "Ethnicity and the Slave Trade: 'Lucumi' and 'Nago' as Ethnonyms in West Africa." *History in Africa* 24 (1997): 205–19.

——. *The Slave Coast of West Africa, 1550–1750: The Impact of the Atlantic Slave Trade on an African Society*. Oxford: Clarendon Press, 1991.

Leal, Euripedes Franklin, and Ana Regina Berwanger. *Noções de Paleografia e Diplomática*. Santa Maria: Universidade Federal de Santa Maria, 1992.

Le Goff, Jacques, ed. *A Nova História*. Coimbra: Almedina, 1990.

Leite, Miriam Moreira, ed. *A Condição Feminina no Rio de Janeiro no Século XIX: Antologia de Textos de Viajantes Estrangeiros*. São Paulo: Editora Hucitec, 1984.

Lisboa, Balthazar da Silva. *Annaes do Rio de Janeiro, Contendo a Descoberta e Conquista deste País, a Fundação da Cidade com a História Civil e Eclesiástica, até a Chegada d'el-Rei Dom João VI; Além de Notícias Topográphicas, Zoológicas e Botânicas*. Bk. 7. Rio de Janeiro: Typ. Imp. E Const. De Seignot-Plancher e Cia, 1835.

Lloyd, P. C. "The Political Structure of African Kingdoms—an Exploratory Model." In *Political Systems and the Distribution of Power*, edited by Michael Banton. London, 1966.

Lobo, Maria Eulália Lahmeyer. *História do Rio de Janeiro (do Capital Commercial ao Capital Industrial e Financeiro)*. Rio de Janeiro: IBMEC, 1978.

——. "Historiografia do Rio de Janeiro." *Revista Brasileira de História*, file "Historiografia Propostas e Práticas," 15, 30 São Paulo: ANPUH Contexto, 1995: 45–62.

Lopes, Vânia Penha. "À Venerável Irmandade de Santo Elesbão e Santa Efigênia, ou uma Tentativa de Entendimento da Questão Étnica no Brasil." B.A. thesis, Universidade Federal Fluminense, Niterói, 1981.

Lovejoy, Paul E. "Identifying Enslaved Africans in the African Diaspora." In *Identity in the Shadow of Slavery*, edited by Lovejoy. London: Continuum, 2000.

Luccock, John. *Notas Sobre o Rio de Janeiro e Partes Meridionais do Brasil*. Foreword by Mário Guimarães Ferri. Belo Horizonte: Editora Itatiaia, 1975.

Maggie, Yvonne. *Medo do Feitiço: Relações entre Magia e Poder no Brasil*. Rio de Janeiro: Arquivo Nacional, 1992.

Maia, Moacir Rodrigo de Castro. " 'Quem Tem Padrinho Não Morre Pagão': As Relações de Compadrio e Apadrinhamento de Escravos numa Vila Colonial (Mariana, 1715–1750)." M.A. thesis, Universidade Federal Fluminense, Niterói, 2006.

Malheiro, Perdigão. *A Escravidão no Brasil: Ensaio Histórico, Jurídico, Social*. 2 vols. Petrópolis: Vozes, 1976.

Mapas Históricos Brasileiros. São Paulo: Abril Cultural, n.d.

Martins, José de Souza, ed. *A Morte e os Mortos na Sociedade Brasileira*. São Paulo: Hucitec, 1983.

Mascarenhas, Luiz de Almeida Soares Portugal Alarcão Eça Mello Silva e (Marquês do Lavradio). "Relatório." *Revista do Instituto Histórico e Geográfico Brasileiro* 4 (1842): 453–76.

——. "Relatório." *Revista do Instituto Histórico e Geográfico Brasileiro* 76 (1913).

——. "Memórias Públicas e Econômicas da Cidade de São Sebastião do Rio de Janeiro para Uso do Vice-rei Luiz de Vasconcellos por Observação Curiosa dos Anos de 1779 até o de 1789." *Revista do Instituto Histórico e Geográfico Brasileiro* 47, pt. 1 (1884): 25–51.

Mattoso, Kátia M. de Queiróz. *Bahia, Século XIX: Uma Província no Império*. Rio de Janeiro: Editora Nova Fronteira, 1992.

——. *Ser Escravo no Brasil*. São Paulo: Editora Brasiliense, 1988.

Maurício, Augusto. *Templos Históricos do Rio de Janeiro*. Rio de Janeiro: Gráfica Laemmert Limitada, 1947.

Mauro, Frédéric. *Le Portugal et l'Atlantique au XVII Siècle (1570–1670): Étude Économique*. Paris: École Pratique des Hautes Études Sixième Section S.E.V.P.E.N., 1960.

McEvedy, Colin. *Atlas da História Moderna (até 1815)*. São Paulo: Editora Verbo, 1979.

Meillassoux, Claude. *Antropologia da Escravidão: O Ventre de Ferro e Dinheiro*. Rio de Janeiro: Jorge Zahar Editor, 1995.

——, ed. *L'Esclavage en Afrique Précolonial*. Paris: Maspero, 1975.

Mello Junior, Donato. *Rio de Janeiro: Planos, Plantas e Aparências*. Rio de Janeiro: Edição da Galeria de Arte do Centro Empresarial Rio, 1988.

Monteiro, John M. *Negros da Terra: Índios e Bandeirantes nas Origens de São Paulo*. São Paulo: Companhia das Letras, 1994.

Mota, A. Teixeira. *Topónimos de Origem Portuguesa na Costa Ocidental de África: Desde o Cabo Bojador ao Cabo de Santa Caterina*. Bissau: Centro de Estudos da Guiné Portuguesa, no. 14, 1950.

Mott, Luiz. "Acotundá: Raízes Setecentistas do Sincretismo Religioso Afro-Brasileiro." In *Escravidão, Homossexualidade e Demonologia*. São Paulo: Ícone Editora, 1998.

——. "Cotidiano e Vivência Religiosa: Entre a Capela e o Calundu." In *História da Vida Privada no Brasil I*, edited by Laura de Mello e Souza, ed. São Paulo: Companhia das Letras, 1997.

——. *Escravidão, Homossexualidade e Demonologia*. São Paulo: Ícone Editora, 1998.

——. *Rosa Egipcíaca: Uma Santa Africana no Brasil*. Rio de Janeiro: Bertrand Brasil, 1993.

Mulira, Jessie Gaston. "A History of the Mahi Peoples from 1774–1920." Ph.D. diss., University of California, Berkeley, 1984.

Mulvey, Patricia Ann. "The Black Lay Brotherhoods of Colonial Brazil: A History." Ph.D. diss., City University of New York, 1976.

Nardi, Jean Baptiste. O Fumo Brasileiro no Período Colonial: Lavoura, Comércio e Administração. São Paulo: Brasiliense, 1992.

Nascentes, Antenor. Efemérides Cariocas. Rio de Janeiro: Prefeitura do Distrito Federal, 1965.

Neves, Guilherme Pereira. "E Receberá Mercê: A Mesa da Consciência e Ordens e o Clero Secular no Brasil (1808–1828)." Ph.D. diss., Universidade de São Paulo, 1995.

Nora, Pierre. "Entre Mémoire et Histoire: La Problématique des Lieux." In Les Lieux de Mémoire: La République, edited by Nora. Paris: Gallimard, 1984.

Novais, Fernando A. Portugal e Brasil na Crise do Antigo Sistema Colonial (1777–1808). São Paulo: Editora Hucitec, 1981.

———, ed. História da Vida Privada. Vol. 1: O Cotidiano da Vida Privada na América Portuguesa. São Paulo: Companhia das Letras, 1997.

Nsondé, Jean. "Les Relations Culturelles et Commerciales entre Populations de Langue Kongo et Européens du XVIe au XVIIIe Siècle dans la Région du Bas-Congo." In Les Assises du Pouvoir: Temps Médiévaux, Territories Africains, edited by Jean Devisse. Saint-Denis: Presses Universitaires de France, 1994.

Nunes, Antonio Duarte. "Almanaque Histórico da Cidade de São Sebastião do Rio de Janeiro." Revista do Instituto Histórico e Geográfico Brasileiro 267 (April–June 1965): 93–214.

Oliveira, Anderson José Machado de. "Devoção e Caridade: Irmandades Religiosas no Rio de Janeiro Imperial (1840–1889)." M.A. thesis, Universidade Federal Fluminense, Niterói, 1995.

Oliveira, João Pacheco de. "Elementos para uma Sociologia dos Viajantes." In Sociedades Indígenas and Indigenismo no Brasil, edited by João Pacheco de Oliveira. Rio de Janeiro: Universidade Federal do Rio de Janeiro, 1987.

———. "Os Instrumentos de Bordo: Expectativas e Possibilidades do Trabalho de Antropólogo em Laudos Periciais." In A Perícia Antropológica em Processos Judiciais, edited by Orlando Silva et al. Florianópolis: Associação Brasileira de Antropologia, 1994.

———. "O Nosso Governo." Os Ticuna e o Regime Tutelar. São Paulo: Marco Zero, 1988.

Oliveira, Maria Inês Cortes de. "Quem Eram os 'Negros da Guiné'? A Origem dos Africanos na Bahia." Afro-Ásia 19/20 (1997): 37–73.

Oliveira, Patrícia Porto de. "Batismo de Escravos Adultos e o Parentesco Espiritual nas Minas Setecentistas." Anais da V Jornada Setecentista (Curitiba), 26–28 November 2003.

Oliveira, Roberto Cardoso de. Identidade, Etnia e Estrutura Social. São Paulo: Livraria Pioneira Editora, 1976.

Peixoto, Antonio da Costa. *Obra Nova de Língua Geral da Mina*. Manuscript of the Biblioteca Pública de Évora and the Biblioteca Nacional de Lisboa published by Luis Silveira, with commentary by Edmund Correia Lopes. Lisbon: Agência Geral das Colônias, 1945.

Pereira, Duarte Pacheco. *Esmeraldo de Situ Orbis* [ca. 1506]. Lisbon: Imprensa Nacional, 1892.

Pina, Rui de. *Crônicas de Rui de Pina: D. Sancho I, D. Afonso II, D. Sancho II, D. Afonso III, D. Dinis, D. Afonso IV, D. Duarte, D. Afonso V, D. João II*. Introduction and revision by M. Lopes de Almeida. Porto: Lello e Irmãos Editores, 1977.

Pinheiro, Fernanda Aparecida Domingos. "Confrades do Rosário: Sociabilidade e Identidade Étnica em Mariana, Minas Gerais (1745–1820)." M.A. thesis, Universidade Federal Fluminense, Niterói, 2006.

Polanyi, Karl. *Dahomey and the Slave Trade: An Analysis of an Archaic Economy*. Seattle: University of Washington Press, 1968.

Portugal e os Descobrimentos: O Encontro de Civilizações. Foreword by Vasco Graça Moura. Commissioned for the Universal Exposition of Seville in 1992 [n.d.].

Prado Junior, Caio. *Formação do Brasil Contemporâneo: Colônia*. São Paulo: Editora Brasiliense, 1972.

Rama, Angel. "La Ciudad Letrada." In *América Latina: Palavra, Literatura, e Cultura*. Vol. 1: *A Situação Colonial*, edited by Ana Pizarro. Campinas: Ed. Unicamp, 1993.

Ramos, Arthur. *As Culturas Negras no Novo Mundo*. São Paulo: Companhia Editora Nacional, 1979.

———. *Introdução à Antropologia Brasileira*. 2 vols. Rio de Janeiro: Casa do Estudante do Brasil, 1961.

Reis, João José. "Identidade e Diversidade Étnica nas Irmandades Negras no Tempo da Escravidão." *Tempo* 2, no. 3 (1997): 7–33.

———. "Magia Jêje na Bahia: A Invasão do Calundu do Pasto de Cachoeira." *Revista Brasileira de História* 16 (1988). São Paulo.

———. *A Morte é uma Festa: Ritos Fúnebres e Revolta Popular no Brasil do Século XIX*. São Paulo: Companhia das Letras, 1991.

———. *Rebelião Escrava no Brasil: A História do Levante dos Malês (1835)*. São Paulo: Brasiliense, 1987.

Reis, João José, and Eduardo Silva. *Negociação e Conflito: A Resistência Negra no Brasil Escravista*. São Paulo: Companhia das Letras, 1989.

Revel, Jacques, ed. *Jeux d'Échelles: de la Micro-analyse à l'Expérience*. Paris: Seuil, 1996.

Ribeiro Filho, J. S. *Dicionário Biobibliográfico de Escritores Cariocas (1565–1965)*. Rio de Janeiro: Livraria Brasiliana Editora, 1965.

Rios Filho, A. M. "Evolução Urbana e Arquitetônica do Rio de Janeiro nos Séculos XVI e XVII (1567–1699)." *Revista do Instituto Histórico e Geográfico Brasileiro* 288 (1970): 22–254.

Rocha, Manoel Ribeiro. *Etíope Resgatado, Empenhado Sustentado Corrigido, Instruído e Libertado*. Introduction by Paulo Suess. Petrópolis: Vozes, 1992.

Rodrigues, Cláudia. "Lugares dos Mortos na Cidade dos Vivos: Tradições e Transformações Fúnebres na Corte." M.A. thesis, Universidade Federal Fluminense, Niterói, 1995.

Rodrigues, Nina. *Os Africanos no Brasil.* Brasília: EdUnB, n.d.

Romero, Sílvio. *História da Literatura Brasileira: Contribuições e Estudos Gerais para o Exato Conhecimento da Literatura Brasileira.* 4th ed. organized and with a preface by Nelson Romero. Rio de Janeiro: Livraria José Olympio Editora, 1949.

Rupert, Arlindo. *Expansão Territorial e Absolutismo Estatal (1700–1822): A Igreja no Brasil, III.* Santa Maria: Editora Pallotti, 1988.

———. *A Igreja no Brasil III: Expansão Territorial e Absolutismo Estatal (1700–1822).* Santa Maria: Editora Pallotti, 1988.

Russell-Wood, A. J. R. *The Black Man in Slavery and Freedom in Colonial Brazil.* New York: St. Martin's Press, 1982.

———. *Fidalgos e Filantropos: A Santa Casa de Misericórdia da Bahia, 1550–1755.* Brasília: EdUnB, 1981.

———. "Prestige, Power, and Piety in Colonial Brazil: The Third Orders of Salvador." *Hispanic American Historical Review* 69 (1989): 61–89.

———. "United States Scholarly Contributions to the Historiography of Colonial Brazil." *Hispanic American Historical Review* 65, no. 4 (1985): 683–723.

Salgado, Graça, ed. *Fiscais e Meirinhos: A Administração no Brasil Colonial.* Rio de Janeiro: Nova Fronteira, 1985.

Salvador, Vicente do (Frei). *História do Brasil.* New edition revised and annotated by Capistrano de Abreu. São Paulo: Weisz Flog Irmãos, 1918.

Santos, Afonso Carlos Marques dos. *No Rascunho da Nação: Inconfidência no Rio de Janeiro.* Rio de Janeiro: Secretaria Municipal da Cultura, 1992.

Santos, Antônio Alves Ferreira (Monsenhor). *Arquidiocese de São Sebastião do Rio de Janeiro.* Rio de Janeiro: Tipografia Leuzinger, 1914.

Santos, Corcino Medeiros dos. *O Rio de Janeiro e a Conjuntura Atlântica.* Rio de Janeiro: Expressão e Cultura, 1993.

Santos, Juana Elbein dos. *Os Nagô e a Morte: Pàde, Asèsè e o Culto Égun na Bahia.* Petrópolis: Vozes, 1976.

Santos, Luiz Gonçalves dos (Padre Perereca). *Memórias para Servir à História do Reino do Brasil.* Preface and annotations by Noronha Santos. 2 vols. Rio de Janeiro: Livraria Editora Zelio Valverde, 1943.

Scarano, Julita. *Devoção e Escravidão: A Irmandade de Nossa Senhora do Rosário dos Pretos no Distrito Diamantino no Século XVIII.* São Paulo: Companhia Editora Nacional, 1978.

Schwartz, Stuart B. *Burocracia e Sociedade no Brasil Colonial: A Suprema Corte da Bahia e Seus Juízes. 1609–1751.* São Paulo: Editora Perspectiva, 1979.

———. *Segredos Internos: Engenhos e Escravos na Sociedade Colonial, 1550–1835.* São Paulo: CNPq, 1988.

Serrão, Joel, ed. *Dicionário de História de Portugal.* 3 vols. Porto: Livraria Figuerinhas, n.d.

Silva, Antonio Moraes e. *Dicionário de Língua Portuguesa*. Lisbon: Oficina de Simão T. Ferreira, 1889.

Silveira, Américo Bispo da. "Conferência." Photocopied Manuscript in author's possession. N.p. N.d.

Slenes, Robert. "*Malungu ngoma vem!* A África Coberta e Descoberta do Brasil." *Revista da USP* 12 (December–January–February 1991/1992): 48–67.

Soares, José Carlos de Macedo. "Fontes da História da Igreja Católica no Brasil." *Revista do Instituto Histórico e Geográfico Brasileiro* 20 (July–September 1953).

Soares, Mariza de Carvalho. "A Biografia de Ignácio Monte; O Escravo Que Virou Rei." In *Retratos do Império: Trajetórias Individuais no Mundo Português nos Séculos XVI a XIX*, edited by Ronaldo Vainfas et al. Niterói: EduFF, 2006.

——. "Can Women Guide and Govern Men? Gendering Politics among African Catholics in Colonial Brazil." In *Women and Slavery*. Vol. 2: *Americas*, edited by Gwyn Campbell, Suzanne Miers, and Joseph C. Miller. Athens: Ohio University Press, 2008.

——. *Devotos da Cor: Identidade Étnica, Religiosidade e Escravidão no Rio de Janeiro, Século XVIII*. Rio de Janeiro: Civilização Brasileira. 2000.

——. "From Gbe to Yoruba: Ethnic Changes within the Mina Nation in Rio de Janeiro." In *The Yoruba Diaspora in the Atlantic World*, edited by Toyin Falola and Matt Childs. Bloomington: Indiana University Press, 2004.

——. "Indícios para o Traçado das Rotas Terrestres de Escravos na Baía do Benim, Século XVIII." In *Rotas Atlânticas da Diáspora Africana: Entre a Baía do Benim e o Rio de Janeiro*, edited by Mariza de Carvalho Soares. Niterói: EduFF, 2007.

——. "O Império de Santo Elesbão na Cidade do Rio de Janeiro, Século XVIII." *Topoi* 4 (2002): 59–83.

——. "O Medo da Vida e o Medo da Morte. Um Estudo da Religiosidade Brasileira." M.A. thesis, Universidade Federal do Rio de Janeiro, 1990.

——. "O Missionário e o Rei." B.A. thesis, Pontifícia Universidade Católica do Rio de Janeiro, 1978.

——. "A 'Nação' Que Se Tem e a 'Terra' de Onde Se Vem: Categorias de Inserção Social de Africanos no Império Português, Século XVIII." *Estudos Afro-Asiáticos* 26 (May–August 2004): 303–30.

——. "Nos Atalhos da Memória: Monumento a Zumbi." In *Cidade Vaidosa: Imagens Urbanas do Rio de Janeiro*, edited by Paulo Knauss. Rio de Janeiro: Sette Letras, 1999.

——, ed. *Rotas Atlânticas da Diáspora Africana: Entre a Baía do Benim e o Rio de Janeiro*. Niterói: EduFF, 2007.

Souvenir: Lembranças do Brasil. Introduction by Lygia da Fonseca Fernandes da Cunha. Rio de Janeiro: SEDEGRA, n.d.

Souza, Laura de Mello e. *Declassificados do Ouro: A Pobreza Mineira no Século XVIII*. Rio de Janeiro: Graal, 1986.

Spix, J. B., and C. F. P. Martius. *Viagem ao Brasil, 1817–1820*. São Paulo: Melhoramentos, 1975.

Suess, Paulo. *A Conquista Espiritual da América Espanhola: 200 Documentos—Século XVI*. Introduction by Paulo Suess. Petrópolis: Vozes, 1992.

Vainfas, Ronaldo. *A Heresia dos Índios: Catolicismo e Rebeldia no Brasil Colonial*. São Paulo: Companhia das Letras, 1995.

——. "Moralidades Brasílicas: Deleites Sexuais e Linguagem Erotica na Sociedade Escravista." In *História da Vida Privada no Brasil I*, edited by Laura de Mello e Souza. São Paulo: Companhia das Letras, 1997.

Vainfas, Ronaldo, and Marina de Mello e Souza. "Catolicização e Poder no Tempo do Tráfico: O Reino do Congo da Conversão Coroada ao Movimento Antoniano, Séculos XV–XVIII." *Tempo* 3, no. 6 (1998): 95–118.

Varnhagen, Francisco Adolfo de. *História Geral do Brasil: Antes da sua Separação e Independência de Portugal*. Revision and notes by J. Capistrano de Abreu and Rodolfo Garcia. 3 vols. São Paulo: Edições Melhoramentos, n.d.

Velloso, Mônica Pimenta. "As Tias Baianas Tomam Conta do Pedaço . . . Espaço e Identidade Cultural no Rio de Janeiro." *Estudos Históricos* 6, file "Cultura e Povo" (1990): 207–28.

Verger, Pierre. *Dieux d'Afrique: Culte des Orishas et Vodouns à l'Ancienne Côte des Esclaves en Afrique et à Bahia, la Baie de Tous les Saints au Brésil*. Preface by Théodore Monod and Roger Bastide. Photographs by the author. Paris: Éditions Revue Noire, 1995.

——. *Fluxo e Refluxo do Tráfico de Escravos entre o Golfo do Benin e a Bahia de Todos os Santos dos séculos XVIII a XIX*. São Paulo: Editora Corrupio, 1987.

——. *Os Orixás: Deuses Iorubás na África e no Novo Mundo*. São Paulo: Círculo do Livro, 1981.

Vieira, Antônio (Padre). *Sermões*. Authorized edition adapted from the official orthography, with summaries preceding each chapter, and with textual revisions and corrections by Frederico Ozanam Pessoas de Barros under the supervision of Padre Antônio Charbel, S.D.B. [Salesians of Don Bosco] (of the Instituto Teleológico Pio XI) and of Prof. A. Della Nina. 24 vols. São Paulo: Editora das Américas, 1957.

Villalta, Luiz Carlos. "O Que Se Fala e o Que Se Lê: Língua, Instrução e Leitura." In *História da Vida Privada*. Vol. 1: *O Cotidiano da Vida Privada na América Portuguesa*, edited by Fernando A Novais. São Paulo: Companhia das Letras, 1997.

Vovelle, Michel. "Iconografia e História das Mentalidades." In *Ideologias e Mentalidades*. São Paulo: Brasiliense, 1991.

Wolf, Kenneth Baxter. "The 'Moors' of West Africa and the Beginnings of the Portuguese Slave Trade." *Journal of Medieval and Renaissance Studies* 24, no. 3 (1994): 449–69.

Zurara, Gomes Eanes de. *Crônicas de Guiné*. Based on the Paris manuscript, modernized; introduction, notes, commentary, and glossary by José de Bragança. Barcelos, Portugal: Livraria Civilização Editora, 1973.

INDEX

Page numbers in italics refer to illustrations; "t" signifies table.

MARIZA DE CARVALHO SOARES is an associate professor of history at Universidade Federal Fluminense and a researcher funded by CNPq-Conselho Nacional de Desenvolvimento Científico e Tecnológico. She is the author of *Devotos da Cor: Identidade Étnica, Religiosidade e Escravidão no Rio de Janeiro, Século XVIII* (2000) and co-author (with Ricardo Henrique Salles) of *Episódios da História Afro-Brasileira* (2005). She also edited the collection *Rotas Atlânticas da Diáspora Africana: Entre a Baía do Benim e o Rio de Janeiro* (2007), and co-edited (with Nielson Rosa Bezerra) the collection *A Escravidão Africana no Recôncavo da Guanabara* (2011).

Library of Congress Cataloging-in-Publication Data

Soares, Mariza de Carvalho.
[Devotos da cor. English]
People of faith : slavery and African Catholics in eighteenth-century Rio de Janeiro /
Mariza de Carvalho Soares ; translated by Jerry Dennis Metz.
p. cm. — (Latin America in translation/en traducción/em tradução)
Originally published as: Devotos da cor : identidade étnica, religiosidade e escravidão no Rio de Janeiro, século XVIII (Rio de Janeiro : Civilização Brasileira, 2000).
Includes bibliographical references and index.
ISBN 978-0-8223-5023-1 (cloth : alk. paper)
ISBN 978-0-8223-5040-8 (pbk. : alk. paper)
1. Slavery—Brazil—Rio de Janeiro—History—18th century.
2. Africans—Brazil—Rio de Janeiro—Ethnic identity.
3. Africans—Religious life—Brazil—Rio de Janeiro.
4. Slaves—Religious life—Brazil—Rio de Janeiro.
I. Title.
II. Series: Latin America in translation/en traducción/em tradução.
HT1129.R53S6313 2011
306.3'62098153—dc22
2011015701